A CANOEING AND KAYAKING GUIDE TO GEORGIA

Once there was a legend that told of a river that went to hear a fountain sing. The song was so beautiful that the river decided to sing it to the ocean. All the way to the shores of the ocean the river sang. Soon, the mountains heard of the song that the river was singing and came from all over the land to listen. And because the song was so beautiful the mountains settled down and stayed to listen forever.

—Algonquin Indian Legend

A CANOEING AND KAYAKING GUIDE TO GEORGIA

Suzanne Welander, Bob Sehlinger, and Don Otey

MENASHA RIDGE PRESS
Birmingham, Alabama

Portions of this book originally appeared in *A Paddler's Guide to Northern Georgia* and *A Paddler's Guide to Southern Georgia*
Published by Menasha Ridge Press
Distributed by The Globe Pequot Press
Printed in the United States of America
First edition, first printing, 2004

Library of Congress cataloging-in-publication data
Welander, Suzanne
A Canoeing and Kayaking Guide to Georgia/by Suzanne Welander, Bob Sehlinger, and Don Otey
p.cm.

ISBN 0-89732-558-3

1. Canoes and canoeing—Georgia—Guidebooks.
2. Kayaking—Georgia—Guidebooks. 3. Georgia—Guidebooks. I. Sehlinger, Bob, 1945– II. Otey, Don. III. Title.

GV776.G4W45 2004
797.122'09758—dc22

2003071016

Cover photo © 2003 by Jon Soderstrom, Stock Up Image Source
Interior photos © as noted
Cover design by Bud Zehmer
Text design by Ann Marie Healy

Menasha Ridge Press
P.O. Box 43673
Birmingham, Alabama 35243
www.menasharidge.com

DISCLAIMER
While every effort has been made to insure the accuracy of this guidebook, river and road conditions can change greatly from year to year. This book is intended as a general guide. Whitewater paddling is an assumed-risk sport. The decision to run a river can only be made after an on-the-spot inspection, and a run should not be attempted without proper equipment and safety precautions. The author and publisher of *A Canoeing and Kayaking Guide to Georgia* are not responsible for any personal or property damage that may result from your activities. By using any part of this guide, you recognize and assume all risks and acknowledge that you are responsible for your own actions.

Table *of* **Contents**

part**One**

THE SAVANNAH RIVER WATERSHED

part**Two**

THE TENNESSEE WATERSHED

part**Three**

THE COOSA RIVER WATERSHED

part**Four**

CHATTAHOOCHEE AND FLINT RIVERS WATERSHEDS

part**Five**

THE ALTAMAHA RIVER WATERSHED

part**Six**

SOUTHEAST AND SOUTH CENTRAL GEORGIA

part**Seven**

THE GEORGIA COAST

part**Eight**

NOTEWORTHY RIVERS IN NEIGHBORING STATES

appendixes

Map Legend

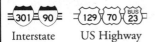
Interstate

US Highway

State Highway

County Road

Forest Service Road

Unpaved Road

Wayne Co.

GEORGIA

NATIONAL PARK

Athens

North Indicator

Trail

Railroad Track

County Line

State Line

Park or City Boundaries

City or Town

Hill or Mountain

Waterway, Lake or Pond, Marsh

Profiled River

Powerline/ Pipeline Crossing

Water Gauge

Access Point

Alternate Access Point

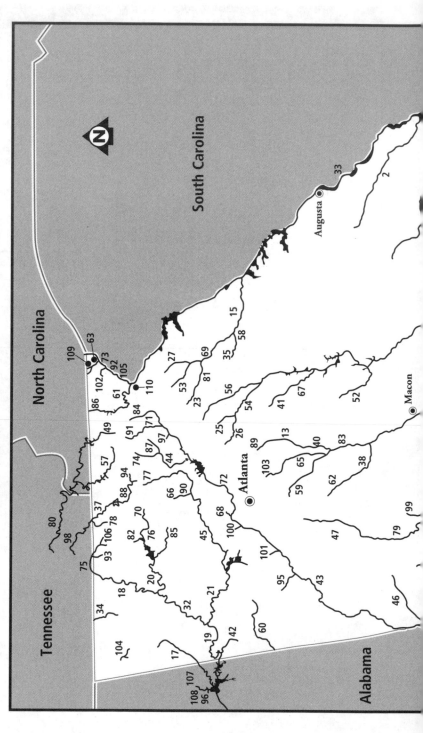

River-Locator Map

Tennessee

North Carolina

South Carolina

Alabama

Atlanta

Augusta

Macon

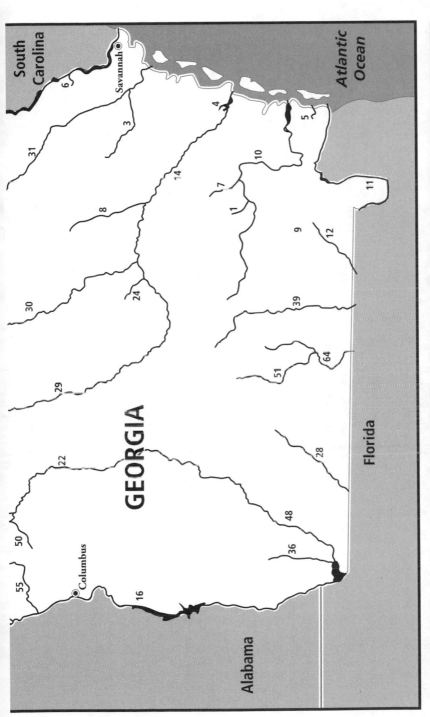

Map Key on next page

River-Locator Map Key

Tidal and Smoothwater

1 Alabaha River — p. 310
2 Brier Creek — p. 88
3 Canoochee River — p. 302
4 Cathead Creek — p. 351
5 Crooked River — p. 348
6 Ebenezer Creek — p. 91
7 Little Satilla — p. 312
8 Ohoopee River — p. 295
9 Okefenokee Swamp — p. 318
10 Satilla River — p. 305
11 St Marys River — p. 314
12 Suwannee River — p. 328

Class I

13 Alcovy River (below US 278) — p. 258
14 Altahama River — p. 285
15 Broad River (below GA 172) — p. 75
16 Chattahoochee River (below Columbus) — p. 177
17 Chattooga River of Chattooga County — p. 171
18 Conasauga River (below US 411) — p. 115

Mild (or Portagable) Whitewater

39 Alapaha River — p. 331
40 Alcovy River (below CR 213) — p. 258
41 Apalachee River (above GA 186) — p. 253
42 Big Cedar Creek — p. 169
43 Chattahoochee River (Sweetwater Creek to Columbus) — p. 177
44 Chestatee River (Copper Mine to Lake Lanier) — p. 198
45 Etowah River (GA 136 to Lake Allatoona) — p. 155
46 Flat Shoal Creek — p. 214
47 Flint River (above GA 18/74) — p. 218
48 Flint River (below Lake Blackshear) — p. 218
49 Hiawassee River — p. 95
50 Lazer Creek — p. 228
51 Little River of Southern Georgia — p. 337
52 Little River of Putnam County — p. 256
53 Middle Fork Broad River — p. 68
54 Middle Oconee River (below GA 330) — p. 240

75 Conasauga River (GA 2 to US 411) — p. 115
76 Coosawattee River (above Carters Lake) — p. 130
77 Etowah River (above GA 136) — p. 155
78 Fightingtown Creek — p. 107
79 Flint River (GA 18/74 to GA 137) — p. 218
80 Hiwassee River — p. 368
81 Hudson River (below GA 106) — p. 72
82 Mountaintown Creek — p. 138
83 Ocmulgee River (above Macon) — p. 271
84 Soque River — p. 192
85 Talking Rock Creek — p. 140
86 Tallulah River (above Plum Orchard Road) — p. 59
87 Tesnatee Creek — p. 203
88 Toccoa River (above Blue Ridge Lake) — p. 102

Class III + Creeks and Class IV–IV + Rivers

89 Alcovy River (above Alcovy Road) — p. 258
90 Amicalola Creek (below GA 53) — p. 150

Moderate Whitewater

Class V Rivers and Creeks

Using the River-Locator Map

Use the preceding locator map to find rivers within your paddling expertise located near your geographic region. Following the map is a key that groups Georgia's rivers in six difficulty categories:

• *Tidal and Smoothwater* rivers that present no significant obstacles.

• *Class I* rivers, some with fast current and/or a rare Class I shoal. May contain dams that require portaging.

• *Mild (or Portagable) Whitewater* of Class I and II with a general demeanor of smoothwater or Class I rapids but with more difficult Class II–IV rapids interspersed at wide intervals. The more difficult drops can either be portaged by novice paddlers or, depending on road access, can present park-and-play opportunities for those wishing to avoid the intervening flatwater.

• *Moderate Whitewater* that presents a more consistent whitewater experience with a difficulty level of Class II or Class III. May contain a more significant rapid with a higher difficulty rating that can usually be portaged.

• *Class III+ Creeks and Class IV–IV+ Rivers,* includng some with continuous whitewater and some with a drop-and-pool character. Portaging the larger drops is generally possible, though it can be difficult. On steep creeks portaging the more difficult rapids is challenging to impossible.

• *Class V Rivers and Creeks,* many in extremely remote settings where rescue would be difficult.

Rivers are listed alphabetically within each category. The numbers on the map correspond to the category lists. Note that some rivers are listed in more than one category. In such cases, river divisions are delineated in detail within the text. Some waterways, particularly longer river sections, display a greater variety of difficulty than can be represented here; read the full description of the river section to tailor your trip to your skill level. The page number for each description is shown alongside each river's name. Remember that rivers are grouped based on their characteristic under ideal conditions, and high water levels may greatly increase risk. See "Rating the River" (page 3) to gain a deeper understanding the difficulty classes and the skills required to paddle each.

Acknowledgments

A varied group of paddlers contributed expert assistance to this guidebook. This project has been a group effort; the Editrix wishes to acknowledge their contributions, which greatly enhanced the completeness and accuracy of this new edition.

Two individuals in particular had a significant influence on the content:

Dr. William "Hawk" Reeves took the initiative to ensure that a sample of Georgia's steep creek runs would be included, providing the source material used to describe Potato, Cooper, Sope, Mossy and Warwoman Creeks.

Roger Nott, in addition to writing the description for the Jacks River, freely lent editorial advice, his encyclopedic knowledge of north Georgia's whitewater streams, and twenty-five years' worth of archived newsletters (including a virtual treasure-trove of trip reports, experiential articles and an early guidebook) from the Georgia Canoeing Association.

The following paddlers wrote descriptions new to this edition:

Mark D'Agostino	Little River Canyon
Julia Franks	Tallulah Gorge
Dan Grissette	Cathead Creek
Allen Hedden	Upper Ocoee River
Mark Hicks	Upper Alcovy and Overflow Creek
Slick	Crooked River, Upper Ocmulgee

The following paddlers substantially edited content from the previous edition:

Julia Franks	Chattooga Section IV
Allen Hedden	Middle Ocoee
Lindsay Meeks and Brookie Gallagher	Okefenokee Swamp

These local experts provided essential input for new content:

Clay Wright	Bear Creek
Dave Chafin	Ebenezer Creek
Steve Braden	Georgia Coast
Michael Moody and Charlie Ford	Altamaha River

Gratitude also belongs to the following fine folks: Michael Moody for editorial assistance and descriptions of the Broad River watersheds; Dick Hurd, who volunteered updates and a new map for the Cartecay River; Dan Roper who scouted access and shared his paddling experiences on the upper Ogeechee River; Dr. Richard Greene for providing a virtual trip down the Flint River using the sights, experiences and detailed notes compiled on his

solo journey to the Gulf; Dave Gale for providing updates and advice for the Upper Chattahoochee; Jed Dugger and his maps of the Little River Canyon; Dick Sturtevant for freely answering questions and volunteering information on the Alapaha and Withlacoochee Rivers; Mark Hicks for sharing his knowledge and enthusiasm for high-water Piedmont play-spots within driving distance for an after-work (or lunch hour) run; Will Reeves and Brad Roberts for editorial guidance on steep creek inclusions (as well as a copy of "Fault Line" from Will's vault); and Elizabeth Carter for advice on Georgia's smoothwater streams.

Of course, this revision would not had existed without the original version written by Bob Sehlinger and Don Otey (with the support of others who guided that project including Gary DeBoucher and Russ Ryder). In reformatting and updating the original material, every effort was made to preserve the delightful flavor of their writing, including such descriptive gems as "veritable whitewater gymnasium."

Lastly, I owe a debt of gratitude to Slick: for always knowing who to contact for what, writing the section on water quality, countless hours editing my text, helping to scout access points, and enthusiastically paddling runs more off-beat than our usual fare.

These paddlers shared selflessly so that others can enjoy the same exhilaration, beauty and respite found on Georgia's riverine sanctuaries—where the only means of entry is paddle.

How to Use This Guide

Georgia is the largest state east of the Mississippi. Its rivers are varied and long. This guidebook groups rivers by watershed (with the exception of "Part Eight: Waterways of Special Mention"). Within each part, rivers are listed starting with the watershed's origins upstream and moving downstream. Each river profile begins with a brief introduction, followed by a list of the county and US Geological Survey (USGS) topographical maps that include the river.

In the interest of including descriptions of as many navigable miles as possible, the waterways covered in this book are divided into sections according to river character and required skill level. Consequently, many river sections are very long and not possible to tackle in a day.

Accompanying each river profile is a map, on which access points are labeled as A, B, C, and so on. A table showing the river miles lying between these access points is also provided on the map. For rivers with numerous access points, determine how many miles you want to cover, and use the table to tailor your trip. The typical paddler will traverse between 6 and 12 miles in a day. Allow more time for portaging around deadfalls when paddling in the upper reaches of a small river, or for scouting and/or portaging rapids.

To help you choose which river or river section to paddle, an at-a-glance data sidebar accompanies each river section. The sidebar includes:

Class: Using the International Scale of River Difficulty, the rating of the section under normal conditions. Parentheses are used to note the presence of a more difficult feature anomalous to the rest of the run. S is used to designate smoothwater and T to designate tidal bodies of water. For more information see "Rating the River" on page 3.

Length: Total number of river miles within the section.

Time: A conservative estimate of the time required to paddle the section under normal conditions based on typical current speed and likely portages or scouting. Time estimates presented in days and/or weeks are based on five hours paddling time per day. For streams that enter larger bodies of water, the time estimate is from put-in to take-out. Shuttle and carry times are not included. The best guideline is your own experience; expect variances from the estimate based on the amount of time you spend playing the river, if more or less scouting and portages are needed, or if you're paddling tandem.

Gauge: The type of gauge(s) available for obtaining water levels for that section. Web refers to data transmitted from gauging stations and posted, with a short time lag, on Internet sites. Phone indicates levels available via recorded messages or from local outfitters. Visual refers to staff gauges planted in the streambed or markings painted onto bridge pilings that can be checked prior to or during a run.

Level: The generally accepted minimum level required by most paddlers, listed in feet or flow volume (cubic feet per second, cfs) where noted.

Gradient: The average drop in elevation per mile from the highest put-in to the lowest take-out within each section. For streams that empty into larger bodies, the gradient listed is to the confluence. If noteworthy, the highest feet-per-mile drop in elevation is listed in parentheses. Gradient is not equivalent to difficulty; the Chattahoochee through Helen has a surprisingly steep gradient but no significant rapids.

Scenery: An A–F grade assigned to views from the river with a bias toward natural environments. A+ = spectacular wilderness; A = exceptionally beautiful with no development visible from the stream; B = beautiful, with an occasional road and/or houses visible from the stream; C = pretty, with pastures, roads and/or lots of houses commonly visible; D = fair, passing through a city or industrial corridor; F = poor.

SAMPLE

class	I–VI, S or T
length	Miles
time	Hours, days, or weeks
gauge	Web, phone, or visual
level	Feet or cfs
gradient	Feet per mile
scenery	A–F

The written description of each river section conveys what paddlers will encounter moving sequentially from the highest to the lowest access points. The location of rapids, scenery, hazards, or other specific features of note are listed here. Use this information along with the mileage charts to select which portion of the river you are interested in paddling.

Shuttle instructions follow the written description. For most river sections, they are provided starting from the nearest town of size or Interstate exit to the lowest take-out, and from there to the highest put-in. Shuttle driving directions use the US prefix for federal highways, GA for state highways, FR for forest service roads, CR for county roads, and P for public roads. The maps included in this book are intended to get you to the river and help you conduct your shuttle, not replace US Geological Survey (USGS) topographic quadrangles or county road maps.

Each river section concludes with detailed gauge information, including where to get current streamflow information and recommended water levels. See "River-Level Information" on page 6 for Internet addresses of Web sites that provide levels. Phone numbers for outfitters and the rivers that they serve are listed in Appendix B.

Rating the River

For years, paddlers have sought to objectively rate rivers. Central among their tools is the International Scale of River Difficulty. This globally accepted system provides a nomenclature that facilitates a quick comparison between rivers by grouping them into six classes. The scale is presented in a table on the following page.

The International Scale has its drawbacks. The character of rivers varies within regions; the huge watersheds of the western United States, for example, produce Class II rivers that contain bigger water than the typical Georgia Class II river. Additionally, stronger, smaller, and more nimble boats and new paddling techniques have pushed many rapids formerly considered unrunnable Class VI waterfalls into the Class V category.

The classifications used to describe rivers in this book are those that have been applied traditionally to specific rapids and river sections. However, some exceptions and deviations from the International Scale were made.

To address the wider range of rapid difficulty compressed within the Class V category, additional numbering is used, where helpful, to differentiate difficulty within this category (i.e., 5.0, 5.1, 5.2, 5.3). The order of magnitude of difficulty separating each of these designations is similar to the difference between Class IV and Class 5.0.

On the other end of the spectrum, greater refinement was used within Class I rivers in this book. Rivers that contain minor rapids, swift current, wide channels and/or are characterized by banks choked by trees and brush can produce significant dangers for paddlers not able to execute the basic navigational moves required to avoid obstacles. Georgia's rivers that exhibit these characteristics (outside of extreme conditions) are classified as Class I in this book.

Georgia contains other flatwater streams that present less danger for the novice paddler. These rivers are characterized by slower current even in periods of higher water, less deadfall and vegetation on the banks, and contain no rapids. Current is moving, requiring the paddler to maneuver their craft; however, the likelihood that a novice paddler will capsize and the difficulty of

INTERNATIONAL SCALE OF RIVER DIFFICULTY

CLASS I Easy

Description Fast moving water with riffles and small waves. Few obstructions, all obvious and easily missed with little training.

CLASS II Requires Care

Description Straightforward rapids with wide, clear channels which are evident without scouting. Occasional maneuvering may be required, but rocks and medium sized waves are easily missed by trained paddlers.

CLASS III Difficult

Description Maneuvering in rapids necessary. Rapids with moderate, irregular waves which may be difficult to avoid and which can swamp an open canoe. Complex maneuvers in fast current and good boat control in tight passages or around ledges are often required; large waves or strainers may be present but are easily avoided.

CLASS IV Very Difficult

Description Intense, powerful but predictable rapids requiring precise boat handling in turbulent water. Depending on the character of the river, it may feature large, unavoidable waves and holes or constricted passages demanding fast maneuvers under pressure. Rapids may require "must" moves above dangerous hazards. Risk of injury to swimmers is moderate to high, and water conditions may make self-rescue difficult.

CLASS V Utmost Difficulty, Near the Limit of Navigability

Description Extremely long, obstructed, or very violent rapids which expose a paddler to added risk. Drops may contain large, unavoidable waves and holes or steep, congested chutes with complex, demanding routes. Rapids may continue for long distances between pools, demanding a high level of fitness. What eddies exist may be small, turbulent, or difficult to reach. At the high end of the scale, several of these factors may be combined. Swims are dangerous, and rescue is often difficult even for experts.

CLASS VI Extreme and Exploratory

Description These runs have almost never been attempted and often exemplify the extremes of difficulty, unpredictability and danger. The consequences of errors are very severe and rescue may be impossible.

Source: American Whitewater Safety Code, revised 1998. For entire descriptions, refer to section VI of the code in Appendix D.

photo © Ben Sumpter

A break in the Class IV Narrows on Section III of the Chattooga River

self-rescue is lower. These rivers carry a classification of "S" for smoothwater in this book.

Finally, a designation of "T" for tidal is used to designate conditions on rivers and creeks near the coast whose dominate current is dictated by ocean tides.

Ratings are assigned to rivers based on their difficulty under normal conditions. River conditions, however, are dynamic—what is normally a placid Class II river can transform into a raging Class V condition at flood stage! Difficulty levels increase with higher water flows and/or low air or water temperatures. Re-evaluate the difficulty level based on the conditions that you encounter at the river on the day you are paddling to determine if the river still remains within your skill level.

A map and key cross-referencing each river section by difficulty can be found on pages x–xiii. Use this illustration to quickly pinpoint the waterways within your skill level and their corresponding page number within the book. For a precise explanation of the skill-level groupings given in the key, see page xiv.

Gathering Information

When planning a paddling trip, besides evaluating your own skills and equipment you must reckon with two related external factors: weather and water levels. The sources of information given below will help you to ensure that when venturing out to paddle you find the conditions you anticipate.

WEATHER INFORMATION

Wind speed, air temperatures, and precipitation conspire to create conditions that are favorable or adverse to paddling. When planning a paddling trip, obtain a reliable weather forecast; the Web sites listed below offer detailed forecasts throughout the day. Be mindful not only of thunderstorms or a strong headwind, both of which can scuttle a river trip, but also intense sunshine, which necessitates bringing extra drinking water and sunscreen. Pack for the best and worst weather possible. Choose appropriate apparel once you're at the river, leaving unnecessary garments in the car.

Weather sites on the Internet include:

NOAA: Visit **www.nws.noaa.gov** for National Weather Service forecasts and **www.srh.noaa.gov/ffc/html/rainresrc.shtml** for precipitation forecasts and rainfall monitoring. Meteorological statisticians' calculated precipitation probabilities are available at **www.nws.noaa.gov/mdl/forecast/graphics/MAV.**

USGS: Current rainfall data and a 30-day rainfall record are at **http://ga.waterdata.usgs.gov/nwis/current?type=precip.**

Georgia Automated Environmental Monitoring Network: The Web page **www.griffin.peachnet.edu/bae** provides forecasts, current conditions, and historical climate data.

RIVER-LEVEL INFORMATION

Throughout this guidebook, relevant stream-flow information is provided for each river. This includes how the water level is measured, whether that information is available remotely (i.e., via Internet or phone), and what levels are adequate for paddling.

Internet Sites

Gone are the days of endless phone calls to determine which rivers are running. The first stop for most paddlers is to check river levels on the Internet—a process that requires only a few minutes. Even more convenient, both the USGS and American Whitewater sites can e-mail you daily with levels on the rivers of your choosing.

US Geological Survey (**http://waterdata.usgs.gov/ga/nwis/rt**) The largest single source for Georgia streamflow data is the USGS Internet site. River gauges can be located by map or table. The map is color-coded, making it easy to spot higher or lower than average flows. Table data shows the most recently reported levels. Up to 31 days' worth of data for a single gauge can be requested in graphical or tabular form. This is particularly helpful for understanding whether the river level is on its way up or down, in addition to anticipating how quickly the level will fall after a rainfall. USGS gauge information can also be used to infer water levels for neighboring rivers that lack on-line gauging stations.

Tennessee Valley Authority (**http://lakeinfo.tva.gov/htbin/ streaminfo**) A few Georgia rivers flow north into the Tennessee Valley Authority (TVA) system; current levels for free-flowing streams are provided on this TVA site. Release schedules for rivers downstream of TVA dams are found at **http://lakeinfo.tva.gov.**

American Whitewater (**www.americanwhitewater.org/rivers/ state/GA**) Based on automated sources of streamflow data (in Georgia these are the USGS and TVA Internet sites listed above), the American Whitewater site provides a table that color-codes each entry according to generally accepted minimum and maximum flows. In some cases, flows in rivers and creeks without gauges are estimated using data from nearby streams. Hyperlinks will take you to detailed descriptions and photos.

Other Scheduled recreational releases are provided for paddlers on the Ocoee River and in the Tallulah Gorge. The annual release schedule for the Tallulah River is available from **http://gastate parks.org/info/tallulah.** The Ocoee release schedule is online at **www.tva.gov/river/recreation/ocoeesched.htm.**

Phone Sources
Gauge readings are sometimes available by phone (often on pre-recorded messages), and relevant numbers are provided. For some rivers, numbers are given for public land-management offices that can provide water-level estimates or other helpful information. Phone numbers for local outfitters are provided in Appendix B.

Visual On-site Gauges
On-site gauges come in two forms: staff gauges or more informal markings painted onto bridge supports. Staff gauges are essentially big yardsticks or rulers stuck in the riverbed or fastened to bridge supports. Many are located at the same USGS sites linked to the Internet. Visual inspection of staff gauges

generally provides the most reliable water levels, although staff-gauge readings sometimes differ from online gauges. When possible, conversion methods are provided to help correlate differing gauges on the same waterway.

Finding Your Way

Even with the best maps, finding your way to the put-in and take-out can be challenging. Roads aren't always marked and shuttle routes frequently include dirt roads that don't see much traffic. The most comprehensive maps of public roads are produced by the Georgia Department of Transportation (GDOT); these were used as the basis for the maps found in this book.

When searching for the right road, pay attention to the numbers affixed to the posts of stop signs; these often refer to the county or forest service road number. In rural areas, county road numbers are often printed in smaller type on ordinary street name signs. Unless noted in the shuttle directions, the shuttle roads included should be passable for ordinary passenger cars. Wet conditions can make some dirt roads difficult or impossible to negotiate. Use your judgment.

MAP SOURCES

County Road Maps: Individual county road maps can be purchased by mail or phone from:

> Georgia Department of Transportation
> Map Sales
> 2 Capitol Square
> Atlanta, GA 30334
> (404) 656-5336.

County maps can be downloaded from the Internet (at no charge) at **www.cviog.uga.edu/Projects/gainfo/gamaps.htm.**

DeLorme Gazetteer: DeLorme publishes an atlas containing topographical maps, with details of back roads, covering the entire state. It does not distinguish between private and public roads or between paved roads and cow paths. It is generally available in outdoor sporting-goods stores, by calling (800) 452-5931, or via the Web site **www.delorme.com.** The same maps are also available in electronic form.

USGS Topographical Maps: Topographical maps, or topos, can be obtained via the Internet at **http://terraserver-usa.com** and at **www.topozone.com.** Computer programs such as National Geographic's Topo! and TopoUSA from DeLorme provide maps

on CDs along with software for viewing, manipulating, and printing the portions you select. Traditional paper maps can be ordered from the state at:

Georgia Geologic Survey
19 Martin Luther King Jr. Drive, Suite 400
Atlanta, GA 30334
(404) 656-3214
http://gcsstore.dnr.state.ga.us

The same topos are available through the USGS on-line at **http://store.usgs.gov,** or by calling (888) 275-8747. Inquiries about maps should be directed to:

United States Geological Survey
Information Services
Box 25286
Denver, CO 80225
(303) 202-4200
(303) 202-4633 (fax)

NOAA Coastal Charts: Ordering information and a list of selling agents for coastal charts by the National Oceanic and Atmospheric Administration (NOAA) is available at **http://chartmaker.ncd. noaa.gov/nsd/states.html,** or by calling (800) 638-8972.

National Forest Maps: Detailed maps of the Chattahoochee and Oconee National Forests, Cohutta Wilderness, and the Chattooga Wild and Scenic River can be ordered on-line at **www.fs.fed.us/conf/maporder.htm** or by calling (770) 297-3000. Maps of the southern district of the Cherokee National Forest (covering the Ocoee and Hiwassee Rivers) are available at (423) 476-9700. National Forest maps are particularly helpful for locating federally owned lands within the National Forests bordering the upper reaches of the Conasauga, Oconee, Ocmulgee, and Tallulah Rivers, as well as Jacks River, Toccoa River, Little River (Putnam County), and Cooper Creek.

OTHER HELPFUL INTERNET RESOURCES

A number of Web sites offer other information helpful to paddlers, particularly if you are interested in camping:

Georgia Department of Natural Resources (GA DNR): The site **http://georgiawildlife.dnr.state.ga.us** provides information on hunting seasons, boat ramps, and state Wildlife Management Areas (WMAs), all managed by the DNR.

Georgia State Parks: An on-line listing, location map, and hyperlinks to a detailed profile of the services available at each

state park are found at www.gastateparks.org. State Parks are managed by the Georgia DNR.

Wildlife Management Areas (WMAs) and County Parks: A locator map for state WMAs is found at **www.n-georgia.com/ wildlifemap.htm.** The home page for the same site lists county-managed parks.

Georgia Department of Industry, Trade, and Tourism: Under its "Tourism" page, **www.georgia.org** provides listings of hotels, campsites, etc. The "Plan Your Trip" option generates a quick list of the businesses you're interested in locating within the region you're planning on visiting.

Georgia River Fishing: Ever wonder what's lurking below the surface of your favorite Piedmont stream? The Web site **www.georgia riverfishing.com** provides information on the types of fish, suggestions on how to catch them, and supporting resources.

Hazards and Safety

Recreational boating has inherent risks, whether the paddler is aware of them or not. The good news is that most accidents can be avoided, and harm minimized, by eliminating a handful of major risk factors.

The single best learning tool for mitigating your risk of serious injury or death is to read accounts of real accidents that occurred on real rivers. Two such collections include the book *River Safety Anthology* and the accident database maintained on American Whitewater's Web site, **www.americanwhitewater.org.** The accounts, compelling and grim, are accompanied by pertinent details and analysis to help other paddlers avoid similar accidents.

In addition to paddler inexperience, the most common factors that contribute to accidents and death on the river are:

• cold water

• flood conditions

• poor or inappropriate equipment

• unfamiliarity with the river

• lack of personal flotation devices (PFDs)

• alcohol consumption

• foot entrapments

• persistent river hazards such as low head dams, strainers, and hydraulics

American Whitewater publishes safety recommendations for paddlers running whitewater. The AW Safety Code is in Appendix C (page 384). Anyone spending much time around popular rivers can observe that competent and respected paddlers not only follow the safety code, they endorse it . . . often evangelically. The reasons are simple. First, while the consequences of accidents are deadly, the risks are highly manageable with the right knowledge and attitude. Secondly, attempting to rescue an accident victim in moving water is particularly risky. Paddlers take a dim view of inexperienced boaters exceeding their safety zone, potentially obligating friends or strangers to put themselves in harm's way should a mishap occur.

Learning swiftwater rescue techniques has the effect of teaching you to spot hazards and avoid accidents before they happen. Appendix A contains a list of local and national paddling clubs, many of whom conduct safety and rescue training under the auspices of the American Canoe Association (ACA). Training in basic first aid is also a good idea since injuries, when they do occur, tend to happen far from outside help.

HYPOTHERMIA

Because it is one of the most common and one of the most easily mitigated risks, hypothermia merits some additional discussion. Any time you get in your boat, it's a good idea to ask yourself how you would feel if you took a swim right then and there— how would you complete the trip afterward? If you don't like the answer, chances are you don't have the appropriate apparel and safety equipment for the conditions.

Hypothermia is a risk when the sum of air and water temperatures (in degrees Fahrenheit) is below 120. Below 100, the risk of lethal hypothermia is substantially greater. At this point, cold becomes a risk-inducing situation requiring continuous attention and management. Obeying early signs of chilling, experienced paddlers will take a break and spend time on shore warming up and refueling. Failing to warm one's self until genuinely comfortable on land before get back on the water is highly dubious, particularly since the muscle coordination necessary for paddling is an early casualty of hypothermia. If you can't warm up, consider the possibility of walking off the river.

Even dry paddlers are at risk of hypothermia on a cold day. Being wet in cold weather, however, drains the body of precious heat at an alarming rate since water conducts heat away from the body twenty times faster than air. You don't have to be immersed to be wet; paddlers wet by spray or from waves splashing into an

open boat have almost as much risk of hypothermia as a paddler completely immersed after a spill.

The best safeguards against cold weather hazards are:

- preventing exposure to cold by wearing proper clothing (fleece, wool, and waterproof outerwear, wet suits, or dry suits)

- eating sufficient food for metabolic fuel

- drinking water to prevent dehydration

- knowing how the body gains, loses, and conserves body heat

- immediately addressing the early symptoms of hypothermia

- knowing how to treat advanced hypothermia.

Specialized paddling apparel is the best tool for preventing hypothermia; ordinary street clothes lose their insulating properties quickly when wet. Cold-weather paddlers should bring along an extra set of clothes in addition to fire starting material, food, and warm liquids. Snug-fitting PFDs contribute to cold-weather survival because they keep swimmers warm in addition to keeping them afloat.

The symptoms of hypothermia progress quickly when a paddler gets wet. The body, in an attempt to conserve heat, reacts to immersion by reducing blood flow to the arms and legs, making heavy work and coordination difficult. When the body's temperature drops appreciably below the normal 98.6 °F, sluggishness and shivering set in, breathing becomes difficult, coordination is lost to even the most athletic person, pupils dilate, speech grows slurred, and thinking becomes irrational. Cold water robs victims of their judgment, and eventually the ability and desire to save themselves. Body temperatures below 90 °F lead to unconsciousness, and a further drop to about 87 °F usually results in death.

If you find yourself swimming in frigid conditions, exit the water as quickly as possible. If there is no opportunity to exit quickly, conserve body heat by minimizing unproductive swimming, relying upon your PFD to float instead. Muscular activity accelerates heat loss because blood is forced to the extremities where heat is lost. Swim aggressively, however, where necessary to avoid obstacles and when the opportunity to reach shore is present.

The key to successfully bringing someone out of hypothermia is understanding that their body must receive heat from an external source. Put the victim into dry clothes and feed him or her warm liquids—but not alcohol, which is a depressant. Build a campfire if possible. Be prepared to convince the impaired paddler that such actions are necessary.

Skin-to-skin transfer of body heat is by far the best method of getting the body's temperature up. In more extreme situations, strip off all clothes and get the victim into a sleeping bag with another unclothed person; don't let the victim go to sleep. Mouth-to-mouth resuscitation or external cardiac massage may be necessary when breathing has stopped, but remember that a person in the grips of hypothermia has a significantly reduced metabolic rate, so the timing of artificial respiration should correspond to the victim's slowed breathing.

Water Quality

The ecological health of a waterway affects the quality of a paddler's experience in several ways, from increased risks to boaters who take an inadvertent swim to decreased wildlife and vegetation en route. Georgia is home to many caring people who fight to keep local streams clean. The success of their continuous efforts makes it very clear that, when citizens get involved, they have the power to turn the tide against water pollution. A very brief primer in pollution types is provided below. Lists of tools and organizations that combat water pollution follows.

THREATS TO GEORGIA WATERWAYS

- Population increases that drive commercial and residential development near rivers, thereby reducing the land's natural ability to filter pollution out of water draining into streams.

- Sedimentation, due to erosion, which creates a hostile environment for aquatic life by depriving them of vision and respiration and decimating fish's spawning grounds.

- The absence of natural vegetation that holds streambanks in place and provides the cool shady places fish need to rest and spawn.

- Effluent from poultry and hog farms which kills aquatic species by creating algae blooms that rob streams of oxygen.

- Chlorine and stench from sewage-treatment plants.

- Harmful bacteria and protozoa from untreated sewage that overwhelms treatment facilities during rain storms.

- Runoff, referred to as "non-point-source pollution," which flows into streams from streets, lawns, parking lots, and other areas of human and avian activity.

- Toxins which accumulate in fish, harming anglers who eat their catch.

- "Point-source pollution," i.e., municipal and industrial discharge, some of which is permitted by the state Environmental Protection Division (EPD).

- Household trash and roadside litter.

State Law: Georgia's stream buffer laws require all streams having year-round flow, even where crossing private property, to have a buffer of natural vegetation on both sides of the stream at least 25 feet wide. A stricter standard applies to primary trout streams, where the minimum buffer width is 50 feet. The law prohibits any land-disturbing activity within the buffer zone, except that which is temporary and for which best management practices are used to minimize erosion. Despite this law, paddlers across the state witness the continuing creep of single-family residences whose land-use violates the buffer zone, whose denuded yards and banks are not allowed to grow vegetation capable of maintaining healthy streambanks. The lack of compliance indicates that the law is poorly understood and largely unenforced with respect to residential dwellings.

At large commercial construction sites, Georgia put some teeth into its erosion and sedementation law in 2003 when the state legislature appropriated resources for the EPD to hire inspectors who verify that construction sites control soil erosion. Past enforcement was spotty and violators often paid wrist-slap fines without being compelled to cease polluting activities. Now, instead of fines, inspectors levy stop-work orders that shut down noncompliant job sites until they clean up their act. Another new provision of state law requires developers to have employees trained and certified in best-management practices on site while land-disturbing work is performed.

Federal Law: In cases where municipal, county, and state governments have failed to protect streams, federal law in the form of the Clean Water Act has given Georgia citizens the leverage needed to bring polluters into compliance with the law. It has also been used with success to force the state EPD and the national EPA to enforce specific laws protecting streams when those agencies lacked the resources or will to do so on their own initiative.

Greenways: Local governments, aided by private organizations and individual donors, raise money to purchase land surrounding waterways, which is then maintained as green space. By establishing such greenways, these communities protect waterways from reckless development and enhance the quality of life in their neighborhoods.

Education: Less conspicuous outside of agricultural and industrial circles but nevertheless critical to our environment, county extension agencies along with the Georgia Soil and Water Conservation Commission educate farmers and land developers in conservation and best-management practices.

Local Interest: Citizens living in each of Georgia's major watersheds have formed groups, often calling themselves "watershed alliances," that endeavor to protect the health of their respective local streams.

Resources for More Information

Report erosion and sedimentation violations to Georgia's Department of Natural Resources Water Protection Erosion and Sedimentation Control Unit, (404) 675-6240, and its State Soil and Water Conservation Commission, (770) 761-3020. For details, visit the Web site **www.dnr.state.ga.us/dnr/environ.** Enforcement is expected to occur at the county level. For example, Fulton County Soil Erosion and Sedimentation Control Division operates a hotline for erosion (among other) complaints, (404) 730-TELL. Not all counties are as well equipped to address complaints, however.

Upper Chattahoochee Riverkeeper (online at **www.ucriver keeper.org**) continues to write the book on standing up to government and special interests to champion the rights of Chattahoochee watershed residents to have clean, healthy waterways. Behind the scenes of their more visible heroics, a dedicated staff does the yeoman's work of monitoring streams, formulating public policy based on the best available science, taking polluters to court, and educating school children—training them to serve as the environmental stewards of our next generation. The Riverkeeper Web site features contact information for citizens wishing to report erosion and sedimentation violations in counties contiguous with the Chattahoochee as far south as West Point Lake (**www.ucriverkeeper.org/RepInc/Index.shtml**).

Between their two Web sites, the Georgia River Network (**http://garivers.org**) and the Georgia Water Coalition (**www.gwf.org/gawater/aboutus.htm**) provide links to most of the citizen watershed protection organizations throughout Georgia. Both statewide and local organizations promote ongoing stewardship and rally to the cause of clean waterways when streams are threatened.

Similarly, The Georgia Conservancy, which is involved in a wide range of environmental-conservation causes, is a leader in guiding the development of Georgia's stream protection laws.

Their Web site, **www.georgiaconservancy.org,** is an excellent resource for learning about these issues.

Another effective organization, the Georgia Public Interest Research Group (PIRG) publishes "A Citizen's Guide to Fighting Water Pollution in Georgia," which is available online at **www.cleangeorgia.org.**

Paddler's Rights

Because the state of Georgia has yet to codify recreational boaters' right to float, how paddlers conduct themselves on or near the river has a direct impact on boater access. One bad experience can move a landowner to restrict access. Obviously, it pays to know your rights, be courteous, and set an example of responsible stewardship so that you and future boaters can continue to enjoy the waterways of the state.

YOUR RIGHTS ON THE WATER

Dan MacIntyre, an attorney who has toiled in the cause of river-access rights for many years, summarizes the stream-access situation in Georgia:

> *Your legal right of passage down a stream in Georgia [as distinguished from the right of access, discussed below] is governed by both Georgia and federal law. The most recent interpretations of those two bodies of law in 1997 apply inconsistent rules.*
>
> *The Georgia law is based upon the 1863 Georgia Code, which defines a navigable stream as one "which is capable of transporting boats loaded with freight in the regular course of trade either for the whole of part of the year." The Georgia Supreme Court in 1997 found Ichuaway Nochaway Creek in Baker County not to be navigable because there was no proof of historical commercial navigation and the stream would not support contemporary commercial barge traffic. Thus, an owner of both stream banks was allowed to deny passage. The Court specifically noted that its ruling was only based on Georgia law, not federal law.*
>
> *In contrast, The United States District Court for the Northern District of Georgia in 1997 held that the Dog River in Douglas County is navigable under federal law and enjoined an owner of both banks from interfering with passage. The Dog River is a much smaller stream than Ichuaway Nochaway.*

Based on the current state of the law, Georgia's paddlers aren't safe from legal problems unless they are in waters capable of supporting contemporary barge traffic. In practical application, however, conflicts are rare and precipitated by personal issues rather than navigability. The best policy, until the law is clarified, is to avoid areas of known conflict.

Other states, Tennessee included, have adopted a recreational boating test when modernizing their navigability definitions, explicitly providing boaters with the right of passage on streams that can be floated.

YOUR RIGHTS ON LAND

Private land is private; you are trespassing when you stand on it whether you are accessing the river, portaging, camping, or stopping for a lunch break. Landowners' rights to prohibit trespassing on their land along streams, if they so desire, is guaranteed. If you are approached by a landowner, by all means be respectful and understanding and explain what you're doing.

Put-ins and take-outs must be secured at highway rights-of-way, on other publicly owned land, or on private land if permission is secured. If access via private land is required, simply asking the owner for permission will get you the green light in the vast majority of cases. Owners appreciate and sometimes insist on having their authority acknowledged; that is why permission is often denied when it is avoided or assumed and yet is usually so easily obtained by simply asking for it.

In granting you access to a river from their property, landowners are extending a privilege to you such as they extend to hunters who stop by their doors and seek permission to shoot doves in their cornfields. Don't betray landowners' trust; your conduct and courtesy (or lack thereof) will shape a landowner's opinion of paddlers in general. Take up the slack when you encounter evidence that others have been careless or irresponsible. Be sensitive to activities such as changing clothes, relieving yourself, listening to loud music or imbibing alcoholic beverages in view of others.

Your Responsibilities

In all situations, practice good stewardship and treat the land and water with respect. Always pick up your litter, close any gates you open, and respect planted fields. Pick up and carry out garbage you find along the stream or where paddlers park. Often, noisy groups and traffic problems at access points do more to give paddlers a bad reputation than their conduct on

the water. Be mindful of surrounding homes and businesses when getting in or out of the river or when placing a shuttle vehicle.

Likewise, be considerate of other land users. Don't run around in the woods during hunting season; no one expects you to be there. Contrary to some big-city stereotypes, accidentally shooting you is the last thing a landowner wants to deal with. If you are canoe camping, leave your campsite in better shape than you found it. If you must build a fire, build it at an established site, and when you leave, dismantle rock fireplaces, thoroughly drown all flames and hot coals, and scatter the ashes. Never cut live trees for firewood; in addition to destroying a part of the environment, they don't burn. Dump all dishwater away from watercourses, and emulate the cat—bury your excrement.

Georgia's Regions

Georgia can be divided roughly into three geologic regions: Mountains (including the Cumberland Plateau, Valley and Ridges, and Blue Ridge Mountains), Piedmont, and Coastal Plain. Geology, topography, and stream-channel development varies significantly from region to region, creating distinctly diverse river ecologies and paddling experiences.

Climate changes are more gradual throughout the state, varying only slightly by region. Georgia receives an average of about 50 inches of rain a year, most of which comes from warm, moist air masses formed over the Gulf of Mexico. Average rainfall decreases with distance from the Atlantic Ocean and the Gulf up to the Fall Line that separates the Piedmont from the Coastal Plain. North of the Fall Line, average rainfall increases again as air masses are forced to rise and thus precipitate moisture as they pass over the ridges and mountains.

On average, less than half of the water that falls on Georgia finds its way into stream channels. Streamflow has two components: direct runoff from rain and groundwater seepage. What water actually makes it into rivers is heavily impacted by the seasonal demands of plant transpiration and evaporation. Because the elevation of the land, ability of the soil to retain water, and the type and density of vegetation vary dramatically through the state, the amount of rainfall that translates into streamflow varies more significantly than the actual rainfall levels.

A description of the geologic and hydrologic characteristic of each region follows, along with charts illustrating the monthly

rainfall, streamflow, and air and water temperatures for the rivers found within each region.

MOUNTAIN REGION

The mountain region contains two distinct regions. The Cumberland Plateau, including the Valley and Ridge Region, is found in the northwest corner of the state; the Blue Ridge Mountains span the north-central to northeast corner.

The Cumberland Plateau and the Valley and Ridge

The Cumberland Plateau region and the Valley and Ridge region grade one into the other; the Paleozoic sedimentary rocks of the Cumberland lie almost flat, whereas those of the Valley and Ridge are folded. The latter province, which extends into Tennessee and Alabama, gets its name from the long parallel valleys separated by ridges that resulted from the erosion of the folded rocks that extend into Tennessee and Alabama.

Erosion works fastest on the limestone that underlies most of the valleys. Not only is the limestone broken up by other rocks carried by moving water, but it is also dissolved by the water itself. This erosive action has carved an extensive network of interconnected subterranean channels and caverns. Through these large openings, the water moves as freely as it would through a city water main. Since the underground channels are connected under large areas, water that falls as rain in Tennessee may flow underground and emerge in Georgia, or water that falls in Georgia may surface in Alabama.

Both regions are drained by a network of streams that yield substantial river flow. Those in the northwestern part of the state drain north into the Tennessee basin; the remainder drain southwest into the Mobile basin. The streams generally flow in deep channels meandering through wide flood plains. Where they cut through the ridges in water gaps, they are shallow and swift and have numerous rapids under-girded by jagged limestone rocks. Steep slopes give rise to rapid runoff, and flash flooding is common.

The Blue Ridge

The Appalachian Mountains of the eastern United States extend southwestward from the state of Maine to the Blue Ridge province of Georgia. The Blue Ridge Mountain region contains thousands of acres of forest, mountains, and rivers. The area is not farmed extensively nor is it densely populated. The steepness of the topography makes the land more suitable for forest than for farms.

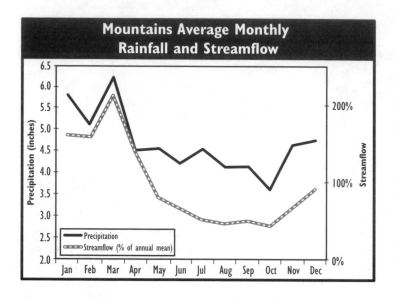

The region is drained by the headwaters of four basins: the Tennessee, Savannah, Chattahoochee, and Coosa. The rivers within the region are small and have small drainages, but they have the highest flow for their size in the state. Their channels are steep and rocky, and water flows swiftly over an abundance of rapids and falls.

The Blue Ridge Mountain region is underlain by rocks that the geologists refer to as crystalline, which includes granite, slate, gneiss, and other dense, hard rocks. The mountains are high and steep and have nearly V-shaped valleys covered with luxurious forests and thick soil, which retard runoff.

The Blue Ridge Mountains are the coolest and wettest part of the state. Average annual rainfall in the region ranges from 55 to more than 80 inches per year, with the greatest amount falling in higher altitudes. The average annual temperature is about 58°F, ten degrees cooler than that in southern Georgia.

The graphic above illustrates the average rainfall and streamflow by month for those streams in the mountain region (mostly the Blue Ridge Mountain streams). The y-axis delineates precipitation in inches; the x-axis marks individual months. Streamflows are expressed as a percentage of the annual average (which equals 100%).

On the Cumberland Plateau, the average annual runoff of streams averages from 18 to 24 inches (compared with a state average of 14 inches). In the Valley and Ridge region, many

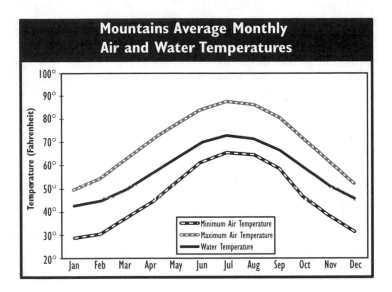

Mountains Average Monthly Air and Water Temperatures

Legend:
- Minimum Air Temperature
- Maximum Air Temperature
- Water Temperature

streams are sustained during dry weather by the numerous springs that are characteristic of the region. Streams of the Cumberland Plateau have lower flow during dry weather because they are not fed by as many springs.

The table above illustrates the monthly high and low air temperatures and average monthly water temperatures for the streams found in the mountains.

PIEDMONT REGION

The Piedmont Region, found directly south of the mountains, is underlain by the same crystalline rocks as the Blue Ridge Mountains but lacks the mountains' heights. Instead, it is an area of rolling plains broken occasionally by narrow stream valleys and prominent hills. The soil cover in the Piedmont is not as thick or as capable of slowing runoff as that of the Blue Ridge.

The region includes parts of several drainages. The Savannah, Ogeechee, Ocmulgee, and Oconee rivers drain into the Atlantic Ocean while the Flint and Chattahoochee drain into the Gulf of Mexico. Throughout most of the region the main streams flow southeastward, with the general slope of the upland, and cross the underlying rock structure at right angles. This creates shelf-like rapids that stretch from bank to bank and rivers that don't run through well-defined channels in comparatively narrow valleys in contrast to rivers like the Chattahoochee. In the northwestern section of the Piedmont, the Chattahoochee and some

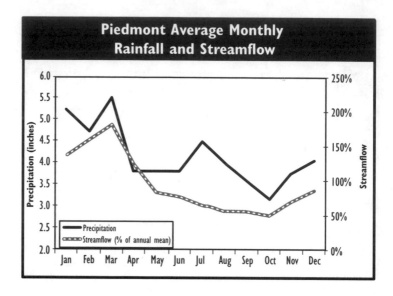

Piedmont Average Monthly Rainfall and Streamflow

streams in the Mobile basin tend to parallel the direction of the rock strata. Rivers there generally have moderate slopes interrupted by occasional rapids and falls and flow in well-defined channels within comparatively narrow valleys.

Ridges between the major drainage systems of the Piedmont are broad and rather sinuous, with the region's primary cities, highways, industries, railroads, and farmlands concentrated atop of them. Towns were first established on the ridges along the old wagon trails and railroads because the ridges were well-drained routes that required a minimum number of bridges and were free from the danger of floods.

Rainfall along the northern Piedmont, the area of highest elevation, averages more than 50 inches annually. To the south and east the rainfall is less. The Augusta area receives less than any other part of the state, a little more than 42 inches annually.

The accompanying table illustrates the average rainfall and streamflow in the Piedmont by month. A second table shows the average monthly high and low air temperatures along with the average monthly water temperature for the Piedmont's streams. The Savannah and Chattahoochee Rivers were not included in the calculation of average water temperature. During the warm months, both rivers are 10 to 20 degrees colder than other Piedmont streams due to cold water releases from their power-generating dams.

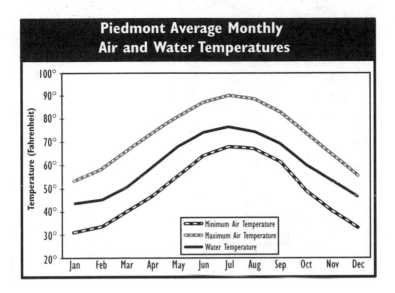

Piedmont Average Monthly Air and Water Temperatures

Legend:
- Minimum Air Temperature
- Maximum Air Temperature
- Water Temperature

COASTAL PLAIN REGION

The Coastal Plain begins immediately south of the Piedmont at the Fall Line—a discernible geologic break between the hard rock strata of the Piedmont and the more easily eroded rock of the Coastal Plain. This line, which roughly parallels the eastern seaboard, is marked by steep cliffs, rapids, and waterfalls.

Cretaceous sand aquifers, a blanket of sand and gravel, begin at the Fall Line and thicken to the south. Rainfall filters into this sand blanket and recharges the sand aquifer with water. When stream levels are high, water moves from the streams into the sands. When the stream levels are low, water feeds back from the sands into the streams.

Streams crossing the Coastal Plain that originate in the Piedmont or in the Blue Ridge transport heavy loads of sediment. The Savannah, Altamaha, Ogeechee, Alabama, and Apalachicola (including the Flint and Chattahooochee) systems carry large sediment loads and are therefore considered alluvial rivers.

The streams that originate in the Coastal Plain generally carry very little sediment. Running over sand and sandy clay, their waters flow clear and sparkling, colored a reddish tea color by tannic acid derived from tree roots and decaying vegetation. Because the reddish water appears glossy and black in direct sunlight, these streams are known as blackwater rivers.

In the southwestern area of the upper Coastal Plain near Albany, limestone-sand aquifers give rise to lime sinks, caves, underground rivers, and artesian wells. These features are formed

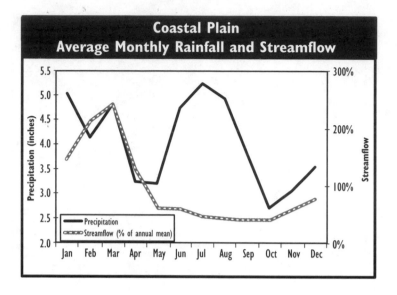

Coastal Plain
Average Monthly Rainfall and Streamflow

by the solvent action of water on limestone. When the limestone is dissolved, caverns and interconnected channels are left below the surface. If the cavern roof collapses, sink holes are created. In low water periods, sink holes can consume the entire flow of these southern rivers, creating a dead-end for paddlers.

The annual rainfall in the Coastal Plain averages from 45 to 52 inches, draining slowly over the flat terrain, with the part that does not sink into the ground quickly evaporated or consumed by vegetation. Table 5 illustrates the average monthly rainfall and streamflow for the streams of the Coastal Plain.

Hydrologists differentiate between streams in the upper Coastal Plain and the lower Coastal Plain. Streams in the upper Coastal Plain have relatively uniform flows and high volume because of minimal storm runoff and large groundwater inflow. The average annual runoff of the larger streams ranges from 12 to 28 inches. The streams are generally sluggish and flow in deep, meandering, low-banked, tree-choked channels bordered by wide, swampy, densely wooded valleys. The very small streams commonly have very little runoff because the permeable soil absorbs rainwater rapidly and the channels are not entrenched deeply enough to intercept much groundwater flow.

The lower Coastal Plain generally has the least runoff of any part of Georgia, averaging from 9 to 14 inches annually. Streams here wander in wide, swampy, heavily wooded valleys separated by very wide and very low flat ridges. Swamp vegetation consumes large quantities of water and evaporation loss is high.

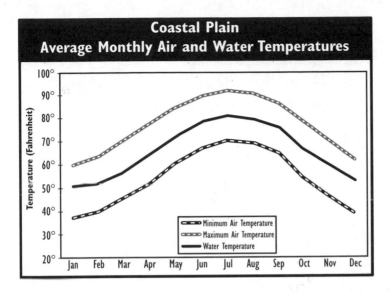

Coastal Plain
Average Monthly Air and Water Temperatures

Legend:
- Minimum Air Temperature
- Maximum Air Temperature
- Water Temperature

The Coastal Plain is the warmest region of the state; monthly temperature averages are shown in the accompanying table.

A Word about Alligators The rivers and streams of the Coastal Plain play host to alligators which can be found as far north as Macon. Their numbers increase the farther south one travels, with particular concentrations southwest of Albany and in the vicinity of the Okefenokee Swamp (Satilla, Suwannee, and St. Marys Rivers).

Generally nonaggressive and retiring in encounters with humans, gators can sometimes be rather unpredictable. Though attacks are exceedingly rare, wildlife experts speculate that they arise from some confusion on the part of the beast as to just what it is attacking. That is of little consolation, since confused alligators neither wreak less damage nor appear any more apologetic than unconfused alligators. The obvious lesson is to preclude confusion. With this in mind, a few simple guidelines should suffice in keeping paddlers safe from encounters with less-than-lucid crocodilians.

1. Never feed alligators; they have difficulty discerning what is and is not food.

2. Never disturb an alligator's nest, even if the mother is momentarily absent. Females with nests are fearless in protecting their eggs and often display remarkably aggressive behavior. Gators are surprisingly fast on land as well as in the water.

3. Do not swim at night. Gators are night feeders.

4. Do not clean fish in camp or leave fish heads or other remains in an area where humans will be.

5. Do not leave children unattended.

6. If possible, leave the family dog at home. See #1 above.

7. Do not make loud or threatening sounds.

Part**One**

THE SAVANNAH RIVER WATERSHED

OVERFLOW CREEK

Overflow Creek is a high-water run for skilled and intrepid boaters. Located in Rabun County, Overflow Creek joins Holcomb Creek and Big Creek at the headwaters of the West Fork of the Chattooga River, and a requisite stint on the latter precedes the take-out. Not for the faint of heart, the entire run is highly technical. The stream is small but very powerful when the water is high. If Section IV of the Chattooga bores you, try Overflow.

MAPS: Satolah (USGS); Rabun (County)

FS 86B TO FS 86 (OVERFLOW CREEK ROAD)

class	IV–V (V+)
length	5 mi
time	4 hr
gauge	Visual
level	0.9 ft
gradient	158 fpm
scenery	A+

DESCRIPTION: You might want to add a parachute to your safety gear for this one. In the 4-mile section between the Overflow Creek access at Three Forks Road (FS 86B) and the take-out where Overflow Creek Road (FS 86) crosses the West Fork of the Chattooga River, this run drops 380 feet. Rapids of Class V+ difficulty dot the route. Scouting is advisable, but is complicated by dense streamside foliage and nearly vertical banks. This run is for experts only, and demands taking all safety precautions.

Overflow starts out as a small stream, but soon begins a rapid descent. There are numerous blind drops; once the paddler in front of you passes over the lip, you do not see them again until you enter the drop yourself. Debris and undercuts are the primary hazards, but vertical pins have occurred on Overflow Creek. There are unnamed drops on this run that would be considered significant rapids on another river.

When you decide to run Overflow Creek for the first time, it is in your best interest to accompany someone who knows the run thoroughly and can give you good instructions en route. There are must-catch eddies, some right before or after a drop, that you are difficult to pinpoint from scouting alone.

Some of the initial drops are Bushwhacker, Peewee, and Roundabout. You may think these are the run's major rapids at

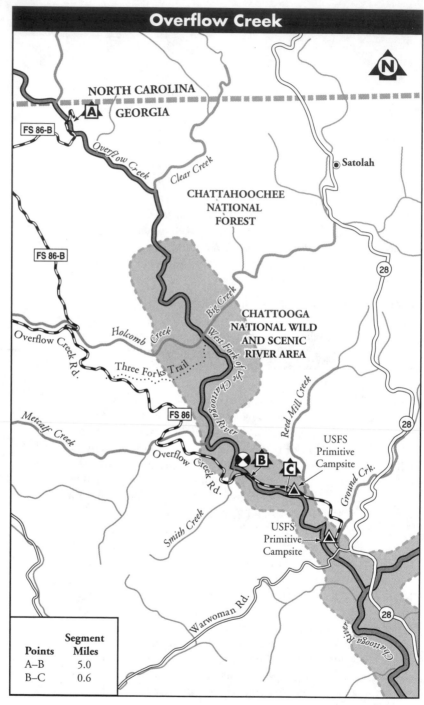

Overflow Creek

NORTH CAROLINA

GEORGIA

FS 86-B

Overflow Creek

Clear Creek

• Satolah

CHATTAHOOCHEE
NATIONAL
FOREST

FS 86-B

Big Creek

CHATTOOGA
NATIONAL WILD
AND SCENIC
RIVER AREA

Overflow Creek Rd.

Holcomb Creek

Three Forks Trail

West Fork of the Chattooga River

Reed Mill Creek

Metcalf Creek

FS 86

USFS
Primitive
Campsite

Overflow Creek Rd.

Smith Creek

Ground Crk.

USFS
Primitive
Campsite

Warwoman Rd.

Chattooga River

Points	Segment Miles
A–B	5.0
B–C	0.6

first, but they are not. The first of the big drops is Blind Falls. Scout on the far right, and when you run it try to stay as far right as you can. Don't let the nose of your boat turn left before hitting bottom, otherwise you will end up in the hole or against the slightly undercut left wall. Gravity, the next rapid, waits not far downstream, so you don't want to swim out of Blind Falls. Eddy out on the right as soon as possible and scout Gravity on the right.

Gravity is Class 5.0 because of the pothole at the base of the drop on river right; it almost took the life of an experienced boater. You must decide whether to portage on the right or to move left at the top of the drop to land on river left and run down the left side. The rapid funnels at the bottom, so if you run it, make sure that when coming down the left side you are not prematurely kicked right. Try to boof the bottom.

Scout and run Singley's Falls on the left. The total drop is close to 37 feet, and at lower water levels it is possible to get your boat completely out of the water onto dry rock on the left. If you boof out of Gravity, you will stay on the left side of the drop; otherwise, you will be funneled into the center. You are already better prepared than past first timers; years ago, guides commonly told unsuspecting paddlers to run the next drop with no warning of its height.

The next drop, Twilight, requires a boof off a mid-stream rock to avoid being smashed against the left wall. After Overflow's confluence with Big and Holcomb Creeks at Three Forks, the first rapid on West Fork of the Chattooga is Igore. Watch for

photo © Rob Maxwell

Gravity rapids at Overflow Creek

undercuts and rock sieves in Igore, and be certain to catch the solitary eddy on river left just after the drop. The eddy must be caught to scout or portage the Great Marginal Monster, the next rapid. Paddling with someone who knows the river and exactly where this eddy is located could be a lifesaver. It is tempting to ignore the eddy and try and take a peak at what lies around the corner. However, missing the eddy normally means you will run the next rapid ready or not, as the current is often too strong to back up.

The entrance to Great Marginal Monster is a little tricky and is normally run on the right, as the hydraulic on the left is stronger than it looks. It can force unfortunate paddlers to swim out of a hole in one of the last places you want to be caught in the water. At normal levels, there is a boat-length flat after the entrance drop and before a boulder in the center diverts the current on both sides into a couple of huge, twin undercuts. A majority of the water in the river goes through these undercuts, and boats have washed through them with up-turned ends. When running this drop, some paddlers boof the rock in the center, while some just continue on the river-left angle with which they finished the river-right entrance drop.

Passing these undercuts without being extruded through them doesn't signal an end to the fun; another big hole can form where the water shooting out of the undercuts converges. Even if you walk this one, putting in right below the hole is still fun. Given the twist at the bottom, you don't want too bury your boat too deeply. Marginal Monster, Gravity, and Pinball are the "Big Three" on this run, in order of increasing difficulty.

Run Pencil Sharpener on far river right to avoid the potential undercut on river left. Pinball, Class 5.1, is a big, long rapid in which it may be difficult to remain upright. Because you don't want to flip over, it's best not to allow your boat to head straight in to the bottom of this drop either.

The last real rapid on this run is Swiss Cheese. This is a blind rapid; even if you have someone leading you down, don't depend on being able to follow their moves visually. Oftentimes, once the person ahead drops over the horizon line, you won't catch sight of them again until it is time to eddy out. It's best to receive verbal instructions on this beautiful rapid.

Longer boats increase the danger level on Overflow. Rapids full of strainers and with no eddies are found above Class V drops. A creek boat, in contrast, allows for nimble maneuvering and more breathing space in the narrow, steep corridors.

In addition to the parachute, bring a flashlight. Unexpected water surges push the creek beyond runnability, and have forced seasoned Class V paddlers to hike out.

SHUTTLE: From Clayton, head east on Warwoman Road. Turn left onto Overflow Creek Road (FS 86) immediately after crossing the West Fork of the Chattooga. Turn right at FS 86B. The put-in is at the end of this road. You will pass several potential take-outs are along the way, the Forest Service campground on the left being the best option.

GAUGE: There is a gauge in the river upstream of the Overflow Creek Road bridge across the West Fork of the Chattooga. Based on paddler postings on American Whitewater's Web site, 0.9 feet is a recommended minimum; exercise caution at levels above 2 feet. Chattooga levels at US 76 can also be used; when the Chattooga is 2.5 feet and on the way up, it may be worth the drive. Knowing whether the creek is on the way up or down is crucial to gauging the feasibility of a run.

Courting Overflow

*Excerpted from American Whitewater's Web site, the following is a conversation about the first runs on Overflow Creek, as relayed by Robin Sayler in the **rec.boats.paddle** discussion forum:*

Not long after you ran Big Creek, Ken, Alan Singley entered West Fork history. He had hiked Overflow, Holcomb, and Big Creeks a good deal by then—as well as the North Fork Chattooga Sections I, Zero, Double Zero, and Minus I, and even Scotsman's Branch. One fine day, I believe in 1975, or maybe 1976, he dropped his boating and camping gear off at the culvert bridge, now famous as the Overflow put-in, drove his truck to the West Fork bridge, and hiked back up to spend the night. The next afternoon, about 5 miles and eight or nine portages later, Alan emerged with wondrous tales of a fantastic whitewater run, with the improbable name of Overflow Creek. The fact that he soloed the exploratory doesn't surprise anyone who knows Alan.

Alan's spectacular, if somewhat unbelievable, tales fascinated everyone, but failed to gain him a partner for another descent. Undaunted, Alan proceeded on

another solo run, this time with five or six portages. Finally he convinced another boater to accompany him, none other than Robert Harrison, an open boater of some renown. Alan and Robert survived, but, alas, Robert's Old Town Tripper was finished, thanks to Pinball. If I recall, Robert made about seven portages on that trip. Should have been eight. Robert's account of that descent convinced everyone that Alan Singley was not only crazy, but a menace to society in general, and to paddlers in particular. It was truly amazing to watch Robert's face as he told us of the Terror That Was Overflow. This sufficiently warned everyone, so again Alan couldn't find anybody to paddle Overflow with him. So, typically, he made the fourth descent solo, this time with four portages. This was sometime in 1977.

That year Diane and I moved to Highlands, North Carolina, situated on top of the ridge that separates Overflow Creek from the Cullasaja River. I was glad to get reacquainted with Alan, who previously had introduced me to the Watauga. One fall afternoon, Alan and I were settin' around jus' doin' nuthin' (that's how it's said up there), and he casually mentioned that I ought to "take a look at" Overflow. Before I knew it, we were crashing through the rhododendrons with our boats, just downstream of the culvert. We put in on this beautiful little gurgling creek, in incredibly beautiful surroundings, and then Alan took off, with me in tow. I can't tell you how many times I followed this young giant, sitting up high in his C-1, down some unforgettable adventure into the unknown, but this was to be the most memorable of them all!

About a mile later, my head was spinning after running some of the most incredible rapids I had ever done. We pulled into an eddy, for the first time since the put-in, and Alan said "what do you think?" I was nearly speechless, but his next sentence struck me dumb!

"We're starting to get close to the big drops, so stay close." "Big drops?" I stammered, "What have we been running for the last mile?" He said nothing, but smiled and peeled out. I got really nervous when he eddied out in a few yards, and said "this is a pretty good one—just stay right and you'll be fine." Then he took off, and disappeared over the edge. I thought I'd seen him for the last time. I scrambled out onto a rock and looked at the horizon line, expecting traces of wreckage, and finally saw the tip of his paddle waving. Not wanting to be left, I swallowed hard and . . .

It was unreal! I asked Alan how many times he had run that 15-foot falls, and when he said "Once—today," I knew the name of that drop immediately—Blind Falls. The rest of the run was like a dream—a whitewater dream. Singley's Falls waited for another day, and we stayed permanently away from Gravity and the Great Marginal Monster.

Then you entered the picture, Ken, and now the whole world knows! Well, maybe it's not just your fault. Anyway, Overflow is too special not to share."

Bo Eakens adds a postscript based on a trip a short time thereafter: "It was the summer of 1978 and the Chattooga had just gotten the big rain. Several of us working for NOC and Southeastern had all our trips cancelled—even Section III was too high for a trip that day. We had all heard about Overflow from the locals, knew there were a few drops still unrun, and decided we'd give it a shot . . . By the time we got to the take-out all the Hollowforms had about 6 inches to 1 foot of the nose pointed towards Heaven. John Kennedy went through the hole at the bottom of Marginal and we watched as his stern seams blew out on both sides. The nose of my Slipper and John Regan's Sauna would require some minimal repairs also . . .

WEST FORK OF THE CHATTOOGA RIVER

Protected within the Chattooga Wild and Scenic River Area, the West Fork contains 4 miles of extremely scenic canoeing for the novice and can be used as an intimate launching pad for a longer trip into Section II of the Chattooga. The river is formed by the unusual symmetrical junction of three creeks: Overflow, Big, and Holcomb. For those interested in visiting the headwaters in addition to the tailwaters, the Three Forks hiking trail to this point is found farther up the same road as the put-in. The camping is good, inviting multiple-day trips within the area.

MAPS: Satolah (USGS); Rabun (County)

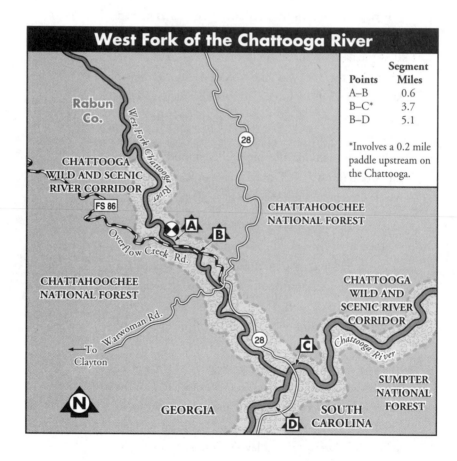

West Fork of the Chattooga River

Points	Segment Miles
A–B	0.6
B–C*	3.7
B–D	5.1

*Involves a 0.2 mile paddle upstream on the Chattooga.

OVERFLOW CREEK ROAD TO THE CHATTOOGA RIVER

class	I–II
length	5.7 mi
time	3 hr
gauge	Visual
level	1.0
gradient	10 fpm
scenery	A-

DESCRIPTION: The river is a popular one for trout fishing and provides one of the best opportunities on the Chattooga to both canoe and fish on the same trip. If floating by a fishing party, minimize any disruption by passing quietly.

The West Fork's rapids are mostly Class I, but two rapids are designated Class II. The first of these is formed by the remains of an old dam, 1 mile below Warwoman Road. The other Class II, Big Slide, is 1.5 miles below the old dam and less than 0.5 miles above the confluence with the main Chattooga.

The most frequently used put-in is at the U.S. Forest Service campground, less than a mile from Warwoman Road. Ample parking is available there, and the carry to the river is short. Take-out either at the GA 28 Russell Bridge, 0.2 miles upstream on the main Chattooga, or drift downstream to the Long Bottom Ford take-out on river left. There is no direct road access at the confluence of the West Fork and the main Chattooga.

SHUTTLE: From US 441 in Clayton, turn east on Rickman Street and then right onto Warwoman Road. Take Warwoman Road 13.4 miles to the river; turn left onto Overflow Creek Road on the far side of the bridge. Potential put-in locations on Overflow Creek Road are 0.9 miles ahead at the U.S. Forest Service campground (primitive camping is available here), or an additional 0.4 miles above that, where the road crosses the river.

GAUGE: See Overflow Creek. The recommended minimum level for running the West Fork of the Chattooga is 1.0 foot.

CHATTOOGA RIVER

The famed Chattooga is one of the nation's most renown rivers. Its reputation is well-deserved—it is a spectacular wilderness river that frolics through rock outcroppings and forest thickets that contain virtually no sign of human habitation. Located along the Georgia–South Carolina border, the river is protected under the Wild and Scenic Rivers Act and managed by the U.S. Forest Service, which divides the river into sections. The river above GA 28 (including Section I from Burrells Ford to the GA 28 bridge) is the only stretch of river in Georgia where paddling is prohibited by law. The remaining three sections consist of 28 miles of pristine whitewater paddling that encompass something for all paddlers, from beginners to experts. Its excellence rivals any river in this country.

MAPS: Satolah, Whetstone, Rainy Mountain (USGS); Rabun, GA, and Oconee, SC (County); Chattooga National Wild and Scenic River (USFS).

GA 28 TO EARLS FORD (SECTION II)

class	I–II (III)
length	7.4 mi
time	4.5 hr
gauge	Web and visual
level	0.8
gradient	11 fpm
scenery	A

DESCRIPTION: Section II of the Chattooga begins at the GA 28 bridge (there is easy access and parking on the Georgia side of the bridge) and continues down river to Earls Ford. This section is approximately 7 miles long and is a good day-trip for beginning boaters. Initially, the stream is shallow and rocky with only a slight gradient. Considerable volume is added when the West Fork of the Chattooga flows in from the right approximately 100 yards below the GA 28 bridge.

The valley through which the upper river flows has a rich history. It was at one time the site of Chattooga Old Town, one of the largest Native American settlements in the Southeast. The town became a major Indian trading center after white men came to the area. The valley was ideally suited for agriculture, and the land-lustful transplants soon appropriated the valley as their own. A large farmhouse owned by the Russell family is one of the few structures from the early agricultural period that is still standing. It lies just off the river on the South Carolina side above Long Bottom Ford, another access point for this section (B).

This area was also visited by colonial naturalist William Bartram and described in his *Travels*. A portion of the Bartram Trail, named in his honor, joins the Chattooga River Trail and parallels the river on the Georgia side throughout Section II down to Sandy Ford Road in Section III.

Chattooga River Map 1

Points	Segment Miles
A–B	1.8
B–C	5.6
C–D	3.1
D–E	2.0
E–F	2.1

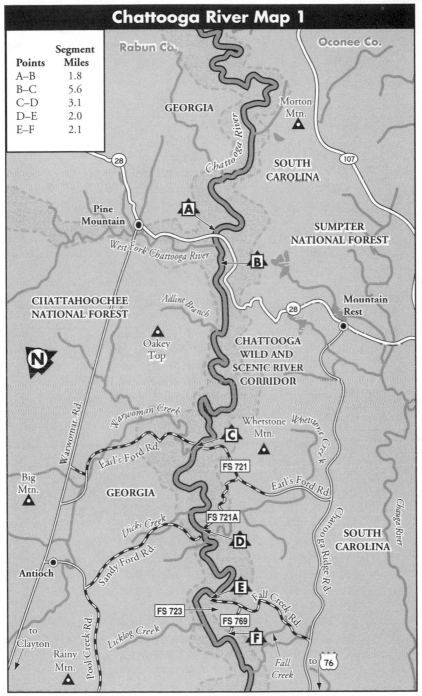

Rabun Co.

Oconee Co.

GEORGIA

Morton Mtn.

SOUTH CAROLINA

28

107

Pine Mountain

A

Chattooga River

SUMPTER NATIONAL FOREST

West Fork Chattooga River

B

CHATTAHOOCHEE NATIONAL FOREST

Adline Branch

28

Mountain Rest

Oakey Top

CHATTOOGA WILD AND SCENIC RIVER CORRIDOR

N

Warwoman Creek

Whetstone Mtn.

Whetstone Creek

C

FS 721

Earl's Ford Rd.

Big Mtn.

GEORGIA

Earl's Ford Rd.

FS 721A

Dicks Creek

D

Chattooga Ridge Rd.

Chauga River

SOUTH CAROLINA

Antioch

Sandy Ford Rd.

E

Fall Creek Rd.

FS 723

FS 769

F

to Clayton

Rainy Mtn.

Pool Creek Rd.

Licklog Creek

Fall Creek

to 76

For the first few miles of Section II the Chattooga is a meandering, gentle, valley stream. Through the valley the river remains close to SC 28, and several seasonal dwellings in private ownership are scattered along the South Carolina shore. Near the end of the valley is the access point at Long Bottom Ford (B). Upon leaving the valley, the terrain begins to revert to a wilderness character and the river quickens its pace. Large hemlocks and white pines thrust from the rocky banks and small islands. In the spring the banks sport a profusion of wildflowers and flowering shrubs, including flame-orange and white wild azaleas.

After passing several large islands in the stream, you will reach the long deep pool that precedes Turn Hole Rapid, the first rapid that most paddlers deem worthy of a name. The rapid is not very difficult, but it can trick the unwary. The approach is through a shallow shoal area that has several possible routes. The main drop is usually entered near the left side. It calls for a quick turn to the right, which is necessary to avoid being pushed into the rocky bank. At average water levels you can run near the center of the stream, straight across the main ledge, if desired. The drop is about 3 feet.

Continuing downstream through another half mile or so of mild Class I and II rapids, you will round the bend to see a group of large boulders and rock slabs extending almost completely across the river. This is Big Shoals, rated Class III by the Forest Service, and it should be scouted. The approach to the rapid is blind due to the large rocks, and occasionally logs or entire trees have become lodged in the main chutes. Scout from the boulders to the right of center.

Big Shoals is a veritable whitewater gymnasium—an excellent place for beginners to play and train. There are several routes to run and a large pool at the bottom for easy recovery. There is also a relatively simple portage back up and over the rocks if you wish to try it again.

The easiest and most popular route at Big Shoals is next to the right bank. There is a nice tongue dropping swiftly into a small reversal wave at the head of the pool below. Other possible routes are over the curler in the right center and, at most water levels, the chute on the far left side.

The remainder of the trip down to Earls Ford has many long, slow pools and a sprinkling of Class I and II whitewater. Look for wildlife in this section; many hawks nest near the stream, and deer are frequently seen early and late in the day.

You will easily recognize the Earls Ford take-out where Warwoman Creek, a fairly large stream, enters the river on the right.

There is a well-trodden sand and gravel beach on the left. If you are getting out here, you are about to begin the worst part of your trip—the quarter-mile carry uphill to the parking lot.

SHUTTLE: Drive east on US 76 out of Clayton to the take-out at Earls Ford. Approximately 2 miles after crossing the river into South Carolina, turn left onto Chattooga Ridge Road. About 6 miles ahead, turn left onto Earls Ford Road and proceed another 3.8 miles to the parking area. Put-ins are reached by returning to the Chattooga Ridge Road and proceeding north another 3.4 miles to SC 28. Turn left here; the entrance to Long Bottom Ford is 4.7 miles ahead or use the GA/SC 28 bridge on the Georgia side of the river.

GAUGE: The minimum runnable level is 0.8 feet; maximum is 3.5. Most boaters refer to the visual gauge located at the US 76 bridge. Levels for this location are also available on the USGS Web site, but are not exactly the same as visual levels. Recently, the staff gauge was unofficially moved in a misguided attempt to remove the discrepancy, resulting in further confusion. Levels provided here refer to the historic position of the visual gauge.

EARLS FORD TO US 76 (SECTION III)

class	II–IV (V)
length	12.2 mi
time	6.5 hr
gauge	Web, visual
level	0.8 ft
gradient	25 fpm
scenery	A+

DESCRIPTION: Section III of the Chattooga stretches from Earls Ford (C) to the US 76 bridge. Multiple access points along this stretch allow for day-trips of manageable length. Depending on the amount of time spent scouting or portaging, paddling all of Section III in one day is difficult, and definitely strenuous.

By the time the river reaches Earls Ford, the volume has increased significantly and the average gradient is much steeper than that of Section II. The first rapid encountered is a fairly straight drop to the right of center over a 3-foot ledge. From the large eddy and pool below this drop, look downstream and to the left for the entrance to Warwoman Rapid. This tricky Class II+ should be entered on the left, heading toward the right. After the small initial drop, make a quick turn to the left and back downstream. The pillowed rock in the center of the chute can pin or capsize your boat if you do not make your turn quickly.

Rock Garden, noted more for its scenic value than for the difficulty of its rapids, is next. You weave between huge boulders and fingerlike slabs of granite that often overshadow the stream. The rapids are mild, but you should stay on your toes.

photo © Tom Welander

Section III on the Chattooga River

Three Rooster Tails Rapid is the next challenge. After a sharp bend in the river, the channel narrows and spills over a series of funneling rocky ledges beneath overhanging rocks. Three pluming waves (the rooster tails) can be seen in the center of the route. The easiest run is just to the right of these pluming waves.

Just below this rapid the river widens and slows to relative tranquility. As you look far downstream you will see Dicks Creek (Five Finger) Falls cascading over a 50- to 60-foot drop into the river on the right. Slightly upstream of this falls, on the Chattooga, is a low shelf of rock that forms part of a definite river horizon line. Stop on this shelf for a mandatory scouting of Dicks Creek Ledge.

Dicks Creek Ledge is given a Class IV rating in Forest Service literature. There are several possible routes; one of them is a portage over the rocks in the center. Most who run the rapid try to make the S-turn over the two drops. Start the first drop heading toward the right, and be prepared to make an extreme cut back to the left at the bottom of the second drop. The S-turn maneuver becomes increasingly difficult at higher water levels.

A short distance beyond Dicks Creek Ledge you will observe a large rocky island. Down the right side of this island is a series of Class III drops called Stairsteps Rapid. This is not one of the major rapids on Section III. If you are doing well at this point, selecting an appropriate course through the Stairsteps should not be difficult.

Just below Stairsteps is another island, which precedes Class III Sandy Ford Rapid. The favored route is also to the right of this island. Sandy Ford, a mid-section access point (D), is located on the left immediately after this rapid. It is recognizable by the sand beaches on both sides of a pooled area. Gravel road access is on both sides of the river, but the Forest Service road on the South Carolina side is recommended.

As you round the bend below Sandy Ford you will come into a large pooled area that leads into the entrance to the fabled Narrows. The Narrows' combination of whitewater, high rock faces, and drooping ferns has made this a favorite spot on the river. If you've brought your camera, this should definitely be recorded on film. To scout the entrance, get out on the lower left end of this pool.

In the Narrows, the river drops over a series of ledges, decreasing in width as it drops. The biggest holes are just to the left of center; the least turbulent path is to the far right. Take your pick. Open canoes needing to bail and others needing a breather may eddy out on the left below the first series of drops. The river continues to narrow and drop until it's only a few feet wide, which creates some strangely turbulent currents. The final drop in the Narrows is around the right side of an under-cut rock midstream. It should be noted that the area immediately below this series of drops has fast moving and highly irregular boiling currents, strong eddy lines, and numerous undercut rocks. For these reasons, the Forest Service has given the Narrows a Class IV rating. If you should find yourself swimming in the Narrows, avoid all contact with rocks, except from the downstream side.

One of the more dramatic rapids on Section III is not far downstream. Second Ledge is a breathtaking and heart-stopping 6-foot vertical drop. It may be scouted from the left bank at any water level, and from the rocks in the center of the stream at lower levels. Most paddlers run straight over the top of the drop on the left. Keep your boat parallel to the current and maintain brisk speed. Be ready to brace firmly when you hit the aerated water at the bottom. Second Ledge is not extremely difficult, but it does get your adrenaline pumping.

Less than 2 miles from Second Ledge is Eye of the Needle, a Class III plunge. Most of the current is pushed against the left bank down a narrow chute that cuts slightly back to the right. The current does most of the work for you in this rapid, but beware of leaning too far to the right as you progress down the chute. You may need a strong brace to stay upright.

For approximately the next 4 miles the river alternates between long pools and Class I and II rapids. Two additional access points are available in this segment; the first is reached by a steep path from the end of FS 723 (E), the second by a half-mile trek from the end of FS 769 (F). The second of these is more easily spotted from the river, and is marked with a post engraved "Fall Creek." The creek itself enters the river downstream of this point, cascading 25 feet into the river. The next two significant rapids are just ahead.

Roller Coaster is a fast, bucking, Class II ride down an extended series of large standing waves. Go for the center of the waves for the most excitement. There is a large pool at the base of Roller Coaster in which to bail and recover if necessary. Immediately around the bend is Keyhole, or Painted Rock Rapid. Much of the current pushes strongly toward a huge undercut boulder at the bottom of the drop. To avoid this rock, begin to the right of center and continue to work right as you descend. You may also run down the extreme left, but a move to the right of the boulder is still essential. If the water level is extremely low, the far left or far right may be your only choices. Painted Rock is rated a Class IV rapid by the Forest Service but is generally considered to be III+ difficulty.

Roughly 3 more miles of Class I and II water (G) brings you to the Class IV+ Bull Sluice. You will know you've arrived at Bull Sluice because of the extremely large boulders extending from the Georgia side of the river, which seem to block the entire stream. Even those who have run this rapid many times before still stop to scout it. Pull out well above these rocks on the Georgia (right) side and walk down to do your scouting. Inexperienced paddlers and those unfamiliar with the sluice have been known to enter the Class III entrance rapids just above it only to find themselves committed to running the thundering lower drops against their will.

Changing water levels alter the difficulty of Bull Sluice considerably and may also alter your plan of attack. Bull Sluice has been run in an infinite variety of crafts by an infinite variety of people. On any given day you will see examples of the worst and best whitewater technique at Bull Sluice. The rapid should not be taken lightly; there have been fatalities here, and on several occasions people, both in and out of their boats, have been stuck in the upper hydraulic for uncomfortably long periods of time. The lower drop is much rockier beneath the surface than it appears. Look at it carefully before you decide to run it. The portage is on the right side over the boulders.

If you decide to run Bull Sluice, here is one of many possible routes. Follow the Class III entrance rapid down the river-left

side and hit the eddy on the left, which is just above the major drop. If you are in an open canoe and have taken on much water, this is the place to bail it out. It is a good spot of level river from which to reconnoiter what lies ahead. Peel out very high from this eddy and head straight over the first of the double drops just to the left of the center of the upper hole. The current will tend to push you to the left, so use it to your advantage to hit the second drop head on. Good luck!

A few hundred yards below Bull Sluice is the US 76 bridge (H). This marks the end of Section III and the beginning of Section IV. Boating access is from the large paved parking lot on the South Carolina side of the bridge. The Forest Service also provides a footpath access to Bull Sluice for those who may want to get a glimpse of the giant rapid without actually getting in the water.

SHUTTLE: The take-out is located on US 76 east of Clayton. The parking lot is the first left immediately after crossing the river. All put-ins for this section are reached via the Chattooga Ridge Road, a left turn 2 miles farther east on US 76. Other access points, from highest to lowest, are at Earls Ford (down Earls Ford Road), Sandy Ford (a left turn on FS 721A off of Earls Ford Road), FS 723 and FS 769 off of Fall Creek Road, and Thrifts Ferry accessible via a dirt road 1 mile east of the bridge on US 76.

GAUGE: Most boaters refer to the visual gauge located at the US 76 bridge (see first section). Levels for this location are also available on the USGS Web site, but are not exactly the same as visual levels. Section III can be run as low as 0.8 feet, but below 1.5 expect to be scraping along, particularly in the higher reaches. It is much more fun at 2 feet and above, and should only be run by expert boaters above 3 feet.

US 76 TO LAKE TUGALOO (SECTION IV)

class	IV–V
length	8.3 mi
time	4.5 hr
gauge	Web, visual
level	0.8 ft
gradient	46 fpm
scenery	A+

DESCRIPTION: In spite of the myriad attractions of Section III, it is probably Section IV's reputation as the ultimate whitewater experience that brings the throngs to the Chattooga. Skilled boaters from throughout North America try to make at least one pilgrimage to Section IV. Because of the greater difficulty and frequency of the rapids on this section, it should only be attempted by those with a high degree of competence. Since it is advisable that only advanced boaters attempt to paddle Section IV, this portion of the guidebook will give attention only to the more hazardous or unusual rapids.

Surfing Rapid, just around the first bend, is exactly what it sounds like—an excellent spot for surfing or playing the river. The best wave is to the far right.

Screaming Left Turn is located approximately 200 yards below Surfing Rapid. Large boulders direct the main stream to the far right. The river then flushes through an extremely sharp turn back to the left—almost all the way to the left bank. The most straightforward route is to follow the main channel, avoiding the shallows on the outside of the curve where strainers sometimes lodge. Screaming Left Turn is designated a Class IV by the Forest Service. Approximately a half mile farther downstream you will reach a point where the river is choked by large mounds of granite; only a horizon line is visible from upstream. This rapid is called Rock Jumble. Several bumpy routes are possible, but the best route is probably to the left of center, following the tongue of deeper water that begins there and washes right and toward the center. Just below, the river calms into a pooled area known locally as Sutton's Hole. It is a popular swimming hole and a good rest stop.

At this point, you are not far from what is probably the most dangerous spot on the river, Woodall Shoals. When you see a granite shelf extending far into the river from the South Carolina (left) side, you are approaching Woodall. Stop on the rocks on the left side to scout. Do not be deceived by the way this rapid appears. The first drop creates a vicious recirculating hydraulic that has taken the lives of many people. Carry around over the rocks to the left and re-enter well below the hydraulic, or take the rock slide near the far right bank if the water is high enough. The rest of the river provides enough thrills, so do not needlessly risk your neck at Woodall. Below the first drop, about 50 yards of Class III water takes you down into a large pool. There is a good dirt-road access via FS 757 on the South Carolina side (I) if you wish to enter or leave the river from here.

Beyond the pool the river begins to narrow and drop swiftly. When the river appears to drop out of sight on the left, stop on the right and scout the next rapid—Seven Foot Falls. A large granite outcropping splits the stream with a sheer 7-foot drop on the left and a more gradual descent to the right, which can only be run at high levels. If you choose the left route, boof the top right-hand corner of the drop with considerable speed. Aim for the aforementioned granite outcropping, expecting that the force of the water will push you left just before the drop. Ideally, you can then drop into the eddy with your hair still dry.

The next few miles provide many Class II–III rapids, with the first sizable series marked by Stekoa Creek cascading in from the

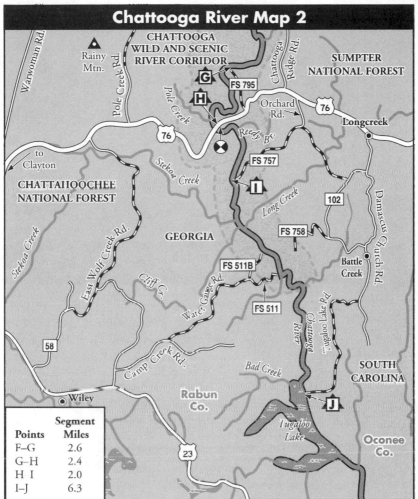

Chattooga River Map 2

CHATTOOGA
WILD AND SCENIC
RIVER CORRIDOR

Rainy
Mtn.

Warwoman Rd.

Pole Creek Rd.

Pole Creek

G

H

FS 795

Chattooga Ridge Rd.

SUMPTER
NATIONAL FOREST

Orchard
Rd.

76

Longcreek

76

to
Clayton

Reedy Br.

FS 757

I

CHATTAHOOCHEE
NATIONAL FOREST

Stekoa Creek

Long Creek

102

Damascus Church Rd.

GEORGIA

FS 758

Stekoa Creek

East Wolf Creek Rd.

Cliff Cr.

FS 511B

Water Gauge Rd.

FS 511

Battle
Creek

58

Camp Creek Rd.

Bad Creek

Chattooga River

Tugaloo Lake Rd.

SOUTH
CAROLINA

Wiley

Rabun
Co.

Tugaloo
Lake

J

Oconee
Co.

23

Points	Segment Miles
F–G	2.6
G–H	2.4
H I	2.0
I–J	6.3

Georgia side. The larger sheer drop of Long Creek Falls entering from the South Carolina side is not too far beyond, and is an excellent place to stop for a break.

As you continue downstream, Deliverance Rock, a gargantuan boulder on the right, looms into view. (It was so named because many of the scenes from the movie *Deliverance* were filmed there.) Approach from the right side of the river. A standard line is to run from the right to the bottom-left of the rapid, steering well clear of Deliverance Rock itself, which is undercut.

Raven Chute is the next challenge, and is easily recognized by the imposing cliffs that loom into view as you round a bend in

photo © Rob Maxwell

Taking the far-left line of Chattooga River's Rock Jumble in Section IV

the river. In the wintertime, when the vegetation is light, you can see the outline of the raven for which this Class IV rapid is named. The bird's head is silhouetted against the sky and his great wings are outstretched on either side. Scouting should be done from the left shore. Though there are several routes through this rapid, be careful about experimenting. Its hidden potholes and sieves have claimed at least one life. A good kayak route starts on the left and follows the top of the long curling diagonal wave to the right. At high water, it becomes very important to stay on the highest point of this curler; erring to the left will slam you against a rock wall and then dump you back upstream into a large recirculating hole. Canoeists sometimes begin their descent further right, paddling across the curler and allowing the pile to push the bows of their boats right.

A mile or so of more moderate water brings you to FS 511, which can be discerned by a sandy beach on the right. FS 511 is a steep unpaved road but it is the last opportunity to exit before the most formidable section of whitewater on the Chattooga—the Class III–V Five Falls.

All of the five drops should be scouted from the shore. The Five Falls section begins when most of the water is channeled to the left of the river; eddy out behind the large boulder in the center of the river. From here you can see a rock garden below you on the left and a large downstream eddy at the edge of the horizon line on river right. Paddle smartly to this right-hand eddy, avoid-

ing the rock garden and sieves on river left. At this point there is an opportunity to scout the actual drop, a 3-foot fall against the right bank followed by a short pool. After the drop, head quickly across to the left bank to scout the second fall, Corkscrew.

From the left bank you can get right on top of the drop and look into the chaos of Corkscrew. There are two big holes on the right-hand side of this rapid, but the left side is shallow and fraught with curler waves that will easily flip you. The preferred route is a sinuous curve that keeps the holes on your right and the shallows on your left. Eddy out on the right at the bottom. If you decide to portage, the right bank is slightly easier.

Scout Crack in the Rock from the right side. Here cracked boulders split the river into three narrow falls, each of which drops about 5 feet. Below 2 feet, the center is the preferred route, but make sure you have enough speed to punch the hole at the bottom. Somewhere above 2 feet, a fourth crack—"far right crack"—opens and is probably the safest route at high water. The left crack is easy to avoid but has nevertheless proven itself to be a consistently fatal funnel for swimmers.

Below Crack in the Rock, ferry to the left bank to scout Jawbone, which is probably the rapid with the greatest number of potential hazards. Jawbone is two soft drops joined by a startlingly fast tongue of water curved like a jawbone. Most people enter this drop at the curve of the jaw and ride it straight to the bottom. Be careful, however, as there are two hazards along the way: the first is an undercut rock to the right of the first drop; the second is the infamous Hydroelectric Rock to the right of the second drop, a round shed-sized boulder with an underwater tunnel at about surface level. Reports of those unlucky enough to take an unscheduled swim through this tunnel confirm that the passage is large enough for a person, but not large enough for a person and a boat. This hole is often lodged with debris; a swim into the hole could be your last. The dangers of Jawbone are further magnified by what awaits accidental swimmers at the next horizon line: an unlucky choice between the bizarrely configured boulder sieve called Puppy Chute, the undercut table rock nicknamed Allison's Rock, or the Class V hole called Sock-Em-Dog, all of which have claimed lives. To scout Sock-Em-Dog, ferry back to the left side of the stream below Hydroelectric Rock.

Sock-Em-Dog, impressive at all water levels, is the last of the Five Falls and is rated Class V by the Forest Service. If you do not like the looks of Sock-Em-Dog, portage on the left. Those running the drop generally begin in one of the two large right-hand eddies. Peel out wide in order to approach from the left of the

channel with a right-hand angle; that way you can drive strongly across the current, which will tend to push you left. There is a smooth hump of water near the center of the top of the drop called the "launching pad." Keep up your speed and go over the top of the launching pad or just to the right of it. Crosscurrents are powerful. Boofing clean over the hole from the launching pad is the most impressive line. But erring to the right of the pad is preferable to landing in the left side of the hole, which is not only the stickier side, but also has a pinning rock known as "Handkerchief Rock." The pool below is a good place from which to watch others or pick up your gear.

At the end of this calm area is Shoulder Bone Rapid. A jutting granite escarpment in the river is reminiscent of a shoulder bone, hence the name. The channel curves around to the left in a C-shape. Follow the water, but don't relax too much, as there is a hole midway down in the middle of the channel.

A few Class II–III rapids remain before the rollicking Chattooga becomes dispassionate Lake Tugaloo. The next 2 miles across the lake to the take-out are painfully slow, so you might as well enjoy the scenery. Take-out on the left at Tugaloo Lake Road. If this road is impassable you must paddle on down to the dam where an access road is on the right.

SHUTTLE: The put-in is at the US 76 bridge parking lot on the South Carolina side. To get to the take-out at Lake Tugaloo from there, take a left out of the parking lot. Turn right at the first paved road, Orchard Road, and follow it until it ends. Turn right onto Damascus Church Road. Pass Damascus Church on the left, and shortly thereafter you will see a sign for the Tugaloo Boat Ramp. Bear right down a windy and steep gravel road that takes you to the ramp. The other take-out is located at FS 757, also accessed off of Orchard Road. The 4-mile trip down FS 511, if needed, is reached by going east on Camp Creek Road from US 441 south of Clayton, then turning left after 1.4 miles onto Water Gauge Road and taking the right fork at FS 511B.

GAUGE: Using levels from the bridge gauge at US 76 (see first section), boaters run this section as low as 0.8 feet. A good first-time level is somewhere between 1.2 and 1.7 feet. At 2.0, the difficulty of the river bumps up to another level; some of the Class IV rapids become Class Vs, and so on. At 2.5 and above, Five Falls is for experts only. The pools between the five falls disappear, Jawbone develops a terminal hole, and Sock-Em Dog becomes a river-wide hole as well.

photo © Rob Maxwell

Running Seven Foot Falls on on the Chattooga

Filming *Deliverance*
— by Doug Woodward

The movie *Deliverance* belongs as much to the GCA [Georgia Canoe Association] as it does to Warner Brothers. Filmed on our home turf, the Chattooga and Tallulah Rivers, three longtime GCA members served as stunt men and technical advisors one golden summer. It was a bit sobering to realize that many of today's GCA members were not even born in 1971 when the filming took place. I'm sure some could care less. But for the few who might like to reminisce, I thought I'd put pen to paper—or finger to computer—before any more years slip by and all of this disappears into the mist of legend. If Claude [Terry] or Payson [Kennedy] has a slightly different perspective of these events—with which our lives in the 1970s were so entwined—then so be it. This is mine.

Back in 1969, when I was living in Maryland, a book had just been published that caught my eye because it appeared to be a story of wilderness river running: James Dickey's *Deliverance*. It wasn't quite an

uninhabited wilderness as it turned out, and the action wasn't all of the whitewater variety. But I read it through at the time, not having the slightest inkling of how involved I would become with that story.

Among the many GCA paddling friends that I made upon moving to Atlanta in the summer of 1970, were the families of Payson and Aurelia Kennedy and Claude and Betty Terry. Payson was librarian of data processing at Georgia Tech and Claude was a microbiologist at Emory University. That fall they asked me if I had read *Deliverance.* "Well," they said, "Warner Brothers is going to film that story down here and they're looking for a river. There's a chance, too, that we might get involved in some way. Can you make it to dinner this Friday?"

I could. In fact, the Dog River running at 3 feet couldn't have kept me away! The dinner, as it turned out, was at the home of Lewis King, a good friend of Payson's. Beside Claude, Payson, and myself, there was one other guest: James Dickey. Lewis King is the real-life Lewis of Dickey's novel. With a tough, wiry body, piercing blue eyes and silver hair, King bore little resemblance to Burt Reynolds, who portrayed the film's Lewis character. But Lewis King was a man of many skills—a number one tennis player for Georgia Tech, an accomplished chess opponent, a canoeist and . . . a champion archer.

Dickey and King grew up together in Buckhead and took a memorable canoe trip on the Coosawatee in Northwest Georgia. Recollections of their trip helped form the basis of the novel. The part of the river they canoed now lies deep underwater behind Carter's Dam. The pair had considerable difficulty in the rapids and ran into moonshiners when trying to leave the river. But, far from being drawn into the web of fear and murder that the story portrays, the two were actually helped out of their troubles by the mountain folks.

We talked whitewater all evening, making equipment and location suggestions. Our first river choice

was the Little River Canyon in Alabama, but in the end settled on the Chattooga and Tallulah. We emphasized that our whitewater experience on area rivers was available should Warner Brothers need further advice. Would they?

As fortune would have it, they did. Film crews had been shooting since mid-May of 1971 before contacting us in July. With much of the cabin, camping, and archery scenes behind them, Warner Brothers was concentrating on the river scenes. Mishaps had occurred already at Rock Jumble and Deliverance Rock on Section IV, where film equipment was lost to the River.

In Tallulah Gorge, where, in the story, the rope breaks and Ed (played by Jon Voight) plunges from the cliff face to the river, a local man had agreed to take the fall. After viewing the spot from below, he told the chief cinematographer Vilmos Zsigmond that he needed to see it from the top of the cliff. Three days later, when the crew finally tracked him down, the local claimed to have "remembered some errands that my wife asked me to do that day." He was replaced by Ralph Garrett, a professional stunt man.

Warner Brothers envisioned using Ralph, teamed with a Rabun County fisherman, for canoeing stunts as well. Though the fisherman knew the Chattooga, neither had ever paddled in moving water before. When they finally emerged at Earl's Ford after a disastrous day on Section II, it was Ralph who demanded that "whitewater experts" be brought in. We later became good friends, and he learned enough to add canoeing to his portfolio of stunts.

And so, we found ourselves in the right place at the right time. On some days—at First Falls, Corkscrew, Jawbone—we were called on to be stunt doubles, Payson and I for Ned Beatty, Claude for Jon Voight. We would report to the makeup station at 7 a.m., dress appropriately, have our hair colored, and then have "cuts and

bruises applied." Instead of Burt Reynolds lying in the bottom of our Grumman, it was his dummy. On other days, we acted as demonstrators, running the easier rapids several times until the principals felt they could do the run themselves. In addition, we were called on for other advice, such as, "Where can we find a rock face with a swift current running past, that Jon Voight can claw at for a finger hold—where we won't lose him down river!" Thus the naming of "Deliverance Rock."

Our advice, however, was not always accepted. Claude and I were made up as doubles for Jon Voight and Ned Beatty, respectively, and had just paddled a green Old Town canoe through several rapids, fighting with the flat-water keel and a load of waterlogged gear to keep the boat on track.

"What they ought to do," Claude expounded, "is rip the keel off of this canoe, substitute Styrofoam for the camping gear, cover it with a tarp and stick the bow and arrows on top." It was the suggestion of an experienced and frustrated canoeist.

Burt Reynolds swiveled around in the stern of his Grumman canoe, fixed his eyes on Claude and snapped, "Look, Candy-ass, you don't go into a scene driving a greyhound bus and come out riding a bicycle!" The silence that followed was one of the few times I've seen Claude at a loss for a reply.

Later that same week, I received my comeuppance in Jawbone Rapid. Ferrying the Grumman and dummy to the next shooting site, I dropped into the large top eddy on river left. However, I had violated a cardinal rule of paddling: Never take to the water with loose rope in your boat. There was a tangle of perhaps 80 feet of ⅜-inch line in the bottom of my canoe, tossed in with unnecessary haste.

As I peeled out into the surging current, I leaned hard on a left draw and . . . my paddle snapped completely in two, plunging me headfirst into the water, the

canoe on top of me. In the next moment, as I was taking my lumps from the rocks, I realized that the Grumman, the dummy, and I were all still connected by rope.

Fortunately, we passed to the left of Hydroelectric Rock, but the canoe was still hell-bent on running Sock-Em-Dog Rapid! It was only through a well-timed assist from Claude in the eddy above that I was able to slip the coils of rope from my ankle.

The Warner Brothers crew was very safety-conscious as well. They were hand-picked for their fitness and desire to work in a remote setting. When we made hazardous runs, there were always alert eyes and ready arms tucked out of the camera's view. A character named "Jimmy the Fish" was particularly alert.

Not all days were as long or as tedious as those at Five Falls. Often we would sit for an hour or two while Zsigmond and director John Boorman decided how to shoot a particular scene. If the day ended at a reasonable hour, we were invited to Kingwood Country Club to see the "rushes" (the previous day's filming).

It was interesting to see other folks worked into the film, too. James Dickey, a large, imposing figure, plays the sheriff. A Rabun County man who was hired to drive cast and crew caught Boorman's eye and was slipped into a deputy's role. Louise Coldren, who fed paddlers for so many years at her Dillard Motor Lodge, played a similar part, serving food to guests near the end of the film.

And in the "Dueling Banjos" scene, the boy, Billy Redden was found waiting tables locally. The scary mountain men, Herbert Coward and Billy McKinney, came from the ghost town at Maggie Valley, North Carolina, where they performed as gun-slinging cowboys.

But not all locals were cooperative. Warner Brothers found the perfect backwoods cabin and gas pump location for the "That river don't go to Aintree!" scene. When they returned a week later to start fine tuning the

set, they were met by the owner who quickly sent them packing: "I just read the book and you're not shooting that filthy story on my place!"

One scene filmed in Tallulah Gorge was a tribute to persistence and ingenuity. Besides the cliff-scaling shots, it was here that the two canoes collided and the Old Town broke apart. Having picked their ideal spot, the crew set about building an artificial rapid of boulders and logs, taking care to not make it a strainer. A track was added so that the Old Town would slide into a broached position in the rapid, the canoe having already been rigged to separate into two halves when a cable was pulled from shore.

Anyone who has hiked or paddled Tallulah Gorge will appreciate the difficulty of just getting boats, camera equipment, and the related gear to river level—not to mention getting them out again. This was accomplished using a cable and pulleys, with a Grumman canoe serving as the "basket." The system ran from the top of the climbing cliff down to the south bank of the Tallulah, 300 feet below. It was a slow and physically demanding process, but vastly better than lugging things in and out by hand.

When the artificial rapid was ready and safety crews set in place, the director radioed Georgia Power for a release from the Tallulah Falls dam to make the rapid come alive. "Too much! Too much! Reynolds and Beatty are swamped!" and another bullhorn would go sailing into the river. It took many takes to finally get it right.

Working in the shadow of experienced filmmakers and actors was a good learning experience and a lot of fun. Burt Reynolds was relatively unknown at the time, having just had his first "exposure" as *Cosmopolitan's* centerfold. He had a quick wit and plenty of self-confidence. Already an accomplished actor, Jon Voight was also a caring individual. Ronny Cox was down to earth and a

pleasure to listen to with his guitar. Ned Beatty, however, was my favorite.

One weekend, the cast and crew went to visit Underground Atlanta, and Beatty missed the early Monday morning bus back. I was asked to fill in for Ned in a non-canoeing scene following Reynolds and Voight's jeep in a station wagon with Ronny Cox along the hairpin turns above Betty's Creek. When Beatty arrived that afternoon, he took time to track me down and thank me for filling in. It was a heartfelt gesture.

Deliverance premiered in Atlanta the next summer (1972), and of course we were there. It soon was in theaters across the country. My mother called from Maryland. "You know, Doug, I've been telling friends at church for a year that you're in *Deliverance*. I just saw it, and I don't think I'll tell anybody else!"

Our screen time could be measured in seconds, but the effect it had on our lives was far-reaching. That same summer, Claude and I started Southeastern Expeditions, running folks by raft down the Chattooga while still hanging onto our jobs in Atlanta. Payson and his family took an even bigger leap as they broke all Atlanta ties and threw themselves into transforming the old Tote-N-Tarry Motel and Restaurant into one of the premier whitewater communities in the world, the Nantahala Outdoor Center. The success of the film also helped boost interest in whitewater paddling and membership in the GCA, which remains instrumental in protecting and securing access to Georgia's waterways.

Reprinted with permission of the author and
the Georgia Canoe Association.

WARWOMAN CREEK

Are you interested in spring creekin' but aren't quite ready for Over-flow, the Chauga, or even lower Amicalola? Try Warwoman up in Rabun County. It drops close to 100 feet in 4 miles before running into the Chattooga at Earls Ford. Warwoman is appropriate for solid intermediate-level paddlers, but the party should include an experienced leader. A dirt road, albeit a short distance away, provides difficult, but do-able, land extraction options. Unusually scenic, Warwoman is a good creek to practice eddy turns, side surfing, boat-scouting drops, and water reading. The water flows at a very rapid rate, helping to create lots of nice relatively technical Class II rapids, even more surfing holes, and three significant Class III drops. Scout the various blind drops, as they are technical and can be dangerous because of undercuts and possible strainers.

MAPS: Rabun Bald, Satola (USGS); Rabun (County)

EARLS FORD ROAD TO SANDY FORD ON THE CHATTOOGA RIVER

class	III (+)
length	4.2 (plus 3.1 on the Chattooga)
time	5 hr
gauge	Web
level	2.5 ft
gradient	22 fpm
scenery	A-

DESCRIPTION: Seldom boated, Warwoman Creek is a delightful, intimate experience for intermediate and advanced paddlers that can only be run when the Chattooga is high. If you get to the put-in and it looks too low, it is. It is possible to limit the run to 4 miles by taking out at Earls Ford, but the shuttle is rather long and you'll miss the opportunity to do the upper reaches of the Chattooga's Section III at high level. Taking out at Sandy Ford on the Georgia side adds another 90 feet of gradient drop.

The run starts just below the Earls Ford Road's bridge crossing the creek. Warwoman begins gently with a Class I–II warm-up. Mattress, the first drop of consequence, is found as the river veers away from the road about 15 minutes from the put-in, and is easily recognized by a distinct horizon line that formerly held a mattress pinned to a boulder. Mattress is a blind, sloping, 10-foot or so drop, which can be scouted from river left or comfortably boat-scouted from the pool. For the more adventurous, there's a small eddy on the right lip. Enter far right and cut left across the face. There is a launch pad in the middle near the top, and a chock-stone at the very bottom of the left-most chute. Mattress ends in a big pool where safety should be set, because if you upend and don't make shore, a narrow gorge will drop you another 10 feet or so over about 100 yards.

Hump is the next major drop. Hump looks quite impressive as you approach its horizon line, but in reality it is a straightforward

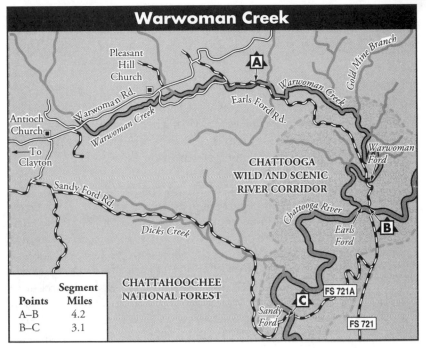

Warwoman Creek

Pleasant Hill Church

Gold Mine Branch

Warwoman Rd.

Earls Ford Rd.

Warwoman Creek

Antioch Church

Warwoman Creek

To Clayton

Warwoman Ford

CHATTOOGA WILD AND SCENIC RIVER CORRIDOR

Sandy Ford Rd.

Chattooga River

Earls Ford

Dicks Creek

Points	Segment Miles
A–B	4.2
B–C	3.1

CHATTAHOOCHEE NATIONAL FOREST

FS 721A

Sandy Ford

FS 721

15-foot slide that can be run anywhere. There is an interesting river-wide surfing wave at the bottom of Hump that becomes awesome at high levels.

Pin Ball, technically the most difficult drop, completes the named rapids. Pin Ball presents with an obvious horizon line and can be scouted from the right bank—the run is down the left chute. The rapids run around a small island (or large boulder). The left chute is obscured by the island and the bottom of the right chute cannot be seen. The right chute looks great from the top, but a large log-strainer half-way down on the left and an invisible cleaver rock obstructing the run-out should preclude intentionally running it. There is a left-hand eddy about 5 feet down (try to backferry into it). Park here to scan the remaining run and position your boat to cut back right and around the island. There is another nifty little eddy a little farther down on the left; don't try for it unless you are fairly confident, because the remainder of the chute is a tight right turn that runs between under-cut banks. Oh, there is also a troll rock at the bottom that will want to kiss anything coming down.

Another 3 miles of sporadic Class I–II water, including a 5-foot ledge below the Warwoman ford crossing of Earl's Ford Road, brings you to the confluence with the Chattooga at Earls

Ford. You still have Warwoman, Rock Garden, Three Rooster Tails, Dicks Creek Ledge, Stairsteps, and Sandy Ford rapids ahead of you if you've opted for the Sandy Ford take-out. Those who have not done Section III above 2 feet should be aware that traditional lines change and more options open up for the significant rapids. Scout the major drops and plan your attack accordingly. Sandy Ford rapid, barely noteworthy at lower levels, transforms into a low–Class IV boat-eater above 3 feet. Stay to the right of the island for the Class III run. The Sandy Ford take-out is on river right, immediately below the island.

SHUTTLE: To get to Warwoman Creek, drive to Clayton. Turn right at the second light (going north and across from the Dairy Queen), follow it to the end, and turn right on Warwoman Road. For the take-out at Sandy Ford, go about 6 miles and turn right onto Sandy Ford Road. Follow it to the very end, about 6 miles. You will ford Dicks Creek; all but the lowest clearance will make the ford at levels up to 3 feet, although four-wheel-drive will help traverse the remaining 1 mile to the river when conditions are wet. The other take-out at Earls Ford is accessed via a very long shuttle to the South Carolina side (see the Chattooga, Section III, for driving directions). To the Warwoman put-in, return to Warwoman Road and turn right; go about 2 miles and turn right onto Earls Ford Road. Put-in at the bridge; there is a large turn-out for parking on the left below the bridge.

GAUGE: There is no gauge on the creek. Chattooga levels can be used to estimate Warwoman's flow, but they are not always correlated. Warwoman is usually runnable after any heavy or sustained rain that leaves the Chattooga at 2.5, and becomes more interesting around 4 feet. The maximum is 5 feet.

TALLULAH RIVER

The Tallulah River is both a small stream of outstanding beauty and a dramatic whitewater run that pushes the limits of navigability. The headwaters are unbelievably clear, attracting avid anglers and occasionally paddlers interested in a technical Class II–III run amid moss-covered boulders. At the other end of the river is the celebrated Tallulah Gorge, home to read-and-run whitewater from Class IV+ to Class V and an exploding wall of water that could only be called The Thing. In between these two extremes are four dams and very little navigable river other than the middle run described below.

MAPS: Hightower Bald, Tiger, Tallulah Falls, Tugaloo Lake (USGS); Rabun, Habersham (County)

COLEMAN RIVER CONFLUENCE TO PLUM ORCHARD ROAD

class	II (III+)
length	4.7 mi
time	4 hr
gauge	Web, visual
level	2.45 ft
gradient	23 (45)
scenery	B

DESCRIPTION: Exceptional scenery and whitewater make this trip very worthwhile. Huge boulders surrounded by draping hemlocks dominate the scene. The run is a fairly technical Class II with two Class III rapids located in the first mile, interspersed with deep pools. Higher water brings some of the rapids to a Class III+ pitch. Its cold, clear waters make Tallulah River an excellent whitewater run in the winter and spring, or after any heavy rain. Hazards include strainers, deadfalls, undercut rocks, and difficult rapids.

The put-in is half a mile above the junction with Coleman River, just above the Forest Service's Tallulah River campground. Above this point is a treacherous Class V run (in the upper gorge) and above that, more Class I–II water. The upper gorge run is more dangerous than the downstream gorge, dropping 250 feet in a 1-mile stretch with numerous undercuts, sieves, and logs constricted into the tight channel. Farther up FS 70 is another Forest Service campground at Tate Branch; primitive camping is available on the east side of the road.

This section of river is popular for trout fishing. Do not trespass onto private property, and do your best not to disturb any anglers you encounter on the river. It is recommended that paddlers take-out on river right at Plum Orchard Road (C) above Lake Burton.

SHUTTLE: From Clayton, take US 76 west, turning right onto Persimmon Road before crossing Lake Burton. Turn left onto Plum Orchard Road (which is also called Cat Gap Road) and continue to the river. To get to the put-in, return to Persimmon

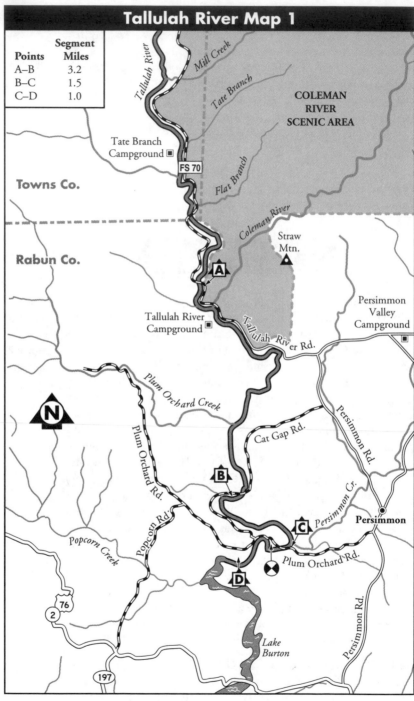

Tallulah River Map 1

Points	Segment Miles
A–B	3.2
B–C	1.5
C–D	1.0

Tallulah River

Mill Creek

Tate Branch

COLEMAN RIVER SCENIC AREA

Tate Branch Campground

FS 70

Flat Branch

Towns Co.

Coleman River

Straw Mtn.

Rabun Co.

A

Persimmon Valley Campground

Tallulah River Campground

Tallulah River Rd.

Plum Orchard Creek

N

Plum Orchard Rd.

Cat Gap Rd.

Persimmon Rd.

B

Popcorn Rd.

Persimmon Cr.

C

Persimmon

Popcorn Creek

Plum Orchard Rd.

D

76
2

Lake Burton

Persimmon Rd.

197

Road and continue north 2.3 miles to make a left onto FS 70 (Tallulah River Road). The put-in is located at the bridge half a mile above the confluence with the Coleman River.

GAUGE: A telemetry gauge is located at the end of this section, and levels are reported on the USGS Internet site for the Tallulah near Clayton. The gauge is readable from the stream, located on the river-right side below the take-out bridge. For additional information, contact the Forest Service's Tallulah District at (706) 782-3320.

TIGER CREEK CONFLUENCE TO TALLULAH FALLS LAKE

class	I–II (III)
length	6 mi
time	3.5 hr
gauge	None
level	Unknown
gradient	13 fpm
scenery	C

DESCRIPTION: The Tallulah is impounded several times before reaching this section, creating three mountain lakes: Lake Burton, Nacoohe Lake, and Lake Rabun. The reservoirs consume most of the upper river's flow, making paddling below the Mathis Dam at Lake Rabun possible only when the local rainfall is sufficient to fuel Tiger Creek, which meets up with the Tallulah at the first crossing of Old US 441 (E). Put in here or on Wolf Creek Road over Tiger Creek, half a mile above the confluence.

The first 2.5 miles of this section of the Tallulah are mostly docile. It's pleasant scenery, though houses and farmland have taken the place of the woods throughout this flatter section. Old US 441 is never far away, and new US 441 crosses the river twice. The 2-mile section after the first crossing contains a couple of small Class II shoals and slides.

One-quarter of the total gradient for this section is concentrated into one Class III rapid that begins immediately above the last crossing of Old US 441 (G). After threading through the boulder slab ledges, the rapid continues as an intermittent Class II for a few hundred yards, ending in a low dam that spills into the lake pool. The road shadows this stretch of river, creating a park-and-play opportunity on the upper reaches of the rapid. The path leading to the river at the small dam above the lake is steep. The take out is 1.6 miles farther down the lake.

SHUTTLE: Approaching Tallulah Falls from the south, turn left onto Main Street immediately before crossing Tallulah Gorge, then right onto River Street to the landing. Parking is available behind city hall. For upper access points, return to US 441 and turn left, taking the immediate left after the bridge onto Old US 441 to reach the access at the first bridge and Tallulah Falls State

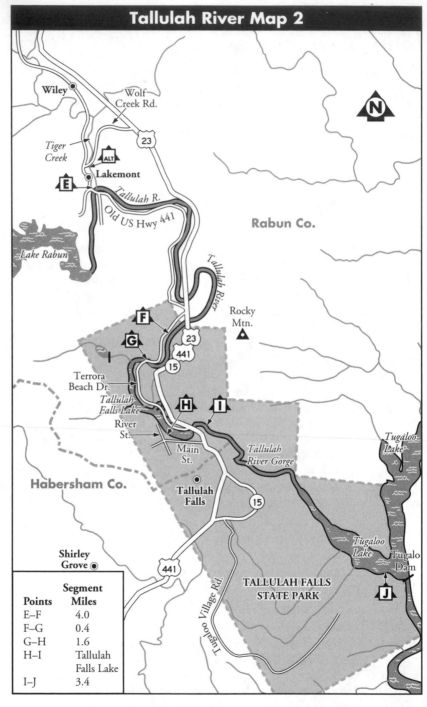

Tallulah River Map 2

Wiley

Wolf
Creek Rd.

23

Tiger
Creek

ALT

E Lakemont

Tallulah R.

Old US Hwy 441

Lake Rabun

Rabun Co.

Tallulah River

N

Rocky
Mtn.

F

G

23

441

15

Terrora
Beach Dr.

*Tallulah
Falls Lake*

River
St.

Main
St.

H

I

*Tallulah
River Gorge*

*Tugaloo
Lake*

Habersham Co.

Tallulah
Falls

15

*Tugaloo
Lake*

*Tugalo
Dam*

Shirley
Grove

441

Tugaloo Village Rd.

TALLULAH FALLS
STATE PARK

J

Points	Segment Miles
E–F	4.0
F–G	0.4
G–H	1.6
H–I	Tallulah Falls Lake
I–J	3.4

Park's Shortline Trail (F). Continuing on US 441 to the third left onto Old US 441 is the easiest way to reach the upper put-in.

GAUGE: None. Runnable only when significant rain falls in the Tiger Creek watershed.

TALLULAH GORGE

class	IV+ (V)
length	3.4 mi
time	2–3 hr
gauge	Web
level	500 cfs
gradient	260 fpm
scenery	A+

DESCRIPTION: Tallulah Gorge has long been a leading attraction in the Southeast. A century before the invention of roto-molded plastic, Royalex, or kevlar, this spectacular 2-mile gorge was nicknamed the "Niagara of the South" by tourists arriving in horse-drawn buggies. The river leaps down 600 feet through five waterfalls—L'eau d'Or, Tempesta, Hurricane, Oceana, and Bridal Veil—carving a magnificent granite gorge more than 1,000 feet deep. Sadly, turn of the century conservationists lost the battle to preserve the canyon's natural state. In 1913, Georgia Power built the dam that to this day generates a portion of Atlanta's electricity and reduces the Tallulah River to a veritable trickle. Since 1997, thanks to the combined efforts of American Whitewater, Georgia Power, GADNR, and several local paddling clubs, the river once again comes to life during release weekends, when Georgia Power releases 500–700 cfs from the top of the gorge.

The first challenge paddlers face is the put-in, which is just below the first three (unrunnable) waterfalls, down some 600 stairs that snake their way down the canyon wall. Last step, the Class IV+ entrance rapid, gives you an idea of the river's speed and is so immediate that the only scouting opportunity is the put-in platform itself. A Class IV boof move off a 6-foot ledge follows, at which point almost everyone eddies out left to scout Oceana (Class V+). A good percentage of those paddlers choose to walk the 100-foot slide on the right bank, sobered by the jagged ledge of granite that runs horizontally across it and creates an almost river-wide break in the face of the slide. The highest point of this abutment is respectfully referred to as The Thing, both for its bizarre geology and for its potential to rearrange both boats and boaters. A significant number of injuries have occurred here. One fact about Oceana that should give you pause is that each year the percentage of Tallulah paddlers who choose to walk the rapid grows higher as more folks assess and re-assess the difficulties and consequences of this rapid.

What follows downstream is a fast section of read-and-run Class IV+ water called The Gauntlet requiring, as one newcomer

photo © Rob Maxwell

Kayaking the quarter-mile Gauntlet on Tallulah River

put it, "a long series of moves and readjustments made on the fly: miss the hole, boof the ledge, brace, grab the eddy—all done faster than you can think it." Significantly, The Gauntlet dumps out directly into the Class V Bridal Veil, a giant slide that ends in a sticky and uniform river-wide hole. Your best bet is to punch The Gauntlet's final hole on river right and then swing immediately far left just as you approach the horizon line of the falls. Scout from river left.

The rest of the river is characterized by a series of slide-like drops, many of which are like Bridal Veil in that they slope directly into sticky holes, and some of which, like the Class III Zoom Flume following Bridal Veil, are friendly enough to warrant such carnival names.

Entrance into the stunning stretch of the river known as amphitheater begins with a boof called Lynch's Wrench and several shallow holes, including one on river right that has earned the name Typewriter. There are several good routes through this section, but whichever one you choose, be assertive about it, especially if you choose to punch the river-right hole. Only after eddying out on the left do you get a clear opportunity to appreciate the height and breadth of the sheer cliff face that gives this section of the river its name.

Several more slide-type drops await around the bend, most notably Tat, the second half of the Class III and IV double slide with the deceptively innocuous name Tit and Tat. Not only does Tat boast Tallulah's most noticeable undercut (on river left), it also has a river-wide hole at the bottom of the slide. To avoid

joining the many paddlers who have suffered the indignity of significant surf time in this hole, run this rapid from top middle to bottom right.

Tom's Brain Buster (IV+) is the next rapid and should be scouted on river right. The line along the right side is straightforward, but keep in mind that this rapid's shallow depths are no doubt responsible for its appellation; Tom's is a good place to keep your boat under you.

Road to Aintree (IV) is harder to scout; a long series of gradually descending shoals ends once again a rough and tumble hole. An assertive run down the right, punching the many sticky holes on the way, is the standard route, although some boaters choose to skirt the holes entirely with a more technical far-left line.

Paddlesnake Ledge (IV), the last significant rapid, is the final slide on Tallulah; run it left of center and angle right. Just around the bend are Powerhouse, with a deceptively sticky hole on river right, Maxwell's Last Drop (don't miss the last good boof on river right), and the mile-long Tugaloo Lake.

Whatever you do on Tallulah, make sure that you take the time to pull over—both for scouting and sightseeing. As one paddler summarized the river: "Tallulah is exquisite: steep walls, and patchworks of sun and shade spattering patterns on clear cold water. The river even smells clean. I know, because a portion of it ended up in my sinuses."

SHUTTLE: The gorge is open only to private boaters with qualified craft and Class V paddling skills. To get to the put-in, take US 441 north from Clarkesville and turn left into the grassy parking area immediately before crossing the river. There is a small fee for parking. Use the walkway under the bridge to cross the road and reach the stairs that lead to the put-in. As of 2001, permits are no longer required and you need only to sign a release form before entering the gorge. To relieve parking congestion at the take-out, a number of organizations provide shuttle service back to the put-in. Use of the gorge is restricted to the developed put-in and take-out facilities to protect the native persistent trillium, which is on the federal list of endangered species. Strictly minimize all contact with the river banks while in the gorge and pack out all your trash.

GAUGE: Flows are usually 500 cfs on Saturday and 700 cfs on Sunday of scheduled release weekends, which are currently the first two weekends in April and the first three weekends in November. Releases begin at 9:30 a.m.; the last runs of the day must start down the put-in stairs by 3:00 p.m. The USGS reports data online for the gauge located above the powerhouse.

Birth of a Waterfall

One of the most exciting developments in the last 20 years of Georgia paddling was the test and subsequent opening of the Tallulah Gorge. In W*hitewater Classics—Fifty North American Rivers Picked by the Continent's Leading Paddlers,* Tyler Williams recounts:

". . . in the early 1990s, the seeds of the river's rebirth were planted when paddler/activist Pete Skinner spread the word to other politically active boaters to look for empty riverbeds in their regions that might benefit from the federal re-licensing process.

"The Federal Energy Regulatory Commission (FERC) must reevaluate licenses granted to hydropower projects every 50 years. In 1991, the Tallulah license was up. Through the efforts of local paddlers Kent Wiggington, David Cox, Risa Shimoda, American Whitewater, the Georgia Canoe Association, and several other groups, momentum for scheduled recreational releases was begun, and all interested parties were brought together to discuss proposals. The result was a flow study in 1993 in which Risa and other top paddlers of the region were sequestered to make a first descent of the gorge."

Ten lucky paddlers were selected for the coveted test run, accompanied by additional boaters and local rescue crews playing the role of safety from the shore. Four runs were planned at different flow volumes. Tyler continues: "The event was quite possibly the most publicized first descent in history. Four Atlanta-based television stations showed up to film the run, newspapers from around the region sent reporters to the scene, and a bevy of local police and Georgia Power representatives scuttled about the put-in. Completing the media circus, a helicopter circled overhead. Several of the paddlers declined requests from the media to attach cameras to their boats

for the run. Apparently the cameramen were unaware of the inherent violence contained in Class V rapids like Oceana, the Tallulah's signature drop."

As fate would have it, a Georgia boater on the safety team was pulled from the shore to replace Walt Lynch, who had the misfortune of dislocating his shoulder early in the first run. (As a consolation prize, the offending rapid, Lynch's Wrench, a.k.a. Ticket Puncher, carries his name.) John Bell, the surprised walk-on paddler, recalls the unusual treatment they received at the end of the first run: "We took-out immediately below at the powerhouse. Georgia Power was waiting with a cooler full of soft drinks and snacks. We filled out a 20-question survey about our impressions of the river. We got interviewed by the press. We were thoroughly videotaped. We put on earplugs and walked through the turbine room of the powerhouse. We rode the cable car to the rim of the gorge. A chauffeur drove us to a catered lunch. Just your typical day on the river . . . "

Shimoda recalls that the emotional highlight of the day "combined the thrill of discovering how 'runnable' the river is—that our hunch about its feasibility was in fact solid—with the realization that the window we were opening (collectively) looked out on both the past grandeur of this destination and the future of the area for 30–50 years (hopefully, longer!)."

Four-and-a-half years of concentrated negotiations followed by a flurry of last-minute preparation ensued, leading to the historic first release day on November 1, 1997. One hundred and twenty paddlers descended the nearly completed walkway to experience firsthand what Shimoda fondly refers to as "an incomparable seasonal resource for those in the southeast who love beautiful rivers."

MIDDLE FORK BROAD RIVER

The Middle Fork Broad River is born in the Chattahoochee National Forest east of Cornelia. Though adventurous boaters have plied the rapids nearer the headwaters, the river is not usually considered paddleable until found in its tamed form outside the town of Franklin Springs. The section described below includes some mild Class I–II rapids near the beginning of the run; farther downstream, the river subsumes the flow of the North Fork before joining the Hudson River to form the Broad River. The proximate terrain throughout this area is rolling forested hills, but occasional intrusions of farmland make human activity easily felt.

MAPS: Carnesville, Danielsville North, (USGS); Franklin, Madison (County)

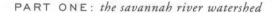

ATKINSON BRIDGE TO GA 281 ON THE BROAD RIVER

class	I (II)
length	14.5 mi
time	7 hr
gauge	None
level	Unknown
gradient	5 fpm
scenery	B-

DESCRIPTION: Immediately above this section, the Middle Fork's gradient is less than 2 feet per mile. In periods of favorable rainfall, canoeing may be possible, although frequent portaging around deadfalls should be expected. Bridge crossings are common, usually less than 2 miles apart, so access is good if the river becomes impassable.

Atkinson Bridge, the put-in for this section, marks the beginning of the hospitable section of the Middle Fork. The gradient increases, and the most notable Class I–II shoals of the lower river are encountered before the North Fork Broad joins the river from the left 4.4 miles from the put-in. Below this point, the Middle Fork offers a largely relaxing experience. The moderate gradient creates a current that is quite powerful at times, and there are very few rapids. The river passes near many towns but goes through none of them, so much of the scenery remains unspoiled woodland or minimally developed agricultural land. Wildlife is abundant, particularly birds, small mammals, and turtles. When the Hudson joins in from the right below US 29, you are now on the Broad River.

After Atkinson Bridge (A), access is available at GA 51 (near the intersection with GA 145), US 29 (the very steep path to the river makes this a better put-in than take-out), and GA 281 on the Broad River. Bond Bridge Road, which crosses the Middle Fork after the confluence with the North Fork, does not provide good access.

Middle Fork Broad River

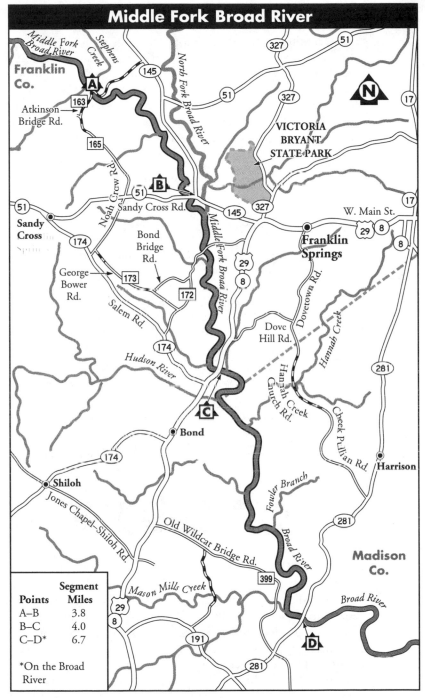

Points	Segment Miles
A–B	3.8
B–C	4.0
C–D*	6.7

*On the Broad River

SHUTTLE: The take-out is at the Broad River's intersection with GA 281, northeast of Danielsville. The easiest access is available at the outfitter's site; make appropriate arrangements for the convenience. From the take-out to the highest put-in take GA 281 back toward Danielsville and turn right onto Old Wildcat Bridge Road, then right again onto US 29. Turn left onto GA 145 outside Franklin Springs. Stay on GA 145 as it crosses the North Fork Broad River and veers to the north. Turn left onto Atkinson Bridge Road and proceed to the river.

GAUGE: There is no gauge on the river. Visually scout the flow from the put-in, or call the local outfitter.

NORTH FORK BROAD RIVER

The North Fork Broad River has its headwaters in Stephens County near Toccoa. The section described below provides a mild journey through a mostly wooded environment near the end of the river. Although not covered here, the river can also be navigated in the hilly areas of southern Stephens County; the consistently mild gradient produces few rapids or shoals. After entering Franklin County, passage becomes difficult, as a great deal of the river's course becomes slow-flowing and marshy. Deadfall portages are frequent from the crossing of GA 145 north of Carnesville downstream to Jackson Bridge Road. To avoid an unpleasant experience, it is inadvisable to attempt this section above Jackson Bridge unless there has been above-average but not torrential rainfall.

MAPS: Carnesville, Danielsville North (USGS); Franklin (County)

JACKSON BRIDGE TO US 29 ON THE MIDDLE FORK BROAD RIVER

class	I–II
length	9.9 mi
time	5 hr
gauge	None
level	Unknown
gradient	9 fpm
scenery	C

DESCRIPTION: Most paddlers prefer to begin at Jackson Bridge Road, or for a shorter trip, 3.4 miles father downstream at GA 51 (B). Here the progress is aided by an increase in flow volume and a gradient of over 13 feet per mile. The streamside environment provides miles of secluded paddling and potential wildlife encounters. After GA 145 crosses the stream at access point C (near the intersection with GA 51), the North Fork is subsumed by the Middle Fork. GA 145 is the easiest take-out point; the US 29 access point 3.5 miles farther downstream involves a steep carry-out on the river-right side.

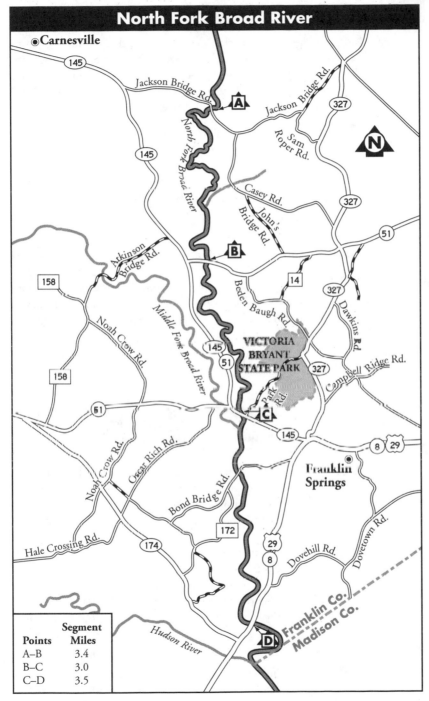

North Fork Broad River

Carnesville

Jackson Bridge Rd.

A

Jackson Bridge Rd.

327

Sam Roper Rd.

145

145

North Fork Broad River

N

Casey Rd.

John's Bridge Rd.

327

51

B

158

Atkinson Bridge Rd.

14

327

Noah Crow Rd.

Middle Fork Broad River

Beden Baugh Rd.

Dawkins Rd.

158

145

51

VICTORIA BRYANT STATE PARK

327

Campbell Ridge Rd.

61

C

Park Rd.

Noah Crow Rd.

Oscar Rich Rd.

145

8 29

Franklin Springs

Bond Bridge Rd.

172

Dovetown Rd.

Hale Crossing Rd.

174

29

8

Dovehill Rd.

Franklin Co.
Madison Co.

Hudson River

D

Points	Segment Miles
A–B	3.4
B–C	3.0
C–D	3.5

SHUTTLE: From Danielsville, take US 29 north to the bridge over the Middle Fork Broad River. Access is available via the dirt road on the right just before the start of the bridge guardrail. To get to the put-in, continue on US 29 toward Franklin Springs and turn left onto GA 145. Follow GA 145 as it turns to the northwest after crossing the North Fork; turn right onto Jackson Bridge Road and follow the road to the bridge and river.

GAUGE: There is no gauge on the river. The local outfitter may be able to provide advice over the phone.

HUDSON RIVER

The Hudson River, the prettiest of the Broad River tributaries, is born in western Banks County, north of Athens. In contrast with the Broad River, its course is narrow and intimate. The scenery remains pleasing despite the growth of houses near the stream. In the upper section, passage can be difficult due to the river's small channel and numerous deadfalls. As the Hudson nears the confluence with the Middle Fork Broad River (forming the Broad River), rapids increase, making for a pretty and enjoyable paddling experience.

MAPS: Homer, Ashland, Ila, Danielsville North (USGS); Banks, Franklin, Madison (County)

GA 59 TO GA 106

class	I
length	13.1 mi
time	8 hr
gauge	None
level	Unknown
gradient	3 fpm
scenery	B-

DESCRIPTION: Cruising does not become sensible until the Hudson crosses GA 106 (E), but for those paddlers who desire an athletic experience portaging over, under, and around many deadfalls, it is possible to put in at GA 59. Below this point the Hudson is quite narrow and shallow, and deadfalls blocking the stream are frequent. If rainfall has been adequate for paddling, this section can provide a scenic tour for the adventurous, who exercise the caution required to avoid deadfalls in the stream. When scouting the river level, be aware that the black-sand river bed will create the illusion of a deeper channel. At low water levels, poling, prodding, and pulling may be required to move the boat downstream.

SHUTTLE: From Commerce, take GA 98 east to Ila. Turn left onto GA 174, then left onto GA 106. The take-out is on GA 106 north of Fort Lamar. To reach the put-in, continue north on GA 106 and turn left onto Bold Springs Road. Bold Springs will

Hudson River

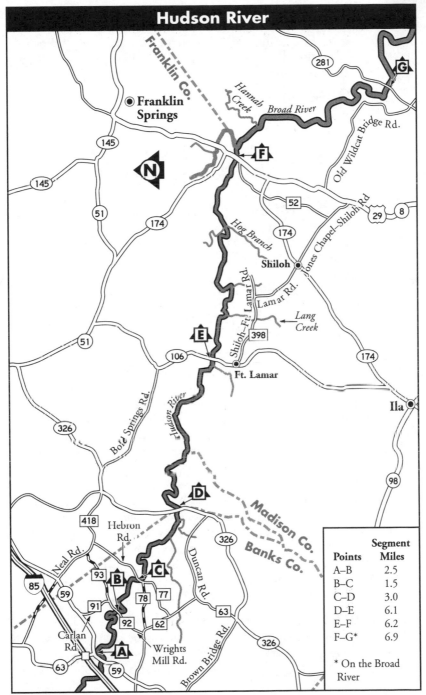

	Segment
Points	**Miles**
A–B	2.5
B–C	1.5
C–D	3.0
D–E	6.1
E–F	6.2
F–G*	6.9

* On the Broad River

merge with GA 326; continue west onto CR 418 as GA 326 turns to the south. At GA 59, turn left and proceed to the put-in at the bridge. Intermediate bridges are accessible from Bold Springs Road at GA 326 (D), Hebron Road (C), and Wrights Mill Road (B).

GAUGE: There is no gauge, but the local outfitter can relay information on river levels in the area.

GA 106 TO BROAD RIVER

class	I–II
length	13.1 mi
time	7 hr
gauge	None
level	Unknown
gradient	8 fpm
scenery	A-

DESCRIPTION: Still beautiful and intimate below GA 106 (E), the Hudson changes its character and becomes more lively. Many rippling shoals keep the boater entertained, but none of the shoals is a problem to navigate. Most of the Class I–II rapids are located downstream of GA 106; then the waters calm until reaching the last shoal right before the river's junction with the Middle Fork Broad. Though some cartographers disagree, the locals consider this point to be the beginning of the Broad River, and they apparently control the signage in the area.

A pleasant 13.1-mile trip can be had by putting in at GA 106, paddling to the confluence, and taking-out 5.7 miles farther downstream on river right, immediately below the GA 281 bridge (G). This take-out is owned by the local outfitter; make appropriate arrangements to use it. The mid-run take-out at US 29 involves a steep scramble up to the road via steps cut into the dirt, and is consequently easier used as a starting point for a trip.

SHUTTLE: The take-out is at the Broad River's intersection with GA 281, northeast of Danielsville. To reach the put-in from the take-out, take GA 281 south toward Danielsville. Turn right onto Old Wildcat Bridge Road, then left onto US 29. (A right turn on US 29 will lead to the mid-run access point.) Turn right onto Jones Chapel–Shiloh Road, which turns into Lamar Road after passing through Shiloh. Turn left onto Shiloh–Fort Lamar Road, then take a right onto GA 106. The bridge is ahead.

GAUGE: There is no gauge. The local outfitter can provide an opinion on current levels over the phone. Alternately, visually scout access points if there's been adequate rainfall.

BROAD RIVER

The Broad River is, along with the Chattooga, one of the major northern tributaries of the Savannah River. With 50 miles of navigable river from its inception to Thurmond Lake, the Broad offers nearly year-round opportunities for canoeing and camping except in periods of extreme drought. The 6 miles of river in the upper section contain most of the river's rapids. In the lower section, the Broad becomes a pastoral stream eminently suited for beginning canoeists and those desiring a relaxed canoe-camping experience. Locals consider the Broad to start at the confluence of its two largest tributaries: the Middle Fork Broad and Hudson Rivers. For those interested in floating the entire length of the Broad River US 29 provides access to both of these rivers upstream of the confluence.

MAPS: Carnesville, Danielsville North, Carlton, Elberton West, Jacksons Crossroads, Broad, Chennault (USGS); Franklin, Elbert, Madison, Oglethorpe, Wilkes, Lincoln (County)

GA 281 to GA 172

class	II (III)
length	5.7 mi
time	3 hr
gauge	Phone, Web, visual
level	2.5 (Web)
gradient	8 (17)
scenery	B

DESCRIPTION: It is in this popular section that the Broad River is at its most exciting. The river widens considerably but maintains the wilderness quality found upstream. Frequent shoals offer 5.7 miles of Class I and II rapids at normal water levels. Take out at the GA 172 bridge on the left side, or call in advance to arrange use of the outfitter-owned take-out 0.5 miles below the bridge on the right.

At high water levels, the Broad is for expert boaters only. With its large watershed, the water gets big, particularly in the winter and early spring. Rapids increase in difficulty level to Class III, with at least one Class IV. At levels over 5 or 6 feet, the waterfall on the river's right, downstream of the major pipeline crossing, turns into a keeper hydraulic that works in tandem with a ledge downstream of it to create a serious threat (akin to the hole at Woodall Shoals), particularly for anyone caught out of a boat. With the wide characteristic of the river, a bomb-proof roll or strong self-rescue skills are necessary at higher water levels to avoid permanent loss of boat.

SHUTTLE: From Danielsville go north on US 29 to a right-hand turn onto GA 281; follow GA 281 to another right turn onto Transco Road. Follow this road less than a mile to a left turn onto David's Home Church Road. After 3.7 miles, turn left onto GA 172. The take-out path is on the far side of the bridge. An alternative take-out is available, with permission, at the outfitter's property 0.5 miles farther downstream. To get there, turn right onto the dirt road just before the bridge. To return to the put-in, backtrack to GA 281 and turn right. The put-in is ahead on the right at the outfitter's, before the bridge.

GAUGE: Data is available on the USGS Web site for the Broad near Carlton. This is miles downstream of this section. Using this gauge, the absolute minimum is 2.5 feet, though a more enjoyable and less scrape-prone minimum is 3.5 feet. The ideal level for this section is 4 to 4.5 feet. Water starts getting pushy above 6 feet. Waves start to increase in size as the water rises above this level; the river has been played by expert boaters at levels as high as the teens and twenties. There is a visual gauge at the GA 281 bridge that gives readings approximately 3 feet lower than the Internet gauge downstream. Levels can be provided over the phone by the outfitter.

GA 172 TO THURMOND LAKE

class	I (II)
length	38.7 mi
time	Up to 4 days
gauge	Web, visual
level	1.5
gradient	<2 fpm
scenery	B

DESCRIPTION: The gradient slows and the river adopts a pastoral character below GA 172 (B). Multiple access points along the remaining 38.4 miles of river allow for trips of varying lengths. The river is ideally suited for relaxing multiple-day trips since it passes through miles of undeveloped woodlands and farmland. The Broad feels remote because it has managed to avoid industrial development.

The only noteworthy rapid on this section is Anthony Shoals, just above Thurmond Lake (formerly Clarks Hill Lake). Anthony Shoals is a very long series of rapids of Class II difficulty. Here the river is quite wide, so even though the gradient is steeper, the river is shallow and its force is diluted. At low water levels, the only feasible route is through the channel cut through the ledges to accommodate the barges that formerly traveled upstream. The shoals have three sections, the last of which is a channel with standing waves that ends at the lake. At higher water levels, the rapids at the shoals wash out. It is possible to take-out on river right above Anthony Shoals using county roads for access.

Broad River Map 1

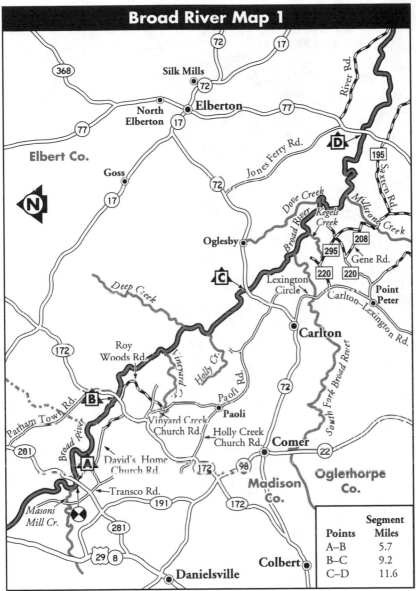

Points	Segment Miles
A–B	5.7
B–C	9.2
C–D	11.6

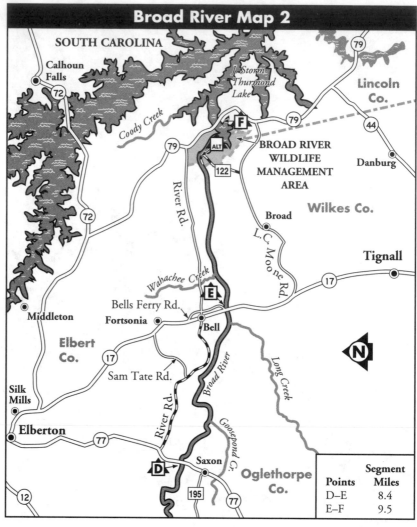

Broad River Map 2

SOUTH CAROLINA

Calhoun Falls
72

Coody Creek

J. Storm Thurmond Lake

79

F

ALT

79

122

River Rd.

72

79

44

Lincoln Co.

Danburg

BROAD RIVER WILDLIFE MANAGEMENT AREA

Wilkes Co.

Broad

L. C. Moore Rd.

Tignall

17

Wahachee Creek

E

Bells Ferry Rd.

Middleton

Fortsonia

Bell

Elbert Co.

17

Sam Tate Rd.

Silk Mills

Elberton

77

River Rd.

Broad River

Long Creek

N

Goosepond Cr.

D

Saxon

Oglethorpe Co.

12

195

77

Points	Segment Miles
D–E	8.4
E–F	9.5

At the shoals, many grassy islets and the rocky streambed combine with the rushing water to make a picturesque setting. This is the only place on the Broad River that supports the rare shoal lilies that live on the fall line rivers of the Southeast. The area also includes remains from previous settlements, including Native American mounds and the ruins of old mills and factories from the 1700s.

Camping and secure parking is available at the last take-out for the river at the Broad River Campground, maintained by the

Army Corps of Engineers. The campground is located on the right side of the lake, 1 mile below Anthony Shoals.

SHUTTLE: From Elberton, take GA 72 east; turn right onto GA 79 and proceed to the lake. Access is at the Broad River Campground. The highest put-in for this section is reached by returning to Elberton via GA 79 and GA 72. In Elberton, take GA 17 northwest to a left turn onto GA 172 at the town of Bowman. Proceed to the bridge over the river. Put-in at the bridge, or secure permission to use the put-in owned by the outfitter 0.5 miles downstream on river right. Most of the mid-run access points are at the junction with state highways. There is a public boat ramp at GA 17, making it the easiest place mid-run to get down to the river. Other access points are available at GA 72 west of Elberton, and at GA 77 south of Elberton. There is one additional access point above Anthony Shoals that can be reached from CR 193 in Wilkes County.

GAUGE: Using the USGS Web site reading for the Broad above Carlton, the minimum level is 1.5 feet and maximum is 12 feet.

SOUTH FORK BROAD RIVER

The South Fork Broad River is a short but sweet Broad River tributary. Rising in northwestern Madison County, it flows southeastward through predominantly agricultural land before entering the Broad River east of Athens. The most noteworthy rapids are found in the lower section. An extensive shoal that can reach up to Class III intensity is located below the dam at Watson Mill State Park.

MAPS: Danielsville South, Carlton, Elberton West (USGS); Madison, Oglethorpe (County)

GA 22 TO WATSON MILL STATE PARK

class	I
length	5.3 mi
time	3.5 hr
gauge	None
level	Unknown
gradient	3 fpm
scenery	B-

DESCRIPTION: At most water levels the uppermost access for boating is at GA 22, just south of the city of Comer. The South Fork takes a lazy winding course with no measurable rapids down to Watson Mill State Park (B). The park is home to one of the few remaining covered bridges in Georgia. At 229 feet, the vintage 1885 bridge is the longest covered bridge in the state. Immediately downstream of the covered bridge is a small dam that must be portaged if you are continuing downstream. Take-out above

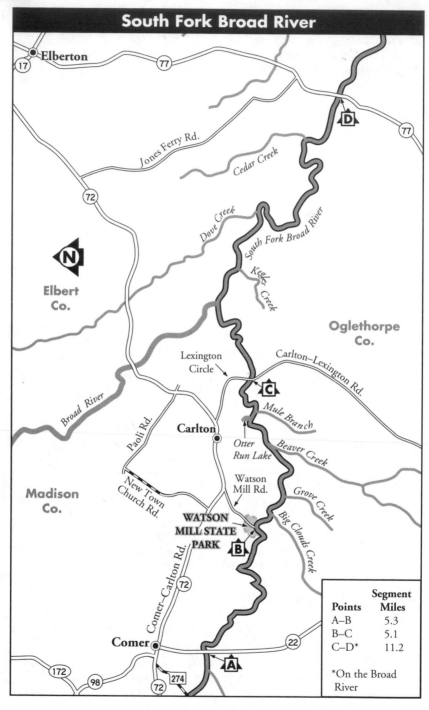

South Fork Broad River

Elberton

Jones Ferry Rd.

Cedar Creek

Dove Creek

South Fork Broad River

Keg Creek

Elbert Co.

Oglethorpe Co.

Broad River

Lexington Circle

Carlton–Lexington Rd.

Paoli Rd.

Carlton

Mule Branch

Otter Run Lake

Beaver Creek

New Town Church Rd.

Watson Mill Rd.

Grove Creek

Madison Co.

WATSON MILL STATE PARK

Big Clouds Creek

Comer–Carlton Rd.

Comer

Points	Segment Miles
A–B	5.3
B–C	5.1
C–D*	11.2

*On the Broad River

the dam regardless. Picnicking and camping facilities are available at the park.

SHUTTLE: To the take-out from Athens, take GA 72 northeast toward Elberton. Follow signs for Watson Mill State Park after passing through the town of Comer. To the put-in, return to GA 72 and turn left. At Comer, turn left on GA 22 and proceed to the bridge.

GAUGE: None.

WATSON MILL STATE PARK TO GA 77 AT THE BROAD RIVER

class	I–II (III)
length	16.3 mi
time	1–2 days
gauge	None
level	Unknown
gradient	8 fpm
scenery	B-

DESCRIPTION: At Watson Mill State Park, the put-in for this section, there is a small dam with rapids below that may be run if water conditions are favorable. These rapids may reach Class III difficulty in high water. Put-in below the dam, or below the rapids. Beyond the park the river continues its sinuous meandering to its junction with the main Broad River. A mid-section access point at Carlton–Lexington Road (C) divides this section into two—5.1 miles above and 11.2 miles below this point.

The only other shoals of appreciable difficulty appear below the bridge at Carlton–Lexington Road. A 3-foot dam at Andrew's Mill creates a slack backwater just downstream of the bridge. The dam should be portaged and rapids below it scouted. The rapids are usually a solid Class II difficulty; at high water they reach Class III difficulty. One final series of shoals is approximately 2 miles farther downstream, just above the Broad River junction. The next access point is 8 miles down the Broad River at GA 77.

SHUTTLE: From Athens, take US 78 east. Just past Lexington, turn left onto GA 77 and proceed to the bridge over the Broad River. To reach the put-in, continue northeast on GA 77. Turn left onto Jones Ferry Road and take it to GA 72. Turn left here. After passing through Carlton, watch for signs for Watson Mill State Park, the put-in for this section.

GAUGE: None.

SAVANNAH RIVER

One of Georgia's longest and largest rivers, the Savannah originates in Hart County in northeastern Georgia. Flowing southeast, the Savannah travels approximately 300 miles and drains an area of 10,600 square miles before emptying into the Atlantic Ocean near the city of Savannah. The journey of the Savannah from source to mouth is a study of contrasts. It originates clear, cool, and free-flowing in the Blue Ridge Mountains. However, its mountain tributaries are dammed and impounded many times before even reaching the Savannah. The Savannah itself comes into being not as a surging, vibrant stream, but as a still mass of backwater in the Hartwell Reservoir, into which the Savannah's parent tributaries, the Tugaloo and the Seneca, empty.

MAPS: Clarks Hill, Evans, Martinez, North Augusta, Augusta East, Mechanic Hill, Jackson, Shell Bluff Landing, Girard Northwest, Girard, Millett, Allendale, Hilltonia, Peoples, Shirley, Hardeeville Northwest, Ringon, Port Wentworth, Lime House, Garden City, Savannah, Fort Pulaski, Savannah Beach North (USGS); Columbia, Richmond, Burke, Screven, Chatham (County)

THURMOND DAM TO SAVANNAH

class	I
length	210.1 mi
time	Up to 4 weeks
gauge	Web
level	N/A
gradient	3; <1 below Augusta
scenery	B–C-

DESCRIPTION: Released below Hartwell Dam, the Savannah is never again clear or free-flowing. As it traverses the Piedmont it flows reddish to light brown and transports a massive suspension of sediment and silt. Its flow is regulated by a series of impoundments, so there is less than 30 miles of free-flowing river between the Hartwell Dam and Augusta. Below Thurmond Dam, the Savannah averages 350 feet in width and runs through deep, well-defined, sandy, clay banks for approximately 6 miles before entering the backwaters of Stevens Creek Dam. Since Thurmond Dam is responsible for ensuring adequate water for navigation on the lower Savannah, releases are more uniform and predictable than at Hartwell. Runnable levels are therefore assured all year.

Three miles below the GA 28 bridge is the Stevens Creek Dam, followed shortly downstream by a navigation dam with locks. Both of these must either be portaged or locked through. Immediately following the navigation lock and dam the Savannah broadens, and shoals appear again and run intermittently until the river narrows and winds to the left before passing the city of Augusta. It is at this point that the Savannah emerges

Savannah River Map 1

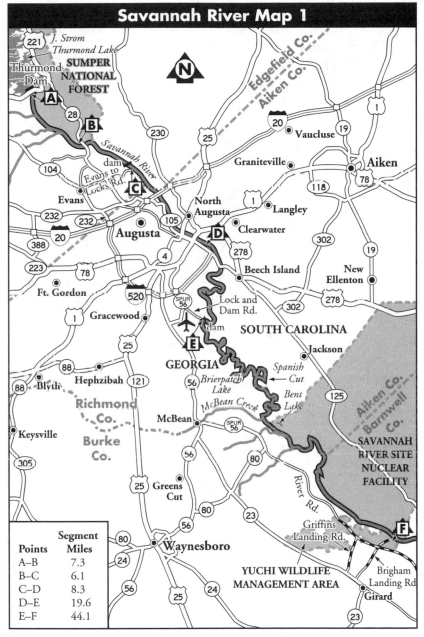

Points	Segment Miles
A–B	7.3
B–C	6.1
C–D	8.3
D–E	19.6
E–F	44.1

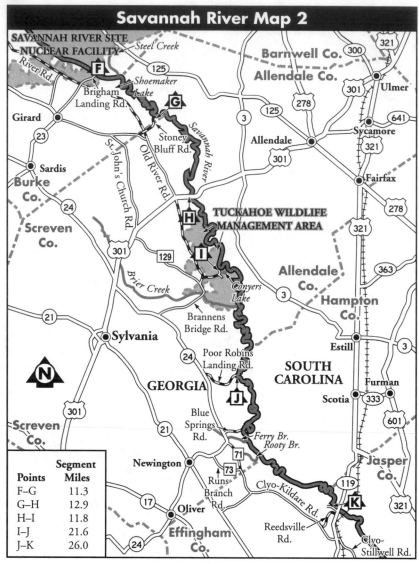

Savannah River Map 2

SAVANNAH RIVER SITE
NUCLEAR FACILITY   *Steel Creek*
River Rd.   **F**

Shoemaker Lake
Brigham Landing Rd.   **G**
Girard   125

23   *Stoney Bluff Rd.*

Sardis
Burke Co.   24

Screven Co.   301   129

Brier Creek   *Conyers Lake*

Brannens Bridge Rd.

21   **Sylvania**

Poor Robins Landing Rd.   24

GEORGIA   **J**

301   Blue Springs Rd.   21

Screven Co.   Runs Branch Rd.   17   **Oliver**

Newington   71   73

Effingham Co.   24

Barnwell Co.   300   321
Allendale Co.
301   **Ulmer**
278   641
125   3   **Sycamore**
Allendale   321
301   **Fairfax**
278
TUCKAHOE WILDLIFE MANAGEMENT AREA   321
I   363
Allendale Co.   3
Hampton Co.
Estill   3
SOUTH CAROLINA   **Furman**
Scotia   333   601
Ferry Br.
Rooty Br.   **Jasper Co.**
Clyo-Kildare Rd.   119
K   321
Reedsville Rd.   Clyo-Stillwell Rd.

Points	Segment Miles
F–G	11.3
G–H	12.9
H–I	11.8
I–J	21.6
J–K	26.0

from its wooded corridor into a heavily populated and industrialized area. Flowing first past the levees of downtown Augusta and then through the heavy industry and junkyards on Augusta's southeast river bank, the Savannah leaves the Piedmont behind and begins to change character as it plods irrevocably towards the Atlantic Ocean. River access in the Augusta area is rare at bridge crossings, and is better sought at private and public boat ramps.

For paddlers, the Savannah has its good points and bad. On the negative side the water is usually not aesthetically pleasing. On the positive side, there is plenty of that funny-looking water, since upstream dams and hydroelectric plants must release sufficient water daily to support navigation in the Coastal Plain. Further, except in the environs of large cities and at two or three isolated industrial sites, the river corridor is surprisingly isolated and pristine, and is rich in flora and fauna. Islands in the Piedmont and meandering bypasses (islands formed when a meander loop is cut off) in the Coastal Plain provide opportunities for canoe-camping.

Below Augusta, as the Savannah sweeps across the Coastal Plain towards the sea, the river is left more or less to its own devices. The river's character changes markedly as it bids farewell to the rolling hills of the Piedmont and enters the agricultural flats and bottom lands of the Coastal Plain. Here the river deepens and constricts to an average 250 to 300 feet, and flows beneath well-defined, sandy clay banks of 2 to 6 feet in height. Where the Savannah was shallow and turbulent upstream, it is now deep and calm. Islands are smaller and much less common, and the straight sections give way to broad meanders and horseshoe loops, complete with lowland swamp and oxbow lakes.

While a forest corridor continues to cradle the river, it frequently yields to lowland swamp on the far side of the river's natural levee. Nevertheless, the streamside forest remains diverse and beautiful. Dominant along the Savannah in the Coastal Plain are bald cypress, tupelo, overcup oak, water hickory, green ash, and swamp black gum, with understory vegetation consisting of swamp privet, swamp dogwood, and swamp palm. Frequently encountered inhabitants of the Savannah along the Coastal Plain include the marsh rabbit, muskrat, several species of bat, mink, opossum, raccoon, gray squirrel, bobcat, long-tailed weasel, red fox, striped skunk, white-tailed deer, beaver, and river otter. Reptiles and amphibians are numerous, and include several species of rattlesnake as well as the southern copperhead and the eastern cottonmouth. The many species of birds are too numerous to list.

Paddling is enjoyable and the setting pristine and remote, with the exception of several isolated riverside power plants and industries, including the nuclear power plant located across the river from Burke County. Hazards to navigation are limited to power boat traffic (which is far from overwhelming) and to a dam 8 miles south of Augusta that must be portaged. The level of difficulty is Class I throughout. Access is good in Richmond and Burke Counties but somewhat limited in Screven and Effingham Counties.

After passing beneath I-95, the Savannah enters the Savannah National Wildlife Refuge. Formerly the site of many plantations, the rice pools have been allowed to revert to grassy marsh and now serve as the wintering grounds for waterfowl. Here begins a series of alternate cuts, canals, and river passages that branch off the main Savannah channel and parallel it to the east, return to the main channel at the southern end of the wildlife refuge, and immediately fork again around Hutchinson Island. Beyond doubt, several days of pleasant paddling can be had while exploring the wildlife refuge.

Moving south beyond the refuge your choice is to paddle through Savannah city and port or to bypass the harbor on the less-trafficked Back River. While the Savannah waterfront is not without historical, industrial, and cultural interest, it is nevertheless somewhat dangerous due to the busy maritime traffic. Our advice is to view Savannah harbor from the deck of a sight-seeing boat.

SHUTTLE: The lowest access is near Port Wentworth at the county park where GA 25 crosses the river. Upriver access points are shown on the map.

GAUGE: There are online gauges on the USGS Web site. The Savannah is runnable year-round. For more information on the upper river, contact the Metter Fisheries Office at (912) 685-2145. For the lower river, the Richmond Hill Fisheries Office can be reached at (912) 727-2112.

Savannah River Map 3

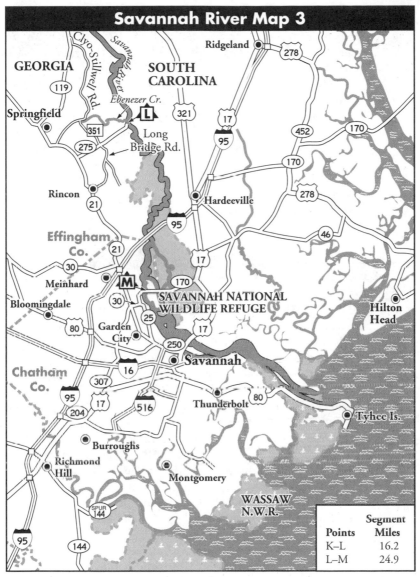

GEORGIA

SOUTH CAROLINA

Ridgeland ● —278—

Clyo-Stillwell Rd.

Savannah River

119

Ebenezer Cr.

Springfield ●

L

321

17

95

452

170

351

Long Bridge Rd.

275

170

Rincon ●
21

● Hardeeville

278

95

170

Effingham Co.
21

46

17

M

170

Meinhard ●

SAVANNAH NATIONAL WILDLIFE REFUGE

Hilton Head

30

Bloomingdale ●

30

25

Hilton Head

80

Garden City ●

17

Chatham Co.

250

16

● Savannah

95

307

17

80

204

516

Thunderbolt ●

Tybee Is. ●

● Burroughs

Richmond Hill ●

● Montgomery

WASSAW N.W.R.

SPUR 144

95

144

Points	Segment Miles
K–L	16.2
L–M	24.9

BRIER CREEK

An intimate stream of primeval beauty, Brier Creek's birthplace lies near the fall line west of Augusta. Unlike most Georgia rivers of its latitude, Brier Creek threads a winding path through dense vegetation reminiscent of the Coastal Plains. Shallow, sloping banks of red clay cradle the stream; trees festooned with Spanish moss arch overhead. In the section described here, it is a sizable creek, averaging 30 to 50 feet wide in the upper sections and up to 60 to 85 feet at the mouth, where it mingles with the Savannah River in a lowland swamp.

MAPS: McBean, Idlewood, Alexander, Hilltonia, Peeples (USGS); Burke, Screven (County)

GA 56 TO SAVANNAH RIVER

class	S
length	78.2 mi
time	10 days
gauge	Web
level	Unknown
gradient	<3 fpm
scenery	B

DESCRIPTION: Runnable downstream of the GA 56 bridge except during dry weather, the current on Brier Creek is generally slow as it flows a comparatively straight course beneath a luxurious canopy of bald cypress, sycamore, willow, and sweet gum. Graceful Spanish moss mysteriously drapes trees at streamside, which adds to the primitive atmosphere. The surrounding terrain consists of a wooded corridor with pine dominating the low, barely rolling swells beyond the river banks.

One segment of creek is considered private by the landowner and maintained to be off-limits to boaters. The property in question begins a few miles below the bridge at Murray Hill Road (C), stretches past Millhaven and ends a couple of miles above Hilltonia Creek Road (D). Other than this stretch, the creek is exceptionally easy to access and open to public use.

As the creek approaches its mouth in Screven County, the high ground gives way to lowland swamp and bogs. Hazards to navigation consist primarily of deadfalls that may require portaging; there are no rapids.

SHUTTLE: The lowest take-out on the creek is reached via GA 24, east of Sylvania. Turn east onto Brannens Bridge Road and the take-out. The next downstream access is 27 miles beyond this point on the Savannah River at Moon Change Swamp (also accessed from GA 24 south). All upstream access points are easily reached from GA 24 north.

Brier Creek Map 1

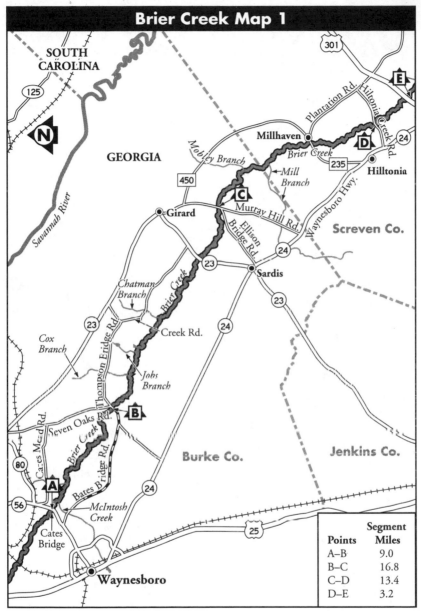

SOUTH CAROLINA

125

N

GEORGIA

Savannah River

Mobley Branch

301

E

Plantation Rd.

Hiltonia Creek Rd.

Millhaven

Brier Creek

D

24

Mill Branch

235

Hilltonia

450

C

Murray Hill Rd.

Waynesboro Hwy.

Girard

Screven Co.

Ellison Bridge Rd.

23

Sardis

24

23

Chatman Branch

Brier Creek

Creek Rd.

24

Cox Branch

Thompson Bridge Rd.

Jobs Branch

B

Seven Oaks Rd.

Burke Co.

Jenkins Co.

Cates Mead Rd.

Brier Creek

Bates Bridge Rd.

80

A

24

56

McIntosh Creek

25

Cates Bridge

Waynesboro

Points	Segment Miles
A–B	9.0
B–C	16.8
C–D	13.4
D–E	3.2

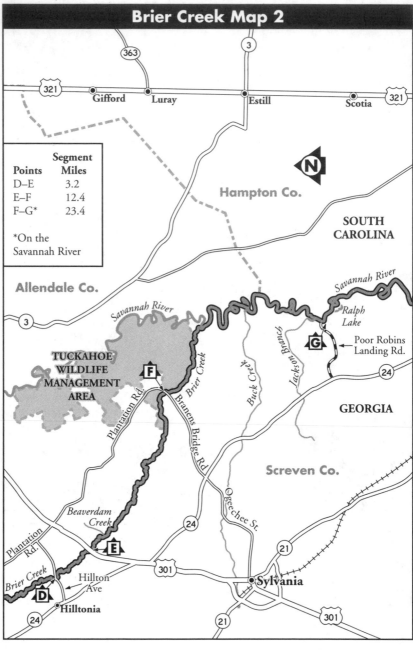

Brier Creek Map 2

Points	Segment Miles
D–E	3.2
E–F	12.4
F–G*	23.4

*On the
Savannah River

GAUGE: Flow data for two tributary streams is available online from the USGS. The minimum level for running the creek using these gauges is unknown. The maximum level is flood stage during the spring. The creek may not be runnable during the fall dry season, especially in low rainfall years.

EBENEZER CREEK

A blackwater tributary of the lower Savannah River, Ebenezer Creek boasts a rich history cast within a distinctly rare natural environment. This 13-mile run passes through ancient dwarf cypress and tupelo forests drowned in small shallow lakes that shelter a wide variety of bird and animal species. The sanctuary that the creek has historically provided is now reciprocated by the state; it is one of only four waterways designated as a Georgia scenic river, and is a National Natural Landmark.

MAPS: Hardeeville Northwest (GA/SC), Rincon (GA/SC), Springfield South (USGS); Effingham (County)

LONG BRIDGE ROAD TO SAVANNAH RIVER

class	S
length	13.5 mi
time	7 hr
gauge	Web
level	Unknown
gradient	<1 fpm
scenery	A–B+

DESCRIPTION: When the water is high, trips can begin at the uppermost access just outside Springfield at Run's Creek. From there, less than a mile of paddling will bring you to Ebenezer landing, potentially the site of the first settlement by the German Salzburgers in 1733. In Georgia, the Salzburgers found freedom to live according to their religious beliefs. Settling at the creek at the direction of Governor Ogelthorpe, the Salzburgers befriended the Creeks of the area, but found that the swamp environment didn't agree with them. After two years of disease and struggle, they migrated down the creek to found New Ebenezer on higher ground at the confluence. The community thrived until the Revolutionary War, when it was mostly destroyed. The church, however, survived, and is the oldest public building standing in Georgia. Some visitors still see, in the bricks of the church, the fingerprints of the women and children who helped build it.

Nearly 100 years later, the creek was the site of a less-well-documented tragic incident during the Civil War when hundreds (or thousands) of freed slaves became caught between opposing armies. Seeking protection from Union Gen. Jefferson C. Davis,

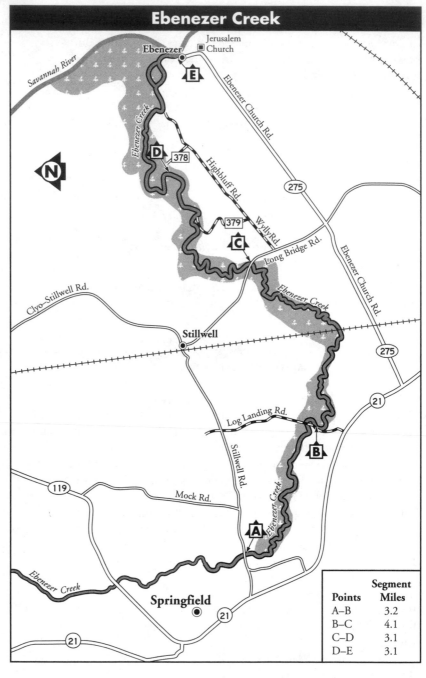

Ebenezer Creek

Savannah River

Ebenezer
Jerusalem
■ Church

E

Ebenezer Church Rd.

Ebenezer Creek

D 378

Highbluff Rd.

N

275

379 Wylly Rd.

C

Long Bridge Rd.

Ebenezer Church Rd.

Clyo–Stillwell Rd.

Ebenezer Creek

Stillwell

275

21

Log Landing Rd.

B

119

Mock Rd.

Stillwell Rd.

Ebenezer Creek

A

Ebenezer Creek

Springfield

21

21

Points	Segment Miles
A–B	3.2
B–C	4.1
C–D	3.1
D–E	3.1

the refugees trailed his army to the creek; the army took the flooded creek as opportunity to strand the refugees on the opposite shore. Panic rose as the Confederate Calvary closed in from the other direction, and countless refugees drowned or were killed as they tried to flee.

Today, the paddle down the creek is a profoundly peaceful one. Periodic high water flows of the Savannah (modulated now, due to the influence of upstream dams) force water to flood in the creek, creating shallow lakes. The resulting ecosystem has been referred to as one of the best examples of a backwater swamp in the state. The elongated lakes provide habitat for an unusual forest of virgin dwarfed bald cypress, located 0.5 miles above Long Bridge Road. Huge foundations support the comparatively small trunks of these trees, some estimated to be in excess of 1,000 years old. The swamp's low nutrient levels, partly responsible for this dwarfing, have facilitated the invasion of non-native plant species that threaten the natural diversity of the creek's native flora. One of the most scenic portions of the creek lies near its mouth, where a forest of swamp tupelos tower above the reflective blackwater. Their regular pattern and lack of intervening vegetation inspire comparisons to a temple or cathedral.

A wide variety of animals thrive within the creek's shelter, including elusive alligators. Birds flock to the area, making birdwatching a major attraction for paddlers. The creek's waters provide spawning grounds for spotted bass.

The creek passes intermittently along flooded swamps and between banks. When the water is high, the creek jumps out of its banks to thread through the swampland forest. You can too, but take care not to get lost, particularly below Long Bridge Road. Even in high water the current is imperceptibly slow. Dry landings are rare in the 3 miles below the Tommy Long boat ramp and at other spots when the water's up. The creek's path is obvious when the water is low; exposed strainers are present, but don't present a problem.

SHUTTLE: From Savannah, go north on I-95, Exit 109 for GA 21 north, to a right-hand turn at GA 275. The boat ramp is at the end of the road. To get to the ususal put-in, take GA 275 west to a right turn onto Long Bridge Road and continue to the creek. A bike trail can be used for a canoe–bicycle loop. Historical sites, including the church and a museum, are located at the confluence in New Ebenezer.

GAUGE: Consult the USGS Web site for Ebenezer at Springfield. The creek is runnable all year. Higher levels make side exploration of the swamps and sloughs possible.

HIAWASSEE RIVER

The Hiawassee River is a coldwater mountain stream with its head-waters on the northern side of Unicoi Gap in Towns County. Flowing north, the river becomes the major feeder stream for Lake Chatuge near the town of Hiawassee. The community jealously guards the river and its fish. "No trespassing" signs are posted prominently at most access points, and strung across the river itself are at least two signs warning against entry. The most easily accessed trip through the gentle valley portion of the river is described below. Downstream of the dam, the river emerges in Tennessee with a new spelling: Hiwassee.

MAPS: Tray Mountain, Macedonia (USGS); Towns (County)

GA 17/75 TO LAKE CHATUGE

class	I–II
length	8.3 mi
time	5 hr
gauge	Web, visual
level	2.5 ft
gradient	13 fpm
scenery	C

DESCRIPTION: The reaches of the Hiawassee above this section roughly parallel GA 17/75. The stream is occasionally visible from the highway, but it is too small to be considered feasible for boaters. It is not until after Soapstone Creek and Corbin Creek have added their flow that the river becomes suitable for canoeing. If you can manage to secure access permission from the private landowners, this Class II stretch is runnable only when the water is fairly high.

There are no difficult rapids below the first crossing of GA 17/75, only pretty rippling shoals that are stilled after 4 miles by the swampy backwaters of the lake. Signs of civilization are never far from the river and increase in frequency as the lake is approached. There are few easy options for taking-out above Lake Chatuge. The best exit points are at the public boat ramp on the lake (D), or less than a quarter mile upstream on Hightower Creek at Kelly Bridge Road (C).

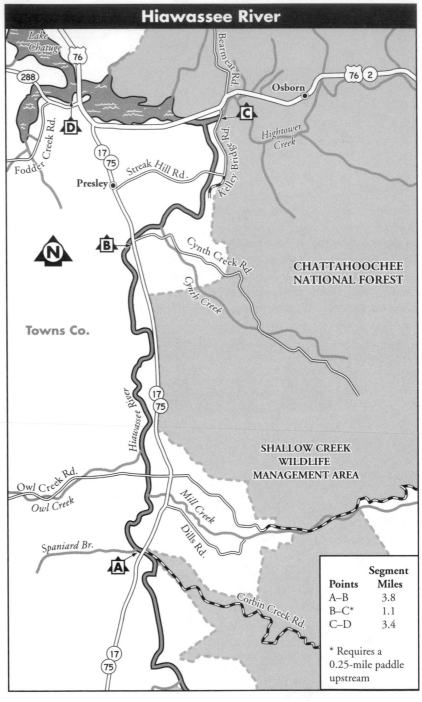

Hiawassee River

Lake Chatuge

76

288

Bearmeat Rd.

Osborn

76 2

C

Hightower Creek

D

Fodder Creek Rd.

17 75

Presley

Streak Hill Rd.

Kelley Bridge Rd.

N

B

Cynth Creek Rd.

CHATTAHOOCHEE NATIONAL FOREST

Cynth Creek

Towns Co.

Hiawassee River

17 75

SHALLOW CREEK WILDLIFE MANAGEMENT AREA

Owl Creek Rd.

Owl Creek

Mill Creek

Dills Rd.

Spaniard Br.

A

Corbin Creek Rd.

17 75

Points	Segment Miles
A–B	3.8
B–C*	1.1
C–D	3.4

* Requires a 0.25-mile paddle upstream

SHUTTLE: From the town of Hiawassee, take US 76 east to the public boat ramp located on the south side of the highway at the intersection with GA 288. To reach the put-in, return to US 76 and continue less than a mile east to a right-hand turn onto GA 17/75. GA 17/75 will cross the river twice; the second time is the uppermost potential put-in. Access may also be available at Owl Creek Road.

GAUGE: This section of river is free-flowing and dependent on rainfall. The TVA provides real-time cfs levels for the gauge at Presley on the unregulated flows page of their Web site, listed in the Introduction. The visual gauge is located on Hightower Creek near its confluence with the Hiawassee. Using this gauge, the minimum level is 2.5 feet and the maximum is 6 feet.

NOTTELY RIVER

The Nottely River is a hospitable, small stream with its headwaters high in the mountains of Union County southeast of Blairsville. It flows northwestward across the county and is the major source stream for the Tennessee Valley Authority's Nottely Lake. Vistas of mountain farmland on both sides of the river frequently give way to houses and businesses located near and sometimes almost in the river. Most of the river's mild rapids are located in the first 2 miles; the deepest woodlands are found in the final 2 miles above the lake. The river is named for an early Cherokee Indian settlement on the stream near the current Georgia–North Carolina border.

MAPS: Coosa Bald, Mulky Gap, Blairsville, Nottely Dam (USGS); Union (County)

GA 180 TO US 76 (NOTTELY LAKE)

class	I–II
length	10.5 mi
time	6 hr
gauge	Web, visual
level	2.0 ft
gradient	12 fpm
scenery	C+

DESCRIPTION: Portions of the river above GA 180 have excellent scenery, but there is insufficient flow volume for boating. It is not until the Nottely has reached the valley floor that it becomes navigable. In the first 2.4 miles, this run drops over 40 feet but creates no rapids above Class II difficulty.

For the first 5 miles, the stream never leaves earshot of US 19. As the river approaches Blairsville, signs of civilization increase and creep ever nearer to the river. The river maintains its pleasant mountain-stream characteristic regardless; the water is clear and

trips lightly over small shoals. Bridge crossings are frequent, and access throughout this stretch is good.

Farther downstream, approximately 2 miles below the bridge at Lower Owltown Road (E), the last rapid is passed at the ruins of an old bridge. After this point, the river leaves the road for 2 miles. The waters of the Nottely are mostly stilled by the lake as the take-out at US 76 is approached.

The river can also be paddled north of Nottely Lake downstream of the dam. This additional 1.7 miles of river from the dam to Smith Bridge contains no rapids above Class I difficulty.

SHUTTLE: To reach the take-out from Blairsville, take US 76 west to the bridge crossing the river. Easiest access is on the northwest corner of the bridge. Returning to the put-in, take US 76 east into Blairsville and follow signs for US 19 south. Continue approximately 8.3 miles to a left-hand turn onto GA 180. The bridge and river are directly ahead. Multiple alternative access points are easily reached off of US 19. Lower Owltown Road, Hudson Road, Jimmy Nicholson Road, and the bridge over the river at US 19 all offer options for varying trip lengths.

GAUGE: The river is free-flowing above the dam. The TVA provides real-time cfs readings on their Web site. A visual gauge is located near Lower Owltown Road. Using this gauge, the minimum level is 2 feet, maximum 8 feet.

Nottely River

Points	Segment Miles
A–B	1.2
B–C	1.4
C–D	1.4
D–E	1.3
E–F	5.2

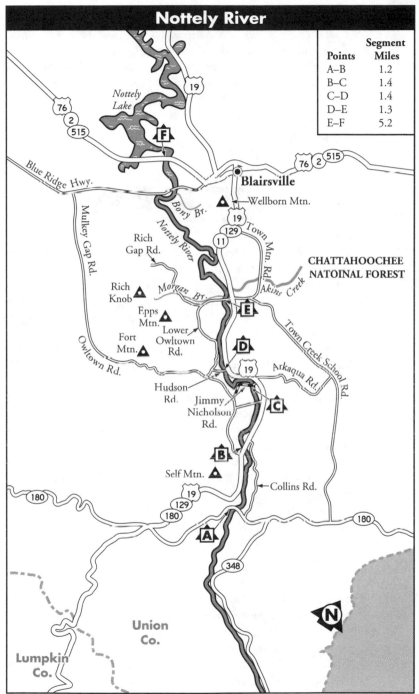

COOPER CREEK

Cooper Creek is a delightful introduction to creeking and is suitable for intermediate or advanced paddlers. The creek runs through pristine wilderness and is one of the most primitive small streams in the state. It's small and tight, and consequently hosts a fair number of deadfalls. Scouting and portaging are possible at most major rapids. The creek is a major tributary of the Toccoa River.

MAPS: Mulky Gap (USGS); Union (County); Chattahoochee National Forest (USFS).

FS 33A TO MULKY CAMPGROUND

class	I–III (IV in high water)
length	5.2 mi
time	4 hr
gauge	None
level	N/A
gradient	60 fpm
scenery	A

DESCRIPTION: Cooper Creek starts with Class I and II rapids and almost never has a flat section without something of interest. A mile or so from the put-in, a huge rock in the center of the stream and an obvious horizon line presage the first interesting rapid, Corner Pocket (Class III-). Scout the 5-foot drop from the large granite rock in the center of the stream. It can be run on either side, but the right side has a good surfing hole. Cooper Falls (Class III) follows almost immediately. This drop is a 16-foot slide which can't be scouted, but shouldn't be any trouble.

After the slide the river gains in gradient and Class II rapids increase in frequency. After another mile or so the creek takes a sharp right turn. In about an eighth of a mile the last big drop occurs. This rapid is known as Grunch (an 8-foot waterfall) and should be scouted from the right bank. Run it on the left side, but be careful, as Grunch has smashed the deck plate of more than one canoe. Below Grunch, Cooper picks up even more in gradient and is almost continuous Class II for several miles. What looks like a low head dam is approached under the FS 236 bridge; don't worry, it's a simple Class II drop. Soon after the last drop and a few more Class I ripples, the takeout comes into view, and you should be able to see your car.

SHUTTLE: From Dahlonega, take GA 60 north. Stay on GA 60 to Suches; after passing into Suches, turn right onto GA 180 east. Continue on this road until you reach Lake Wilfred Scott Recreation Area. Immediately past the recreation area, turn left onto Cooper Creek Road, FS 33. Turn left when FS 33A branches off to the right. The unpaved road will become paved again and travel past some houses and farms, but don't get worried. Turn

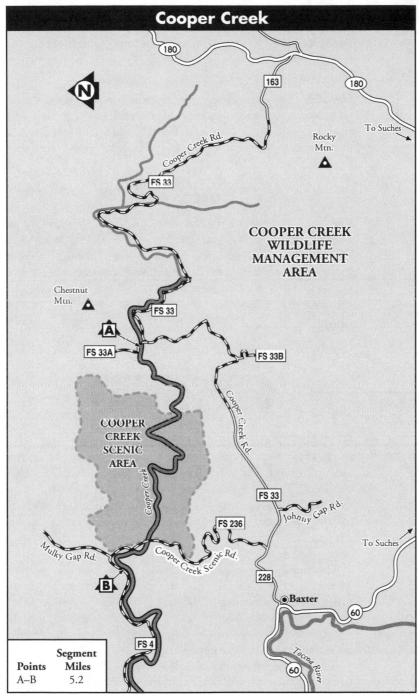

Cooper Creek

N

180

163

180

To Suches

Rocky
Mtn.

Cooper Creek Rd.

FS 33

**COOPER CREEK
WILDLIFE
MANAGEMENT
AREA**

Chestnut
Mtn.

FS 33

A

FS 33A

FS 33B

Cooper Creek Rd.

**COOPER
CREEK
SCENIC
AREA**

Cooper Creek

FS 33

Johnny Gap Rd.

FS 236

To Suches

Mulky Gap Rd.

Cooper Creek Scenic Rd.

228

B

●**Baxter**

60

FS 4

Toccoa River

60

Points	Segment Miles
A–B	5.2

right onto FS 236 and continue on this road until you come to a stop sign at the FS 4 junction. Turn left on FS 4 and proceed to the Mulkey Creek Campground on the left, the take-out for this run. To reach the put-in, return to FS 33A. The put-in is at the bridge over the creek.

GAUGE: There is no gauge. Cooper will only be runable during rainy season or after a major rain. If the small island at the put-in is under water, it is runnable. If it looks too honkin' high, it probably is.

TOCCOA RIVER

The Toccoa is a purely delightful mountain stream. Its upper reaches harbor a primitive woodland paddling experience with mostly mild rapids. Unregulated by dams, the river's flow becomes the major feeder for Blue Ridge Lake. Below the dam, the river widens as it weaves through settled lands on its way to McCaysville and into Tennessee, where it is thereafter known as the Ocoee River.

MAPS: Suches, Noontootla, Wilscot, Blue Ridge, Mineral Bluff (USGS), Fannin (County)

DEEP HOLE CAMPGROUND TO BLUE RIDGE LAKE

class	I–II (III)
length	17.5 mi
time	1–2 days
gauge	Web, phone, visual
level	250 cfs
gradient	13 fpm
scenery	A

DESCRIPTION: While it is navigable by canoe or kayak above the junction with Cooper Creek in Fannin County, the highest usual put-in is the U.S. Forest Service campground at Deep Hole on GA 60. The first 3-mile segment traverses some farmland, some woodland, and intersects with a couple of roads before veering into the fragrant realm of the undisturbed forest. Putting in downstream of the campground where GA 60 passes near the river (C) brings the forest's entrance 1.8 miles closer.

Flowing through the national forest on the back side of Tooni Mountain, the river becomes a sheer delight for beginning canoeists, canoe campers, and trout fishermen. Water quality is good, and trout fishing is excellent. Add beautiful scenery, wooded seclusion, and mild rapids, and you have the perfect environment for an overnight trip.

Within the forest section, fairly continuous Class I rapids keep things lively. A half-mile of Class II+ activity begins below the Rock Creek junction. The Benton McKay Trail, a loop of the

Toccoa River

Points	Segment Miles
A–B	1.2
B–C	0.6
C–D	6.2
D–E	1.0
E–F	2.6
F–G	1.8
G–H	1.6
H–I	2.5
I–J	4.2
J–K	Lake Blue Ridge
K–L	6.8
L–M	6.4
M–N	1.6

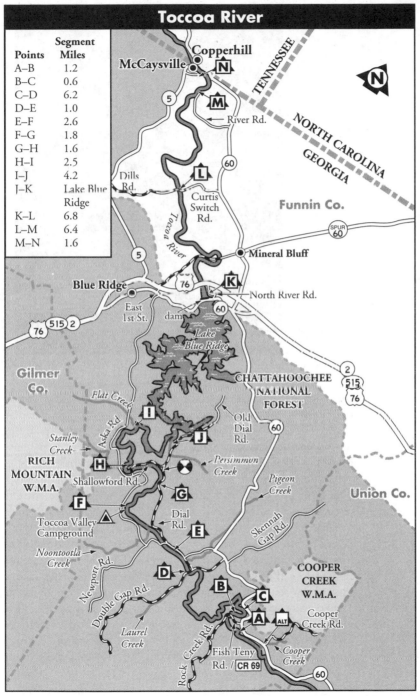

Toccoa River seen from the Benton McCay Trail bridge

photo © Tres Hombres del Rio

Appalachian Trail, crosses the river via suspension bridge at this point, providing a good vantage point for scouting the largest rapid. The loop trail makes a good hiking side-trip up Tooni Mountain. Best in winter and early spring, the view of the surrounding valleys carved by the river is worth the climb.

Gradually the river leaves the seclusion of the forest and enters a picturesque valley upstream of Swan Bridge (D). The current remains swift and busy, with Class I activity for the next 9 miles to Blue Ridge Lake. The surrounding views are fairly pastoral, giving way to civilization mingled with intermittent brushes with forest after passing Dial Road. There are no major rapids until right before the final take-out, where the river narrows into a short series of Class II rapids that become more challenging at higher water levels. After this point, the river is quickly stilled into the backwaters of Lake Blue Ridge. Occasionally, when the lake pool is down 40–50 feet, an additional section of continuous Class II rapids is exposed. This can be run with a take-out on river right at Persimmon Creek.

Access is good throughout the upper section and easily accommodates shorter trips. A 7.2-mile stretch that includes the most remote forest segments and challenging rapids can be created by putting in at GA 60 and taking-out on Dial Road (E). The upper section also encompasses the 15-mile U.S. Forest Service Toccoa Canoe Trail, which stretches from Deep Hole Campground to the Sandy Bottom take-out (G). The trail makes for one busy or two relaxed days of paddling. Downstream, a quick 5.4-mile trip begins at the campground put-in on Aska Road (F) and ends below the last rapid. At low lake levels, more Class II rapids open up between access points I and J.

SHUTTLE: From GA 2/515 in Blue Ridge, turn east onto Windy Ridge Road. The road quickly comes to a stop sign; turn left. After 0.2 miles, turn right onto Aska Road. The lowest usual take-out point (I) is 7 miles ahead on the left. Ample parking is available at the bend in the road near the top of the rapid; if you choose to run the rapid, your car can easily be moved to the more restricted pull-out near the bottom for loading. To get to the put-in, continue in the same direction on Aska Road. Along the way, you'll pass most of the intermediate access points, with the exception of the Sandy Bottom take-out and Swan Bridge. Aska Road will eventually dead-end into Newport Road. Turn left here, then right at the next dead-end into Dial Road. Take Dial Road until it reaches GA 60; turn right. The turn for Deep Hole Campground is on the right, approximately 0.5 miles after the road rejoins the river.

GAUGE: The TVA provides data for the gauge at Dial Road on their Web site or by calling (800) 238-2264. The river can be run as low as 250 cfs, but is more enjoyable above 400. Experienced boaters will continue to enjoy the river at levels above 1,000 cfs, but beginners will be imperiled, particularly upstream of Dial Road, since laurel thickets eliminate eddies and block safe access to the banks in many spots. A visual gauge is located on river right between the Toccoa Valley Campground and Shallowford Bridge. Using this gauge, the minimum level is 0.7 feet, maximum 6 feet.

BLUERIDGE DAM TO McCAYSVILLE

class	I
length	14.8 mi
time	6
gauge	Web, phone
Level	1,600 cfs
gradient	5 fpm
scenery	C+

DESCRIPTION: Below Blue Ridge Lake the river's gradient becomes (and remains) gentle for the 14 miles to McCaysville. Both the river and the valley widen considerably, and signs of civilization become more prevalent. Railroad tracks parallel the river most of the way. At McCaysville the river enters the Copper Basin area and is known thereafter as the Ocoee River.

SHUTTLE: From McCaysville, go east on GA 60/5 and take GA 60 south toward Mineral Ridge. Turn right onto River Road and follow it a few miles to Horseshoe Bend River Park. To the put-in, continue south on GA 60 toward Blue Ridge. Turn right onto GA 2/515; after 1.3 miles, turn left on North River Road. The put-in is at the Powerhouse River Access, less than a mile ahead. Mid-run access is reachable from GA 60 at Curtis Switch Road.

GAUGE: The TVA provides data for the Toccoa below the dam on their Web site or by calling (800) 238-2264; Blue Ridge Dam is currently option #23 within their phone system. Standard operating flow when the dam is generating is 1,600 cfs, which provides plenty of water for this section and no real hazards.

FIGHTINGTOWN CREEK

Fightingtown Creek tumbles off the eastern slopes of the Cohutta Mountains in Gilmer County. Flowing north toward Tennessee to become a tributary of the Ocoee River (known as the Toccoa in Georgia), its steady grade and narrow width combine to create a quick and lively Class I to II ride. Despite its frequent road crossings and proximity to McCaysville, the stream manages to maintain the aura and aroma of a wild and loamy forest.

MAPS: Cashes Valley, Epworth (USGS); Fannin (County)

POWER DAM ROAD TO MCCAYSVILLE

class	I–II
length	12.7 mi
time	7 hr
gauge	Visual (difficult to reach)
level	Unknown
gradient	16 fpm
scenery	B

DESCRIPTION: Although it is small in its upper reaches, Fightingtown Creek gets sufficient rainfall in its watershed to make it suitable for canoeing many months of the year. Winter, spring, and early summer are the most dependable. The creek is usually no more than 20 to 30 feet wide and a canopy of trees keeps the paddler in nearly perpetual shade.

Current is swift, creating Class I–II rapids as it drops an average of close to 20 feet per mile. There are no heart-stopping drops—the largest drop is 4 feet—but you should remain alert and be sure to maneuver precisely at times. Hazards are mostly in the form of deadfalls and strainers. Boaters must frequently carry over or slide under trees that block the stream, particularly in the upper stretches. The section located between Madola Road (C) and West Tennessee Street (D) is the most popular, as it is both the longest stretch uninterrupted by bridges and harbors the greatest gradient change.

Access may be available upstream of Power Dam Road (A) at the creek's crossing with GA 2, and again from the side roads off of Chestnut Gap Road. These properties appear to be private, and permission should be obtained before using them. Putting in at GA 2 adds another 4.6 miles of river to the trip; the put-in next to Chestnut Gap Road is another 1.7 miles farther upstream. Downstream of the GA 2 crossing an old bridge has fallen into the creek; large beams and protruding spikes create potential danger.

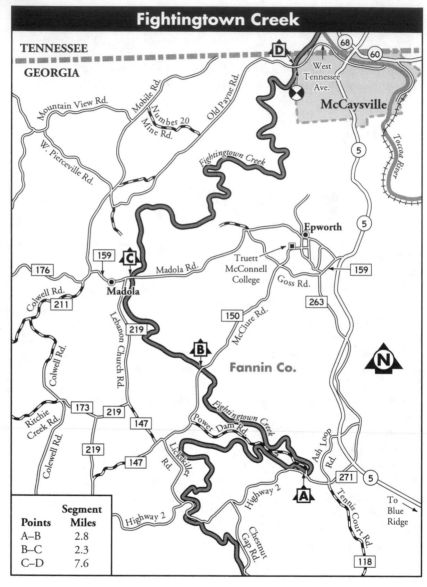

Fightingtown Creek

TENNESSEE

GEORGIA

Mountain View Rd.

Mobile Rd.

Number 20

Mine Rd.

Old Payne Rd.

68

60

West Tennessee Ave.

McCaysville

Toccoa River

W. Pierceville Rd.

Fightingtown Creek

5

5

Epworth

159

Truett McConnell College

Goss Rd.

176

159

Colwell Rd.

211

Madola Rd.

Madola

150

McClure Rd.

263

Lebanon Church Rd.

219

B

Fannin Co.

N

Colwell Rd.

Colwell Rd.

Ritchie Creek Rd.

173

219

147

Fightingtown Creek

Power Dam Rd.

Ash Loop Rd.

Colwell Rd.

219

147

Lickskillet Rd.

Highway 2

A

271

5

To Blue Ridge

Tennis Court Rd.

Highway 2

Chestnut Gap Rd.

118

Points	Segment Miles
A–B	2.8
B–C	2.3
C–D	7.6

SHUTTLE: Entering McCaysville from the south on GA 5, turn left onto West Tennessee Avenue before crossing the Toccoa River. Follow this street 1.3 miles to the take-out on the far side of the bridge. To get to the put-in, return to GA 5 and turn right. Turn right onto GA 2. The put-in is from the bridge at Power Dam Road.

GAUGE: There is a visual gauge upstream on river right at West Tennessee Road, but it is located on private property and difficult to reach. Alternatively, visually check the stream's flow at the desired access points. The TVA online gauge for the Toccoa River at Dial may give some idea of rainfall in the area. A rough estimate of Fightingtown volume can be calculated using the TVA-supplied levels for the Ocoee at Copperhill (unregulated flow), minus the flow for the Toccoa below Blue Ridge Dam, divided by two. The estimated minimum paddleable level using this method is 350 cfs.

SOUTH CHICKAMAUGA CREEK

South Chickamauga Creek is a long, winding, valley-floor stream in the northwest corner of the state. It flows north from Ringgold over the border into Tennessee and Chattanooga before entering the Tennessee River. As it weaves between the steep ridges that border the valley, the creek exposes you to numerous sites of cultural and natural interest.

MAPS: Ringgold, East Ridge, East Chattanooga (USGS); Catoosa GA, Hamilton TN (County)

LAFAYETTE STREET TO US 11/64 IN CHATTANOOGA, TN

class	I
length	19.5 mi
time	2 days
gauge	Web, visual
level	180 cfs
gradient	4 fpm
scenery	C–D

DESCRIPTION: At lower levels, South Chickamauga Creek makes for a placid, Class I float within easy reach of the urban area of Chattanooga, Tennessee. Along the way the creek passes by caves, springs, sinks, bluffs, farmland, Civil War historical sites, a wildlife sanctuary, and the old Swanson Mill at Graysville, Georgia. The mill's dam is only 100 feet below the access at the Graysville bridge (C), an intermediate access point. Be sure to take-out at this bridge to portage around the dam.

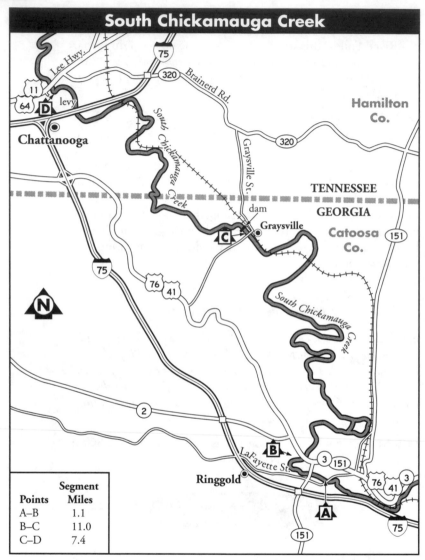

South Chickamauga Creek

Points	Segment Miles
A–B	1.1
B–C	11.0
C–D	7.4

Upon emerging from the riverine environment at the US 11 take-out in Chattanooga (D), you may encounter wildlife of another sort, including the 15-foot-high giant orange lizard and his ilk rendered in cement at the local miniature golf course.

SHUTTLE: From I-75 just over the border in Chattanooga, take Exit 4 for TN 320. Turn west onto Brainerd Road and proceed to a left turn onto Lee Highway, US 11. The take-out is less than a mile ahead on the left. Park between the levee and Brainerd Village Shopping Center. To get to the put-in, return to Brainerd Road. Continue 3.8 miles to a right turn onto Graysville Street. After 2 miles, the road will make a sharp right turn and head toward the creek. An alternative access point (C) is available down the side road on the right, immediately after crossing the railroad tracks. To get to the uppermost put-in, continue down Graysville Street. Turn left onto US 41 and go about 5 miles to a right turn onto Lafayette Street. The highest put-in is on the right at the bridge.

GAUGE: The TVA provides real-time stream flow data for South Chickamauga Creek at Chickamauga, Tennessee on their Web site. Minimum runnable water level is 180 cfs; maximum is flood stage. A staff gauge is located on river left, upstream from the bridge at US 11.

BEAR CREEK

A relatively recent addition to Georgia's steep creek portfolio, Bear plunges off the slopes of Lookout Mountain for a run through one of the gorges at Cloudland Canyon State Park. Amid the steep creek hazards of undercut boulders, tightly constricted passages, potentially ill-placed migrating wood, rocky landings, and precipitous portages lies the heart of Bear: a steep, fast, ride down some of the best Class V creekwater in the state.

MAPS: Durham (USGS); Dade (County)

GA 189 TO CANYON VIEW ROAD

class	V
length	3 mi
time	2.5 hr
gauge	Visual
level	9 inches
gradient	270 (475) fpm
scenery	A+

DESCRIPTION: Access at Bear Creek was for a short period denied by the state, fearing carnage and the accompanying cost of rescue. Enter American Whitewater, who negotiated passage for paddlers through the state park. There have been no recent access issues, but be well aware of the skill level required before paddling this creek. This is a run for advanced boaters only.

At the put-in, the creek barely appears worthy of its Class V rating. Beware—after a warm-up of quick and continuous Class II–III water, Bear starts to roar. No less than 14 significant drops are packed into the middle of the run as the gradient crescendos to a peak of 475 feet per mile. Technically a drop-and-pool stream, the water runs quickly from one rapid to the next. Eddies are small, making the run conducive to running from one rapid to the next without pause, *if* you know the lines and have confirmed that the channel is clear. The creek can be run more than once in a day.

The first significant rapid is Surrealistic Pillow (Class 5.0). Choose the far-right slot at medium levels, avoiding the undercut and log in the main channel. Portaging is the best option when the water is low. Surrealistic kicks off a series of technical drops separated by Bear's signature fast water. The largest—Class 5.2 Stairway to Heaven—falls 45 feet in three stages. The second stage drops 15 feet onto a bone-crushing slab of rock; back, rib, and head injuries have all occurred here. The daunting portage is in the channel on river left.

Should you need it, a trail on river left at Stairway leads up to a picnic area in the park. Turn right at the top of the hill and follow the faint path out. To minimize the risk of a misdirected and potentially cold walk through the woods, case the park before your run to get a sense of where this path ends.

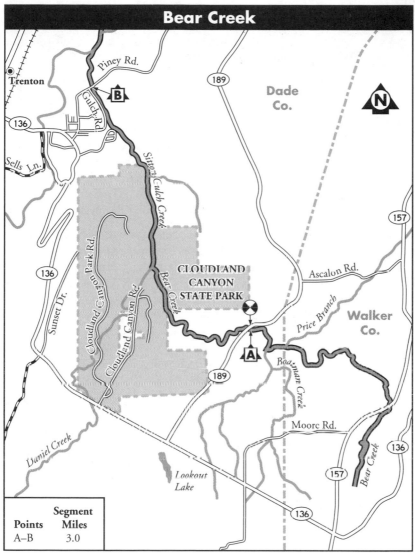

Bear Creek

Points	Segment Miles
A–B	3.0

After Stairway, the next significant drop is Big Bang (also Class 5.2). The portage here is a jump into the pool on river left, or run it with a boof close to the bank on river right. A few more technical rapids, including the Class 5.0 Momentary Lapse of Reason, are encountered before Daniel Creek enters from the left. A half mile hike up Daniels reveals more rapids.

Below the confluence with Daniel, Bear changes names to the less-than-poetic Sitton Gulch Creek. Technical rapids continue

in quick succession, culminating in Omega, where a nasty river-left sieve swallows half the creek's flow. The sieve isn't difficult to avoid, unless the continuous rapids leading into it lull you into letting your guard down.

SHUTTLE: From I-59, take Exit 11 in Trenton for GA 136. Head east, toward the ridge, following GA 136 as it jogs to the right. Before heading up the hill, turn left and take the first right into the gravel parking lot; this is the take-out. Visually confirm adequate flow here; if it looks good, there's sufficient water for the entire run. To get to the put-in, continue up the hill on GA 136. Turn left at the flashing yellow light, cross Daniel Creek, and pass the entrance to the park on the left. Turn left onto GA 189; parking is on the left before crossing the creek.

GAUGE: A gauge is painted on the river-right, downstream side of the bridge at the put-in. The absolute minimum is 9 inches; 1 foot is optimal, and 18 inches a healthy maximum. A USGS gauge is located on Lookout Creek at New England, a short distance downstream of the confluence with Sitton Gulch. Recommended levels using this gauge are unknown.

part**Three**

THE COOSA RIVER WATERSHED

CONASAUGA RIVER

The Conasauga leaps to life high on the pristine slopes of the Cohutta Wilderness of northwest Georgia. Adventuresome paddlers with the favor of the rain gods smiling upon them can catch the adrenaline rush through the upper section, a steep Class III–IV+ descent through an isolated forest wilderness. After bounding to its meeting with the Jacks River, the Conasauga ratchets down a notch as it veers north into Tennessee and takes a serpentine course along the Tennessee-Georgia border before turning south into Georgia for good, transformed into a meandering valley river that becomes increasingly burdened with the by-products of human activity as it approaches its junction with the Coosawattee near Calhoun.

MAPS: Tennga, Parksville Tennessee, Beaverdale, Chatsworth, Calhoun Northeast, Dalton South, Calhoun North (USGS); Murray, Polk TN, Bradley TN, Whitfield, Gordon (County); Cohutta and Big Frog Wilderness (USFS)

CHICKEN COOP GAP TO OLD GA 2 BRIDGE

class	III–IV (IV+)
length	5.9
time	4 hr
gauge	Visual
level	Unknown
gradient	82 (125) fpm
scenery	A+

DESCRIPTION: During high-water periods, experienced boaters usually begin their trip at Chicken Coop Gap off FS 17 at the edge of the Cohutta Wilderness Area. Accessing this put-in requires determination, as you must belay your boat and equipment approximately one-quarter mile down into the gorge. Above all, a high skill level is required to successfully navigate the river down to the Alaculsy Valley. This is rugged and wild terrain. The river drops more than 100 feet per mile in some areas, creating intense, lengthy rapids of Class IV+ difficulty. It can only be run in high water, and when the water is high all conditions combine to create a potentially lethal situation. It is no place for beginners.

For those with the above-mentioned qualities, however, the rewards are great. The scenery is pristine and stunningly beautiful. The water is crystalline and contains native trout. After 2 miles

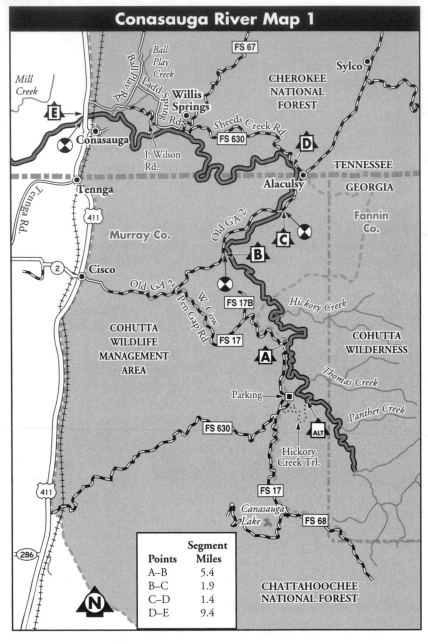

Conasauga River Map 1

Mill Creek

Ball Play Creek

FS 67

Sylco

Ball Play Rd.

Ladd Spring Rd.

Willis Springs

CHEROKEE NATIONAL FOREST

Sheeds Creek Rd.

E

Conasauga

FS 630

D

J. Wilson Rd.

TENNESSEE

Tennga

Alaculsy

GEORGIA

411

Old GA 2

Fannin Co.

Murray Co.

C

2

Cisco

B

Old GA 2

W. Cow Pen Gap Rd.

Hickory Creek

FS 17B

COHUTTA WILDLIFE MANAGEMENT AREA

FS 17

A

COHUTTA WILDERNESS

Thomas Creek

Parking

Panther Creek

FS 630

ALT

Hickory Creek Trl.

411

FS 17

Canasauga Lake

FS 68

286

N

Points	Segment Miles
A–B	5.4
B–C	1.9
C–D	1.4
D–E	9.4

CHATTAHOOCHEE NATIONAL FOREST

photo © Tom Welander

The Upper Conasauga River

of warm-up rapids, difficulty crescendos to Class IV+ with Room of Doom (a.k.a. Boof or Consequences or Undercut) and Whale Tail. Scouting is frequently necessary around blind drops and turns. All rapids on this section have been run, but portages may be prudent under some circumstances.

The near pass of Old GA 2 (B), also known as East Cow Gap Road, is the most popular take-out for this section. Here the river enters the Alaculsy Valley, where it remains until the Jacks River junction. The valley is pretty, to be sure, but in comparison to the upper section, it might produce either ennui or welcome relief to the paddlers using the take-out at the Old GA 2 bridge (C) 1.9 miles farther downstream.

SHUTTLE: On US 411 in Cisco, turn east onto Old GA 2 which turns into East Cow Pen Gap Road. A convenience store selling Cohutta Wilderness information is located on the west side of US 411 at the turn. The usual take-out is found at the first near pass of the river after the Alaculsy Valley opens up. The trip to the put-in is 8.6 miles from this point. To get to there, backtrack 2 miles to West Cow Pen Gap Road (FS 17) which dead-ends into East Cow Pen Gap Road at a Forest Service information station (which you passed on the way in). Turn left and follow the road up the hill. Continue, veering right where the road forks. The put-in is ahead—listen for water and look for a steep incline on the left. Another 3-mile section of river with 375 feet gradient is above Chicken Coop Gap. To drive to this put-in,

continue on FS 17 to a left-hand turn at to the Hickory Creek trailhead and get ready to hike 1.5 miles to the river. Using this put-in commits you to an 8.9-mile run to the valley.

GAUGE: A staff gauge is located in the stream at access point B and another gauge is painted on the river-left side of the Old GA 2 bridge 2 miles farther downstream. Without aid from the uniquely anthropomorphic "elbow tree" that has served as the main gauge for this section, minimum and maximum correlations to these newer gauges are unknown. A level of 2.0 on the staff gauge at the take-out and 6 inches on the Old GA 2 bridge is ample. If the USGS gauge at Eton is at 12 feet or higher, it's worth checking the upstream gauges, but keep in mind that the river empties rapidly and Eton is far downstream of this section.

OLD GA 2 BRIDGE TO US 411

class	I–II(III)
length	10.8 mi
time	5.5 hr
gauge	Web, visual
level	5.0/1.0 ft
gradient	19 fpm
scenery	A

DESCRIPTION: The most visited section of the Conasauga for boaters, campers, and anglers begins at the Forest Service campground where the Jacks River meets the Conasauga (D). The added flow of the Jacks doubles the volume of the Conasauga and makes boating practical over a greater portion of the year. Access is much easier than in the upper section, as a well-maintained Forest Service road leads directly to this point. Access to the Cohutta Wilderness backpacking trails is available nearby.

Here, the river resumes a character similar to its upper section, with sparkling water bracketed by dense forests, but gradient and therefore rapids are greatly moderated. One series, known locally as simply The Falls, is generally considered a Class III. Get out on the right above the rapid and follow the trail if you wish to scout the rapid. Portage on the right if it appears too difficult. Many of the remaining rapids are challenging, but none is as tricky as The Falls.

The scenery alone makes this trip worthwhile. Many enticing camping spots beckon to boaters. Even though this section can be done in one day, this is a pleasant area in which to linger. Class I–II rapids appear sporadically until reaching the valley a few miles above US 411. A ripply ride past occasional houses, accompanied by the aroma of wild bluebells blooming in early spring, brings you to the take-out on river right.

SHUTTLE: To reach the take-out at access point E, take US 411 north out of Chatsworth to where the road crosses the river

photo © Tres Hombres del Rio

A rock-garden ledge on the Conasauga

north of Tennga and the Tennessee border. The take-out is accessed via a dirt road on the left just past the bridge. As of early 2004, access is restricted here, but remains possible for a small fee. The put-in is reached by continuing north, briefly, on US 411, turning right onto Ball Play Road. Follow Ball Play over the tracks and to a stop sign, turning right onto Ladd Spring Road, or take the short-cut by turning right onto J. Wilson Road before reaching the stop sign (this will necessitate a right turn at the stop sign after you wind around to Ladd Spring Road). Follow this road, taking a slight right-hand turn where it becomes gravel FS 221, until you reach the Forest Service campground on the right at the Jacks River.

GAUGE: A gauge is painted onto the take-out bridge; a rocky run is possible at 1.0; levels above 1.5 feet are better. At 2.0 (around 12.0 at Eton) the run is cushy and fast, and somewhat reminiscent of the Nantahala. The maximum level is not known. The USGS gauge listed on the Internet is 24 miles downstream near Eton, but can be used to decide whether the trip is worth the drive. Recalling that the upper river drains quickly, an Internet level of 7.0 feet or higher is enough to inspire a trip. At 5.0 feet on the Internet gauge, this section will be passable but rocky.

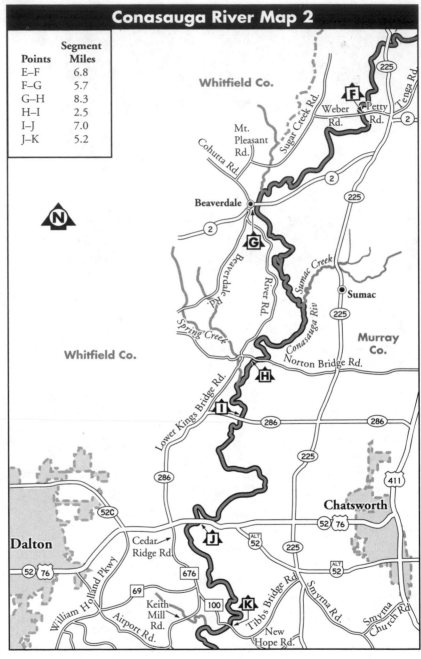

Conasauga River Map 2

Points	Segment Miles
E–F	6.8
F–G	5.7
G–H	8.3
H–I	2.5
I–J	7.0
J–K	5.2

Whitfield Co.

Sugar Creek Rd.

Weber Rd.   Petty Rd.

Tenga Rd.

225

2

Mt. Pleasant Rd.

Cohutta Rd.

2

225

Beaverdale

N

2

G

Beaverdale Rd.

River Rd.

Sumac Creek

Sumac

Conasauga Riv

225

Murray Co.

Spring Creek

Whitfield Co.

Norton Bridge Rd.

H

I

Lower Kings Bridge Rd.

286   286

225

286

411

52C

Chatsworth

52 76

J

ALT 52

225

Dalton

Cedar Ridge Rd.

ALT 52

52 76

William Holland Pkwy

676

Smyrna Rd.

Tibbs Bridge Rd.

Smyrna Church Rd.

69

100

K

Keith Mill Rd.

Airport Rd.

New Hope Rd.

Conasauga River Map 3

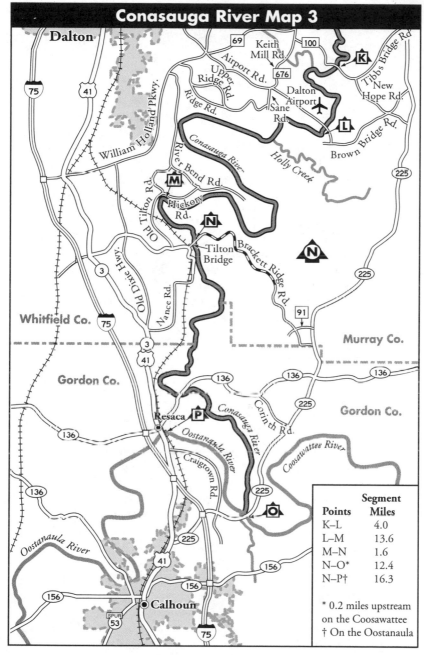

	Segment
Points	Miles
K–L	4.0
L–M	13.6
M–N	1.6
N–O*	12.4
N–P†	16.3

* 0.2 miles upstream
on the Coosawattee
† On the Oostanaula

US 411 TO THE OOSTANAULA RIVER

class	I
length	71 mi
time	Up to 9 days
gauge	Web
level	N/A
gradient	3 fpm
scenery	C

DESCRIPTION: In this section, the Conasauga is a distinctly pastoral stream. Some attractive wooded sections remain, but all pale in comparison to the delights of the mountainous region. Rapids disappear, replaced by farms, settlements, and then industrial facilities as the river nears its junction with the Coosawattee outside Calhoun, to form the Oostanaula. If you are paddling to the end of the Conasauga, take-out 0.2 miles upstream on the river-left side of the Coosawattee, or paddle another 3.7 miles downstream to the next access on the Oostanaula in Resaca.

SHUTTLE: To take-out on the Coosawattee, take I-75 to Exit 317 for GA 225 North. The take-out is at the boat ramp on the left side of the road before crossing the Coosawattee. For the Oostanaula take-out, take I-75 to Exit 320 for GA 136 East. Turn right onto US 41; the take-out is straight ahead on the left prior to crossing the bridge. The upper access points are all easily reached from picturesque and historical GA 225 North.

GAUGE: See previous section. The lower river is runnable except in periods of extreme drought or flooding.

JACKS RIVER

The Jacks River is a spectacularly beautiful "steep creek," which drains a high mountainous area of northern Gilmer and western Fannin Counties, and flows northeast to join the Conasauga River just north of the Tennessee Border. Two sections totaling over 17 miles drop at an average rate of 90 feet per mile, and are runnable by advanced and expert boaters after heavy rains. The Jacks flows almost entirely within the 36,977-acre Cohutta Wilderness of the Chattahoochee National Forest, and offers some of the finest white-water in the Southeast. Its wilderness designation protects the river's pristine beauty and excellent water quality, but presents major access problems, since all of the roads which lead to its most navigable parts have been closed to vehicles 3.5 or more miles from the river, since 1975.

MAPS: Hemp Top, Tennga (USGS); Murray, Fannin, Polk TN (County); Cohutta and Big Frog Wilderness (USFS)

JONES MILL TO JACKS RIVER BRIDGE

class	II–V
length	18.2 mi
time	14 hr
gauge	None
level	N/A
gradient	82 (263, 232) fpm
scenery	A+

DESCRIPTION: One can drive to the river's edge in the Jones Mill community, but the stream here is extremely small (15 feet wide), and putting in here commits you to running to the Conasauga, over 18 miles, a long day-trip under ordinary river conditions. However, the challenges of the Jacks are anything but ordinary! The river descends about 40 feet in the first 2 miles; the first 4.5 miles contain numerous deadfalls, often forming river-wide blockages. The difficulty and danger increase exponentially after the second mile, just past Bear Branch, as the river cuts a deep, narrow, twisting gorge and plummets 495 feet in the next 2 miles. Both banks are steep, and the precipitous, twisting, often blind drops are very difficult to scout or portage.

The Jacks River hiking trail joins the river at Bear Branch and parallels it for 15 miles to the take-out, mostly along the bed of an old logging railroad used between 1915 and 1930 by the Conasauga River Lumber Company to log 70 percent of the present wilderness. It fords the river almost 50 times and should not be hiked when the river is high. While this trail generally runs close to the river and is wide and level, along this most dangerous part of the Upper Jacks the trail is steep and narrow and usually high above the river. The trail could be used here to portage long sections of river, but seldom is near enough to be useful in portaging individual rapids. The river gradient lessens near mile 5 past the entrance of Sugar Cove Branch on the left, but very frequent Class II and III and occasional Class IV rapids continue to the confluence with the Conasauga River, whose flow is doubled by the Jacks.

To avoid many of the difficulties and dangers of the uppermost stretches of the river, you can carry-in to one of several lower access points. The most practical lower entry to the Lower Jacks is from the north along the Beech Bottom Trail. You will need a good portaging system, such as balancing your boat on a backpack frame with a good waist-belt, allowing you to transfer most of the weight to your hips and to keep your arms at your sides. Beech Bottom Trail is wide and provides good footing. The first 1.3 miles of the trail descend to a creek, but most of the rest is uphill, until you're near the spectacularly beautiful Jacks River Falls.

The entire trail is 3.5 miles, but after 2.75 miles you can carry or slide down to a point about 300 yards upstream of the

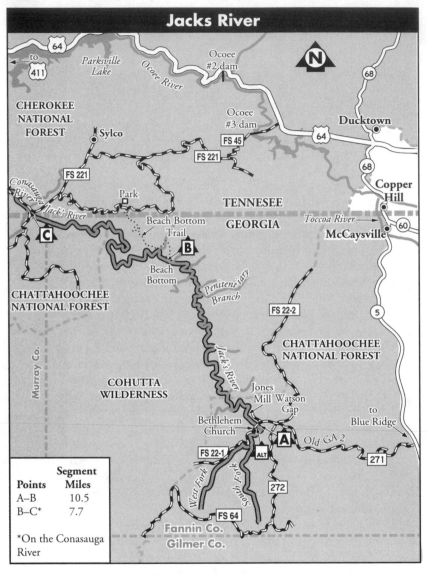

unrunnable, 40-foot Jacks River Falls. The descent here is about 200 feet vertically, on about a 35-degree incline. To avoid having to portage the falls (on the right) and run the 0.4 miles of Class IV immediately below it, you might slide down to the river in a southwesterly direction at mile 2.5 of the Beech Bottom Trail. Downstream of this point nothing normally rates above a hard

Class III, although the gradient exceeds 100 feet per mile after about 3 miles in the dramatic horseshoe bend area. Nevertheless, all of the Lower Jacks is very technical and continuous, and offers a most wonderful 7.7-mile slalom run.

The shuttle is about 2 hours each way! This should be done the day before if you are running the full 18 miles. If you attempt the Upper and Lower Jacks and plan to run it in one day, it would be best to go in May or June and put-in before sunrise. One group of three kayakers left the Jones community at 6 a.m. in mid-June and reached the Jacks River Bridge at 9:45 p.m.!

SHUTTLE: Although a shorter route is available on dirt roads through the Cohutta Mountains, it is much quicker to use a 65-mile shuttle along paved highways. To get to the take-out, take GA 5 north from Blue Ridge into Tennessee and continue on TN 68 to Ducktown. Go west on US 64 and south on US 411 to near the Georgia state-line. (This point can alternatively be approached from the south on US 411 out of Chatsworth.) Turn left onto Ball Play Road, the last paved road before crossing the Conasauga. Follow Ball Play over the tracks and to a stop sign, turning right onto Ladd Spring Road. Follow this road, staying to the right when it turns into the gravel FS 221, until you reach the Forest Service campground on the right at the Jack's River confluence. (You can also leave US 64 in Tennessee and cross the Ocoee at Powerhouse #3, go a few miles and take the first right, go to the end of the road and turn left onto Sylco Creek Road. It becomes Sheeds Creek Road, and leads to the Jacks River bridge at the northwestern trail-head of the Jacks River Trail.)

To reach the highest put-in at Jones Mill (A), return to GA 5 north of Blue Ridge and take Old GA 2 west from Gravely Gap, about 4 miles north of Blue Ridge, for about 10 miles to Watson Gap, about 2 miles past the end of the pavement. Go straight onto FS 126, following the signs to Jones Mill and Bethlehem Church, and put-in at the bridge at the bottom of the hill or just upstream past Bethlehem Church at the confluence of the West and South Forks of the Jacks. Parking at the bridge is very limited, but is on National Forest land. All the land adjacent to the river downstream for 2 miles is private property.

To drive from the take-out at Jacks River Bridge (C) to the Beech Bottom Trail put-in (B), go north-notheast on Sheeds Creek Road (the dirt road on river right, across the bridge at the take-out) toward the community of Sylco. After 1.25 miles turn sharply right onto FS 62, towards Simmons Gap. This will lead you to the parking lot for the Beech Bottom Trail in about 6 miles.

GAUGE: There is no gauge on the Jacks, but the USGS gauge near Eton on the Conasauga is helpful as much for its rainfall readings as for river height or flow. A level of 1,200 cfs to flood stage on this gauge warrants further evaluation. It is important to determine if the river is rising or falling and how quickly it is doing so when studying this considerably downstream gauge's readings. If it is falling, you will need a much higher flow. After a heavy rain the river peaks and runs off quickly, particularly when the water table is low, typically in the summer and fall. Ideally you want to embark in the rain or shortly after its end. Running the Upper Jacks would usually need a recent heavy rain of at least 2 inches. Gauges on the upper Conasauga, which is runnable at the same times and is similar in character to the lower Jacks, can aid in determining suitability of the level.

CARTECAY RIVER

The Cartecay is one of the most popular whitewater rivers in the mountains of northern Georgia. The first 3 miles of scenic paddling are a placid prelude to 7 miles of outstanding whitewater. Many people live on the banks of the Cartecay; lawns that stretch down to the edge of the river are common below Lower Cartecay Road. Paddlers and area residents maintain a generally amicable relationship that becomes strained from time to time. Be on your best behavior as you play alongside their backyards.

MAPS: Tickanetly, Ellijay (USGS); Gilmer (County)

HOLT BRIDGE ROAD TO DNR TAKE-OUT

class	I–III
length	9.8 mi
time	4–5 hr
gauge	Phone, visual
level	1.6 ft
gradient	9 to 40+ fpm
scenery	B-

DESCRIPTION: Below Holt Bridge Road (A), the first few miles of the Cartecay are slow and easy paddling through a scenic mountain valley. Thickets of mountain laurel, large pines, and various hardwoods will often suddenly part to expose rolling pasture and views of the surrounding mountains. The flow in the valley is Class I, with the only hazard occasional downed trees that may block the entire narrow stream bed. Another access point is located near the end of the valley on Lower Cartecay Road (C). Here both sides of the river are owned by outfitters who supply parking and shuttles. Most paddlers take advantage of the convenience as this put-in is closer to the excitement below.

Cartecay River

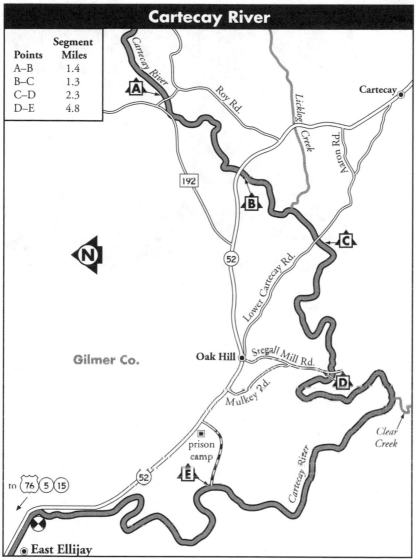

Points	Segment Miles
A–B	1.4
B–C	1.3
C–D	2.3
D–E	4.8

As the valley ends, the gradient gets steeper, and easy Class II rapids begin to appear. The Cartecay, like the Chattooga, is a drop-and-pool stream, with rapids coming in sudden bursts interrupted by long, nearly placid stretches. The first rapid of significant technical difficulty is S-Turn. Scout from river left if desired; the bank here is private property, so keep your visit brief. This rapid can be run down the middle, but more typically it is run down the chute

S-Turn on the Cartecay River

on river left. Eddy out to the right after the first drop, or make a tight turn to the left and run the forceful current into the pool below, eddying out right or left in order to avoid being driven into the large boulder at the end of the pool.

The next two rapids, separated by 100 yards, are nearby when the river narrows. The first is Surfing Wave, with a deep pool below it. The next, more vigorous drop has a clear channel through it and a whirlpool on the right which is best avoided at high levels.

A long pool breaks up the action and serves as a warning for the first big drop on the river, Stegall Mill Falls (also known as Blackberry Falls). This should be scouted on the left. Again, this is private property, so stay on the rocks as you scout. Although not technically difficult, this rapid looks quite impressive, and a very small pool is all that separates it from several tight rapids just below. The falls may be run straight down the center over the pluming wave in the main chute, or through the channel on the left. Be ready to brace and recover for the technical turns that follow. The mid-run access point at Mulkey Road (D) is located on river right just below the covered bridge. Parking is limited here and there have been conflicts with property owners in the area. The local outfitters run shuttles to this point to alleviate the pressure.

Below the covered bridge, the river continues to carom along through its drop and pool pattern for another 5 miles. Get ready for more action the next time the rocks move down to the river

photo © Rob Maxwell

Clear Creek Falls on the Cartecay

level. A pointed rock shaped like half a football announces the next rapid, Mr. Twister. Scout on the left. The rapid is typically run on the right, avoiding the souse wave on the left. There is a long recovery pool at the bottom.

The second major drop of the river is close when you reach two islands. Run the long rapid with several drops to the left of the islands, and pull out onto the rock shelf on the left immediately after the second island to scout Clear Creek Falls, also known as the Narrows at Clear Creek. At normal water levels, run this near the left bank. At water levels above 3 feet, a potentially hazardous hydraulic reversal develops at the base of the drop. Portage is easiest on the right.

For the remainder of the distance to the final take-out, the river's pace remains brisk, entertaining the boater with some interesting Class II ripples before reaching the DNR public access on the right (E).

SHUTTLE: From East Ellijay, turn right onto GA 52. Follow GA 52 for 2.7 miles to a right-hand turn onto an unmarked road at the bottom of a large hill. There is a sign there for the Rich Mountain Wildlife Management Area. Follow the unpaved road straight ahead to the take-out. To reach the Holt Bridge put-in, return to GA 52 and turn right. Turn left onto Big Creek Road, then right onto Holt Bridge Road. The put-in is directly ahead. Intermediate access points are available at GA 52, Lower Cartecay Road, and Mulkey/Stegall Mill Road, which intersect with GA 52 from the south.

GAUGE: A staff gauge is located on GA 52 east of GA 5/515. Local outfitters can provide river levels by phone. There is no Internet gauge for the Cartecay, but levels for the Coosawattee near Ellijay on the USGS Web site are considered comparable up to 2.5 feet. The river has been run as low as 0.8 (from Lower Cartecay Road to Mulkey Road); a more enjoyable minimum is 1.6 feet. Around 2 feet is comfortable; above 3 feet, boaters should be experienced. The maximum runnable level is 4 feet for open boats and up to flood stage for decked boats.

COOSAWATTEE RIVER

The Coosawattee River is the lost gem of North Georgia's whitewater streams. Said to have rivaled the Chattooga River, the most dramatic portions of the Coosawattee now lie stilled beneath the surface of Carters Lake. A sense of what the Coosawattee was and what it has become is masterfully conveyed by James Dickey's poem "On the Coosawattee." It has been suggested that Dickey's experiences on the river before it was dammed were a major influence on his novel Deliverance. *The Ellijay and Cartecay Rivers meet in Ellijay to form the Coosawattee; 9.3 miles of pleasing Class I and II rapids remain of the upper section. Below the dam, the Coosawattee snakes along a sedate course across Gordon County before it merges with the Conasauga River to become the Oostanaula River.*

MAPS: Ellijay, Webb, Oakman, Redbud, Calhoun North (USGS); Gilmer, Murray, Gordon (County)

GA 5 ALT. TO CARTERS LAKE

class	I–II
length	13.1 mi
time	6 hr
gauge	Web
level	0.7 ft
gradient	18 fpm
scenery	B-

DESCRIPTION: Below Ellijay the scenery remains breathtaking at times, though residential development has supplanted the forested banks of the upper stretches. Early in the run, boaters will find several fish weirs that supposedly date back to the Cherokees. These create small ledges but no real hazard to navigation. Fishing is good for those who care to try their luck. The river has produced trout of record size for the state.

The 9.3 miles to the backwaters of Carters Lake are not dull, but rapids never get above a solid Class II level under normal conditions. Rapids start out small, building in difficulty throughout the run to the lake. There are many long, pooled sections, but enough Class I and II action intervenes to keep you

Coosawattee River

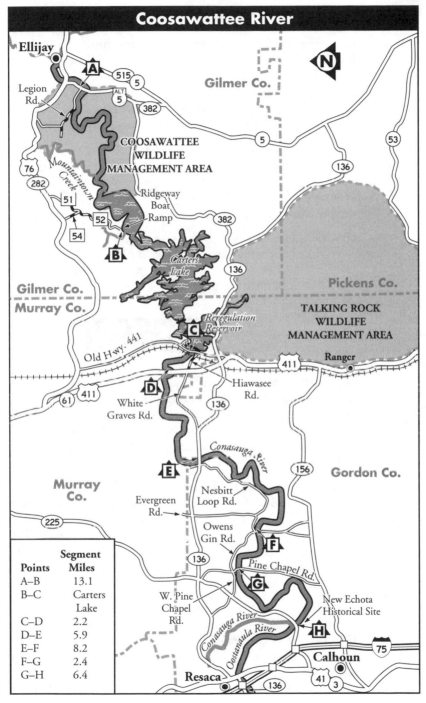

Ellijay

515
5

ALT
5

382

Legion Rd.

5

53

Gilmer Co.

136

COOSAWATTEE WILDLIFE MANAGEMENT AREA

76

282

Mountaintown Creek

51

52

54

Ridgeway Boat Ramp

382

B

136

Carters Lake

136

Gilmer Co.
Murray Co.

Pickens Co.

TALKING ROCK WILDLIFE MANAGEMENT AREA

Reregulation Reservoir

C

Old Hwy. 441

411

Ranger

61   411

D

Hiawasee Rd.

White Graves Rd.

136

Conasauga river

E

156

Gordon Co.

Murray Co.

Evergreen Rd.

Nesbitt Loop Rd.

225

Owens Gin Rd.

136

F

Pine Chapel Rd.

W. Pine Chapel Rd.

G

New Echota Historical Site

Conasauga River

Oostanaula River

H

75

Calhoun

Resaca

136

41   3

Points	Segment Miles
A–B	13.1
B–C	Carters Lake
C–D	2.2
D–E	5.9
E–F	8.2
F–G	2.4
G–H	6.4

from becoming too complacent. Rapids become more frequent after Mountaintown Creek enters from the right, significantly increasing the stream's volume. Soon after the rapids begin to hold your interest they come to an abrupt end in the backwaters of the lake. The lake is pretty and powerboat traffic is usually light, but you should allow ample time to reach the first public access point at Ridgeway Boat Ramp, almost 4 miles ahead. The ramp is hidden within a cove that stretches back to the right.

SHUTTLE: From GA 5/515 in East Ellijay, take GA 282 west approximately 7.5 miles to the left turn for the Ridgeway Boat Ramp at Carters Lake. To get to the put-in, return to Ellijay and turn right onto SR 5 Alt. Continue 0.8 miles to a left turn into the last entrance into the park.

GAUGE: The USGS Web site provides data for the gauge at East Ellijay. The minimum is considered to be 0.7 feet; around 2 feet is a comfortable run. The maximum is 4 feet for open boats and up to flood stage for decked.

CARTERS REREGULATION LAKE DAM TO CONASAUGA RIVER

class	I
length	25.1 mi
time	Up to 2.5 days
gauge	Web
level	Unknown
gradient	2 fpm
scenery	C

DESCRIPTION: Below the Carters Lake reregulation reservoir, the Coosawattee becomes a higher volume valley river that meanders through more populated areas. Farmland, industrial plants, and some woodland make up the streamside environment. The Coosawattee merges with the Conasauga near Resaca and is thereafter called the Oostanaula River.

SHUTTLE: To get to the lowest take-out, take Exit 317 off of I-75 and proceed east on GA 225. The boat ramp is a left turn before crossing the river. For the highest put-in, continue north on GA 225. Turn right onto GA 136. After crossing US 441, turn left onto Old US 441/Old Reservoir Road. Watch for the right-hand turn into the recreation area below the dam, 1.2 miles past the bridge over the river. Stay to the right.

GAUGE: Flows are dependent on dam releases from the reregulation reservoir, and can be found on the USGS Web site for the Coosawattee at Carters or Pine Chapel, Georgia, or by calling the Army Corps of Engineers at (706) 334-2248. The Corps adheres to a required minimum flow of 240 cfs. While the levels don't change rapidly, a call to check the release schedule in advance of your trip is recommended.

A River Ran Through It:
The Story of the Coosawattee River Gorge
— by Daniel M. Roper

Every year an average of 6 feet of rain and snow fall on North Georgia's Blue Ridge Mountains. This precipitation runs off steep mountain slopes and percolates through soil and rock, creating countless creeks and streams which unite to form rivers like the Chattahoochee, Chattooga, and Coosawattee.

Born at the junction of the Ellijay and Cartecay Rivers in downtown Ellijay, the Coosawattee River tumbles westward through rolling mountains. Until it was dammed in the 1970s, the river cascaded over a series of ledges and shoals in the Coosawattee River Gorge. Through this narrow, scenic gorge the Coosawattee once carried runoff from its 376-square-mile watershed into the vast, nearly level, region northeast of Calhoun known as the Great Valley.

Prone to flood during the winter, the Coosawattee posed a constant threat to adjacent farms and, further downstream, the cities of Calhoun and Rome. Periodically, these cities experienced devastating floods. To eliminate this problem, Congress enacted legislation in 1945 that eventually resulted in construction of a dam at the mouth of the gorge (near the community of Carters).

While constructing the dam, it was necessary to divert the river through a tunnel blasted through the mountain. During construction, which began in 1962, all trees within a 100-foot-wide swath of the gorge's high-water mark were removed, clearing the future lakebed of navigation obstacles. The dam consists of compacted rock over an earth core. It is 2,053 feet long, 452 feet high, and at its base, 1,650 feet wide. Flooding of the gorge, began in November, 1974, took several years.

The Coosawattee River's impending demise did not go unnoticed. Awareness of its rapids and scenic gorge spiked in 1970 with the publication of James Dickey's novel *Deliverance*. The setting for this popular novel, a riveting, disturbing tale of survival against the forces of man and nature, is the fictional Cahulawassee River in north Georgia. Four Atlanta businessmen, while making a final canoe trip down the Cahulawassee before it is dammed, are assaulted by a pair of ruthless, depraved hillbillies. The novel was made into a successful film featuring banjo picking, abundant profanity, and stunning mountain scenery and whitewater footage. In the movie, mountain folks are generally portrayed as dirty, backward, violent people who dislike strangers. *Deliverance* did for them what *Jaws* would later do for sharks.

Although *Deliverance* was filmed on the Chattooga and Tallulah rivers, it is widely believed that Dickey drew his inspiration for the story from an experience on the Coosawattee River. In a 1995 interview, Dickey, who passed away in 1997, responded to this rumor. "Deliverance was inspired by my experiences on four or five different rivers including the Coosawattee, Chattooga, and Chattahoochee." Asked whether he had endured any experiences like those immortalized in *Deliverance*, Dickey coyly replied, "I can't say. The statute of limitations hasn't expired yet."

Claude Terry, an acquaintance of Dickey who was a stuntman and technical advisor for the movie's canoeing scenes, is familiar with the story's origins. "It was rough in the mountains", he explains, "twenty or thirty years ago. You could get killed at the drop of a hat. But today, people have forgotten that."

According to Terry, Dickey and two friends (Lewis King and Al Braselton) organized a canoe trip down the Coosawattee. While Dickey and Braselton canoed the river, King was to drive to a point downstream and pick them up.

photo © Dan Roper

A now-submerged rapid on the Coosawattee

"King," Terry says, "found a rugged, remote logging road that seemed to head towards the river. When he stopped to check a map, he was suddenly confronted by a man and his son, both armed, who demanded to know what he was doing there." King explained his presence to them, but they apparently suspected he might be a revenuer. The father told his son to take his shotgun and accompany King to the river. He was told to return "alone" if no one came down the river to confirm King's story and prove that his presence was innocent.

"Afraid that Dickey and Braselton might already have passed downstream," Terry says, "King sweated bullets until, an hour or two later, they rounded a bend in the river." Satisfied now that they posed no threat, the boy helped King, Dickey, and Braselton carry their canoe and gear to the pickup truck. The older man told them to go on their way, wishing them well.

This sobering encounter proved to be the seed which, planted in Dickey's fertile mind, yielded *Deliverance*. When the novel was later adapted for film, however, the slopes of the Coosawattee had already been sheared in preparation for the creation of Carter's Lake.

Consequently, rafting scenes were shot along Section IV of the Chattooga and in Tallulah River Gorge. Horsepasture River Valley served as the fictional Cahulawassee dam construction site in the final scene, which depicts the dismantling of an old church and the removal of coffins from its cemetery.

Growing awareness that the Coosawattee was the inspiration for *Deliverance,* and of its impending disappearance, led to a flurry of eleventh-hour canoe trips.

Jerry Bearden, a biologist with the Georgia Department of Natural Resources, rafted the river with his wife Pam in July, 1974, just four months before the gorge was flooded. "It was a fast ride with a lot of white-water," he recalls. "About halfway through, there was one particularly tough set of rapids. The river was divided there by an island. On the right side much of its water was forced through a narrow gap between the island and a sheer rock wall. Having been warned to avoid this, we carried our raft across some rocks on the opposite side of the river."

Earlier that year Bearden had been given the responsibility of coordinating a trip for state dignitaries who wanted to experience the river before its demise. This, Bearden says, nearly turned into a disaster. "Several inches of rain had fallen the previous evening and the river was rising. I dropped them off and was to pick them up downriver that afternoon. Only none of them ever arrived. When we found them alongside the road, staggering out of the woods, it was nearly midnight." The novices, who had simply been overwhelmed by the river, lost three of their five canoes.

Jack Weems, a former president of the Georgia Canoeing Association, paddled the river in April, 1974, and remembers the falls. "It was beautiful", he says, "but obviously dangerous. I had heard of people who were accidentally swept over and drowned." In one instance, Weems says, a canoeist, stranded on the island by high water, was rescued by a helicopter.

Ellijay resident Bill Middleton recalls a fatality at the falls. "In 1966", Middleton says, "Jimmy Wright got in the river to cool off and drowned after being swept over the falls." Middleton, who often went there to fish, believes that the falls were 10–15 feet high. Forever submerged 400 feet under the surface of Carter's Lake, however, the falls no longer pose a threat.

James Dickey did not recall a public outcry against construction of the dam. "The damming of the Coosawattee," he said, "began before America became conscious of the environment." It was a time when no one doubted the wisdom of converting a remote gorge into a source of hydroelectric power, flood control, and recreation.

Both Dickey and Terry later contributed to efforts to protect the Chattooga River, which remains undeveloped as a federally designated Wild and Scenic River. Dickey addressed both houses of Congress. Terry took then Governor Jimmy Carter down Section III of the Chattooga. According to Terry, "I believe that we were the first pair to run Bull Sluice (a notorious Class V rapid) in a tandem canoe." Later, Terry was present when Carter telephoned an influential, undecided congressman and persuaded him to vote in favor of designating the Chattooga a Wild and Scenic River.

The recreation, flood control, and power generation attributes of Carters Lake are undeniable. Without exception, however, those interviewed for this story expressed a sense of loss arising from the flooding of the gorge. "You know", reflected Dickey, "I will probably never get in another canoe. But I remember those days when I paddled the Coosawattee with great favor. Progress—so called—is a dreadful thing."

Originally published in the Summer 1995 issue of *North Georgia Journal,* P.O. Box 127, Roswell, GA 30077. Reprinted with permission of the author and publisher.

MOUNTAINTOWN CREEK

Located west of Ellijay, Mountaintown Creek is a delightful stream that moves at a good clip through many Class I and II rapids that build in frequency and intensity before the creek ends 6 miles below the put-in. Paddling Mountaintown Creek commits you to an additional section of easy whitewater on the wide Coosawattee and a paddle down the still waters of Carters Lake to reach the nearest take-out point. Although the lake paddling portion is less than exciting, Mountaintown Creek itself never bores.

MAPS: Dyer Gap, Webb (USGS); Gilmer (County)

GA 282 TO CARTERS LAKE RIDGEWAY BOAT RAMP

class	II
length	11.1 mi
time	4.5–6 hr
gauge	None
level	N/A
gradient	28 fpm
scenery	B

DESCRIPTION: Don't miss the antique cars embedded in the bluff on river right at the put-in; they are, along with the tires ingeniously recycled to form the steps down to the river, the sole visual remains of the automobile junkyard that once occupied this spot. The scene quickly changes as the river cruises by stretches of riverside housing narrowly separated from the river by a low bank. The development continues until well downstream where the primitive forest reasserts itself.

The main attraction of this run is the stream itself. From the beginning, the pace is steady and quick. The creek barely pauses between rapids, preferring to ripple over the shallow bed than to pool before the next drop. Rapids start out easy and become more challenging; several significant, technical, Class II drops are found near the end of the creek. The pace is unforgiving for paddlers without a functional ferry or eddy turn.

After 6 miles of the creek and a similarly lively 1.5-mile section of the Coosawattee, the backwaters of Carters Lake put the brakes on the current, silencing the rapids. Around this point, the flotsam swept east off the lake announces the formal entry into Carters Lake.

The remaining 3.8 miles seem to pass slowly in comparison to the fast pace of the creek. On a windy day, forward progress can be difficult. The take-out is at the Ridgeway Boat Ramp, which is not visible from the main channel. Look to the right shore for a long cove that bends back to the right. A small island lies just offshore from the boat ramp. The next access area is many miles down the lake, so make sure you do not miss the take-out.

SHUTTLE: From GA 5/515 in East Ellijay, take GA 282 west approximately 7.5 miles to the left turn for the Ridgeway Boat Ramp at Carters Lake. Note the put-in on GA 282, 3.8 miles before the boat ramp road.

GAUGE: There is no gauge. The local outfitter can provide information on flows via phone.

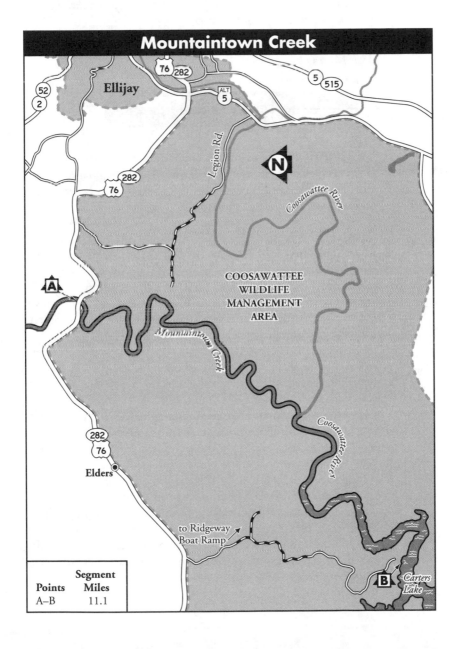

Mountaintown Creek

Ellijay

Legion Rd.

Coosawattee River

**COOSAWATTEE
WILDLIFE
MANAGEMENT
AREA**

Mountaintown Creek

Coosawattee River

Elders

to Ridgeway
Boat Ramp

Carters
Lake

Points	Segment Miles
A–B	11.1

TALKING ROCK CREEK

Catching the elusive Talking Rock Creek is a bit like sighting a rare and beautiful bird. Its watershed is narrow, making it difficult to find the creek at a navigable level that will hold out for the two days normally required to paddle it. Journeying through a small gorge environment that remains mostly wild and remote even by today's standards, Talking Rock after a good rain serves up a rollicking fast Class II ride that is worth the wait.

MAPS: Talking Rock, Oakman (USGS); Pickens, Gilmer, Gordon, Murray (County)

GA 5 ALT. TO CARTERS LAKE REREGULATION RESERVOIR

class	I–II (III)
length	19.4 mi
time	10 hr
gauge	Web
level	300 cfs
gradient	19 (30+) fpm
scenery	A–B

DESCRIPTION: Talking Rock Creek is navigable from the old GA 5 in Pickens County to the Carters Lake reregulation reservoir where the creek merges with the Coosawattee River. At its highest possible access, the stream is quite small as it flows through a valley toward Swan Bridge (B), a distance of almost 2 miles. Although this section is scenic and pleasant to paddle when the water is high, most boaters prefer to put-in downstream of this point. Below Swan Bridge, the streamside environment becomes much steeper and the flow volume is more conducive to easy floating due to Town Creek's entry just above the bridge. Shoals become more frequent but are not extremely difficult to negotiate.

Below the first crossing with GA 136 (C), you will enter an isolated 14-mile stretch of river unspoiled by bridges. The terrain becomes rugged, and sheer walls often rise 100 feet or more above the stream. The seclusion in this section is interrupted by a smattering of human settlements that have carved homesteads out of the banks of the creek, exposing large swaths of unprotected and eroding earth. For the time being, the density of this activity is low and the forested hills quickly prevail.

There are many rapids on this section, some quite long, but few beyond Class II difficulty. Numerous deep, quiet pools give ample opportunity for swimming, fishing, or just relaxing. There are sites suitable for camping, and this section is long enough for two full, relaxed days. Attempts to traverse it in one day should maximize daylight time on the river. There is no good access until GA 136 crosses for the second time.

Talking Rock Creek

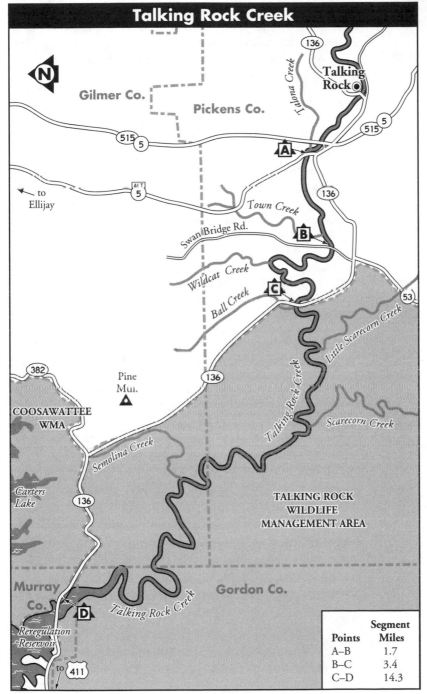

Points	Segment Miles
A–B	1.7
B–C	3.4
C–D	14.3

Of particular interest is the natural scenery along the entire route. At low water levels there are many small islands of river grasses and flowers in midstream that create a maze for canoeists. Sheer rock walls will often be on the sides of the stream. The name Talking Rock Creek probably came from the echoes that reverberate from the cliffs when any loud noise is made. One imposing bluff on the right side about two-thirds of the way down this section contains what appears to be the entrance to a cave that is well above stream level. The gorge also holds one of the last stands of virgin timber in the state.

Eventually, the rapids are stilled and you will enter the final leg of the trip across 2 miles of backwater formed by the Carters Lake re-regulation reservoir. Powerboat traffic can be encountered on the river after this point.

Talking Rock Creek is subject to rapid fluctuations in water level, and the difficulty of navigation is appreciably increased in extreme high water. Because of the lack of easy access and the difficulty of evacuation should problems arise, inexperienced boaters are advised to float this section only when the water is moderate to low.

SHUTTLE: To the take-out, take GA 5/515 north from Atlanta; above Jasper, turn left onto GA 136. The put-in at GA 5 Alt. is an immediate right turn. Return to GA 136 west to get to the take-out. Alternate access points are passed along the way at Swan Bridge Road and the first crossing of the creek with GA 136. Continue on GA 136 another 8.2 miles past the first crossing to get to the take-out at the second. Ignore signs to turn right for the Carters Lake boat ramp, and turn left instead onto the small paved but unmarked road next to the GA 136 bridge.

GAUGE: Real-time data for the creek levels at Hinton are available on the USGS Web site. The bare minimum level is 200 cfs or 1.5 feet; a more enjoyable minimum is 300 cfs. While planning your trip, keep in mind that the flow drops rapidly. The maximum is 4 feet for open boats and 6 feet for decked.

Speak to Me, Talking Rock:
A river tells many secrets to those who listen
— by Reece Turrentine

"We must be close to Cedar Cliffs," I called back to Dick in the rear of our canoe. Dave, the third member of our party, was canoeing solo and out of earshot.

"Couple-a more bends," Dick grunted, timing a stern stroke to send us neatly through a chute in the rapids of Talking Rock Creek.

Until then his estimates had been perfect, so I started scanning the steep riverbanks for the cliffs we had waited all morning to see.

The day before, while scouting the river, we heard the story of Cedar Cliffs from Mr. Low.

In the hamlet of Talking Rock, a sign on one side of the road read "Low's Pulp Wood." A sign on the other side advertised "Low's General Store." Through the middle of town ran Talking Rock Creek.

"I think Mr. Low's the man to talk to, don't you?" I asked Dick.

We found him inside the general store, sitting at a rustic check-out counter and surrounded by shelves that held everything from pins to plows.

"What can I do for you, gentlemen?" he asked, barely glancing up from his ledger as we walked toward him.

We introduced ourselves as he rang up a purchase for a customer.

"We'd like to know more about Talking Rock Creek," I said.

Though our introductions had rated little interest, this request created an immediate reaction.

"Yeah?" he responded, turning in our direction. "What do you want to know about it?"

"To begin with," I said, "can you tell us where it got its name?"

Mr. Low leaned forward, and for the next half-hour, except when he stopped to ring up a sale, we had his undivided attention.

A Native American tribe, he told us, once lived on the creek right across from Cedar Cliffs. Braves would gather on the edge of the creek to dance and shout questions to the overhanging rocks. They asked where to hunt, how to avoid floods, whether or not to go to war. The cliffs gave back echoes—became talking rocks—faithfully answering important questions in the life of the tribe.

"There are other stories about how Talking Rock Creek got its name," he said, "but that's the most accepted. I got it from my father and he got it from folks further back.

"Dad," he said, his voice lowering and faltering, "was a rural mail carrier on and around this creek for 42 years. He walked it, crossed it, lived along it, but he had never been all the way down it in a boat. So when he was 70 years old, I put him in a raft with me to make the trip. Just below Cedar Cliffs, the raft punctured and we had to walk out." Mr. Low recalled the memory with a smile, but the smile quickly faded. When he spoke next, it was with great difficulty.

His father, he said, had been killed a few days before. "Dad still insisted on driving around in his little pickup. A few days ago a big truck hit him just as he turned onto the bridge over Talking Rock Creek."

Dick and I apologized for bringing up a topic so linked to his recent sorrow, but Mr. Low didn't seem to resent that. Talking Rock is a part of his life. To avoid mention of the creek would be to stifle all conversation. For the Lows, and many families before, Talking Rock Creek flowed through all their memories. Yet it was an

awesome thought, as we discussed it later, that one man's life could be so bound up with a river that he was born near it, played in it, worked beside it, and then tragically—yet, somehow appropriately—died on it. In this sense all creeks and rivers could be called "talking." All could tell of the lives and loves and losses of the generations who lived and died along their banks.

We speed over creeks and rivers on modern bridges and seldom give them a glance or a thought. Why, even that day I had belittled Talking Rock Creek from the GA 156 bridge. "Doesn't look like much from here, does it?" I said. I should have known better. Like most people, creeks don't reveal themselves much at points of public viewing. To discover what they are really like, you must journey into the interior and learn something of history.

The fast-flowing water of Talking Rock brought my mind back to the present. Drawing closer to Cedar Cliffs, we darted through the rapids. It was rugged wilderness, all right—far different from my superficial bridge view the day before. The canyon walls all but blotted out the sun's rays. And under the clefts of the overhanging rocks hung great blocks of ice, still untouched by the warmth of that early spring day.

As we rounded a bend, I saw a distinct break in the tree line on the high ridge above. As we came closer, we caught glimpses through the trees of massive rock outcroppings. Then the trees slid by like a parting curtain, and there in full view was Cedar Cliffs. Long ledges and shelves overlapped their way up to a height of 70 feet or more. Crevices and caves darkened the surface of the weatherworn rock face. We pulled up to a sandbar to view Talking Rock's main attraction.

This was our lunch stop, so Dick unfolded his little camper seat. Dave found a rock to sit on and I located a leaning tree that provided perfect viewing. We sat quietly for a while, eating our lunches and watching the river

run past the cliffs. I don't know what the others were thinking, but I could almost picture in my mind Mr. Low's Indian camp, with its tepees and camp fires. We were probably eating right on the spot where the ceremonial dances took place and the calls went up to the echoing cliffs above.

In my imagination, ancient tom-toms sounded. Dave broke the spell with a dream-shattering question: "I wonder if those Indians back then were like politicians today?"

I took the bait and asked, "What do you mean?"

"Well," he said, "some old chiefs probably stacked the deck before the dance, and had a brave hidden in a cave up there who'd call back the right echoes!"

We chuckled and agreed it was possible.

Dave, who closed the doors of a successful contracting business in Atlanta to open an outfitting and guide service called Wildewood Shop in Helen, contemplated offering guided trips on Talking Rock Creek. "I'll make it an overnight trip, unless all of them are experienced canoeists. This is too hard a push for beginners in one day. Besides," he continued with common sense, "why all the rush? Instead of canoeing 20 miles a day, they should go for 10, and get something out of it."

"And we'd better get started ourselves," I replied.

I was reluctant to leave Cedar Cliffs—with a little more time I believe I could've really heard those distant tom-toms and legendary echoes. But the more exciting rapids lay before us.

I felt a real exhilaration as we shoved the canoes back into the swift current. The creek was more like a friend now than an alien wilderness. We had probed its history, met its people, run its current, and seen its beauty. And also there was the exhilaration of the companionship—really getting to know people. On such a

photo © Tres Hombres del Rio

The bluffs of Talking Rock Creek

trip, you don't just share a river, you share yourself. You meet on a common ground where titles, stations, and professions don't count. Pretenses are lost among the rapids.

Exhilaration is not quite the word. Inspiration is more like it. A canoeing trip contains the necessary ingredients to inspire me: a touch of the visionary to quicken the mind and stir the imagination, balanced with rugged realism, common sense, good humor, and companionship. And that explains why, before slipping into bed bone-weary but contented, I went back to the map—to pick out another river, another place, for another day.

Excerpted from "Brown's Guide to the Georgia Outdoors: Biking, Hiking, and Canoeing Trips" (selected from *Brown's Guide to Georgia*). Reprinted with permission of Cherokee Publishing.

OOSTANAULA RIVER

The name Oostanaula is a derivation of the Cherokee phrase for "Shoal River." The inspiration behind the name is a mystery, since the gradient of the stream averages less than 1 foot per mile. There are occasionally ripples, but rapids are nonexistent as the river loops lazily across Gordon and Floyd Counties on its way to Rome, where it combines with the Etowah to form the Coosa River. Less than 50 miles in length, the Oostanaula is formed by the union of the Coosawattee and Conasauga rivers.

MAPS: Calhoun North, Sugar Valley, Calhoun South, Plainville, Armuchee, Shannon, Rome North (USGS); Gordon, Floyd (County)

GA 225 TO ROME

class	I
length	49 mi
time	5.5 days
gauge	Web
level	N/A
gradient	1 fpm
scenery	C–D

DESCRIPTION: The Oostanaula River stands prominently in Cherokee history as a major artery for trade and the site of the Cherokee Nation's capital, New Echota, located at the head of the Oostanaula where the Conasauga and the Coosawattee meet. The town was the center of government and culture for the Cherokees, and was where, in 1826, Sequoyah began printing the *Cherokee Phoenix,* a newspaper printed in the Cherokee alphabet. Although the Cherokee people won the legal battle to retain the sovereignty of their nation, President Andrew Jackson refused to obey the ruling, resulting in the tragic removal of the people who had inhabited these lands long before the arrival of the settlers. The New Echota State Historical site, located in what is now known as Calhoun, memorializes the historic Cherokee presence, and is part of the Chieftains Trail of historical sites that threads through northwest Georgia.

Navigation of the river itself is uncomplicated. The current is slow and downstream momentum is dependent on the will and stamina of the paddler. The streamside environment is agricultural, with some woodland. The scenery is visually pleasing, but the river begins and ends in urban areas, with accompanying sewage treatment facilities. The city of Rome, which grew from the Cherokee trading village of Chiaha, anchors the mouth of the Oostanaula where it meets the Etowah. Man-made flood control levees in Rome block some evidence of the city's presence and create a park-like atmosphere.

Oostanaula River

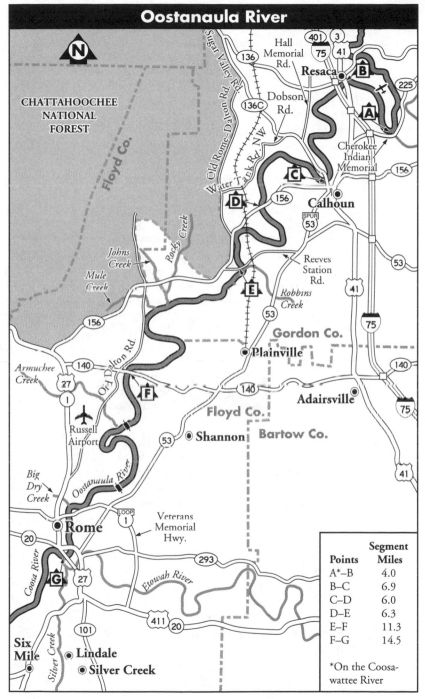

Points	Segment Miles
A*–B	4.0
B–C	6.9
C–D	6.0
D–E	6.3
E–F	11.3
F–G	14.5

*On the Coosawattee River

SHUTTLE: The last opportunity to take-out is on river left immediately before the entry of the Etowah on the same side. Access is from the parking lot located behind the buildings at the corner of West First Street and Broad Street in downtown Rome. See the map for the location of upper access points.

GAUGE: Data is available at the USGS Web site for gauges located at Resaca and Rome. The river is large and usually runnable, unless at flood stage.

AMICALOLA CREEK

The Amicalola gets its name from the Cherokee phrase for tumbling water. It's called a creek on most maps, but if it is merely a creek, it is an awesome one. The scenery is spectacular, and the rapids are sometimes stupendous. It is hard to describe this stream without superlatives, so if it is really just a creek, it is simply the best whitewater creek in the state. Located entirely in Dawson County, its upper east fork, Little Amicalola Creek, contains the famous Amicalola Falls.

MAPS: Nimblewill, Amicalola, Nelson, Juno, Matt (USGS); Dawson (County)

GOSHEN CHURCH ROAD TO GA 53

class	I–II+
length	10.3 mi
time	7 hr
gauge	Visual
level	0.6 ft
gradient	18 fpm
scenery	A

DESCRIPTION: For the most part, the first 4.3 miles of the upper section from Goshen Church Road (A) to the campground off of Amicalola Church Road (B) provides easy floating, quiet beauty, and a few small rapids. The put-in at Goshen Church Road is surrounded by private property. Please be extremely courteous and respectful of the rights of landowners in this area. Note that with sufficient water (over 1.0 foot), a wilderness run through 5 miles of Class I–II rapids, with one Class III at an abandoned mill, opens up above this section.

The access point at the campground (B) is commonly called "6-mile" in reference to the 6 miles of river between there and GA 53 (D). Downstream of the campground, the stream turns east and comes to a shallow and rocky series of Class II ledges. Tornado activity from 2002—not the first tornado to upend trees into the river corridor—is evident in this section; watch for deadfall as the stream may be partially to completely obstructed. In mid-run, Cochrane Creek enters on the left and increases the stream volume considerably. In the next half mile are three good rapids that may require scouting. The first is a wide, 5-foot ledge.

The third ledge on upper Amicalola Creek

Look for a little chute into a pool just left of the downstream island. The next rapid is more complex; from a right-side approach several routes are possible. The third rapid is a 3.5 foot ledge that can be sneaked through on the extreme right; the main route left of center can be a boat buster. The remaining miles to Steele Bridge Road provide easy floating.

By the time the stream reaches Devils Elbow above Steele Bridge Road (C), the Amicalola has a more respectable volume. Starting flat and building gradually to several Class II rapids, the next 2.3-mile stretch is a good training course for beginners. It is also the most popular section of the river for anglers. In addition to the fish, they are looking for solitude, so give them a wide berth. The last Class II rapid, just a quarter mile from the GA 53 bridge, has a feisty little hole at the bottom that creates a good surfing wave. There is a good recovery pool here if upsets occur. The developed take-out is around the bend. Use the parking area at the top of the hill during your run; you can easily drive down to load up afterwards.

SHUTTLE: From Dawsonville, take GA 53 west to the take-out on the right. Check the gauge where GA 53 crosses Amicalola Creek. Two of the put-ins above this point are easiest to reach by continuing west another 1.5 miles on GA 53 and turning right onto Amicalola Church Road. The 6-mile put-in is 4.3 miles ahead on the right. For the uppermost put-in, continue to the stop sign at Afton/Lois Cantrell Road and turn right, then turn left onto Goshen Church Road and proceed to the bridge and

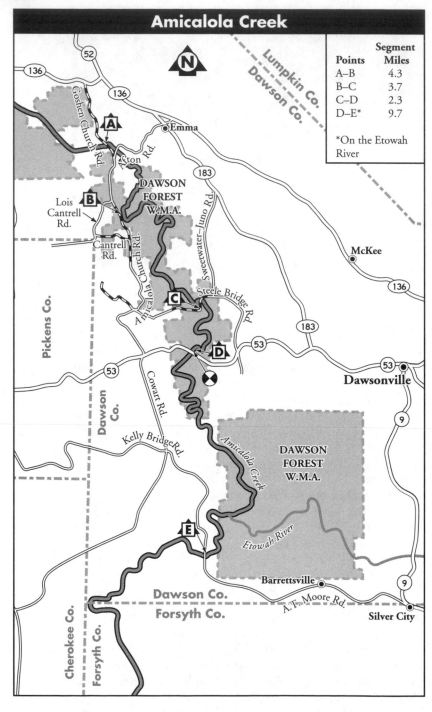

Amicalola Creek

Points	Segment Miles
A–B	4.3
B–C	3.7
C–D	2.3
D–E*	9.7

*On the Etowah River

photo © Tres Hombres del Río

The five-foot ledge on upper Amicalola Creek

put-in. The fastest route to the Steele Bridge Road put-in from GA 53 is from the other side of the river. To get there, take GA 53 1.5 miles east, turn left onto Sweetwater-Juno Road, and continue 2 miles to a left-hand turn onto Steele Bridge Road.

GAUGE: The staff gauge is located at GA 53 in the pool upstream of the bridge on the river's left side. An enjoyable minimum for this section is 0.8, though the river is runnable below this level, particularly between 6-mile and Steele Bridge for boaters who don't mind the practice dodging rocks. The maximum is 2.5 feet for open boats, 3.5 feet for decked.

GA 53 TO THE ETOWAH RIVER AT KELLY BRIDGE ROAD

class	III–IV (V)
length	9.7 mi
time	5 hr
gauge	Visual
level	0.6 ft
gradient	22 (39) fpm
scenery	A+

DESCRIPTION: Below GA 53 the Amicalola is for experienced boaters only. Here the rapids crescendo to Class IV+ heights when the water is high, and even at low water they rate a solid Class III. At levels above 1.2 feet, all boaters should be very competent. The first 2 miles below the highway have an average gradient of 39 feet per mile. The first mile is almost continuous rapids, so be adept at self-rescue.

The Edge of the World is the name of the first set of rapids below the bridge. You will see a definite rocky horizon line all across the river. To scout, take out on the left approximately 100

yards before the drop. The trail does not continue far enough downstream to be used as a portage route. A large log jam in the center of the stream provides an alternative vantage point.

The Edge is composed of two large drops of 5 to 6 feet each with several smaller drops interspersed. Begin on the left side for the first drop and work all the way across to the right side over the smaller ledges. The second large drop is a straight shot near the right bank. The Class II–III action continues for another half mile of maneuvering before slowing to any sizable pool. Pools interspersed with Class II rapids continue for another half mile to Off the Wall rapid. Off the Wall can be recognized by the steep sloping granite face on the right bank. A large portion of the stream flow is diverted by boulders into a narrow channel on the right. Here the water rebounds off the granite face and makes a quick drop. Draw to the left of the protruding rock at the bottom of the chute.

Class I–II rapids are abundant and quickly bring you to Split Rock. Here the stream divides into three channels, with the center channel seeming to split a large boulder. The left channel is often blocked by fallen trees, but the center (preferable) and right channels are usually runnable.

The action begins to moderate, but the streamside environment remains extraordinary. Scenery surpasses the expectations of most travelers on their first descent. Lacy hemlocks and towering pines jut out from rocky precipices. Sheer walls occasionally rise several hundred feet above water level. Tributary streams cascade into the crystalline Amicalola and the influences of nearby civilization are rarely seen. Savor it.

Just about the time that you're starting to think that the Amicalola has shown you all of its thrills, you'll reach Roostertail Rapid. The stream drops steeply with good routes along the left (the rooster tail) and the far right. The center is usually too shallow and rocky.

The intense whitewater is now ended and the stream begins to change character altogether. With the exception of one last surfing wave, rapids become less frequent and the current eventually becomes almost slack. The Etowah River merges from the left a few miles below Roostertail Rapid, increasing the volume but not velocity of the flow. Relax and enjoy the contrast to the adrenaline rush of the upper rapids, or stroke hard if the day is waning. It always takes longer than you think it will. The takeout is on the right bank at Kelly Bridge Road (E).

SHUTTLE: From GA 400 north of Atlanta, turn left onto GA 369 and follow it to a right-hand turn onto GA 9. At A. T.

Moore Road, turn left. Follow this road to the bridge over the Etowah. The take-out is on the far side of the bridge on the right; the gate is not locked. This is private property, and there is a per person fee for parking here. Ensure that access continues at this site by paying it, not littering, and keeping the gate closed. To get to the put-in, continue west on what is now Kelly Bridge Road. Turn right onto Cowart Road, then right again onto GA 53 and proceed to the put-in by making a left turn over the bridge.

GAUGE: See the upper section for gauge location. The lower section can be run as low as 0.5 feet, but the going is technical. At 0.6 feet the water starts becoming more enjoyable; it's less rocky at 0.9 and above. Maximum levels are the same as the upper section.

ETOWAH RIVER

Tumbling out of the southern slopes of the Blue Ridge Mountains, the Etowah is a strikingly beautiful stream suitable for beginners during most seasons of the year. Only after nearly 140 miles of navigable river does the Etowah change names, becoming the Alabama-bound Coosa as it meets the Oostanaula in Rome. In the upper sections, the Etowah delights paddlers as a pristine whitewater stream surrounded by primitive woodlands, then it winds through forests and valley farmland, making a brief subterranean plunge through a mining tunnel. After being impounded by a dam, the lower Etowah emerges as a larger river that curls through the barely rolling farmland spotted with industry east of Rome.

MAPS: Campbell Mountain, Dawsonville, Coal Mountain, Matt, Ballground East, Ballground West, Canton, South Canton, Allatoona Dam, Cartersville, Kingston, Wax, Rome South, Rome North (USGS); Lumpkin, Dawson, Forsythe, Cherokee, Bartow, Floyd (County)

HIGHTOWER CHURCH ROAD TO GA 136

class	I–II (IV)
length	27.9 mi
time	Up to 3 days
gauge	Web
level	300 cfs
gradient	13 (17) fpm
scenery	B+

DESCRIPTION: In the mountains northwest of Dahlonega where this section begins, the Etowah slips through dense thickets of mountain laurel, rhododendron, and hemlock that crowd the shoreline. Quite small at first, the river is prone to deadfall blockages. Many feeder streams enter, however, as the river skirts Campbell Mountain and the volume increases rapidly. At normal

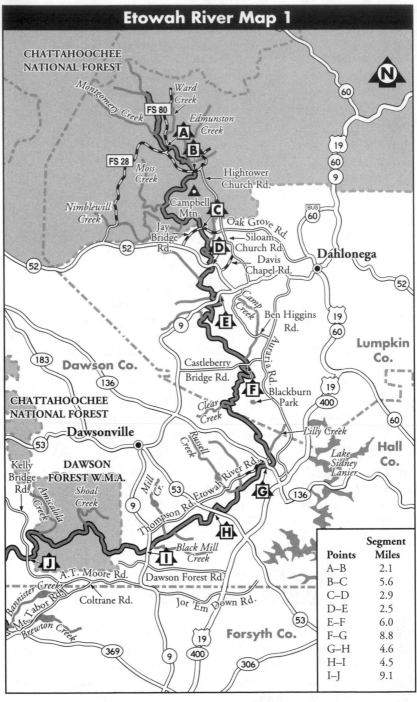

Etowah River Map 1

Points	Segment Miles
A–B	2.1
B–C	5.6
C–D	2.9
D–E	2.5
E–F	6.0
F–G	8.8
G–H	4.6
H–I	4.5
I–J	9.1

water levels, a few small ledges in this section create rapids of Class II difficulty. Some of these become borderline Class III at higher water levels. Trout fishing on this upper section is good, and for this a canoe provides the best access since the area roads are infrequent and primitive.

If the rocks in the rapids above the bridge at Hightower Road (A) are covered, putting in farther upstream at Montgomery Bridge on FS 28 becomes feasible, adding another 2.1 miles and 72 feet of gradient to the trip. The Class I–II flow in the section-above access point A passes through scenery even more remote and native, though again, be prepared to deal with the inevitable trees that block passage at times.

After rounding Campbell Mountain, the river enters a narrow farming valley. The gradient becomes more gentle and remains reasonably constant past GA 52 (D) and on to the river's first crossing with GA 9 (E).

The most popular and possibly the most scenic section of the Etowah lies between GA 9 and Auraria's Castleberry Bridge (F). The environment reverts to woodlands (now sprinkled with houses); high rock bluffs often rise above the river and rapids become more frequent as the gradient increases. Of particular interest are Chuck Shoals and Etowah Falls. Class II Chuck Shoals, approximately 0.75 miles below the GA 9 bridge, is usually run from the left, angling right toward the center chute. Scout from the right side. For the next 2 miles, the river generally moves at a brisk pace down to the Class IV Etowah Falls, easily recognized by their sound and the distinct horizon line they form. Advanced boaters can find a clean line through the falls at higher flows. Otherwise, this rapid is usually portaged using the trail on river right. Continuing its lively flow, the Etowah produces several more Class I–II rapids before Castleberry Bridge. Move to the right of the small islands encountered a short distance above the bridge to access the take-out on river right.

The portion of the Etowah below Castleberry Bridge begins to flatten, and rapids diminish in frequency and intensity. Far from boring, this stretch contains a unique and mysterious feature: 3.5 miles below the bridge, the river disappears into the earth as a portion of the stream's flow enters an old mining tunnel, traveling nearly 0.25 miles through a mountain. The tunnel and the small drop inside of it can be run safely at medium-to-low water levels if there is no debris blocking the passage. Stop at the entrance to the tunnel and lower your face to the water level, peering closely within for any logs or brush that may be lodged inside. Do not enter the tunnel under any circumstances

if the daylight at the far end of the tunnel is obstructed in any way. If you do not wish to go through the tunnel, follow the original stream bed to the right around the mountain. The frequent Class I–II rapids that preceded the tunnel are replaced by mostly flat moving water for the remainder of the trip down to GA 136 G).

The tunnel, constructed in the 1930s, is a reminder of the mining activity that is part of this area's history. Gold fever seized settlers in the early nineteenth century and became a major impetus for the land-grab that culminated in the removal of the native tribes to western lands in 1838. Nearby Auraria was, at the time, the hub of mining activity; all that remains of the community today are the ruins of an old hotel and a historical marker.

SHUTTLE: North of Atlanta on GA 400, turn left onto GA 136 and follow to the bridge for the final take-out. To reach the usual highest put-in at Hightower Church Road, take GA 60 north into Dahlonega, turning left onto Bus GA 60, Bus US 19. After leaving town, turn left onto Oak Grove Road. Turn right onto Hightower Church Road at the four-way stop (the Jay Bridge intermediate access point is straight ahead) and proceed to the bridge over the river. Other intermediate access points are easily reached from GA 9.

GAUGE: See the following section. Look for submerged rocks above Hightower Church Road if you hope to run the uppermost section.

GA 136 TO KNOX BRIDGE BOAT RAMP ON LAKE ALLATOONA

class	I
length	65.4 mi
time	Up to 6.5 days
gauge	Web
level	200 cfs
gradient	4 fpm
scenery	B+–C

DESCRIPTION: In this long section, the Etowah's gradient is lower, producing an occasional Class I rapid, as it moves alternately through farmed valleys and forest. Soon after putting in at GA 136, the topography opens into a broad, flat plain referred to as a savannah on some maps. The river, still small in size, spends the next 10 miles snaking through the farms that populate this wide valley.

The section of river that commences with the second crossing of GA 9 (I) bears special mention, since most of the subsequent 9-mile run passes under the pleasantly wooded canopy of the Dawson Forest Wildlife Management Area (WMA). Diminutive and lively at the onset, the river is still small

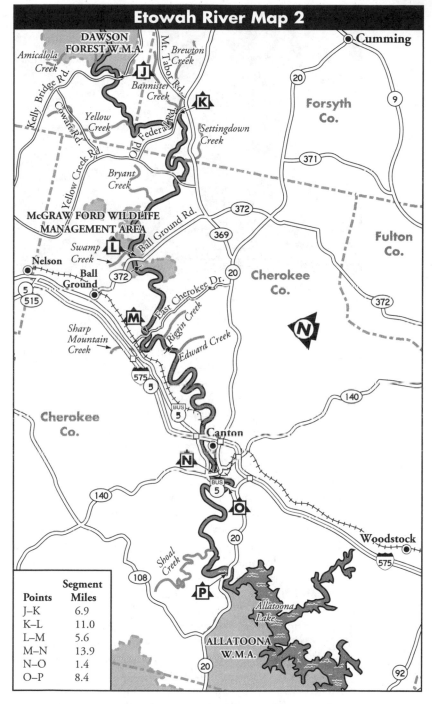

Etowah River Map 2

DAWSON FOREST W.M.A.

Cumming

Amicalola Creek

Brewton Creek

J

Bannister Creek

K

Mt. Tabor Rd.

Kelly Bridge Rd.

Cowart Rd.

Yellow Creek

Old Federal Rd.

Settingdown Creek

Forsyth Co.

20

9

Yellow Creek Rd.

Bryant Creek

371

McGRAW FORD WILDLIFE MANAGEMENT AREA

Ball Ground Rd.

372

369

Fulton Co.

Swamp Creek

L

Nelson

Ball Ground

372

20

Cherokee Co.

372

5

515

East Cherokee Dr.

M

Riggin Creek

N

Sharp Mountain Creek

Edward Creek

140

575

5

BUS 5

Cherokee Co.

Canton

N

BUS 5

140

O

Woodstock

575

20

Shoal Creek

108

P

Allatoona Lake

ALLATOONA W.M.A.

20

92

Points	Segment Miles
J–K	6.9
K–L	11.0
L–M	5.6
M–N	13.9
N–O	1.4
O–P	8.4

Canoeing the Etowah River

enough to contain a fair amount of deadfall. The fallen trees require maneuvering but usually pose little nuisance. As the flow increases, the forest deepens and deadfall encounters lapse. An occasional road passes through the forest, but there are few other signs of civilization, making this an ideal camping section. The rapids do not surpass Class I in difficulty, and are generally stilled by the time the second major creek, Amicalola, enters on the right, approximately two-thirds of the way through the run. A good take-out at Kelly Bridge Road (J) is on private property. A small, per-person fee helps ensure continued access at this facility.

The river's descent below Kelly Bridge to the lake remains mellow with only scattered shoals and no serious rapids. The scenery alternates between farmland and forest, including the McGraw Ford WMA, for over 20 miles until light industry and suburban developments make their presence known. Soon thereafter, the river passes through the center of Canton. The best access here is in the county park (Boling Park) located on the river-right side, downstream of the GA 5 (Bus) bridge (O). Since the trip from here to the last take-out (P) is mostly on the Army Corps–managed lake, the shores are thickly forested and devoid of development. With the exception of powerboats that can come upriver from the lake, the woodlands are quiet and frequented by wildlife, making good spots for camping. The boat ramp at Knox Bridge is closed when the lake is at low pool.

SHUTTLE: To the take-out at Lake Allatoona, take GA 20 west of Canton and turn left into the boat ramp road after crossing the bridge over the lake. Call the Army Corps of Engineers at (770) 382-4700 to check on availability, or to request that the gate be opened in the off-season. See the map for the location of upper access points.

GAUGE: Using the levels supplied by the USGS for the GA 9 gauge near Dawsonville, the upper sections are runnable with a minimum of 300 cfs. Downstream at the Dawson Forest section, 200 cfs on the Dawsonville gauge is sufficient. Using data from the USGS Canton gauge for the river below Ball Ground, the minimum level is 0.9 feet; maximum is 6 feet.

ALLATOONA DAM TO THE OOSANAULA RIVER

class	I
length	48.4 mi
time	Up to 5 days
gauge	Phone, web
level	Unknown
gradient	2.5 fpm
scenery	B–C-

DESCRIPTION: The flow volume in this 48-mile section varies dramatically based on releases at Allatoona Dam. When the dam is not generating power, normal flows are 300 cfs; the power-generating flow is nearly 7,000 cfs greater than this. Needless to say, this is not a situation that you would want to encounter unaware. The turbulent power-generating flows dislodge trees and other brush, creating dangerous strainers. Before planning a trip anywhere below the dam, call the Army Corp of Engineers for a release schedule. The Corps does attempt to limit these extreme releases to weekdays.

Outside of the weekday diurnal flush, there are many opportunities for relaxing flat-water trips on this section. There is good access to the river at the top of this section below Allatoona Dam at Coopers Furnace Day Use Area (Q). Downstream of the dam, glimpses of the recreation and industry found in the town of Cartersville fill the initial views from the river. Approximately 3.5 miles downstream from Allatoona Dam, a smaller, private dam blocks the stream and can be portaged on the left. At non-generating flows, paddlers can approach the dam to portage at their ease. A treacherous recirculating hole forms below the dam at power-generating flows, making a portage during those times more challenging.

A fascinating historical site is found 3.2 miles downstream of the US 41 bridge (R) at the Etowah Indian Mounds. When approaching the site from the river, Pumpkinvine Creek's entrance on the left followed by a nearly river-wide fishing weir marks the spot—the grassy mounds rise above the river on the

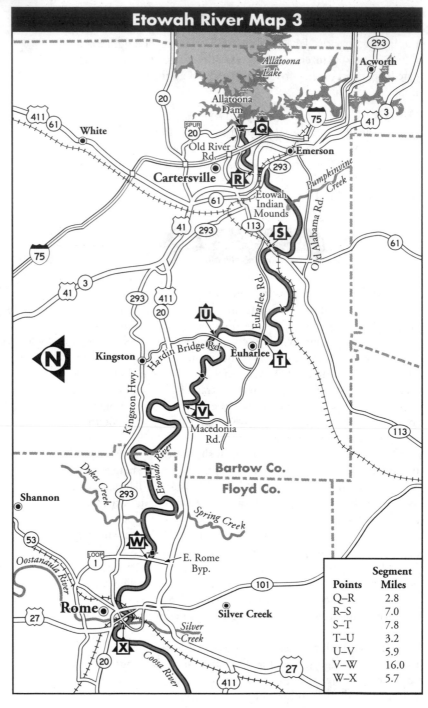

Etowah River Map 3

	Segment
Points	**Miles**
Q–R	2.8
R–S	7.0
S–T	7.8
T–U	3.2
U–V	5.9
V–W	16.0
W–X	5.7

right. The Mound Builders were part of the Mississippian culture that pre-dated the Cherokee and Creek nations in this area.
The artifacts and the mounds themselves give intriguing
glimpses into the lives of the people who inhabited this area as
early as AD 950. The long distance to the parking lot from the
river makes the site more suitable for an educational side-trip
than a starting or ending point for a run. There is a small fee to
visit the park that is payable at the museum.

After exiting Cartersville, the Etowah begins its slow meandering course toward Rome. Multiple access points make for good
sections for beginners or those who like a few lazy days of camping, fishing, and swimming. The banks are all private property, so
respect property owners' rights and be aware of the dam release
schedule when selecting a campsite. The gradient averages less
than 3 feet per mile, so no difficult rapids are found. The most
jarring departure from the scenery is the Bowen nuclear power
plant located above the river's crossing with Euharlee Road (U).

The Etowah meets the Oostanaula and becomes the Coosa
River in downtown Rome. The final take-out for the Etowah
River (X) is located around the corner of this bluff on the river-
left side of the Oostanaula. Be wary of possible turbulence as you
traverse the point; the stairs leading to the parking lot are less
than 100 feet upstream on the Oostanaula.

SHUTTLE: The final take-out is located at the parking lot west
of the intersection of West 1st Street and Broad Street in downtown Rome. Most other access points for this section are easily
reached from GA 20.

GAUGE: The Army Corps of Engineers controls the flow volume emitting from Allatoona Dam. Flow schedules can be
acquired by calling (706) 334-7213. Real-time levels are provided on the USGS Web site.

A Child's Experience of the Etowah
— by Joe Cook

An 80-mile straight-line distance separates the headwaters of the Etowah on the Appalachian Trail and Rome, Georgia, where the river meets the Oostanaula to form the Coosa. However, the course the Etowah takes is anything but straight. In all it winds some 160 miles. On a map the river writhes like a confused and frightened snake, coiling and slithering here and there with little direction.

The communities through which it passes—Dawsonville, Canton, Cartersville, Rome and others—are to some degree uncertain of their course as well. Change is coming fast to the Etowah watershed, and residents are facing difficult questions about what they want the river and surrounding landscape to look like in 20 years, when half-a-million new residents will call the Etowah basin home.

With these fast-approaching changes in mind, my three-year-old daughter Ramsey, her mother Monica, and I set out in the spring of 2002 to canoe the length of the Etowah. Initially we were concerned about how our just-potty-trained daughter would handle a month-long canoe journey, but our fears quickly evaporated as Ramsey settled into her river home. She studied bugs and critters, painted with watercolors using the river as her rinse cup, sang along to songs we played on a small tape player, and splashed at will, hanging legs, hands, and head over the gunwales to take in the river.

By trip's end, she knew the laughing call of the pileated woodpecker and could recognize the river's numerous Native American fish dams. She even mastered the old river runner's motto, "just go with the flow," plaintively using it whenever Monica and I discussed the best course through an obstacle.

The river itself is a gem—shining like the gold that first brought settlers to its banks. While signs of growth and development are commonplace, long stretches of the river and the land around it appear unspoiled. Highlights include the Dawson Forest, portions of northeast Cherokee County, and the run from Cartersville to Rome, which is filled with Native American fish dams.

The journey gave our daughter treasured encounters with natural Georgia, the beginning, we hope, of a lifelong appreciation for wilderness and wildlife. It also modeled self-reliance; on the river, stopping at McDonald's is not an option. Finally, the trip freed her mother and I from the daily concerns of contemporary life, fostering appreciation for our family.

If you're looking for an alternative to Disney World for your next family vacation, you might consider the Etowah or another Georgia river. Just be sure to pick a small, intimate one like the Etowah. Big, open water where the banks are distant seemed to bore Ramsey. The only time she napped during the 26-day trip was during the monotonous paddle across Lake Allatoona.

COOSA RIVER

The Coosa River is formed as the waters of the Etowah and the Oost-anaula merge in downtown Rome. As it chugs along toward Alabama, the river largely leaves the industrial development of Rome behind and the surrounding land reverts to gentle farmland hills. The flow of the river is extremely sluggish through its straighter sections. Upon reaching the Weiss Lake backwaters near the state border, the current stops altogether and the river adopts the meandering habit of a Coastal Plains stream.

MAPS: Rome North, Rome South, Livingston, Rocky Mountain, Melson, Chattoogaville (USGS); Floyd (County)

ROME TO THE GEORGIA–ALABAMA BORDER

class	I
length	29.4 mi
time	Up to 4 days
gauge	Web, visual
level	8.0 ft
gradient	<1 fpm
scenery	C–D

DESCRIPTION: The river's channel is wide and remarkably straight for its first 16 miles. After putting in at picturesque downtown Rome, the first few miles flow through an industrial area. Grassy, man-made levees occasionally separate the boater from this activity. Industry, including a large power plant near GA 100, continues to intrude on the scenery from time to time, reminding the paddler that this is a working river.

Seven miles downstream from Rome, an inoperable lock and dam operation is encountered. The locks were formerly used to open the upper reaches of the river to the large-scale commercial traffic that found it difficult to negotiate this area. The remains of the dam create a rare play spot on the river. At lower water levels, waves develop on the river-left side. If you're passing through from upstream and want to avoid the turbulence, the dam can be portaged on the left. At higher levels, the waves wash out into an obvious downstream channel on the left. The park here is an intermediate access point (B), complete with camping sites and a boat ramp just below the dam on river left. There is a fee for parking and launching.

Farther downstream, the area around Fosters Bend just above Weiss Lake is of particular interest. Here a large oxbow lake and swamp are formed, supporting a small population of cotton-mouths (water moccasins). This snake is usually found only in the Coastal Plain and no other populations are known to be near this area. There are also many plants found here indigenous to the Coastal Plains. On the higher ground near the oxbow, evidence has been found of early Native American settlements.

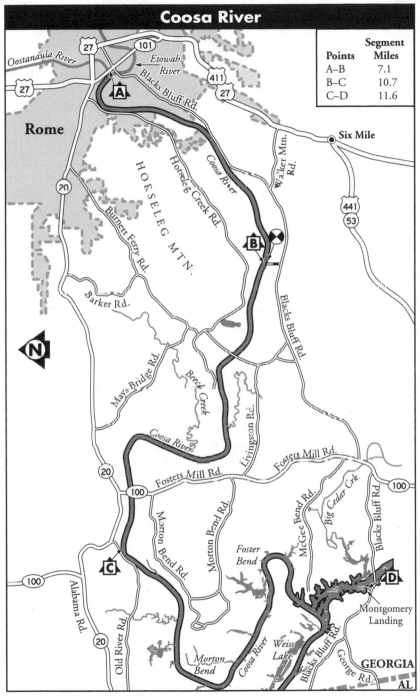

Coosa River

Points	Segment Miles
A–B	7.1
B–C	10.7
C–D	11.6

Oostanaula River

Etowah River

Rome

Blacks Bluff Rd.

Six Mile

Horseleg Creek Rd.

Coosa River

Walker Mtn. Rd.

HORSELEG MTN.

Burnett Ferry Rd.

Barker Rd.

N

Mays Bridge Rd.

Beech Creek

Livingston Rd.

Coosa River

Fosters Mill Rd.

Fosters Mill Rd.

Fosters Mill Rd.

McGee Bend Rd.

Big Cedar Crk.

Blacks Bluff Rd.

Blacks Bluff Rd.

Morton Bend Rd.

Morton Bend Rd.

Foster Bend

Montgomery Landing

Alabama Rd.

Old River Rd.

Morton Bend

Coosa River

Weiss Lake

Blacks Bluff Rd.

George Rd.

GEORGIA

AL

The final access point is on Weiss Lake at the Bushy Branch Park Montgomery Boat Ramp (D). Reaching it requires approximately 3 miles of lake paddling below Fosters Bend. For those who wish to visit Fosters Bend without experiencing the upper part of the Coosa, put in at the boat ramp and paddle back up. A navigational map of Weiss Lake may be helpful for the river below GA 100 as the main channel can be difficult to discern.

SHUTTLE: Leaving Rome on GA 20 for the take-out, proceed west to a left turn onto GA 100. (Continuing farther on GA 100 to a left-turn onto Old River Road to reach the DNR boat ramp on the Coosa, access point C.) After 6.7 miles on GA 100, turn right onto Blacks Bluff Road. The entrance for the Montgomery Landing boat ramp is on the right, after the bridge over the lake. To return to the highest put-in, take Blacks Bluff Road back to GA 100 and turn left. In 0.5 miles, turn right onto the continuation of Blacks Bluff Road. Where the road dead-ends, turn left (a right-hand turn here will take you to Lock and Dam Park, access point B). Take a left at Horseleg Creek Road; a right at Burnett Ferry Road will take you to GA 20, approximately 5.5 miles ahead. Turn right onto GA 20 and follow it into Rome. The road merges with GA 1 as it veers to the right and crosses the Oostanaula River. At the first opportunity over the bridge, turn right into the parking lot and put-in down the stairs into the Oostanaula just above the confluence with the Etowah.

GAUGE: The USGS Web site provides a reading for the Coosa River near Rome. A visual gauge is located at the Lock and Dam Park. Using this gauge, the minimum level is 8 feet, maximum 14 feet for open boats and up to flood stage for decked boats. Water levels can fluctuate dramatically during the day depending on power-generating flows from the Allatoona Dam upstream on the Etowah River. Refer to the gauge information for the final section of the Etowah River (page 155) for more information on dam releases.

BIG CEDAR CREEK

Big Cedar Creek, tucked into the hills southwest of Rome, pleases with a seemingly incongruous slice of central-Tennessee scenery mixed with Class I and II shoals. The glades of large eastern red cedar that inspired the creek's name are mostly gone, supplanted by longleaf pines and mixed hardwoods. Flowing to the northwest out of Polk County, the creek ends as a Coosa River tributary in Weiss Lake on the Georgia–Alabama border.

MAPS: Cedartown East, Livingston, Melson (USGS); Polk, Floyd (County)

CAVE SPRING ROAD TO MONTGOMERY LANDING AT WEISS LAKE

class	I–II
length	20.5 mi
time	12 hr
gauge	Web, visual
level	Unknown
gradient	9 fpm
scenery	B- to C

DESCRIPTION: Boaters may begin their trip on Cave Spring Road (A), northwest of Cedartown in Polk County. The upper section from here to the US 411 bridge (D) is mostly flatwater; it's not far downstream from Cedartown, and the aroma of treated sewage is mildly apparent. Rapids, when they occur, are usually quick ledges under-girded with sharp limestone rocks; you (and your boat) will be happier if there's sufficient water. The one exception is a picturesque Class II drop that may prove challenging for inexperienced boaters.

Water levels change dramatically throughout the year, with high-water periods in the winter and early spring 15 feet or more above the normal summer flows. With its limited watershed, the creek drains quickly after a rain, making the paddling most feasible during these periods. Debris from high water flows is jammed under most bridge trusses, so exercise caution and avoid contact with these when the water is up.

Fish are abundant in Big Cedar Creek and are often visible if you are cautious. The current is slow enough to make fishing from the boat practical, particularly in the lower section below US 411. Below the point where GA 100 crosses the creek, the current becomes slack and progress will be much slower. The scenery is still pleasant and mostly woodland. Almost 2 miles of paddling across Weiss Lake are required to reach the final take-out at Montgomery Landing (H).

SHUTTLE: To the take-out from Cave Spring, go west on US 411 and turn right onto GA 100, then left onto Blacks Bluff Road. Montgomery Landing is the first right-hand turn after crossing the lake. The best upper access points are at GA 100 (F),

Big Cedar Creek

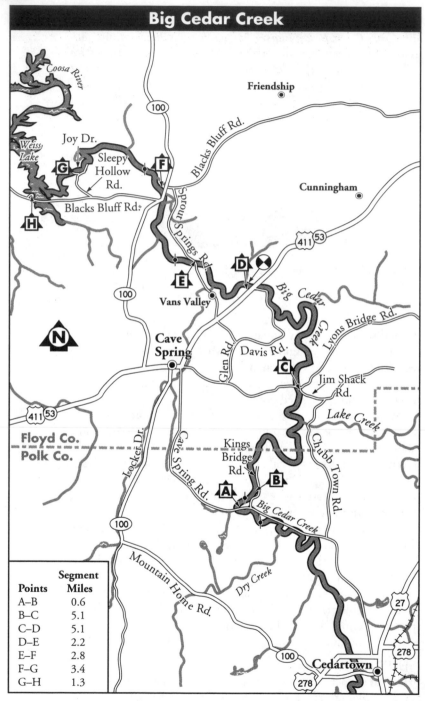

Points	Segment Miles
A–B	0.6
B–C	5.1
C–D	5.1
D–E	2.2
E–F	2.8
F–G	3.4
G–H	1.3

at US 411/GA 53 (there may be a fee for launch use and parking at the convenient campground), and at Kings Bridge Road (B). The highest put-in access is on Cave Spring Road that runs between Cedartown and Cave Spring. Access at Lyons Road and Kings Bridge Road is available with permission of the property owners.

GAUGE: Levels are available on-line from the Southeast River Forecast Center at www.srh.noaa.gov/ffc/html/etowagph.shtml. Allow at least 5 feet; 6 feet would provide more margin to the rocks in the upper section. A gauge is painted on the bridge supports at the river-right, downstream side of the US 411 bridge; pull out on the northeast side of the bridge to check the level. Levels of -1 to -6 inches are required for the lower section. More water, at least in the 0 to 1 foot range, makes the upper section enjoyable. The maximum is 15 feet (flood stage).

CHATTOOGA RIVER OF CHATTOOGA COUNTY

Georgia's other Chattooga River snakes between the Armuchee Ridges in the northwestern corner of the state. Docile in character, the river gurgles gently through the towns and industry of Trion, Summerville, and Lyerly on its way to the Coosa River in Weiss Lake. Sandstone ridges including Dirtseller Mountain and Taylor Ridge rise on either side of the river, making for visually engaging scenery without generating any significant rapids.

MAPS: Trion, Summerville, Chattoogaville, Lyerly (USGS); Chattooga (County)

WALKER COUNTY LINE TO GEORGIA–ALABAMA BORDER

class	I
length	28.7 mi
time	Up to 3.5 days
gauge	Web
level	2.0 ft
gradient	3.5 fpm
scenery	C-

DESCRIPTION: There are two Chattooga Rivers in Georgia—this one is the lesser known. A cascading wilderness whitewater stream this isn't; unlike its namesake, the Chattooga River in Chattooga County holds no significant rapids. The scenery is pleasantly pastoral when not interrupted by reminders of the costs of civilization. In Trion, there is no vegetative facade to screen views of the denim mill and surrounding town. One mile downstream, you will encounter a sewage treatment plant; several miles later (upstream of access point F, the US 27 bridge in Summerville), the river passes a prison. Upstream of the bridge at Lyerly Dam Road (H) is a small dam that is easily portaged.

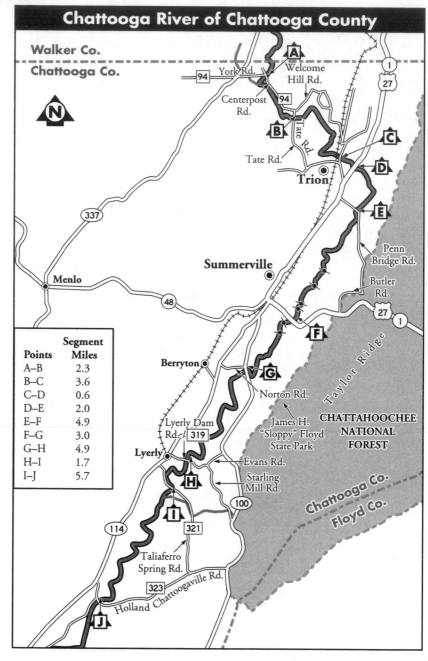

Chattooga River of Chattooga County

Walker Co.

Chattooga Co.

N

York Rd.

94

94

Welcome
Hill Rd.

Centerpost
Rd.

A

B

Tate Rd.

Tate Rd.

Trion

C

D

E

337

Penn
Bridge Rd.

Summerville

Butler
Rd.

Menlo

48

27 1

Taylor Ridge

Berryton

F

G

Norton Rd.

CHATTAHOOCHEE
NATIONAL
FOREST

James H.
"Sloppy" Floyd
State Park

Lyerly Dam
Rd. 319

Lyerly

Evans Rd.

H

Starling
Mill Rd.

100

114

I

321

Chattooga Co.

Floyd Co.

Taliaferro
Spring Rd.

323

Holland Chattoogaville Rd.

J

Points	Segment Miles
A–B	2.3
B–C	3.6
C–D	0.6
D–E	2.0
E–F	4.9
F–G	3.0
G–H	4.9
H–I	1.7
I–J	5.7

Frequent bridge crossings and the proximity of nearby towns make this a highly accessible stream. Roads cross every 2 to 5 miles in the 28.7-mile course from just north of Trion to Holland–Chattoogaville Road. The Chattooga flows from there into Alabama, where it becomes a major feeder for Weiss Lake.

The river's watershed is large, resulting in floatable flows during periods when other rivers are too low to enjoy.

SHUTTLE: The lowest take-out for this Chattooga River is reached from Rome via GA 20 westbound. Turn right onto northbound GA 100, then left onto Holland–Chattoogaville Road in Holland, continuing to the river. Upper access points are easily reached from GA 114 west of the river, and from US 27 above Summerville.

GAUGE: Check the USGS Web site for levels at Summerville. The minimum is 2 feet; maximum 5 feet.

TALLAPOOSA RIVER

Fortunately for those seeking wooded solitude, few paddlers frequent the shy Tallapoosa. Despite the periodic bridge crossings, the river offers seclusion and serene beauty. Rolling hills stretch in all directions, but dense streamside flora and high banks usually block the view. The current is moderate; infrequent small shoals and rocky bluffs add spice. The most enjoyable sections are located due west of Atlanta on the Alabama border in Haralson County.

MAPS: Draketown, Rockmart South, Buchanan, Tallapoosa North, Tallapoosa South (USGS); Paulding, Haralson (County)

ROCKMART ROAD TO LINER ROAD

class	I (II)
length	35.5 mi
time	Up to 4.5 days
gauge	Visual
level	5 ft
gradient	4 fpm
scenery	C

DESCRIPTION: The Tallapoosa River originates in Carroll County, cuts across a corner of Paulding County, and traverses the breadth of Haralson County to enter Alabama just west of the town of Tallapoosa. The winter rains and infrequent summer deluges give the Tallapoosa sufficient volume for boating as high as Paulding County, although the river's width in this area is barely sufficient to turn a typical canoe. In addition to the shallow ledges and twisty boulder shoals, the primary navigation risks are deadfalls and strainers, intensified in the upper reaches, and the water intake rubble dam located upstream of the GA 100 bridge (I).

Tallapoosa River

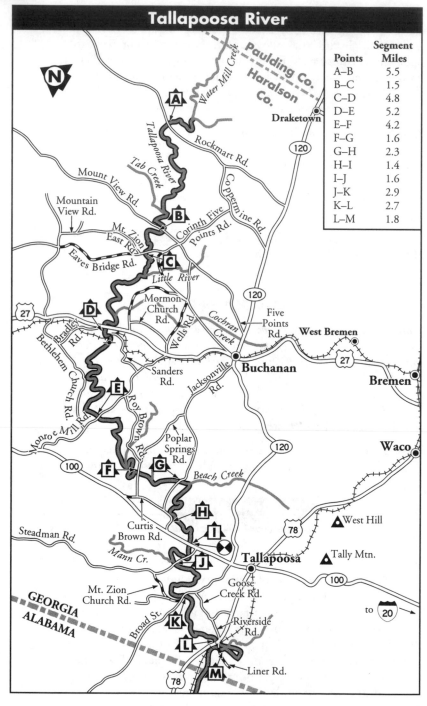

Points	Segment Miles
A–B	5.5
B–C	1.5
C–D	4.8
D–E	5.2
E–F	4.2
F–G	1.6
G–H	2.3
H–I	1.4
I–J	1.6
J–K	2.9
K–L	2.7
L–M	1.8

Most seasons of the year boaters will be forced to launch well into Haralson County. Launching lower in the river's course ensures a more adequate flow and rewards you with the return of a deeper wilderness downstream of the town of Tallapoosa. Bluffs become more prevalent, shoals are visually pleasing, minor and infrequent.

Some bridge access points are steep and can be choked with vegetation along the banks, but fortunately the most difficult can easily be avoided. The best access points are noted on the map. Deadfall pinned to bridge abutments can be extreme and channels completely blocked, even at the lowest access points. Be careful to avoid contact as you paddle by or portage around these nests of logs.

Trips can be extended over the Alabama state border—the next verified downstream access is 18 miles downstream at the AL 49 bridge, although exploration may yield better take-out options. The beauty, seclusion, and speed of the river intensifies as the Alabama border is approached and crossed. Rocky bluffs rise above the stream, one holding a shallow cave.

SHUTTLE: To the lowest take-out located in Georgia, go west on US 78 out of the town of Tallapoosa. After crossing the river, take the first left onto Liner Road, following it to the left as it swings around the railroad tracks. Continue to the bridge; the best access is on the far right-hand side.

GAUGE: There's a staff gauge affixed to the river-left side of the GA 100 bridge north of Tallapoosa. Minimum level is 5 feet, maximum 18 feet.

part**Four**

CHATTAHOOCHEE AND FLINT RIVERS
WATERSHEDS

CHATTAHOOCHEE RIVER

*"The lore of the South could not survive without rivers any better than
the human body could survive without blood," writes Marc Reisner in*
Cadillac Desert. *Every river has its stories—the Chattahoochee could
fill volumes. It is Georgia's longest river and the only one spanning all
three of its geological regions. Sparkling headwaters fall from the
mountains, are temporarily stilled in Lake Lanier, emerge to lope
across the Piedmont hills and through Atlanta, and upon reaching
Columbus, turn south to spill through successive dams throughout the
Coastal Plain, rarely flowing freely. Millions depend on the river—
Atlanta and Columbus drink it—yet the river's waters are polluted
from human contact, particularly in and downstream of Atlanta. As
Atlanta modernizes its sewer system and Columbus talks of freeing the
drowned Coweta Falls, the final chapter has yet to be written.*

MAPS: Jacks Gap, Cowrock, Helen, Leaf, Clarkesville, Lula,
Buford Dam, Suwannee, Duluth, Norcross, Chamblee, Roswell,
Mountain Park, Sandy Springs, Northwest Atlanta, Mableton,
Ben Hill, Campbellton, Palmetto, Rico, Newnan North,
Whitesburg, Lowell, Franklin, Hill Crest, Columbus, Fort
Mitchell, Fort Benning, Union, Omaha, Twin Springs, George-
town, Eufaula North, Eufaula South, Ft. Gaines Northeast, Ft.
Gaines Northwest, Ft. Gaines, Columbia Northeast, Columbia,
Gordon, Saffold, Bascom, Steam Mill, Fairchild, Sneads
(USGS); White, Habersham, Hall, Forsyth, Gwinnett, Fulton,
Cobb, Douglas, Carroll, Coweta, Heard, Muscogee, Chatta-
hoochee, Stewart, Clay, Early, Seminole (County)

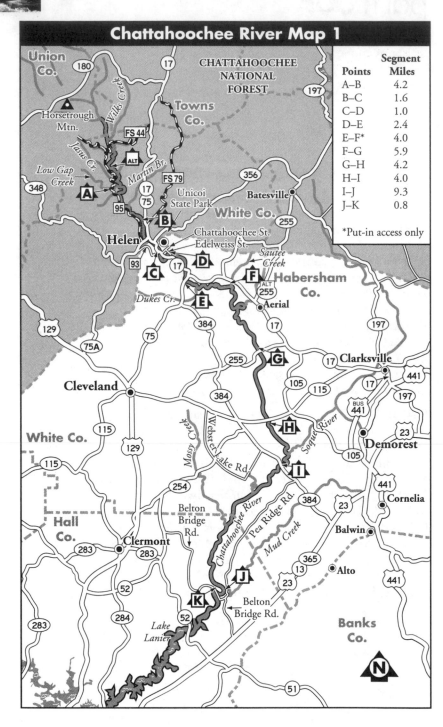

Chattahoochee River Map 1

Union Co.

180

17

CHATTAHOOCHEE NATIONAL FOREST

197

Wilks Creek

Horsetrough Mtn.

Towns Co.

FS 44

ALT

Jasus Cr.

Martin Br.

FS 79

356

Low Gap Creek

348

A

17 75

95

Unicoi State Park

Batesville

White Co.

255

Helen

93

C

17

Chattahoochee St.
Edelweiss St.

D

Sautee Creek

F

ALT 255

Habersham Co.

Dukes Cr.

E

Aerial

129

75

384

17

197

75A

255

G

105 115

Clarksville

17

441

Cleveland

384

17

BUS 441

197

White Co.

115

129

Mossy Creek

Webster Lake Rd.

H

Soque River

Demorest

23

105

115

254

I

441

Belton Bridge Rd.

Chattahoochee River

Pea Ridge Rd.

384

23

Cornelia

Hall Co.

283

Clermont

283

Mud Creek

Balwin

52

365

13

Alto

441

J

23

283

284

52

K

Belton Bridge Rd.

Banks Co.

Lake Lanier

51

N

Points	Segment Miles
A–B	4.2
B–C	1.6
C–D	1.0
D–E	2.4
E–F*	4.0
F–G	5.9
G–H	4.2
H–I	4.0
I–J	9.3
J–K	0.8

*Put-in access only

LOW GAP CREEK TO GA 75 ABOVE ROBERTSTOWN (UPPER UPPER CHATTAHOOCHEE)

class	III–IV
length	4.2 mi
time	3–4 hr
gauge	None
level	N/A
gradient	57 fpm (2 mi at 85)
scenery	A

DESCRIPTION: The river is extremely small in this section, but the scenery and gradient combine to make a run that borders on spectacular—on the rare occasion of the right water level. The river drops extremely fast through a rocky and deadfall-ridden constricted channel bordered by hemlock, mountain laurel, and rhododendron. There are many sections barely wide enough for a boat to pass through and occasional blind turns and drops with little margin for error. Scout as much of the river as possible from the road before putting in, and scout all major drops while on the water. This seldom-traveled run is for expert boaters only.

The recommended put-in is where the Chattahoochee River Road (FS 52) crosses Low Gap Creek, which is sizeable enough to provide passage to the river when it's running. Either carry down the path along the left side of the creek or run the creek down to its confluence with the Chattahoochee. Shortly downstream, the access road rejoins the river. There are multiple opportunities to access the river or to camp in the remaining miles down to the valley. The river is mostly Class II–III below Low Gap Creek and is less choked by trees than in the sections above. The uppermost access is on FS 44, but putting in here is problematic. The wooded upper section often forces boaters to return upstream rather than allowing them to continue downstream. If it is clear, there are four rapids in the first 2 miles of this section that approach the limits of navigability. Portage here is harrowing, involving slick, steep rocks and rhododendron thickets. Another option is to put-in between the highest access point and Low Gap Creek by parking near the gated Forest Service road you encounter on FS 52 after crossing Jasus Creek and sliding down the ridge to the river (bearing north to the river instead of south into the gully). Putting in here adds 1.4 miles of Class II–III water to the run.

SHUTTLE: From Helen, the take-out is north of town on GA 75 before the highway veers away from the river at Spoilcane Creek. To get to the put-in, take GA 75 back toward Helen. Before town, turn right onto GA 75 (Alt.) and take the immediate right onto Chattahoochee River Road on the other side of the river. Follow this road until reaching the Forest Service campground at Low Gap Creek.

GAUGE: There is no gauge for this section. Flow flushes through quickly and the lower river must be near or approaching flood stage in order to find sufficient flow at the headwaters. Scout the level from the road to determine feasibility.

ROBERTSTOWN TO LAKE LANIER (UPPER HOOCH)

class	I–II (III)
length	32.3 mi
time	Up to 3 days
gauge	Web, phone, visual
level	800 cfs
gradient	14 fpm
scenery	A–B

DESCRIPTION: Upon reaching the valley floor, the river calms into steady Class I riffles and remains that way through Alpinized Helen. Other than boisterous summer tubing traffic, there are no immediate obstacles except for one low wooden bridge near Robertstown that may present problems at higher levels. Chattahoochee Street in Helen (D) is the last opportunity to take-out before encountering a dam that cannot be portaged at Nora Mill in Nacoochee.

Below the mill, the river takes a significant bend and passes beneath GA 75 twice. After the second crossing (E), the river flows adjacent to the Nacoochee American Indian Mound. River access is possible at this second crossing on the southeast corner of the bridge, though traffic on the road is fast and heavy, especially on weekends. The Nacoochee Valley offers a pleasant, pastoral float mostly through open farmland with some wooded areas. There are often downed trees, however, that can cause problems. The state has recently purchased the Nacoochee mound and definitely does not allow public digging for artifacts. Please respect these Native American ancestral lands.

From the Sautee Creek junction down to GA 255 (G) lies one of the longest undisturbed stretches of the river. The terrain is heavily forested, with large white pines and frequent rock outcroppings. Evidence of human intrusion is less obvious than earlier, and a pleasant illusion of isolation settles in. This is a good section for camping. Rapids are fairly frequent but never go beyond a mild Class II category. River access is available at the GA 17 bridge over Sautee Creek (F), and is best on the bridge's southwest corner. It is a short float to the main stream of the Chattahoochee; be ready to portage around downed trees, which can easily span the creek.

Rapids become more challenging below GA 255. This segment begins with several Class I rapids and smooth pools. Then the river enters a long, slow area nicknamed the Dead Sea because its stillness offers a marked contrast to the rapids above and below. Large trees on either side form a cool green tunnel of vegetation that occasionally opens into rolling pastured vistas.

The Dead Sea is the first warning sign that Smith Island rapid is near; the next indicator is a large, gently sloping granite face on the right. This rapid should be scouted by first timers or by anyone running the river at extreme water levels. Do not scout from the island, which is private. The left side of the island is the best route. It is a Class II rapid at almost any water level, and at high water it becomes a solid Class III. Enter the rapid from the left side of the main stream at the top of the island, then gradually work back to the right side (left bank of the island) for the final plunging chute. This chute ends in a fairly deep pool next to a large rock face. Recover on the island if necessary.

Whitewater buffs will find the 4 miles starting at the GA 115 bridge (H) the Chattahoochee's most exciting. Rapids are frequent, lengthy, and challenging enough to keep paddlers occupied. The entrance to Buck Shoals, the first rapid of note, is marked by an island not far from the put-in. One quarter mile of fairly continuous Class II water awaits. Buck Shoals has eaten experienced decked boaters at extremely high water levels, when waves may exceed 4 feet in height. At low or average water levels, one encounters a more technical run. The next named rapid is Three Ledges. A large granite outcropping on the right indicates the imminence of this drop. Many consider this to be the most fun or challenging series of rapids of this section. The traditional route is to run just to the left of the flat protruding rock at the first ledge, moving to the center for the second and third ledges. The hole at the base of this rapid is a great place to play. The next long pool, with granite outcroppings on the right, denotes the approach to Horseshoe Rapid (Class II+). A long, low ledge of rocks forces the river to hook around them, thus giving Horseshoe its name. Enter on the left, and be ready to cut hard back to the right. Just below Horseshoe the Soque River enters, followed shortly by a small creek falls; the Duncan Bridge Road take-out (I) is ahead.

The 9-mile section below Duncan Bridge Road offers a few Class I–II rapids similar in character to those above the bridge, and the scenery remains quite good. This section encompasses the entry of Mossy Creek on river right—a potential steep creek run into the Chattahoochee. The state owns a parcel of land at the mouth of the creek. Some good play spots are found in the last mile above Mud Creek at high levels. Paddling up Mud Creek to the bridge is the best take-out before the current stops in the backwaters of Lake Lanier. Once in the backwaters, forward progress is hard work.

SHUTTLE: The take-out for the GA 115 to Duncan Bridge run is reached by going north on I-985, which turns into GA 365,

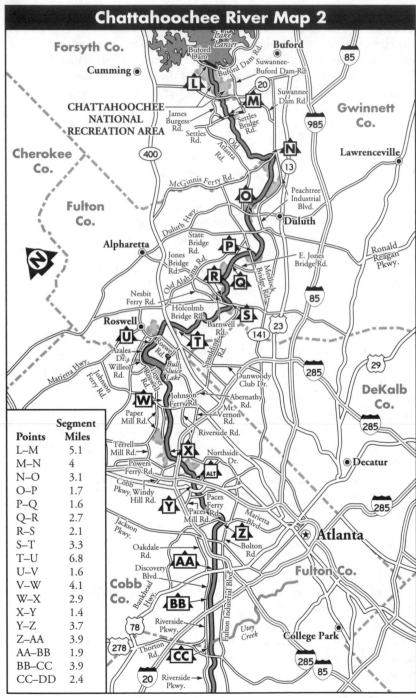

Chattahoochee River Map 2

Points	Segment Miles
L–M	5.1
M–N	4
N–O	3.1
O–P	1.7
P–Q	1.6
Q–R	2.7
R–S	2.1
S–T	3.3
T–U	6.8
U–V	1.6
V–W	4.1
W–X	2.9
X–Y	1.4
Y–Z	3.7
Z–AA	3.9
AA–BB	1.9
BB–CC	3.9
CC–DD	2.4

turning left onto GA 384, Duncan Bridge Road, and following it to the far side of the river before turning right into the outfitters parking lot. There is a small fee for parking here; paddlers typically use the shuttle service to GA 115 since the deluxe put-in at the bridge is on land owned by the outfitter. There is no public parking there. The GA 255 access is on the river-left, or Habersham County, side of the river only. Do not disturb the property owner on the river-right side. Parking here and upstream at the Sautee Creek put-in is tight; shuttle service is available to these points.

GAUGE: There is a gauge in the river 100–200 yards upstream of the GA 115 bridge. It is affixed to an old bridge piling located upstream of a small shoal on river left. Using this gauge, the recommended levels for this section are a scrapey minimum of 0.8 and a maximum of 6.0. The river has been run at levels higher than 6 feet by expert boaters. Levels are also easily acquired online from the USGS Web site by referencing the gauge near Cornelia. The gauge is located at Duncan Bridge Road, below the confluence with the Soque River; readings may not correlate with flows originating from the upper sections of the Chattahoochee. Keeping this in mind, the minimum for this section is 800–900 cfs. The local outfitter can provide information on levels over the phone.

BUFORD DAM TO SWEETWATER CREEK (METRO HOOCH)

class	I–II
length	56.2 mi
time	Up to 6 days
gauge	Web
level	900 cfs
gradient	<3 fpm (11)
scenery	B–D

DESCRIPTION: The Chattahoochee through the Piedmont from Buford Dam to Franklin (industrial Atlanta excepted), is pleasant paddling. Modest bluffs and some exposed rock combine with a young forest dominated by pignut hickory, river birch, tulip poplar, sassafras, water oak, black walnut, box elder, and loblolly pine that approaches and retreats from the river's edge. Undergrowth consists of honeysuckle, various asters, Christmas fern, trumpet creeper, and river cane. Throughout metropolitan Atlanta, the Chattahoochee National Recreation Area protects a patchwork of nearly 10,000 acres of metropolitan riverside land.

Starting at the public park below Buford Dam, the river flows between clay banks of 6–10 feet as it winds through the Piedmont en route to Atlanta. Tree-lined and pleasant, the river averages 120 feet in width and flows with a moderate current. Water is clear with a greenish cast in this stretch during most of

the year. Small ripples and occasional tiny shoals keep the paddling interesting.

Two miles below GA 141 (P), at Medlock Bridge Road, are the backwaters of Morgan Falls Dam. Though the water is slack for the next 16 miles, from this point to the dam, passage through this wealthy suburban residential area is nonetheless interesting because some of Atlanta's finest residential architecture is nestled among the hills and bluffs that border the river. Downstream of the Morgan Falls Dam the parade of homes continues for about 4 more miles.

The short and popular whitewater section known as the "Metro Hooch" begins at the Powers Island put-in above I-285 (X). Half a mile below the I-285 crossing, two stairstep shoals of low Class II difficulty keep paddlers awake. With the exception of the apartment complexes found by the floodplain at the beginning of this run, the scenery offers a refreshing and surprising respite from the nearby asphalt and engines. Rocky bluffs and dense forest rise from the river, creating a natural oasis that recalls the river's native roots. Shoals arrive at equal intervals throughout the run. The last bend introduces first the sounds, then the sights of the city as the I-75 bridge comes into view. The common take-out for this section at the Paces Mill Recreation Area (Y) arrives quickly after passing beneath the bridge.

Continuing downstream, small shoals persist until 1.5 miles below Paces Ferry Road, where there are two partial dams. Both can be run without danger. A clear downstream V marks the route through the first, while the second should be run on the far right. Just upstream of Nancy Creek's entry on the left is a park and play spot known as the Wave. Access this spot via Atlanta Road (Z), paddling upstream from the Nancy Creek confluence.

Water quality worsens as the river progresses through Atlanta. Below the Wave, the Chattahoochee is bordered by sewage treatment facilities and a congested industrial corridor complete with factories, junkyards, and freight yards. Of all sections, this is the most abused, and it smells of it.

SHUTTLE: The Metro Hooch segment is nestled between a web of roads and interstates that offer easy access no matter which direction you come from. The take-out is at the West Palisades/Paces Mill Recreation Area located on US 41 south of I-285 on the north side of the river. To get to the put-in from there, take US 41 north and turn right at Cumberland Boulevard. Cross over I-75 and turn right onto Akers Mill Road. Turn left at the first opportunity to cross under I-285, then take an immediate right onto the access road on the other side. The entrance to the

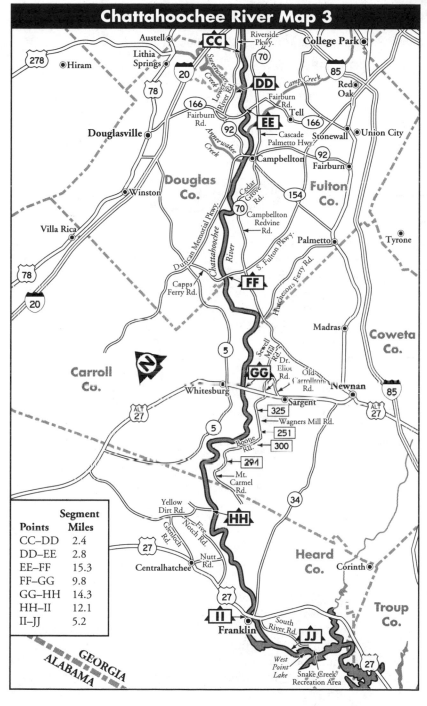

Chattahoochee River Map 3

Austell
Riverside Pkwy.
CC
College Park
278
Hiram
Lithia Springs
70
20
78
DD
Camp Creek
85
Red Oak
Fairburn Rd.
166
92
Fairburn Rd.
Tell
EE
166
Douglasville
Cascade Palmetto Hwy.
Stonewall
Union City
Campbellton
92
Fairburn
Douglas Co.
Cedar Grove Rd.
154
Fulton Co.
Winston
70
Campbellton Redvine Rd.
Villa Rica
Palmetto
Tyrone
78
S. Fulton Pkwy.
20
Capps Ferry Rd.
FF
Hutcheson's Ferry Rd.
Madras
Coweta Co.
5
Sewell Mill Rd.
Dr. Eliot Rd.
Old Carrollton Rd.
GG
Carroll Co.
Whitesburg
Newnan
85
Sargent
ALT 27
325
Wagners Mill Rd.
5
251
Boone Rd.
300
291
Mt. Carmel Rd.
34
Yellow Dirt Rd.
HH
Glenloch Rd.
27
Nutt Rd.
Heard Co.
Corinth
Centralhatchee
27
Troup Co.
II
South River Rd.
JJ
Franklin
27
GEORGIA
ALABAMA
West Point Lake
Snake Creek Recreation Area
27

Points	Segment Miles
CC–DD	2.4
DD–EE	2.8
EE–FF	15.3
FF–GG	9.8
GG–HH	14.3
HH–II	12.1
II–JJ	5.2

Cochran Shoals/Powers Island Recreation Area is on the left after crossing the river. Put-in at the small channel between the island and the shore, or at the larger main channel.

GAUGE: Flows on this section are controlled by releases from Buford Dam. Using the USGS gauge for the Chattahoochee at Atlanta, 1,500 cfs makes the rapids in the Metro Hooch section interesting; from 2500–5000 cfs, they are partially to completely washed out. The minimum is 850 cfs. Higher flows carry more pollution—have the skills necessary to avoid a swim or roll.

SWEETWATER CREEK TO COLUMBUS

class	I (II)
length	59.5 mi
time	Up to 6 days
gauge	Web
level	Unknown
gradient	<2 fpm
scenery	B-

DESCRIPTION: Downstream of Atlanta, agricultural tableland and forest alternately cradle the stream. The river's course tends toward long, straight sections followed by broad, looping bends. Shoals are intermittent and usually consist of small ledges that are straightforward and rarely exceed Class I+ in difficulty. An exception is Bush Head Shoals, a legitimate Class II section about 3 miles upstream of Franklin in Heard County. The best route here is to the right around the large island at the top of the shoals, moving to the middle of the stream at the downstream base of the island to run the lower shoals. Daniel Shoals, farther downstream, is borderline Class II and should present no difficulty. Below Daniel Shoals are the city of Franklin and West Point Lake.

Released at West Point Dam, the Chattahoochee moves from one impoundment to another all the way to Columbus, where four dams within a 3-mile section of river provide a disappointing finale for this dam- and power plant–infested section of the Chattahoochee. Slack water, dull scenery, and an abundance of portages combine to make a paddle trip suitable only for bad dreams. Between Franklin and Columbus (where the river passes from dam to dam) the riverbanks diminish in height marking the river's transition from the Piedmont to the Coastal Plain.

In downtown Columbus below the 13th Street bridge, a Class II–III shoal downstream of the Eagle and Phenix Dam forms a park-and-play spot. When there is water flowing over the dam, sizable surfing waves, holes, and wave trains are to be found. The dam has been purchased by a private party with intention of breaching it (in addition to the next dam upstream), liberating Coweta Falls from where it sits beneath the pool.

Chattahoochee River Map 4

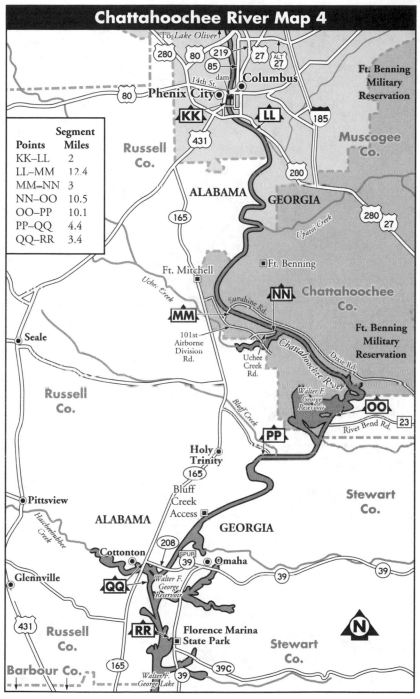

Segment
Points	**Miles**
KK–LL	2
LL–MM	12.4
MM–NN	3
NN–OO	10.5
OO–PP	10.1
PP–QQ	4.4
QQ–RR	3.4

To *Lake Oliver*

280 80 219 27 ALT 27

85

dam

14th St. **Columbus**

Phenix City

KK   **LL**

Ft. Benning
Military
Reservation

80

431

Russell Co.

200

Muscogee Co.

185

ALABAMA   **GEORGIA**

165

Upatoi Creek

280 27

Ft. Mitchell

■ Ft. Benning

Uchee Creek

Sunshine Rd.

NN   **Chattahoochee Co.**

MM

Seale

101st
Airborne
Division
Rd.

Uchee
Creek
Rd.

Chattahoochee River

Dixie Rd.

Ft. Benning
Military
Reservation

Russell Co.

Walter F. George Reservoir

OO   23

River Bend Rd.

Bluff Creek

PP

Holy Trinity

165

Bluff
Creek
Access ■

Stewart Co.

Pittsview

Hatchechubbee Creek

ALABAMA   **GEORGIA**

208

Cottonton

SPUR 39

● **Omaha**

39

39

Glennville

QQ   *Walter F. George Reservoir*

431

RR   ■ **Florence Marina State Park**

Russell Co.

Stewart Co.

165

Walter F. George Lake   39   39C

Barbour Co.

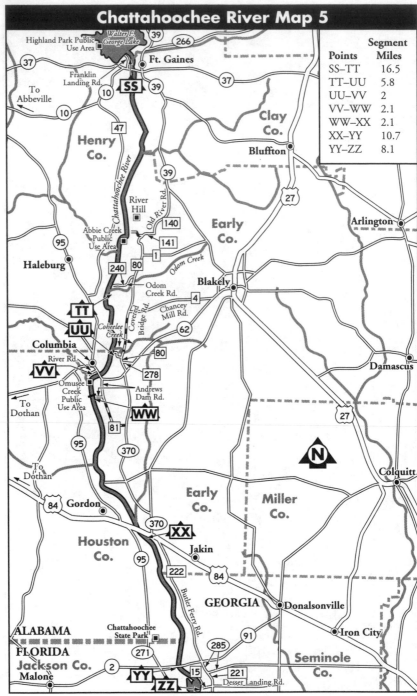

Chattahoochee River Map 5

Segment	
Points	**Miles**
SS–TT	16.5
TT–UU	5.8
UU–VV	2
VV–WW	2.1
WW–XX	2.1
XX–YY	10.7
YY–ZZ	8.1

SHUTTLE: To reach the highest access point for this section at Sweetwater Creek, take Exit 44 from I-20 west of Atlanta, turning south onto GA 6. Continue to a right-hand turn onto Riverside Parkway; access is ahead at the bridge over the creek. Lower access points are most easily reached from GA 166, GA 5, or US 27.

GAUGE: The section above West Point Lake is runnable if Buford Dam is releasing water. The online USGS gauge for the Columbus park-and-play spot is at US 280; levels, controlled by Bartlett's Ferry Dam, vary throughout most days. Minimum and maximum levels on this gauge are unknown; check feasibility visually if you live in the area. The LaGrange Fisheries Office at (706) 845-4180 can provide additional information on floating or fishing this section.

COLUMBUS TO LAKE SEMINOLE

class	I
length	93.1 mi
time	Up to 2 weeks
gauge	Web
level	N/A
gradient	<1 fpm
scenery	C

DESCRIPTION: Flowing south from Columbus in Muscogee County, the Chattahoochee River is impounded frequently as it winds through a farming plateau sprinkled with industry. Its banks average 4–8 feet high and are tree-lined. Towboats and other industrial traffic move up and down the 300-foot-wide stream. From Columbus the Chattahoochee moves down to the Walter F. George Reservoir and from there to Lake Seminole, where it meets the Flint to form the Apalachicola River. The level of difficulty from Columbus to Lake Seminole is Class I; powerboat traffic is the primary hazard to navigation.

SHUTTLE: See map. GA 39 parallels the east side of the upper portion of the river in this section; most access points are easily reached from it. Below Blakely, use GA 62, GA 370, US 84, and GA 91 in addition to GA 39.

GAUGE: Runnable all year. For more information, call the Albany Fisheries Office at (229) 430-4256.

The Persistent, Wild Chattahoochee
— by Joe Cook

When we first told friends and family about our plans to canoe the 540-mile length of the Chattahoochee River system in one long trip, many were incredulous.

"People die down here on the river. Are you sure you want to do this?" we were told. What's more, previous incarnations of this guidebook offered little encouragement, describing portions of the Chattahoochee as a "paddle trip suitable only for bad dreams."

Naive or brazen, or some combination of the two, we pursued our dream of seeing the whole river system. In July of 1995, after 100 days on the Chattahoochee and Florida's Apalachicola River, we triumphantly plunged our canoe in the Gulf of Mexico.

In retrospect, parts of the trip were nightmarish indeed—swarming gnats on Lake Seminole, biting yellow flies in the swamps of Apalachicola and no less than a dozen portages around the river's many dams—but for every hardship, we were rewarded tenfold, with brilliant, playful whitewater in the headwaters, peaceful flat water and shoals in the Piedmont, and the moss-draped, mist-shrouded waters of the coastal plain.

Perhaps the episode that best sums up the trip is our experience paddling what has been referred to as "Dead River"—the 70-mile stretch of the Chattahoochee between Atlanta's Peachtree Creek and West Point Lake

where for years metro Atlanta's treated and untreated sewage has fouled the waters. Despite cautionary words from various guidebooks, we found the so-called "Dead River" very much alive.

Yes, detritus from the city of four million could be seen around each bend, but as we headed west into the sunset, the riverside trees shook in the spring breeze, drawing our attention away from the trash. Billowy white cottonwood seeds began drifting across the river like snow, the sun bathing the seeds in beautiful light. It was a peaceful scene that seemed strangely out of place in this troubled stretch of river. It occurred to us then that paddling the Chattahoochee is like simultaneously paddling through a national park and an industrial park.

To this day, some of my favorite portions of the Chattahoochee lie within that 70-mile stretch below Atlanta. And, it is ironic that perhaps the most breathtaking section of the river—the high, rocky cliffs of the Palisades in the Chattahoochee River National Recreation Area—lie inside Atlanta's infamous I-285 perimeter highway.

From the headwaters to Lake Seminole, that is the paradox of the Chattahoochee. It has been used, abused, and infringed upon, yet it maintains its beauty. There is not a section along its length that is unworthy of exploration . . . and preservation.

Joe Cook is co-author of *River Song: A Journey Down the Chattahoochee and Apalachicola Rivers*

SOQUE RIVER

The Soque is a northern Chattahoochee River tributary with two lives. The top section, a Class I–II mountain stream near the border of the Chattahoochee National Forest, serves up a delightful tour of mountain forests on a flow volume similar to the upper Chestatee, with less dramatic thrills than the nearby upper Chattahoochee. As the river passes through the town of Clarkesville and Habersham Mills below, it metamorphoses from a cool, clear, trout-supporting flow to a warmer, murky one that stains the Chattahoochee brown as it joins the larger stream.

MAPS: Lake Burton, Clarksville Northeast, Clarksville (USGS); Habersham (County)

GA 356 TO GA 197

class	I–II
length	7.0 mi
time	4.0 hr
gauge	None
level	N/A
gradient	18 fpm
scenery	B

DESCRIPTION: The prettiest stretch of the Soque lies in this section. The river dances nimbly over its rocky bottom as it speeds through the mature forest, fragrant with the rich aroma of the ancient Appalachians. Hemlocks and rhododendrons cradle the banks. Rapids in the Class I range start the first mile of the trip, building to numerous Class II rapids that make up the meat of the run. The intensity of the drops falls again to Class I during the final third, as the take-out is neared.

It is worth noting that paddling has been discouraged in the area for years by the largest local landowner, whose residence sits atop a prominent bluff overlooking the river in this section, enabling efficient policing of river usage. Ownership of this property is in a state of transition, which may result in conditions more hospitable toward paddlers. Strictly limit your on-the-ground activities to the public right-of-way found at state highways, and, as usual, leave no trace behind. Warning: The surrounding community believes that this river is not open to paddling, and is well-coached in how to communicate this. Some believe that this is motivated by an upscale trout-fishing resort on the river. Unless and until the situation changes, expect to be challenged.

Soque River

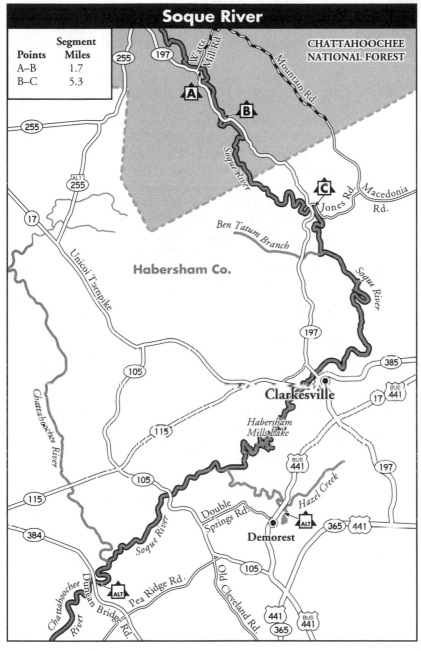

Points	Segment Miles
A–B	1.7
B–C	5.3

CHATTAHOOCHEE NATIONAL FOREST

Watts Mill Rd.

Mountain Rd.

255

197

A

B

Soque River

C

Jones Rd.

Macedonia Rd.

255

ALT 255

17

Ben Tatum Branch

Habersham Co.

Soque River

197

Unicoi Turnpike

Chattahoochee River

105

385

Clarkesville

17 441

BUS 441

Habersham Mills Lake

115

BUS 441

197

Hazel Creek

105

ALT

365 441

Demorest

Double Springs Rd.

115

384

Soque River

ALT

Pea Ridge Rd.

Old Cleveland Rd.

105

441

BUS 441

365

Duncan Bridge Rd.

Chattahoochee River

Habersham Mills owns a big chunk of property on the river, south of Clarkesville. There are two dams on the river here, connected by a dry stretch of river that only runs during heavy rains. The lack of flow and public access points eliminates paddling through this segment. Access is also not available at GA 105, where a new bridge rises high above the streambed. For the determined, Hazel Creek provides an exciting Class III+ approach to the lower section of the Soque. Putting in at Main Street (US 441 Bus.) in Demorest results in a 9.2-mile run to the Duncan Bridge take-out on the Chattahoochee: 3.2 miles down Hazel Creek, 4.9 miles on the lower Soque, and 1.1 miles on the Chattahoochee. A dam is located where Hazel meets the Soque, and a rapid reminiscent of Bull Sluice is found below that. As with the upper section, keep in mind that you will be passing private property along the way, and that landowners in the area feel strongly about their river being off-limits to boaters. Confrontations are not unusual. As the locals recite: "Try the upper Hooch. The rapids are better." Maybe that's not such bad advice.

SHUTTLE: From Clarkesville, take GA 197 north to a right-hand turn onto Ben Jones Road (C). This is the take-out for this section. To get to the put-in, return to GA 197 and continue north to a right-hand turn onto Watts Mill Road. Access is also available where GA 197 crosses the river between these two points.

GAUGE: There is no gauge on this river. If the Chattahoochee gauge at GA 115 is registering 1.5 feet, the Soque is worthy of scouting to determine its runnability. The maximum is 6 feet.

MOSSY CREEK

Mossy Creek is a steep little run found between the rolling hills of the Georgia Piedmont and the Appalachian Mountains. Draining into the mighty Chattahoochee River below the popular whitewater stretch, Mossy attracted little attention until it was "discovered" by local boaters only a few years ago. The unassuming put-in, which resembles most flat pastoral piedmont streams, only furthers the likelihood of folks ignoring this creek. Between the put-in and take-out, Mossy Creek passes over numerous Class III and IV drops. The creek gets even harder when the water gets high, becoming a series of 7-foot waves and huge river-wide holes linked together in long continuous rapids.

MAPS: Leaf, Lula (USGS); Habersham (County)

NEW BRIDGE ROAD TO MUD CREEK OFF OF PEA RIDGE ROAD

class	III–IV (V)
length	2.2 mi (plus 4.5 on the Chatta-hoochee)
time	4 hr
gauge	None
level	N/A
gradient	80 fpm
scenery	B-

DESCRIPTION: Mossy Creek is full of waterfalls and slides and can be truly impressive at flood stage. It starts with 0.25 miles or so of flat-water and Class I shoals. Then comes a cute little warm-up ledge, followed around the corner by an impressive horizon line. It's impressive because the river completely disappears from sight, and in the distance, way, way, way below you, is a meadow with a water wheel. Don't let this horizon line intimidate you. The first rapid, Waterwheel, drops 40 feet or so and is made up of three sliding falls, each bigger and tougher than the previous, but each with a small recovery eddy. It can be run blind, and can be run right, left, or middle. Take note of the rebar on the right. The sluice leads to an apparently functional waterwheel and mill. At high levels Waterwheel becomes one single drop with a keeper hydraulic. If you jettison here at flood levels, your boat will be gone for good. At least it's an easy walk out up the driveway.

There is a nice pool next to the mill, but at the end of this is an even more awesome horizon line marking Ratchet Rapid. It wouldn't hurt to scout here first. Ratchet begins with a 6- or 7-foot vertical drop, which is followed by a series of ledges, each with its own hydraulic. The typical run is far right, cutting river left across the face, dropping into each ledge wherever. If you start far right, you must boof (left or right) to avoid pinning. Ratchet can also be run starting from the far left at the top. The rapid ends in a large pool at the bottom.

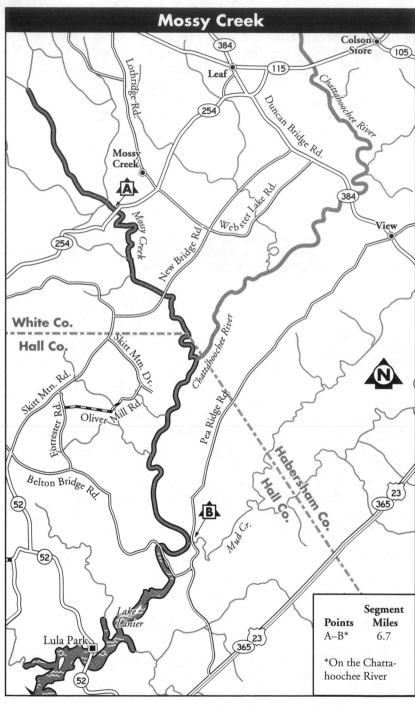

Mossy Creek

Colson Store

105

384

Leaf   115

Chattahoochee River

Lothridge Rd.

254

Duncan Bridge Rd.

Mossy Creek

A

Webster Lake Rd.

384

View

Mossy Creek

254

New Bridge Rd.

White Co.

Hall Co.

Skitt Mtn. Dr.

Chattahoochee River

N

Skitt Mtn. Rd.

Pea Ridge Rd.

Forrester Rd.

Oliver Mill Rd.

Belton Bridge Rd.

Habersham Co.
Hall Co.

52

23

365

52

B

Mud Cr.

Lake Lanier

Lula Park

23

365

52

Points	Segment Miles
A–B*	6.7

*On the Chatta-
hoochee River

The next mile or so following Ratchet includes smaller falls and shoals. Then comes the BIG DROP. . . known as Broken Butt Falls. It will be obvious, and you should seriously consider scouting first. Actually, this advice is superfluous, since the horizon line is truly monstrous and scouting will come naturally. Broken Butt Falls drops at least 30 feet at slightly less of an angle than Oceana in the Tallulah Gorge. The fun run is far left where there are two launching ramps. The smarter run starts on river right and cuts across the face towards the left. There are several little ledges that will help you accomplish the traverse.

A river-wide natural dam and straightforward drop follow Broken Butt Falls. Then come some more drops, a boulder garden, and attendant sieves. The boulder garden is technical, has several interesting slot moves through undercuts, and continues all the way to the Hooch. When the water is high, this section becomes more difficult than the preceding slides. It will take another 45 miles on a relatively flat Hooch (two fun little rapids) to reach the take-out at Muddy Creek.

SHUTTLE: From Gainesville, take US 23/GA 365 north, turning left onto Belton Bridge Road. Follow to Pea Ridge Road and turn right. The best take-out is where this road crosses Mud Creek. To get to the put-in, return to Belton Bridge Road and turn right, crossing the Chattahoochee. Turn right onto Forrester Road, then right again onto Skitts Mountain Road for 1.7 miles, and right onto New Bridge Road. Mossy Creek is the first creek crossing on New Bridge Road, 0.9 miles ahead.

GAUGE: The Georgia USGS Internet site lists real-time data for the Chattahoochee River near Helen. Runnable levels commence at 3 feet, up to 8 feet. Alternatively, water should cover the footings of the river-left piling at the put-in bridge. If Mossy looks too high, it is. Mossy Creek is usually runnable October through June, after heavy or sustained rain.

CHESTATEE RIVER

Easily reached from Atlanta, the Chestatee is best known for provid-ing a mild and beautiful journey through the mountain foothills. Its headwaters are in northern Lumpkin County, northeast of Dahlonega in the same hills the Cherokees first called home. As it flows to the south and into Lake Lanier, the river now plays host to a crop of newer residents. Some reaches still feel relatively remote, resulting at times in a pleasantly secluded paddling experience. The river is presented in two sections, the lower being the most popular and hospitable. The upper section encompasses most of the significant rapids of the river.

MAPS: Neels Gap, Dahlonega, Murrayville (USGS); Lumpkin (County)

US 129 (TURNERS CORNER) TO COPPER MINE

class	I–III (IV)
length	14.7 mi
time	1–2 days
gauge	Web, phone, visual
level	2.1 ft
gradient	19 fpm (60+)
scenery	B

DESCRIPTION: The scenery is beautiful and the rapids can be challenging, but running this section of the river presents a frustrating problem. The stream flows entirely through private property, and landowners have been unfriendly to hostile in the past. In the early 1980s, there was a county ordinance passed that prohibited floating above Copper Mine. Signs from this era remain at Turners Corner and at Damascus Church Road. Enforcing this ordinance is questionable, but discretion is advised.

Once on the water, the scenery and small rapids that mark the first 3 miles of this section are quite pleasant. Damascus Church Bridge (B), also known as Tate Bridge, marks the end of the upper valley. At this point the river begins to drop at a brisk pace, averaging just over 24 feet per mile, past the Town Creek Church Bridge (C), also referred to as the Garnett Bridge, and on to Grindle Bridge (D). Class II rapids are frequent and can be challenging. Play spots start developing here at 2.5 feet, and get better at 3.5 feet.

Below Grindle Bridge is the most significant drop of the river, Class IV Grindle Falls. The falls cascade approximately 60 feet in stages to the river bed below. Routes exist on both the left and right sides of the island at the top. Scout your choice and verify that the channels aren't blocked by trees. Portaging here is difficult; river left is the easiest side. The falls would be a beautiful spot to linger, but the banks are private property, so make your impact minimal and move on.

Chestatee River

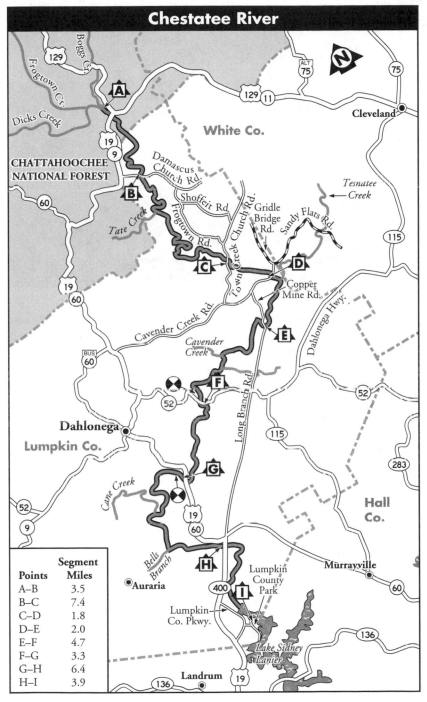

Points	Segment Miles
A–B	3.5
B–C	7.4
C–D	1.8
D–E	2.0
E–F	4.7
F–G	3.3
G–H	6.4
H–I	3.9

photo © Rob Maxwell

Taking a far-left line on Grindle Falls on the Chestatee

Tesnatee Creek, a major tributary, enters from the left just below Grindle Falls. About 1.5 miles farther downstream you will see a concrete bridge. Just upstream from this bridge is a small man-made dam about 2 feet high. There are a few breaks in the dam, so running it is usually no problem. Pull to either shore just past the bridge to scout Copper Mine Rapid, a good Class III drop. The best route is near the center and just to the left of a large boulder that splits the stream. Other routes are possible, however.

Access here is either at river left on the upstream side of the bridge, or below the bridge via the dirt road that reaches river left downstream of the bridge. The dirt road is privately owned and frequently blocked to vehicles. Regardless of which option you choose, parking along the highway near the top of the dirt road is advisable.

SHUTTLE: From Cumming, take GA 400 north to the intersection with GA 60. Continue straight ahead through this intersection; you are now on Long Branch Road. Continue straight through the next intersection (with GA 52); the Copper Mine take-out is ahead on the left before the bridge. There is a dirt road that leads to the river and parking is tolerated at the bottom of this road. For the uppermost put-in for this section, continue north on the same road. At its end, turn left onto Cavender Creek Road, then right onto Town Creek Church Road. There is intermediate access where this road crosses the river at Garnett Bridge (C). Turn left 0.6 miles past the river onto Frogtown

Road (marked "To Hwy 19"). A left-hand turn 1.5 miles ahead will keep you on Frogtown until it dead-ends into Damascus Church Road. Turn left here and proceed to US 19; along the way you'll pass the Tate Bridge access point (B). A right-hand turn on US 19 will take you to Turners Corner a little over 2 miles ahead. Turn left onto US 129; the best access in the area is on the left as the river and road near each other.

GAUGE: The USGS Web site provides data for the Chestatee near Dahlonega, downstream of the upper section. Minimum for the upper valley is 2.1 feet. Levels of 2.3 to 2.4 feet are needed to make paddling below Damascus Church Road feasible. A visual gauge readable from the river is located at GA 52; a staff gauge is found farther downstream at the local outfitter's shop, south of Dahlonega. The outfitter can provide river levels over the phone.

COPPER MINE TO LAKE LANIER

class	I–II (III)
length	18.3 mi
time	1–2 days
gauge	Web, phone, visual
level	1.0 ft
gradient	4 fpm
scenery	B

DESCRIPTION: This section starts with Copper Mine rapid, a Class III drop described above. It is possible to put in at the large pool directly below the rapid. Go to the right of the island downstream of the rapid, as the left is quite shallow.

Below Copper Mine, the river's drop slows to an average of only 13 feet per mile down to the GA 52 bridge (F). Natural scenery remains outstanding, but private residences crowd the view from the river at times. One rapid in this section is worthy of mention. It has become known as Blasted Rock Rapid because of the many sharp rocks in the stream resulting from dynamite blasting in the area many years ago. A slender island divides the stream and the rapid may be run on either side. Be cautious of deadfall on the left. This one becomes more formidable as the water gets higher, but at moderate water levels it is a Class II.

Soon after Blasted Rock Rapid you will pass an active granite quarry on the right. This indicates that you are near GA 52, another access point. The river becomes much smoother and slower from this point until it crosses GA 60. The scenery remains pleasant, consisting mostly of farmland with some residential developments.

Below the GA 60 bridge (G), the river follows the highway corridor closely for 0.5 miles and then veers away from the road into the forest. This section is a good one for family day-trips where beginners or small children are present. The scenery is

photo © Rob Maxwell

The far-right line of Copper Mine Rapid on the Chestatee

excellent, and none of the rapids exceeds Class I. A few hours of paddling will bring you to the next access at the top end of GA 400 (H).

From this point to the backwaters of Lake Lanier, you should be prepared to do a lot of paddling or have plenty of daylight left if you plan to drift. The gradient eases to less than 5 feet per mile for the remainder of the trip, and the current is quite slow as it continues into Lake Lanier where it stops altogether. The riverside environment remains mostly woodland to the Lumpkin County Park on Lake Lanier, the final access point for the Chestatee.

SHUTTLE: From GA 400 south of Dahlonega, turn to the east onto Burnt Stand Road and follow signs to Lumpkin County Park. To get to the highest put-in, see directions to the take-out for the upper section. Alternate access points are available at GA 400 (dirt road at the southwest corner of the bridge), GA 60 (on the west side of the road after the bridge or farther downstream at the outfitters), and GA 52. Camping may still be possible within the lower section, but leaving a car overnight at the Copper Mine put-in is discouraged due to evidence of nighttime activity there.

GAUGE: See preceding section. The minimum level for this section is 1 foot; the lower stretches can be run down to 0.6 feet. The maximum for open boats is 3 feet and up to flood stage for decked boats.

TESNATEE CREEK

A tributary of the Chestatee north of Atlanta, Tesnatee Creek provides an excellent Class I to II day-trip when water conditions are favorable. Draping hemlocks hang over the stream in places, and drifts of mountain laurel cluster with rhododendrons at the banks, making for a spectacular late-spring display. Occasional 20- to 30-foot-high rock faces add to the scenic beauty of this untouched little creek.

MAPS: Cleveland, Dahlonega (USGS); White, Lumpkin (County)

TOWN CREEK ROAD TO OLD COPPER MINE ROAD ON THE CHESTATEE RIVER

class	I-II (III)
length	7.2 mi
time	4 hr
gauge	None
level	N/A
gradient	25 fpm
scenery	B+

DESCRIPTION: Starting near Cleveland, Georgia, only 7 miles of the stream are navigable. The average gradient, however, is over 25 feet per mile, so the pace is usually lively. Most of the rapids do not exceed a Class II difficulty at normal water levels. There is one man-made hazard: a dam that is part of a refurbished power plant located approximately 2.5 miles below the bridge at Gene Nix Road (B). The easiest portage around the dam is on the right. Tesnatee Falls, a 20-foot drop, is immediately below the dam. If running the falls, scout right and portage the dam on the left to set up for the run, avoiding the rock outcropping on the far right.

Soon thereafter, the Chestatee River joins in from the right. An easy paddle up the Chestatee takes you to the base of scenic Grindle Falls. The take-out for the trip is located 1.6 miles down the Chestatee at the bridge above Copper Mine rapid. Exit the stream on river left above or below the rapid, a moderate Class III drop. The Copper Mine rapid is described in the first section of the Chestatee River (see page 198).

SHUTTLE: From Cumming, take GA 400 north to the intersection with GA 60. Continue straight ahead through this intersection; you are now on Long Branch Road. Continue straight through the next intersection (with GA 52); the take-out is ahead on the left before the bridge. To reach the put-in, continue north to where the road ends. Turn right onto Cavender Creek Road. After crossing the Chestatee again at Grimes Bridge, turn right onto Dumas Road (the road name eventually changes to Sandy Flats). This road nears the river, providing an intermediate access point (C), then pulls away. At the stop sign,

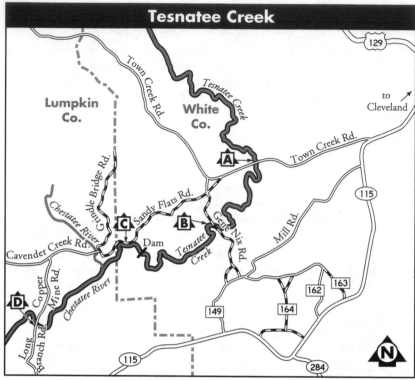

Tesnatee Creek

continue straight ahead (or turn right for the other mid-run access at B). When Sandy Flats ends, turn right onto Town Creek Road; access is available at the business on the left before the river. Ask permission before putting in.

GAUGE: There is no gauge on the creek. Use Chestatee River levels to get a rough idea of feasibility, and scout the river at access points before putting in. A level of 2.2 on the USGS Chestatee Internet gauge is a good minimum for the Tesnatee.

BIG CREEK (a.k.a. VICKERY CREEK)

Big Creek is a tributary of the Chattahoochee River in the northern suburbs of Atlanta. Belying its metropolitan location, the stream is narrow and intimate as it flows between brush-covered banks for most of its length. The sights and sounds of the city are never far away, however. The section described below provides a convenient, although brief, Class II–III paddling experience. Nearly 2 miles of creek is followed by an optional 1 mile paddle down the plains of the Chattahoochee.

MAPS: Roswell, Mountain Park (USGS); Fulton (County)

OXBOW ROAD TO AZALEA DRIVE ON THE CHATTAHOOCHEE RIVER

class	II–III
length	3.0 mi (includes 1.0 on the Chattahoochee)
time	2.5 hr
gauge	Web
level	55 cfs
gradient	42 fpm
scenery	C

DESCRIPTION: Big Creek passes through the residential fringes south of Roswell and thus is no stranger to development. Houses overlook its banks in several sections, and aqueducts feeding water to Roswell cross over the stream occasionally. Though aqueducts present more of an aesthetic blight than a danger, be careful when approaching them at higher water levels. Water quality is typical of urban streams.

The oldest development on the creek is a scenic wonder: a 30-foot-high stone dam that was part of the textile mill complex built in 1838. A mandatory portage of the dam is recommended in order to avoid bodily harm. The rapids below the dam are technical at any time and become more difficult in high water. Normally Class II, when the water is up they approach Class III in difficulty.

The National Park Service maintains a small park with hiking trails near the mouth of the creek that can be used as a take-out. Otherwise, paddle a placid mile of the Chattahoochee and take-out downstream on the river's right.

SHUTTLE: From the Roswell Road bridge over the Chattahoochee, turn west onto Azalea Drive. Georgia Power maintains a public boat ramp on the Chattahoochee River less than a mile ahead on the left. The alternate take-out is in the Chattahoochee River National Recreation Area, 0.1 mile east of Roswell Road on Riverside Road. From either take-out, return to Roswell/Atlanta Road and turn north toward Roswell. Continue 1.3 miles to a right turn onto Oxbow Road. The put-in is at a small park on the right.

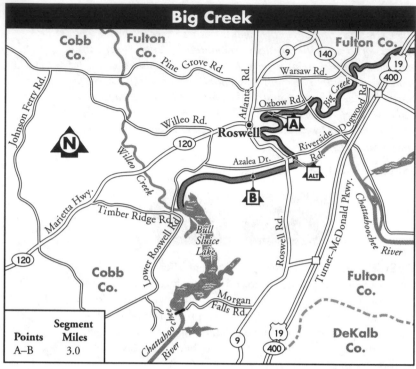

Big Creek

Points	Segment Miles
A–B	3.0

GAUGE: The USGS Web site provides real-time data for the gauge located 7 miles upstream at Kimball Bridge Road in Alpharetta. The minimum runnable level is 55 cfs. The maximum is 250 cfs for open boats and flood stage for decked boats.

SOPE CREEK

If it is raining mid-week and you're an advanced Atlanta-area pad-dler who can take off from work at a realistic time, consider looking at Sope Creek. It takes a lot of water to get the creek up; too much and it jumps out of the banks and develops into a continuous Class V run, with predatory river-wide holes. But when the conditions are right, it's one of the best III–IV whitewater creek runs in Atlanta. You'll want to keep your mouth shut on this one and take a good shower when you get home; the water's filthy.

MAPS: Sandy Springs (USGS); Cobb, Fulton (County)

LOWER ROSWELL ROAD TO COCHRAN SHOALS RECREATION AREA ON THE CHATTAHOOCHEE RIVER

class	III–IV (V)
length	2.5 mi plus 2 on the Chattahoochee
time	2.5 hr
gauge	Web
level	5.0 ft or 300 cfs
gradient	45 fpm
scenery	C

DESCRIPTION: Before you put-in, spend the time to scout the drops above and below the bridge at Paper Mill Road (B). The creek can come up faster than it will register on the USGS Web site—too much water and it quickly becomes more than anyone interested in a Class III–IV run bargained for. Visual scouting can confirm if you're in the sweet spot. If the hole immediately below the bridge is the only thing that looks dangerous, the creek is running at a moderate level. When the water is really high, a river-wide hole develops on the upstream side of the bridge. Paired with the downstream hole that turns into a keeper at these levels, seriously consider catching the creek on another day.

Sope starts out fast flowing and mostly flat before the creek falls over a series of bedrock ledges. Potentially sticky hydraulics can develop at each of these ledges. When the water is high, the four ledges leading to the bridge at Paper Mill Road develop river-wide keeper holes. These ledges can be scouted from the bridge before starting your run. The bridge rapid, at normal flows, involves avoiding the bridge pylons, the massive nearly symmetrical hole below the bridge, and the undercut rock downstream on river right. Scout this to determine the best line at the time. Following this hole is a smaller drop, with its own hole at high water. Class III shoals and drops continue before the creek flattens out. The only other hazards that remain before reaching the Chattahoochee are two pipes and a bridge that cross the stream with low clearance (portage if there's not enough room to go under or over), errant golf balls, and a low head dam below the Columns Drive bridge.

Ample strainers are characteristic of this run, and vigilant scouting is recommended. At high water, eddies disappear,

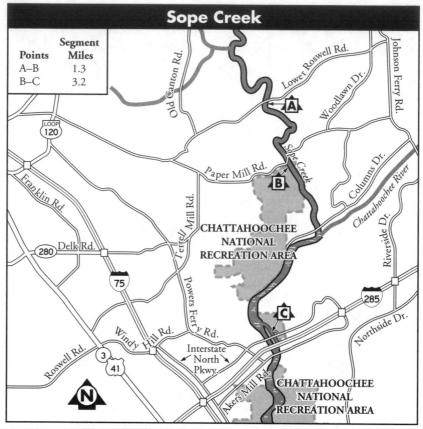

Sope Creek

Points	Segment Miles
A–B	1.3
B–C	3.2

leaving paddlers to scout while surfing. Under normal conditions, all major drops can be portaged and most can be scouted from the bank. The creek's flashy flow catches people unaware; rescue, if you aren't pinned, is as easy as climbing out to someone's house. The take-out on the Chattahoochee is at the Cochran Shoals Recreation Area (Powers Island) on the river-left side of the island, above I-285.

SHUTTLE: The Cochran Shoals/Powers Island Recreation Area is located on Interstate North Parkway and can be easily reached from I-75. Exit at Windy Hill Road (Exit 260) going east. Turn right onto Powers Ferry Road, then left onto Interstate North Parkway. Continue to the first left after crossing the Chattahoochee. To the put-in, turn right out of the parking lot, right onto Powers Ferry Road, right onto Terrell Mill Road (follow signs to stay on Terrell Mill), and right onto Paper Mill Road.

Pull over before the bridge to scout at Paper Mill Road. To the put-in, continue in the same direction on Paper Mill Road, turn left onto Woodlawn, then left onto Lower Roswell Road. Access is before the bridge on the left.

GAUGE: The Georgia USGS Web site lists data for Sope Creek at the put-in. "Real-time" data can tell you if the creek's worth checking out; in the lag time, the situation can change. Use visual scouting from Paper Mill Road to verify the level before you put-in. If it's still raining, take that into account, too. The minimum level is 5 feet (300 cfs); maximum is 8 feet. Above 8 feet, the run turns into a solid, continuous Class V.

SWEETWATER CREEK

Sweetwater Creek is a shady, scenic little stream that drains the corner of Douglas County in suburban Atlanta before emptying into the Chattahoochee River. The creek meanders peacefully between 4-foot-tall banks until encountering the Brevard Fault Zone at Sweetwater Creek State Park. Here, serenity turns to mayhem as Sweetwater crashes over 6-foot ledges and churns through complex rock gardens. As is typical for urban streams, the water quality is poor—this, along with the difficulty and intensity of the rapids, makes the creek suitable only for those paddlers with the technical skills necessary to avoid an unplanned swim in Class III–IV water.

MAPS: Mableton, Austell, Ben Hill, Campbellton (USGS); Douglas (County)

SWEETWATER CREEK STATE PARK TO RIVERSIDE PARKWAY

class	III–IV (IV+)
length	4.1 mi
time	3 hr
gauge	Web, visual
level	1.6 ft
gradient	31 fpm (51)
scenery	B-

DESCRIPTION: The upper 3-mile flatwater section can be circumvented by putting in at Sweetwater Creek State Park. Here, the creek enters its most scenic and exciting section, as it crashes over 6-foot ledges and churns through complex rock gardens for nearly a mile of nonstop action before hurtling over Sweetwater Falls. Access is available at the park via a 500-meter trail from the parking area downhill to the creek. Hiking trails hug the river-right side throughout the run, making this a possible, but extensive, park-and-play spot.

The best routes through the rapids at the park are generally found on river left. The creek retains a lot of wood that relocates

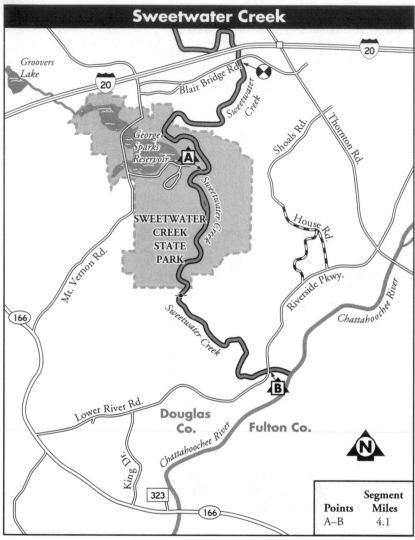

Sweetwater Creek

Groovers Lake

Blair Bridge Rd.

Sweetwater Creek

Shoals Rd.

Thornton Rd.

George Sparks Reservoir

A

SWEETWATER CREEK STATE PARK

Sweetwater Creek

House Rd.

Mt. Vernon Rd.

166

Riverside Pkwy.

Chattahoochee River

Sweetwater Creek

B

Lower River Rd.

Douglas Co.

Fulton Co.

Chattahoochee River

King Dr.

N

323

166

Points	Segment Miles
A–B	4.1

at high flows; actively scout from the river and banks to avoid encounters with logs and overhanging branches. After the first major ledge, the intense bump and grind continues up to the edge of the falls, which are scouted from the observation deck on river right. At flows above 5 feet, the section above the falls contains more than one Class IV drop.

Sweetwater Falls, a broken ledge rapid, is the highest drop on the river, and approaches Class V difficulty above 7 feet. Different lines open up as the water levels change; scout to choose the best route. Below the falls, the creek holds a few more exciting drops and surfing waves before reaching the take-out at Riverside Parkway. Take-out here to avoid an extensive paddle on the Chattahoochee in its most abused state.

SHUTTLE: From I-20, exit at Thornton Road and turn south. Continue on Thornton to Riverside Parkway, the last traffic light before crossing the Chattahoochee. Turn right and continue to the creek 2.5 miles ahead. To get to the put-in at the park, return to Thornton Road north and turn left at Blair Bridge Road, the last traffic light before reaching I-20. At the stop sign at Mount Vernon Road, turn left and follow signs to the park entrance on the left. Continue straight ahead to the dead-end at the trailhead parking lot.

GAUGE: What remains of the traditional gauge is painted on the pilings at Blair Bridge Road south of I-20, on the river left downstream side. Minimum level is 1.6 feet, although up to 2.5 feet can still be scrapey. A good level is 4; 6 is considered high. The maximum is 10 feet, though it has been run at higher levels. The USGS Web site lists gauge data for the creek near Austell, upstream of this section and not correlated with the visual gauge. With the creek's large drainage basin, levels stay up for as much as 3–4 days depending on the season and rainfall. For more information, call Sweetwater Creek State Park at (770) 732-5871.

DOG RIVER

Well, it rained like stink, and the Dog River Reservoir Recreational Complex was accessible to non–Douglas County residents, so . . . a bunch of us petted the hair of the Dog. Hair, of course, is in the eyes of the beholder. The Dog is a nice intermediate creek-run under sane boating conditions. It is exceptionally beautiful, with little evidence of human intrusion and only minimal pollution. The Dog's teeth consist of technical rapids, tricky converging currents, grabby holes, strainers, and undercut rocks and all kinds of private landowners who would prefer you not scout from the bank.

MAPS: Winston, Rico (USGS); Douglas (County)

Post Road to the Reservoir

class	II–III (IV)
length	7.3 mi
time	4 hr
gauge	None
level	None
gradient	17 fpm (50)
scenery	B-

DESCRIPTION: The Dog starts small and easy and consistently increases in size and difficulty. From the Post Road bridge (A) to Banks Mill Road (B) the Dog bounces over intermittent small ledges separated by short pools. Class I rapids build in intensity approaching the GA 5 bridge (C). Some acceptable surfing holes follow as the Dog begins to bite. Then, a couple of miles into it, the river goes through several stages of steep rocky drops and large pools, followed by more steep drops and pools, forming a mile-and-a-half of continuous whitewater. These include some relatively technical Class III rapids that transform into Class IV in high water.

The run changes significantly according to water level. Scout the rapids from your boat, as some land owners can be very sensitive to trespassers walking on their land. The whitewater run includes several islands; all should be run on the left, unless strainers are present.

The confluence of Flyblow Creek on the right signals the end of the most intense whitewater section and the transition to more tranquil water a quarter mile downstream. The Dog ends abruptly when the last Class I rapid simply stops at a lake. It's a short paddle to the take-out at the Dog River Reservoir Recreational Complex on the right. The Complex is open February 20 through Thanksgiving, from 7:00 a.m. until dusk. It is a well-managed, exceptionally nice facility that charges per-person fees for access, launching, and parking. Access to this facility for non-Douglas County residents was secured through the courts.

The river may be tempting because of its easy proximity to Atlanta, but don't trifle with it. When it's runnable at all it's

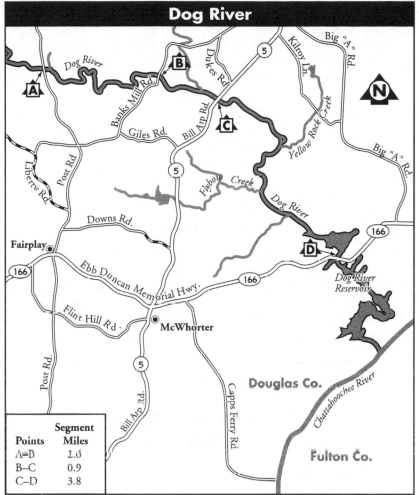

Dog River

Dog River

A

B

Banks Mill Rd.

Dukes Rd.

5

Kilroy Ln.

Big "A" Rd.

N

Giles Rd.

Bill Arp Rd.

C

Yellow Rock Creek

5

Flybow Creek

Dog River

Big "A" Rd.

Liberty Rd.

Post Rd.

Downs Rd.

166

Fairplay

166

Ebb Duncan Memorial Hwy.

166

Dog River Reservoir

Flint Hill Rd.

McWhorter

Post Rd.

5

Bill Arp Rd.

Capps Ferry Rd.

Douglas Co.

Chattahoochee River

Fulton Co.

Points	Segment Miles
A–D	2.0
B–C	0.9
C–D	3.8

pushy, technical in spots, and demanding. Occasional deadfalls add to the danger. Scouting, portaging, and rescue are difficult. Those attempting the Dog for the first time should be experienced with Class III whitewater and should make every effort to accompany someone who knows the run.

SHUTTLE: To get to the reservoir take-out for the Dog, take I-20 to Exit 8, west of Atlanta. Turn south when exiting and stay on GA 5 for some time. Eventually it narrows to two lanes, and a mile or so later it will cross the Dog. Water height can be gauged from here. Continue on GA 5 until it crosses GA 166. Turn left onto GA 166, looking for the sign for The Douglas County

Water and Sewer Authority Dog River Reservoir Recreational Complex. You must make a tricky tight left U-turn to enter. To return to the put-in at Banks Mill Road, return to GA 5 and take it back toward the interstate. Turn left onto Giles Road before crossing the river, then turn right onto Banks Mill at the stop sign. The river and put-in is just ahead.

GAUGE: There is no gauge for the Dog and it must be at flood or near flood to run. You can see one rapid from the GA 5 bridge; if it looks bony, the river is too low; if the river is in the trees, it's probably too high. Consider checking out the Dog if Sweetwater Creek is at 6 feet or so.

FLAT SHOAL CREEK

Flat Shoal Creek, a tributary of the Chattahoochee in middle Georgia, flows southwestward, draining portions of Troup and Harris Counties north of Columbus. Take the name literally: the section described below is mostly flat-water followed by a single, nearly mile-long shoal. Following a fairly constant gradient throughout its length, the shoal sports a dazzling display of shoal lilies in mid-May.

MAPS: Cannonville, Whitesville (USGS); Troup, Harris (County)

GA 18 TO GA 103

class	I–II+
length	5.2 mi
time	3 hr
gauge	Visual
level	3.5 ft
gradient	3 fpm (83)
scenery	B-

DESCRIPTION: An intimate stream except at the broader shoals, Flat Shoals Creek is shady and inviting. The creek runs between steep, sandy, clay banks averaging 4 to 6 feet in height, surrounded by an oak-hickory forest with a plentiful sprinkling of loblolly pines on the rocky points. Paralleled by I-85, this is one of the most easily visited streams in the Piedmont. Though runnable below the US 27 bridge, logjams punctuate the stream in the upper sections. Downstream the channel is clearer, but access is a major problem since very few take-outs are available. Described here is a relatively painless 5-mile run from GA 18 to GA 103, flowing through 4 miles of pleasantly forested flat-water followed by long, delightful, and attention-demanding Class II+ shoals.

In these shoals there are no big drops, but the ledges follow one another almost without interruption. The going here is frequently technical and requires good water-reading ability and

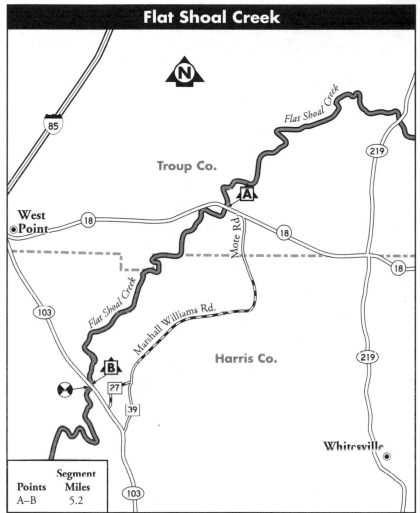

Flat Shoal Creek

Flat Shoal Creek

85

Troup Co.

219

A

Mote Rd.

West
Point

18

18

18

Flat Shoal Creek

Marshall Williams Rd.

103

Harris Co.

219

B

27

39

Whitesville

103

Points	Segment Miles
A–B	5.2

quick thinking. In low water expect to get stuck a few times. In high water beginners may be in for a long tumbling swim. Scout or portage from the right bank as water levels require.

The shoal lilies, when in bloom, cluster on the banks and grow in patches within the shoals themselves. When the water is up, they add another dimension of difficulty to the shoals as you maneuver to avoid them while attempting to find a suitable channel through the rocky ledges. An endangered species indigenous only to the fall-line shoals of Piedmont streams, their habitat is shrinking due to dams and increased siltation in the rivers.

SHUTTLE: From I-85 near West Point, take Exit 2 and get onto GA 18 east, then take GA 103 south. Proceed to the bridge crossing the creek; this is the take-out. For the put-in, go north to GA 18 and turn right. The put-in is on this road.

GAUGE: A gauge is located at GA 103. The creek is runnable most of the year, more reliably in winter and spring. At 3.5 feet the water barely covers the rocks in the shoals and begins washing out the channels.

MULBERRY CREEK

Mulberry Creek flows east off of Pine Mountain and empties into the Chattahoochee River 20 miles north of Columbus. A wilderness stream except for intersecting roads and a dam near US 27, the stream is virtually undisturbed by man. For most of its course it is placid and shaded, with the dramatic exception of the falls located below the last take-out.

MAPS: Cataula, Mulberry Grove, Bartletts Ferry Dam (USGS); Harris (County)

WINFREE ROAD TO GA 219

class	I–II (V+)
length	23.4 mi
time	2.5 days
gauge	None
level	N/A
gradient	5 fpm (162)
scenery	B-

DESCRIPTION: Mulberry Creek is primarily characterized by calm water passing between high banks covered with mulberry and mountain laurel. Kingsboro Dam, located upstream of US 27 (B), must be portaged on the left; a yellow cable stretched across the stream signals the approach of the dam. The cable itself, located 0.5 miles upstream of the dam, presents a dangerous obstruction at higher water levels. The portage is difficult, and lining the canoe through the shoals below the dam may be necessary. Another shoal is located below Hudson Mill Road (C). Near the end of this run, the creek makes an unexpected drop over a 4-foot rock ledge that can be portaged over the center rocks.

This ledge at High Shoals is only a prelude to what lies 0.5 miles below the last take-out at GA 219: a torturous drop that includes a 40-foot falls. The area is a major hazard, and should be avoided at all costs by all but proven expert boaters. If this isn't you, paddle back upstream to the take-out at access point F. Swimming through the falls is highly dangerous.

Mulberry Creek

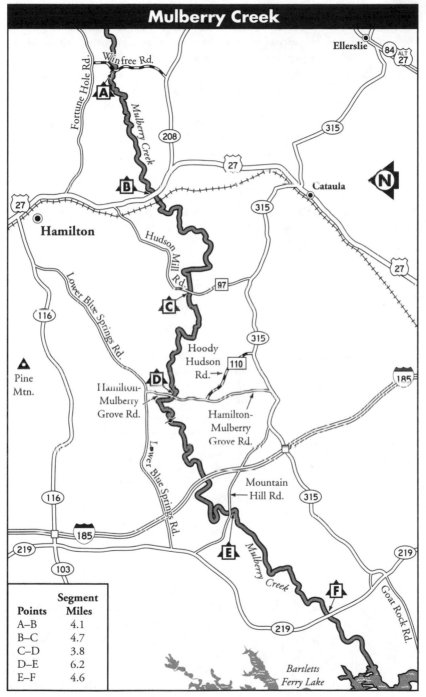

Ellerslie

84 ALT 27

Winfree Rd.

Fortune Hole Rd.

A

Mulberry Creek

208

27

315

Cataula

N

315

Hamilton

Hudson Mill Rd.

B

97

C

116

315

Lower Blue Springs Rd.

Hoody Hudson Rd.

110

315

Pine Mtn.

D

185

Hamilton-Mulberry Grove Rd.

Hamilton-Mulberry Grove Rd.

Lower Blue Springs Rd.

116

Mountain Hill Rd.

315

185

219

E

Mulberry Creek

F

219

103

Goat Rock Rd.

Points	Segment Miles
A–B	4.1
B–C	4.7
C–D	3.8
D–E	6.2
E–F	4.6

Bartletts Ferry Lake

Mulberry Creek crosses the fault line like no other stream, with a gradient similar to Overflow in the worst stretch. If you have the appropriate skills, run it accompanied by someone who has run the rapids before and knows the routes. Numerous holes, undercuts, precipitous drops, and lodged logs make this a hazardous run, and a probably lethal place to be caught outside of a boat. Multiple Class IV and V+ situations are encountered, with no separating pool. Bank scouting is mandatory, and the property owners in the area don't favor paddlers. The take-out after the falls is to carry back up or paddle across Bartletts Ferry Lake.

SHUTTLE: From Columbus to the lowest take-out on the creek, take I-185 north to Exit 10, and GA 315 west to GA 219 north, to its crossing with the creek. For up-river access points, return to GA 315 and turn left.

GAUGE: There is no gauge. Do not attempt at flood stage.

FLINT RIVER

In terms of wilderness beauty and spectacular vistas of varied terrain, the Flint is rivaled by no other large river in Georgia. In the Piedmont alone, the Flint alternately flows broad and narrow, beneath pine covered bluffs and at the foot of high rock walls, over extensive rocky shoals, through winding bottomland swamp, past cities and towns, and between fertile cultivated plateaus. In the Coastal Plain, the Flint meanders through alternating pine forests and swamp and reclaimed crop and pastureland. It is one of Georgia's longest rivers, with headwaters originating near Forest Park south of Atlanta and tailwaters in the extreme southwestern corner of the state, where it meets the Chattahoochee River in Lake Seminole. The Flint is suitable for both weekend paddling and epic canoe-camping trips.

MAPS: Brooks, Hollonville, Haralson, Gay, Woodbury, Sunset Village, Roland, Lincoln Park, Prattsburg, Fickling Mill, Roberta, Reynolds, Garden Valley, Montezuma, Pennington, Methvins, Drayton, Leslie Southeast, Albany Notheast, Albany East, Albany West, Baconton North, Baconton South, Newton, Branchville, Hopeful, Cooktown, Steinham Store, Bainbridge, Fowlstown, Faceville (USGS); Fayette, Spalding, Pike, Meriwether, Upson, Talbot, Taylor, Crawford, Peach, Macon, Lee, Worth, Cougherty, Baker, Mitchell, Decatur (County)

WOOLSEY TO GA 18/74

class	I–II (III)
Length	39.5 mi
time	Up to 6 days
Gauge	Web
Level	150 cfs
gradient	8 fpm
scenery	B

DESCRIPTION: The Flint is runnable all year but is subject to sudden flash flooding during the winter and spring, particularly in the Piedmont. Late summer and fall are prime paddling times that offer clearer water and exposed sandbars for camping. Though a passage can be forced in the headwaters, an epidemic of deadfalls (largely the result of beavers) restricts paddling upstream of Woolsey in Fayette County.

Heading downstream from the Hampton Road bridge east of Woolsey (A), Class I riffles and small ledges combine with more deadfalls to keep paddlers awake. The stream winds continuously and is well insulated in a canopy of willow, ash, birch, and silver maple. Half a mile below the crossing of GA 92 (B) is a rip-rap dam that must be portaged. As far downstream as the GA 16 bridge west of Griffin (D), deadfalls can completely block the stream forcing paddlers to portage; after Line Creek's entrance 1 mile below GA 16, deadfall blockages become rare. There is a shoal on the river above the mouth of Line Creek.

Below GA 362 (F) the river curves slightly less and broadens from 45 to 65 feet wide on average. Bottomlands to either side of the stream are swampy and inundated with water and vegetation. Small shoals persist at approximately half-mile intervals, with each shoal only 30–40 feet in length, and the river widens to about 90 feet midway through Pike County. Here, an agricultural plain encroaches on the stream's wooded corridor but never robs the Flint of its remote atmosphere.

Passing beneath the David Knott Bridge west of Concord on Flat Shoals Road (G), old bridge pilings sometimes obstruct the stream by catching driftwood and debris to form strainers. Below the pilings is a larger shoal more complex than the others upstream. Extending several hundred yards, this Class II (borderline Class III) stretch is basically an exercise in route selection with several alternatives available. No further shoals of significance interrupt the tranquil flow of the Flint until downstream of the GA 18 bridge (H).

SHUTTLE: To reach the final take-out for this section, take US 41 south from Griffin, turn right at GA 18, and proceed to the river. The upper access points are most easily reached from GA 74 on the west side of the river.

GAUGE: The USGS Web site lists data for a gauge station near Griffin. The river is floatable with as little as 150 cfs, though is

more pleasurable at higher flows. Due to the high number of trees and beaver dams in stream, the river should be avoided at levels approaching flood stage.

GA 18/74 TO GA 137

class	II (III)
length	50.9 mi
time	Up to 6 days
gauge	Web, phone, visual
level	7.0
gradient	8 fpm
scenery	A

DESCRIPTION: In this section the terrain alters dramatically, with the river expanding to over 250 feet and descending a long series of ledges where steep wooded hills and small mountains converge to form an intimate and spectacular valley. Tall bluffs alternate with steep, sloping, forested hills and exposed rock walls and ledges. Pine Mountain looms majestically above the stream as the Flint passes along the Upson–Meriwether County line. This area narrowly escaped being inundated by a dam that was proposed to pen the river in at Sprewell Bluff.

Due to the breadth of the river, the vistas are unobstructed and overwhelming. So too is the forest, which is spectacularly diverse, with both mountain and Coastal Plain species. Here the ravines, slopes, and bluffs support beech, black gum, sourwood, sweet bay, white oak, chestnut oak, hickory, buckeye, and tulip poplar. Evergreens include loblolly and shortleaf pines and red cedar. Along the streamside, tupelo gum and black willow are common and mountain rhododendron grows side by side with such swamp shrubs as cyrilla. High on the mountains, exposed rock outcroppings colored with moss punctuate the green slopes. Of special geological interest is Dripping Rock, a quartzite outcrop located below the mouth of Elkins Creek at the northeastern terminus of Pine Mountain. Fabulously, this eclectic botanical mix is heavily draped with Spanish moss at Yellow Jacket Shoals, where an occasional palmetto encroaches on the scene.

The most formidable whitewater on the Flint occurs in the 9 miles between Sprewell Bluff (I) and Po Biddy Road (L). Below Sprewell Bluff to the GA 36 bridge, shoals remain easy Class II, although they tend to be more continuous than upstream. In low water the current pools above each ledge. In high water, however, the current is appreciably faster and precipitates the formation of some respectable holes.

Approximately half a mile beyond the GA 36 bridge (J) lies Yellow Jacket Shoals. At low water this long borderline Class III is technical, with a couple of big drops and some hidden boat-eating

Flint River Map 1

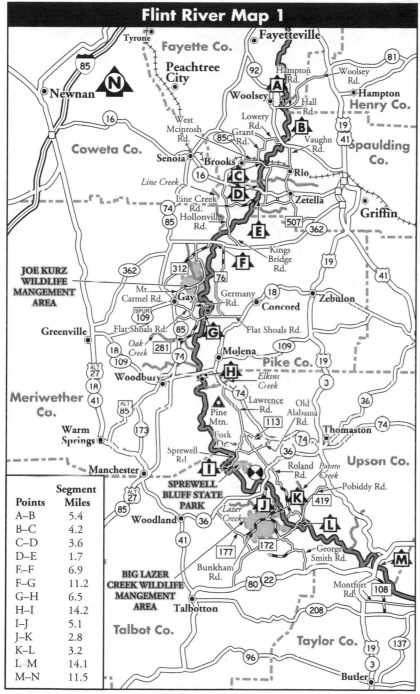

Points	Segment Miles
A–B	5.4
B–C	4.2
C–D	3.6
D–E	1.7
E–F	6.9
F–G	11.2
G–H	6.5
H–I	14.2
I–J	5.1
J–K	2.8
K–L	3.2
L–M	14.1
M–N	11.5

rocks. Since this rapid defies a "straight through" approach, paddlers attempting Yellow Jacket Shoals should possess skills in water reading, eddy turns, and ferrying. At higher levels the eddies disappear and the rapid becomes more intense. Fortunately, alternate routes become more numerous.

A series of islands divides the channel below Yellow Jacket Shoals, creating occasional narrows as the Flint passes them. Shoals persist through the island section but occur less frequently and never exceed Class II. Lazar Creek enters on river right at Hightower Shoals, announcing a sizeable tract of Big Lazer Creek WMA land on the right. The dirt road to the boat ramp here succumbed to erosion from high waters in 2003, but access from the road is still possible, though challenging due to the steep banks. The surrounding terrain remains mountainous, spectacular, and remote until the final approach to Po Biddy Road.

Downstream of Po Biddy Road the rugged, steep slopes begin to recede and taper down to an agricultural plateau by the time the river reaches the US 80 bridge (M). White kaolin bluffs start appearing in this section, as do cattle pastures. The gradient diminishes, and though the current remains swift, the shoals are smaller and occur less often. Passing an island midway between US 80 and GA 137, the last significant shoal is found where the river winds between high banks and rocky clay bluffs surrounded by cultivated tableland. The river narrows to 85–110 feet and flows swiftly, though flat and calm, with large sandbars appearing on the inside of turns at low water. This marks the Flint's departure from the Piedmont and its arrival onto the Coastal Plain.

SHUTTLE: Most access points in this section are easily reached from Thomaston. For the final take-out at GA 137 (N), take US 19 South to GA 208 East, which will intersect with GA 137 East at Pickling Mill. Follow the road to the river and the boat ramp on the far side. Sprewell Bluff State Park is reached from GA 74 west of Thomaston; turn left at Old Alabama Road and follow signs to the park.

GAUGE: A gauge is painted on the pilings visible from the outfitter located at the GA 36 bridge; call the outfitter for levels (see Appendix B). The USGS provides data for the gauge at Culloden, which can be used to estimate the bridge level. Divide the Culloden flow in half and add 6 feet. Using the bridge gauge, 7.0 is the recommended minimum. The river becomes enjoyable above 8.0. The park management has been known to turn people

Flint River Map 2

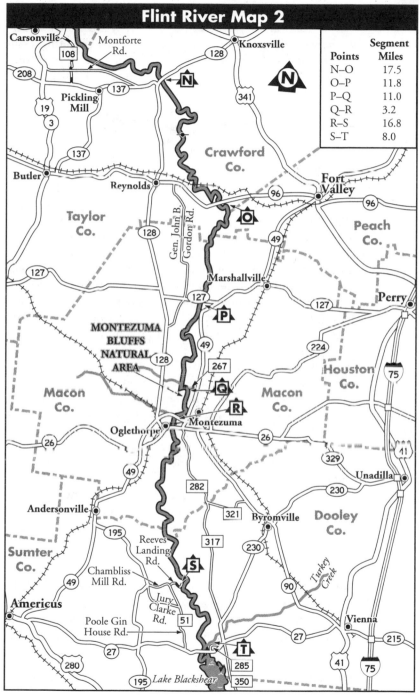

Points	Segment Miles
N–O	17.5
O–P	11.8
P–Q	11.0
Q–R	3.2
R–S	16.8
S–T	8.0

away from putting in at Sprewell Bluff when the bridge gauge is over 11 feet; call at (706) 646-6026 to verify access before leaving home if the gauge is headed over 10 feet. The outfitter will run shuttles to their property at Goat Mountain, upriver from Sprewell, for experienced paddlers under those conditions.

GA 137 TO LAKE BLACKSHEAR

class	I
length	68.3 mi
time	Up to 5 days
gauge	Web
level	300 cfs
gradient	1 fpm
scenery	B

DESCRIPTION: After crossing the Fall Line, the Flint River changes quickly. Four miles below the GA 137 bridge (N) on the Taylor–Crawford County line, the valley farm belt beside the Flint River reverts to forest, which expands almost immediately into a thick corridor on both sides of the stream. As the valley widens, the Flint begins meandering, and very shortly forms horseshoe bends and occasional oxbow lakes. Seasonally wet bottomland surrounding the Flint makes up the Magnolia Swamp, which slows the flow of the current. Through most of this section (to GA 49), pretty sandbars beckon travelers closer to the forest.

As the stream passes east of Reynolds and into Macon County, the banks begin to rise as it leaves the swamp. All through Macon County, a wooded corridor dominates the terrain, with farm or pastureland occasionally wedging in near the tree-lined riverbanks. The Flint reveals its ancient past with fossilized oyster shells and sharks' teeth embedded in its banks, evidence that this land was once under the ocean floor. By the time it reaches the end of this section, the Flint fully represents Coastal Plain flora and fauna, including alligators, cypress trees, and lily pads.

About 10 miles below the GA 49 bridge at Montezuma (R), the river corridor becomes swampy once again approaching the backwaters of Lake Blackshear. Feeder creeks and backwater sloughs make possible various side explorations. Wildlife, including birds, is exceptionally diverse in this area.

SHUTTLE: The final access point for the section above Lake Blackshear (T) is via a fish camp located on Turkey Creek immediately above GA 27 west of Vienna. Access points above this are evenly spaced and reached via roads that mirror the river on the east and west sides.

GAUGE: See the preceding section. This section of the Flint is generally runnable year-round, and is well-suited for extended

Flint River Map 3

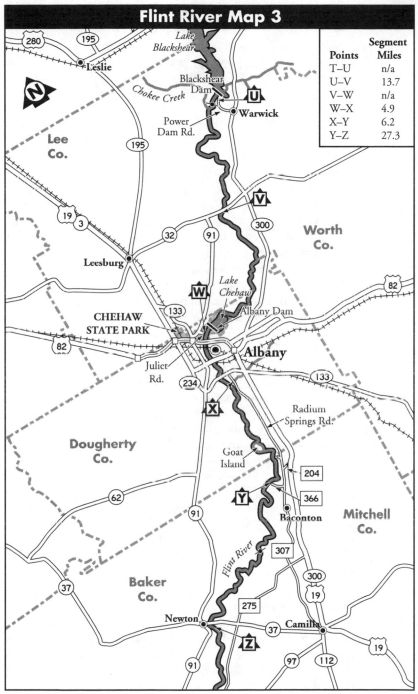

Points	Segment Miles
T–U	n/a
U–V	13.7
V–W	n/a
W–X	4.9
X–Y	6.2
Y–Z	27.3

canoe-camping trips. The Albany Game and Fish Office at (229) 430-4256 can provide additional info.

LAKE BLACKSHEAR DAM TO LAKE SEMINOLE

class	I (II)
length	87.5 mi (excluding Lake Chehaw)
time	Up to 2 weeks
gauge	Web
level	N/A
gradient	1 fpm
scenery	B+

DESCRIPTION: Below Blackshear Dam the Flint continues its journey through the Coastal Plain, flowing in long straightaways and broad, seemingly endless bends through a wooded corridor surrounded by fertile farmland. Averaging 210–255 feet in width, the current is slower than in the Piedmont sections, and the water is a clear to split-pea green when sediment concentrations are low. Banks average 5–20 feet in height and begin sporting a curious undercut feature, extending slightly over the edges of the river and occasionally displaying micro-caves. Pine, sweet gum, sycamore, willow, and ash congregate above the water, mingling at times with large cypress trees. Due to the width of the stream and the height of the banks, the river is almost totally exposed to the sun. Significant amounts of empty mussel shells litter the banks, testifying to the river's health and the abundant presence of wildlife.

As the Flint approaches the environs of Albany it is backed up by the Flint River Development Dam on the northeast edge of the city. The lake created is small and rather interesting since a number of swamp marshes and sloughs occur to either side of the main channel. Downstream of the dam, the Flint runs through downtown Albany, where, below the second railroad bridge, Class II Albany Shoals awaits. The river picks up some litter at this point, washed downstream out of the city.

Leaving Albany, the Flint winds through an agricultural plateau punctuated by many small- and medium-sized towns and a power plant at Goat Island. The scenery remains substantially unchanged at streamside (with the exception of clear-cutting visible in Baker County), and there are no additional shoals. Medium-sized rounded rocks line the banks, which continue displaying caves and shadowy overhangs. Powerboat traffic begins increasing above Bainbridge in the pool of Lake Seminole, which signals the end of moving water on the Flint. Beyond Bainbridge in Lake Seminole, the Flint unites with the Chattahoochee to form the Apalachicola River, which continues downstream below the Jim Woodruff Dam to flow into Florida en route to the Gulf of Mexico.

   The level of difficulty on the Flint River below Lake Blackshear is Class I except for Albany Shoals. Dangers are limited to the dam in Albany and powerboat traffic. Access is good.

SHUTTLE: The boat ramp on GA 311 north of Bainbridge offers the easiest access before encountering too much of the backwaters of the lake. The highest access point in this section is the Marine Corps Ditch Boat Ramp (X) on the river-left side below the dam at Albany.

GAUGE: The USGS on-line gauge at Newton provides data for the Flint south of the dams in Albany. The river generally has sufficient flow year-round but should be avoided during floods.

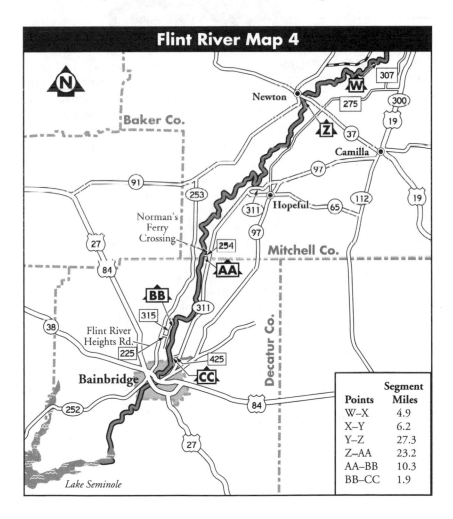

Flint River Map 4

| | Segment |
Points	Miles
W–X	4.9
X–Y	6.2
Y–Z	27.3
Z–AA	23.2
AA–BB	10.3
BB–CC	1.9

Baker Co.

Mitchell Co.

Decatur Co.

Newton

Camilla

Hopeful

Norman's Ferry Crossing

Flint River Heights Rd.

Bainbridge

Lake Seminole

LAZER CREEK (a.k.a. BIG LAZER CREEK)

Located in the west-central part of the state, Lazer Creek flows north-eastward through undisturbed forested banks into the Flint River just below Hightower Shoals near Thomaston. Its headwaters are on Pine Mountain. A creek of significant size, the paddling is mostly flat-water, occasionally interrupted by Class I and two solid Class II shoals. Hazards consist of the shoals themselves, which should be scouted, and the occasional hornets' nests hanging from overhead branches. Lazer Creek is remarkably free of deadfalls and strainers.

MAPS: Roland, Lincoln Park (USGS); Talbot, Upson (County)

HENDRICKS/SUNRISE ROAD TO THE FLINT RIVER

class	I–II
length	8.3 mi
time	5
gauge	None
level	N/A
gradient	13 fpm
scenery	A-

DESCRIPTION: Talbot County is 93-percent forested, and Lazer Creek remains a virtually undisturbed wilderness. Thickly overgrown, only now and then are signs of human activity visible. The hills rise to 200 feet over the water in some sections, surprisingly mountainous territory for this part of the state. The stream bed is predominantly sandy and rocky. Narrow and intimate at the beginning of its canoeable length, Lazer Creek becomes 80 yards wide or more toward its mouth. The Flint, on which this section ends, is 150 yards or more wide.

While the stream is mostly placid, quartzite ledges occasionally cross the calm stream, causing shoals of Class I and II difficulty. Two solid Class II rapids in the second half of the run deliver whitewater excitement guaranteed to wake anyone lulled by the prevailing flat-water and beauty of the surrounding terrain. The first is Big Shoals, a river-wide stair-step ledge whose first drop may be as much as 5 vertical feet depending on the line chosen. Below this ledge, the creek's largest tributary, Coleoatchee Creek, enters on the left. The second noteworthy rapid occurs near the confluence with the Flint.

For its last quarter, Lazer Creek is bordered on the right by the local Wildlife Management Area. If you're camping in the area, be mindful of hunting seasons. The game calendar on the GADNR Web site provides hunting season dates.

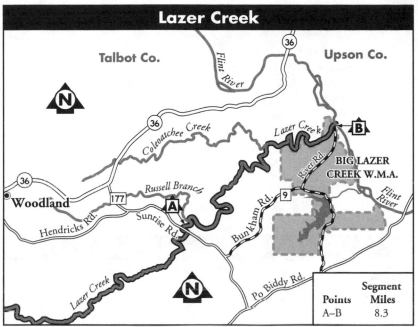

SHUTTLE: From Thomaston, take GA 36 west. After crossing over the Flint, look for Hendricks/Sunrise Road and turn left there. Cross over the creek (the put-in for this section) and continue another 1.3 miles to a left turn onto Bunkham Road. A little less than 3 miles ahead, turn left onto River Road. Follow River Road a similar distance until it dead-ends at the river. This is the take-out. The cove that leads to this spot can be difficult to spot from the river at the end of the day, so note the surrounding features well.

GAUGE: There is no gauge for the creek. The seam in the pilings of the bridge on river right at the put-in can be used to judge feasibility; 3 feet below the seam has proved to be ample flow. The creek is most likely runnable if the Flint is running over 8.5 feet at GA 36. Avoid the creek when the Flint is over 11 feet.

POTATO CREEK

The sleek blue C-1 completed the ferry above the big waterfall, spun, and plunged over the edge into the huge exploding hole at the base. A satisfied smile crossed the boater's face as he punched the hole and cleared the rapid; eddying to the right, he watched as three more boats surged over the falls and plummeted into the hole. Now you might think it's flat down south of Atlanta, but that's not entirely true. A series of faults cross Georgia, creating spectacles like Potato Creek. With an average gradient in the 1-mile rapid stretch exceeding 100 feet per mile, Potato Creek is intense.

MAPS: Thomaston, Sunset Village (USGS); Upson (County)

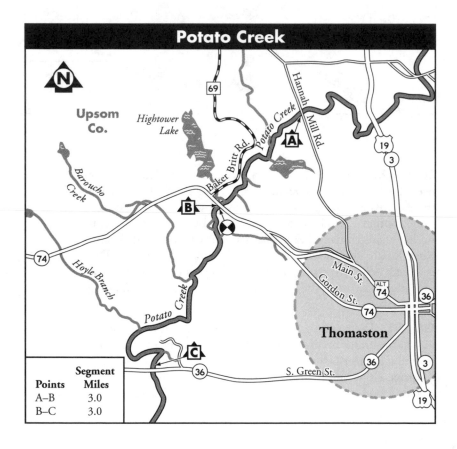

GA 74 TO GA 36

class	III (IV)
length	6 mi
time	3.5 hr
gauge	Visual
level	0
gradient	47 fpm
scenery	B-

DESCRIPTION: An optional 3-mile, Class II warm-up precedes the popular whitewater stretch that begins at GA 74 (B). The bottom drops out about a half click below the GA 74 bridge with a remarkable 40-foot horizon line. The entire drop is divided by an island two-thirds of the way down. Both sides are runnable, but river left is the usual route, avoiding the undercut rock three-quarters of the way down. On river right a big vertical drop—Oh! Cool—plummets into a pool and is followed by several more smaller drops. A small pool below the island allows for regrouping and a good view downstream.

Horizon lines stretch off to the limit of sight. The drops are continuous and sometimes blind. The best lines are not always obvious and change with the level; it helps to have someone who knows them with you the first time. Fools Falls and Impact Falls are some of the most dangerous drops. Both are sheer and should be boofed or ski-jumped to avoid being pinned in the shallow water below. The rapids have ample play spots, especially a great surfing wave in Mr. Potato Head Rapid, located near the bottom of the run. The rapids stretch ends after about a mile with a long, technical, boulder sieve.

A mile of flat-water follows, and then you'll arrive at the take-out bridge (C) just before Potato Creek Falls. You can hear the falls well before you see its horizon line. Falling over 80 feet, three back-to-back waterfalls comprise the cascade. Paddle down to the lip to check its runability; the bridge is an acceptable take-out and the last completely legal one. Meat Grinder is the first of two sliding drops and ends in a shallow pool. Run on the right or center. Then comes Mashed Potato, another sliding drop; run on the far right. The last drop, Potato Creek Falls, is about 20 feet through a very steep, twisting slide into an enormous exploding and curling hole. Don't worry; it usually doesn't hold boats, especially since you are moving at such a great speed. Following the falls are sets of nasty boulder sieves on either side of an island dividing the stream. The take-out is on the left. This is a semi-private road, so be brief and mind your manners.

SHUTTLE: Potato Creek is in the vicinity of Thomaston, south of Atlanta. To get there follow GA 74 west from Thomaston towards Woodbury. Turn right on FS 69, immediately after the Potato Creek bridge. The put-in is via the tiny feeder stream that

The top of the GA 36 rapid on Potato Creek

photo © Rob Maxwell

runs under the bridge and into Potato Creek. Be courteous, as this might be private land. The take-out is back to Thomaston, then a right at the light onto GA 36 west. Park at the bridge. It is possible to take the last left before the bridge, but this is a private road and you will need to ask for permission to park there. The three drops—Meat Grinder, Mashed Potato, and Potato Falls—are all visible from the GA 36 bridge.

GAUGE: The gauge is painted on the bridge piling at GA 74. A level even with the bottom of the slab on the pillar at GA 36 is considered zero. While runnable at this level, high water runs start at 1 foot. It is usually runnable after rain in October through June.

SPRING CREEK

Exotic and beautiful, Spring Creek is located in the southwestern corner of the state. Its flows are spring-fed and clear, revealing the creek's interior habitat. With its headwaters in Clay and Calhoun Counties, the creek flows directly south into the Flint and Chattahoochee Rivers at Lake Seminole. Its level of difficulty is Class I(+), with numerous deadfalls being the primary hazard to navigation.

MAPS: Colquitt, Boykin, Bronson, Desser, Reynoldsville (USGS); Miller, Decatur (County)

US 27 TO SMITH LANDING

class	I (+)
length	27.9 mi
time	3 days
gauge	Web
level	125 cfs
gradient	<2 fpm
scenery	A

DESCRIPTION: Spring Creek is runnable below US 27 in Miller County. Vastly different from other Coastal Plains streams in the state, Spring Creek is largely spring fed. When high water subsides following the spring rains, the water in the upper sections is crystal clear and reveals a beautiful array of underwater plant life, spring "boils," and a bottom that is often solid limestone, sometimes pitted by erosion with jagged cutting edges. Fish and mollusks are plentiful and can be observed from a canoe. Cypress and planer trees line the banks, which rise high from the stream, thereby eliminating much of the usual wet floodplain flora. Limestone outcroppings add to the wilderness beauty of the partially shaded stream, and small shoals and rocky shallows enliven the paddling. Pine and hardwood forests surround the water.

The stream is intimate and diminutive until the lake pool is encountered near the Seaboard Coast Line rail crossing. From here the run remains interesting as the creek slowly widens to become the Lake Seminole Waterfowl Management Area. Except in the spring and in the lake pool of Lake Seminole, the water is too shallow for powerboat traffic but is perfect for paddle craft.

SHUTTLE: From nearby Bainbridge, take GA 253 west toward Lake Seminole. Before reading the lake, turn right onto GA 310, then left onto Smith Landing Road. The creek access (E) is at the end of the road. For upstream access, return to GA 310 and turn left. All other access points can be reached from this road, including US 84, Lane Bridge Road, CR 190, and US 27 (the northernmost put-in). Access is good at all points and becomes progressively more developed proceeding downriver.

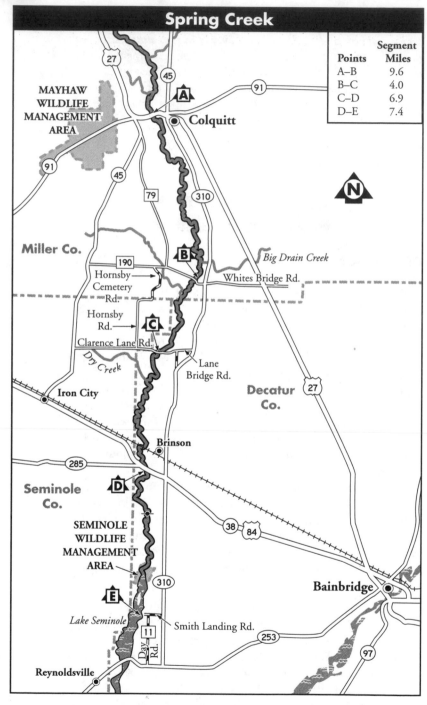

Spring Creek

Points	Segment Miles
A–B	9.6
B–C	4.0
C–D	6.9
D–E	7.4

MAYHAW WILDLIFE MANAGEMENT AREA

Colquitt

Miller Co.

190

Hornsby Cemetery Rd.

Big Drain Creek

Whites Bridge Rd.

Hornsby Rd.

Clarence Lane Rd.

Lane Bridge Rd.

Dry Creek

Iron City

Decatur Co.

Brinson

285

Seminole Co.

SEMINOLE WILDLIFE MANAGEMENT AREA

Bainbridge

Lake Seminole

Smith Landing Rd.

Day Rd.

Reynoldsville

GAUGE: The USGS Web site lists data for Spring Creek at Lane Bridge Road near Iron City. Runnable levels commence at 125 cfs; maximum level is flood stage. Spring Creek is usually runnable upstream of US 84 from November to June and all year below US 84.

part**Five**

THE ALTAMAHA RIVER WATERSHED

NORTH OCONEE RIVER

One of Athen's rivers, the North Oconee begins as a small river that meanders through the agricultural land of Jackson County. Upon entering Clarke County and the city, the river becomes more navigable as it forms the center of the North Oconee Greenway, 3 miles of parkland that shelter the well-vegetated banks of the river as it stretches south to the University of Georgia campus. The Sandy Creek Nature Center, located at the confluence of the river with Sandy Creek, anchors the north end of the greenway and promotes public awareness of the importance of preserving the riparian habitat along the river corridor. Below Athens, the river meets up with the Middle Oconee to form the main Oconee River.

MAPS: Nicholson, Athens West, Athens East (USGS); Oconee, Clarke (County)

NEWTON BRIDGE ROAD TO BARNETT SHOALS ROAD ON THE OCONEE

class	I (II)
length	18.4 mi
time	2 days
gauge	Web
level	Unknown
gradient	6 fpm
scenery	C–D

DESCRIPTION: Though it is possible to paddle the North Oconee starting as high as Maysville, it not usually pleasant. The stream is small and frequently blocked by deadfall, making frequent portaging necessary. The surrounding area consists of farms, some of which are sizeable industrial operations. Hurricane Shoals County Park offers seasonal day-use recreation at the GA 82 crossing (25 miles above access point A). The rapids below the dam in the park may reach as high as Class II intensity in high water.

Paddling becomes reasonable at Newton Bridge Road (A). Sandy Creek soon enters from the left, ensuring a more reliable flow. The nature center is located here. Though not accessible from the river, the center offers educational displays and programs as well as hiking trails that extend up Sandy Creek.

Through the city, the river is mostly placid, with a handful of exceptions. The first obstacle encountered is an aqueduct crossing

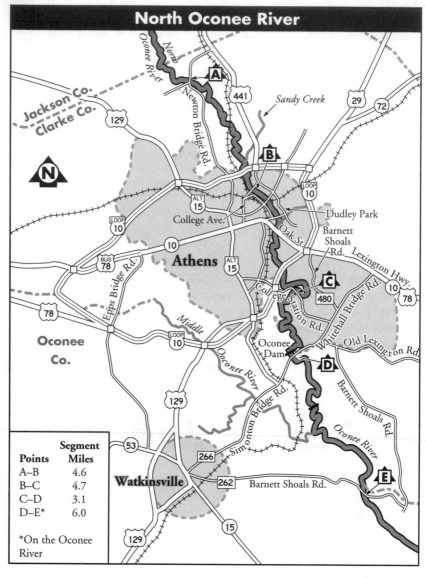

North Oconee River

Points	Segment Miles
A–B	4.6
B–C	4.7
C–D	3.1
D–E*	6.0

*On the Oconee River

the stream downstream of College Avenue (B); a pile of rubble downstream of the water intake structure is used to back up water for the intake. The pipe and rip-rap below is passable at lower levels, but becomes dangerous at higher flows. Portage this if the clearance is insufficient to pass beneath it. Two miles downstream below the crossing of Lexington Highway are rapids created by the remains of an old dam at Easley's Mill. This rapid ranges in difficulty from Class II to Class III, depending on the water level. Scout before running it. Upstream of the College Station Bridge (C), you will encounter a sewage treatment facility and its distinctive smell.

Below the College Station Bridge, the river slows and becomes the backwater for another small dam, the Oconee Dam, located approximately 2.8 miles below the bridge. Portage on either side. Just below the dam is a series of Class II rapids that extend almost to the Whitehall Bridge (D). An aqueduct crosses the river immediately below the bridge; pass underneath this only if there is sufficient clearance. Otherwise, portage. Downstream of Whitehall, there are 3 miles of mostly wooded shorelines and rippling shoals (and one more dam) before reaching the confluence with the Middle Oconee. Approximately 3 miles of paddling brings you to the next access point (E) at the Barnett Shoals Road bridge over the Oconee River.

SHUTTLE: From Watkinsville, take Barnett Shoals Road east to the Oconee River and the final access point for this section. The highest put-in at Newton Bridge Road is accessed off of US 441, north of Athens.

GAUGE: The USGS gauge is located at College Avenue; data for this station is provided online. Recommended minimum levels using this gauge are unknown. If the Middle Oconee is at 1.2 feet, the North Oconee is probably runnable. Avoid the river at flood stage.

MIDDLE OCONEE RIVER

The Middle Oconee flows across the broad pasturelands of Jackson County before entering Clarke County and flowing through southwest Athens. Below the city, it meets up with the North Oconee to form the main Oconee River. In the upper section, the river is small and has very little gradient. Downstream, farmland gives way to signs of suburban development as the river adopts the typical Piedmont habit of long flat-water stretches interrupted by an occasional shoal.

MAPS: Pendergrass, Winder North, Jefferson, Athens West (USGS); Jackson, Barrow, Clarke, Oconee (County)

OLD PENDERGRASS ROAD TO GA 330

class	I
length	17.6 mi
time	Up to 2 days
gauge	Web
level	Unknown
gradient	<2 fpm
scenery	C-

DESCRIPTION: Though potentially navigable above this section given sufficient rainfall, runoff from a poultry-processing plant and frequent deadfalls may preclude an enjoyable paddling experience. Below Old Pendergrass Road (A), the river remains small and susceptible to blockage by deadfalls. For the first 5.5 miles (to access point C at Johnson Bridge), it moves slowly through a swampy area where long stretches of the stream have been artificially channeled. This segment of the river has proven to be good for duck hunting. Below Johnson Bridge, the river's gradient remains gradual as it passes through pastures and woodlands. The flow volume is increased by the entrance of the Mulberry River below Double Bridges Road (D). There are no significant rapids on this section.

SHUTTLE: From Athens to the last take-out for this section, take US 129/GA 15 Alt. north to a left turn onto GA 330. Proceed to the river; access is on the west side of the bridge. The upstream access points can all be reached by returning to US 129 north.

GAUGE: The USGS site provides data for the Middle Oconee near Arcade, although runnable levels are unknown using this gauge.

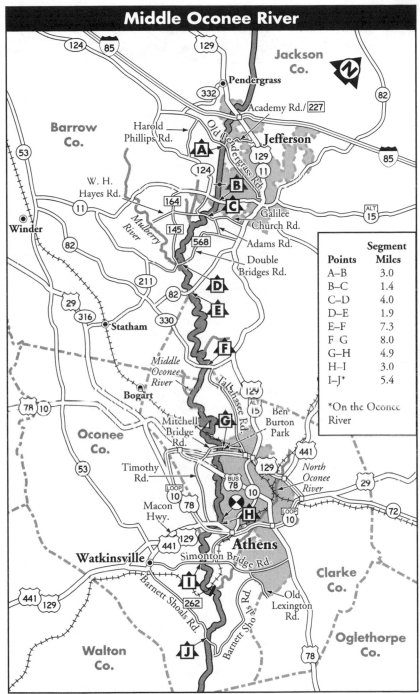

Middle Oconee River

	Segment
Points	**Miles**
A–B	3.0
B–C	1.4
C–D	4.0
D–E	1.9
E–F	7.3
F G	8.0
G–H	4.9
H–I	3.0
I–J*	5.4

*On the Oconee River

GA 330 TO BARNETT SHOALS ROAD ON THE OCONEE

class	I–II
length	21.3 mi
time	Up to 2.5 days
gauge	Web, visual
level	1.6 ft
gradient	8 fpm
scenery	C

DESCRIPTION: In this section, the Middle Oconee offers a pretty trip through the woodland suburban fringes of the city. Rapids are few; small dams create the main obstacles. The first dam is located below the GA 330 bridge (F); portage on the right to run the Class II rapids below. A broken dam is located above Ben Burton Park (G); the tower on river left marks the site. The remains of this dam can be run, but watch for the boat-shredding rebar supports that remain imbedded in the river. The park itself is a pleasant place to stop, if not being used as an access point.

Below the park, the river becomes very wide and rocky and the woodlands become more predominant. No formidable rapids are encountered; the only major blight is the dumping from a sewage treatment plant near Macon Highway. One final dam is located less than a mile above the confluence with the North Oconee River. The Middle Oconee river ends here and the main Oconee River begins. Another 2.8 miles of paddling brings you to the first access point on the Oconee at Barnett Shoals Road.

SHUTTLE: From Watkinsville, take Barnett Shoals Road east to the Oconee River; this is the final access point for the lower section. The best upper access points for this section are listed on the map.

GAUGE: A gauge is located in the river 0.5 miles upstream from GA 29. Runnable levels start at 1.6 feet. The maximum is up to flood stage. Data is also provided online for the USGS gauge located on the river in Athens. Minimums using this gauge are unknown.

MULBERRY RIVER

The Mulberry River is a small stream that flows into the Middle Oconee River northwest of Athens. Originating in Hall County, the river flows to the southwest, dividing Jackson and Barrow Counties. The Mulberry's gradient is gentle and there are no significant rapids as it drains the surrounding pastoral terrain.

MAPS: Winder North, Jefferson (USGS); Jackson, Barrow (County)

GA 11 TO GA 82 ON THE MIDDLE OCONEE

class	I
length	8.7 mi
time	6 hr
gauge	None
level	N/A
gradient	5 fpm
scenery	C+

DESCRIPTION: A small stream, the Mulberry must be caught at a favorable water level to make boating pleasant. Deadfalls are frequent and at high water create potentially hazardous strainers. On the other hand, the stream is sometimes too low to run at all. Wait for periods of moderate to heavy rainfall and be prepared to avoid debris clogging the streambed. The best access for canoeing is from Hancock Bridge Road (B) to the GA 82 bridge over the Middle Oconee (D).

The scenery is not dramatic, but it is pleasing to the eye. Hardwood forests alternate with pastures that at times lack adequate buffer vegetation. The concentration of large-scale chicken farms on this section is noticeably lower than on other rivers in the area.

SHUTTLE: The final take-out on the Middle Oconee is on GA 82 south of Jefferson. To the highest put-in at GA 11, continue south on GA 82 to a right turn onto GA 330, to a right turn onto GA 211 and a final right onto GA 11. Intermediate access is available at Hancock Bridge Road, which is reached by turning right onto Pleasant Hill Church Road from GA 211.

GAUGE: There is no gauge. Visually scout the stream's flow from the access points.

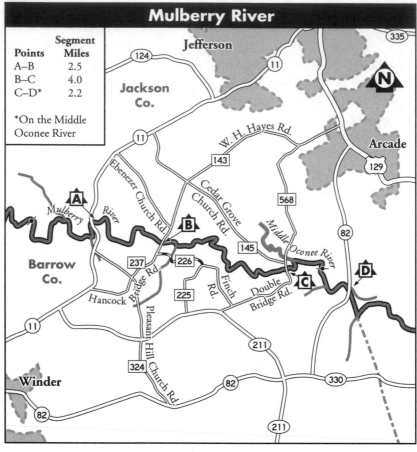

Mulberry River

Points	Segment Miles
A–B	2.5
B–C	4.0
C–D*	2.2

*On the Middle Oconee River

Jefferson

124

11

335

Jackson Co.

11

W. H. Hayes Rd.

143

Arcade

129

Ebenezer Church Rd.

Cedar Grove Church Rd.

568

A

Mulberry River

B

145

Middle Oconee River

82

Barrow Co.

237

226

C

D

Hancock Bridge Rd.

225

Finch Rd.

Double Bridge Rd.

11

Pleasant Hill Church Rd.

324

211

Winder

82

82

330

211

N

OCONEE RIVER

The Oconee River is born south of Lake Lanier in Hall County, where several small feeder streams supply the North and Middle Forks of the Oconee. Flowing southeastward and draining Jackson County, the forks join to form the Oconee River south of Athens. From Athens to Lake Oconee, the river has been smoothed by a series of dams, and now contains very little in the way of whitewater save for an occasional riffle. The current is lively between the dam pools and the wooded and well-vegetated 4- to 7-foot clay banks. Below Lake Sinclair, the river essentially enters the Coastal Plain, where it winds past occasional sandbars to its meeting with the Ocmulgee, forming the Altamaha River.

MAPS: Barnett Shoals East, Greshamville, Buckhead, Harmony, Liberty, Rockville, Lake Sinclair West, Lake Sinclair East, Milledgeville, Irwinton 15', Gumm Pond, Tooomsboro, Oconee, Cowhell Swamp, Dublin, Rentz, Minter, Rockledge, Lothair, Glennwood, Mt. Vernon, Uvalda, Hazelhurst North (USGS); Clark, Oconee, Oglethorpe, Greene, Putnam, Baldwin, Wilkinson, Washington, Johnson, Laurens, Treutlen, Wheeler, Montgomery (County); Georgia Department of Natural Resources; Oconee National Forest (USFS)

WATKINSVILLE TO LAKE OCONEE

class	1+
length	19.7 mi
time	Up to 2.5 days
gauge	Web
level	580 cfs
gradient	<4 fpm
scenery	B-

DESCRIPTION: As with most streams draining the Piedmont, the Oconee carries a large amount of sediment that adversely affects the aesthetic appearance of the water, causing it to vary in color from a greenish-brown to a pale, mustard yellow. Between Athens and Lake Sinclair signs of habitation are rare and the river setting is generally secluded. The Oconee National Forest borders the stream on the east starting at the Big Creek confluence and on both sides of the river downstream of the Rose Creek confluence until the vicinity of the I-20 bridge near the south end of Lake Oconee.

The surrounding terrain rises quickly from the Oconee's narrow floodplain to a gently dipping plateau and valley topography. Wildlife is plentiful and stream flora diverse, with river birch, sycamore, sugarberry, and green ash interspersed with several varieties of bottomland oak and stands of sweetgum and box elder.

Other than the pool behind Barnett Shoals Dam south of Athens, moving current in the Piedmont section of the Oconee terminates in the National Forest below the GA 15 bridge (B),

where the river encounters the backwaters of Lake Oconee. Below Wallace Dam the waters of the Oconee are simply transferred from Lake Oconee to Lake Sinclair.

The level of difficulty for the Oconee from its inception below Athens to Lake Oconee is Class I, with dams and occasional deadfalls being the primary hazards to navigation. The river averages 70–110 feet wide where moving current exists; channel configuration usually tends toward a moderate to long, straight or gently turning section followed by a sharp bend. The upper Oconee is runnable all year providing the Barnett Shoals Dam and Powerhouse are releasing.

SHUTTLE: A campground with boat ramp access is located on GA 15 north of Greensboro in the National Forest; other ramps are located on Lake Oconee. The highest put-in below the confluence of the forks is east of Watkinsville on Barnett Shoals Road.

GAUGE: The USGS Web site provides levels at Penfield, near the end of this section. The minimum is 580 cfs; maximum up to flood stage. Additional information, including a map of access points, can be provided by the Game and Fish Division's Fishery Management section, East Central Regional Office, at (770) 918-6418.

SINCLAIR DAM TO ALTAMAHA RIVER

class	I+
length	143.2 mi
time	Up to 4 weeks
gauge	Web, phone
level	N/A
gradient	<2 fpm
scenery	B

DESCRIPTION: Technically still a Piedmont stream below Lake Sinclair, below the dam the Oconee slips sluggishly through what is left of Furman Shoals (Class I+) before being impounded once again, this time by a 7-foot dam in Milledgeville that reaches out from both sides of an island in midstream. Land on the island to carry around.

Departing the populated and developed environs of Milledgeville, the river slips into a wooded lowland corridor and runs unobstructed in broad bends and long straightaways for 6 miles before assuming the looping serpentine course that will typify its path the remainder of the way to the Altamaha. A large river in the Coastal Plain, the Oconee broadens from 110 feet below Milledgeville to 250 to 280 feet at Dublin to almost 320 feet as it approaches its mouth at the Altamaha south of Charlotteville.

Throughout the Coastal Plain, sandbars suitable for camping become common on the insides of the bends, and some oxbow

Oconee River Map 1

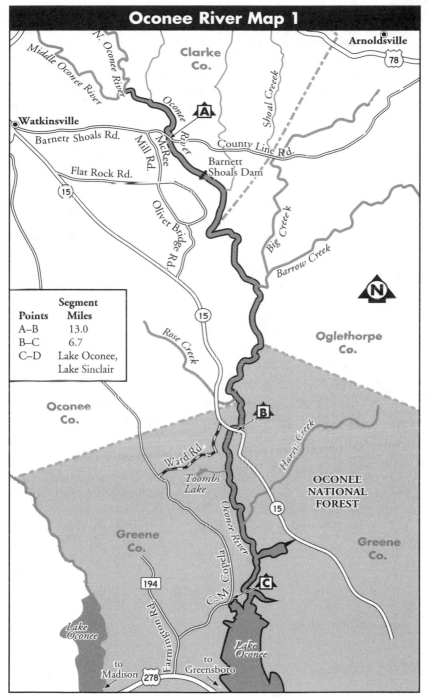

Clarke Co.

Arnoldsville

78

Middle Oconee River

N. Oconee River

N. Oconee River

Oconee River

Shoal Creek

A

Watkinsville

Barnett Shoals Rd.

McRee Mill Rd.

County Line Rd.

Barnett Shoals Dam

Flat Rock Rd.

15

Oliver Bridge Rd.

Big Creek

Barrow Creek

15

N

Points	Segment Miles
A–B	13.0
B–C	6.7
C–D	Lake Oconee, Lake Sinclair

Rose Creek

Oglethorpe Co.

Oconee Co.

B

Harris Creek

Ward Rd.

Toombs Lake

OCONEE NATIONAL FOREST

15

Greene Co.

Oconee River

Greene Co.

194

C. M. Copela

C

Lake Oconee

Farmington Rd.

Lake Oconee

to Madison

278

to Greensboro

lakes and meandering bypass islands appear. Surrounding the river is an often-flooded bottomland forest. In sections where the forest is flooded more than six months of the year, bald cypress, tupelo gum, and swamp black gum predominate. In areas inundated less than half the year, overcup oak and various water hickories combine with laurel, willow, oak, red maple, American elm, and green ash to form the lowland forest. On the bank, willow, cottonwood, river birch, some silver maple, sycamore, and bald cypress are common. Extremely remote, the forested bottomland swamp that surrounds the Oconee is more than 2 miles wide above Dublin, and expands below Dublin to a breadth approaching 4 miles. In Cow Hell Swamp north of Dublin, bald cypress grace the river in ever-increasing numbers and algae-covered backwater sloughs and oxbow lakes teem with wildlife.

As the Oconee enters Dublin, it flows through a well-defined channel below 15-foot banks before slipping back into the lowlands and swamp on the southeast side of the town. From here to the Altamaha the scenery remains similarly beautiful, with little change other than the appearance of pine on the natural levee and on the perimeter of the swamp. The level of difficulty throughout is Class I, with floating and stationary deadfalls being the only hazards to navigation. The current is slow and the water generally murky brown with sediment. The Oconee below Lake Sinclair is runnable all year.

SHUTTLE: From US 221 south of Uvalda, turn right at Bells Ferry Road for the last boat ramp on the Oconee, or continue straight ahead to the first ramp on the Altamaha at the bridge. See the map for the location of upper access points.

GAUGE: Runnable up to flood stage. Levels are posted on the USGS Web site for Milledge. For additional information, call the DNR Fisheries office in LaGrange at (706) 845-4180.

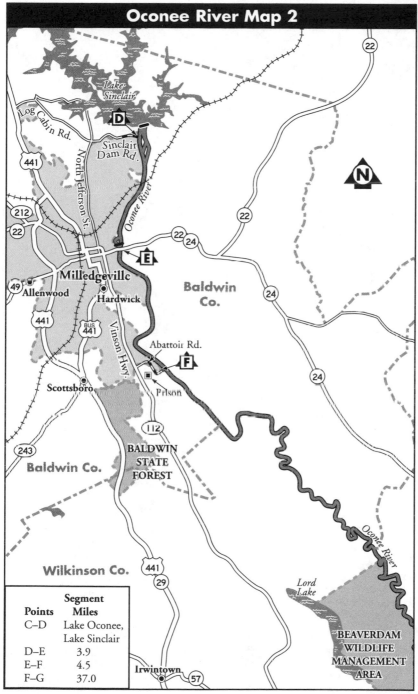

Oconee River Map 2

Lake Sinclair

D

Log Cabin Rd.

Sinclair Dam Rd.

441

North Jefferson St.

Oconee River

212

22

22 24

22 24

E

N

Baldwin Co.

24

Milledgeville

49 Allenwood

Hardwick

441

BUS 441

Vinson Hwy.

Abattoir Rd.

F

24

Scottsboro

Prison

112

243

BALDWIN STATE FOREST

Baldwin Co.

Oconee River

Wilkinson Co.

441

29

Lord Lake

BEAVERDAM WILDLIFE MANAGEMENT AREA

Irwintown

57

Points	Segment Miles
C–D	Lake Oconee, Lake Sinclair
D–E	3.9
E–F	4.5
F–G	37.0

Oconee River Map 3

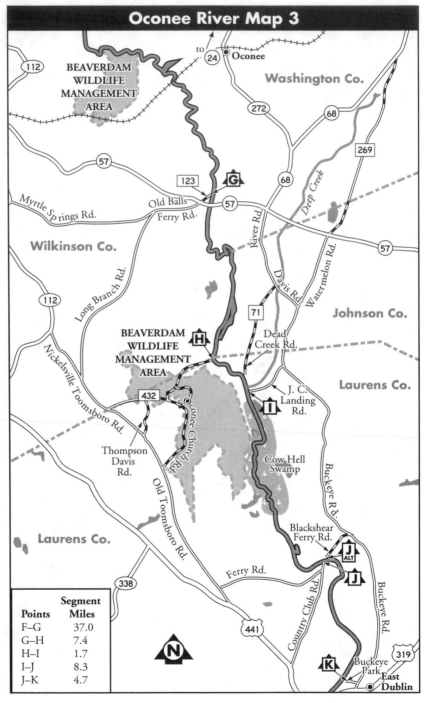

Points	Segment Miles
F–G	37.0
G–H	7.4
H–I	1.7
I–J	8.3
J–K	4.7

Oconee River Map 4

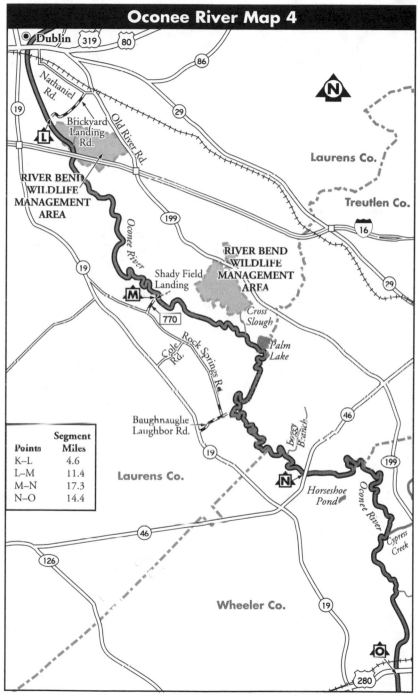

Dublin

319 80

86

Nathaniel Rd.

19

Brickyard Landing Rd.

L

Old River Rd.

29

N

Laurens Co.

Treutlen Co.

16

RIVER BEND
WILDLIFE
MANAGEMENT
AREA

199

Oconee River

RIVER BEND
WILDLIFE
MANAGEMENT
AREA

19

Shady Field Landing

M

29

770

Cross Slough

Cole Rd.

Rock Springs Rd.

Palm Lake

Baughnaughe Laughbor Rd.

Boggy Branch

46

19

199

Points	Segment Miles
K–L	4.6
L–M	11.4
M–N	17.3
N–O	14.4

Laurens Co.

N

Horseshoe Pond

Oconee River

46

126

Wheeler Co.

19

Cypress Creek

O

280

Oconee River Map 5

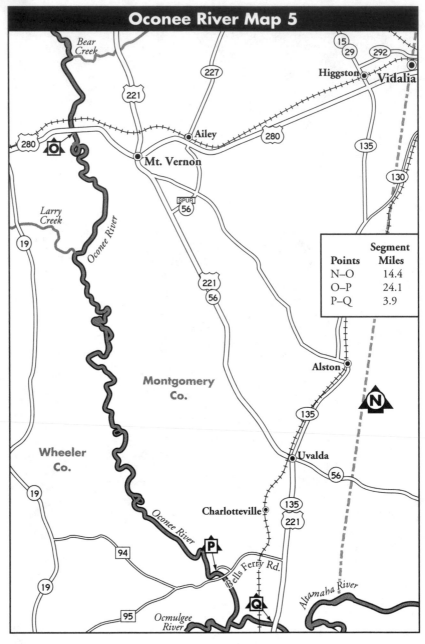

Points	Segment Miles
N–O	14.4
O–P	24.1
P–Q	3.9

APALACHEE RIVER

The Apalachee reaches from Gwinnett County to Lake Oconee and is a major tributary of the Oconee River. Its character combines features of lowland swamps and streams of the Piedmont; at times it is a river, at times a virtually impassable swamp. The sections described below are the most easily paddled. The upper section is the milder of the two and contains three portages around dams. The lower section begins with a dramatic Class IV drop and ends with a solid Class III. Both rapids can be accessed via nearby roads for those not interested in paddling the mostly mild water in between.

MAPS: Statham, High Shoals, Watkinsville, Apalachee (USGS); Walton, Oconee, Morgan, (County)

TREADWELL BRIDGE ROAD TO GA 186

class	I (II)
length	11.1 mi
time	6–7 hr
gauge	Web
level	Unknown
gradient	7 fpm
scenery	B-

DESCRIPTION: Though access is good for the 12.5 miles above this section, the stream is quite small and moves slowly through swampy areas replete with deadfalls and strainers. At times forward passage can be challenging. The highest feasible access is at the abandoned bridge at Tanners Bridge Road on the south side of the river for those interested in tackling all or portions of this section.

Below Treadwell Bridge Road (A), a dirt road on the river's right lacking its namesake bridge, the river becomes more lively and less barred by deadfall. Most of the Apalachee's course from this point to the bridge at GA 186 (C) is characterized by a gentle gradient with rapids that do not exceed Class II difficulty. There are three dams on this section that must be portaged. The first is a small dam just above US 78 at Caruthers Mill. The next dam is at Snows Mill Road just above the bridge; portage on the left shore. The last and highest dam is at the end of this section in the community of High Shoals at GA 186. If continuing downstream into the lower section, the dam can be portaged on either side, but the right is easier. The take-out for this section is located before the bridge and upstream of the dam at river right. This is private property, so be sure to follow the directions posted for contacting the landowner and asking permission.

SHUTTLE: From Watkinsville, take US 129/441 south toward Bishop. Turn right on GA 186. Continue to the take-out on the right on the far side of the bridge. To weave your way to the

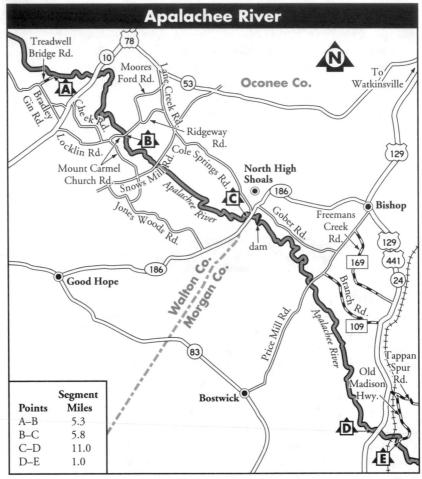

Apalachee River

Treadwell Bridge Rd.

Moores Ford Rd.

Oconee Co.

To Watkinsville

Bradley Gin Rd.

Creek Rd.

Lane Creek Rd.

Locklin Rd.

Ridgeway Rd.

Cole Springs Rd.

Mount Carmel Church Rd.

Snows Mill Rd.

Apalachee River

North High Shoals

Bishop

Jones Woods Rd.

Gober Rd.

Freemans Creek Rd.

dam

Good Hope

Walton Co.
Morgan Co.

Price Mill Rd.

Branch Rd.

Apalachee River

Bostwick

Old Madison Hwy.

Tappan Spur Rd.

Points	Segment Miles
A–B	5.3
B–C	5.8
C–D	11.0
D–E	1.0

put-in, continue east on GA 186 and turn right onto Jones-woods Road. Turn right onto Snows Mill Road, then left onto Mount Carmel Church Road. Follow this road to the river for the mid-run access point (B), or for the highest access point turn left onto Locklin Road before reaching the bridge. Next, turn right onto Creek Road, which will take you to US 78. A left onto US 78 followed by a quick right onto Snip Dillard Road brings you to Bradley Gin Road. Turn right here; Tread-well Bridge Road is less than a mile ahead on the right.

GAUGE: The USGS Web site provides data for the gauge near Bostwick. Ideal minimum and maximum levels are unknown.

GA 186 TO OLD MADISON HIGHWAY

class	I–III (IV)
length	12.0 mi
time	6 hr
gauge	Web
level	350 cfs
gradient	12 fpm
scenery	B+

DESCRIPTION: This section is characterized by stretches of moving water interspersed with a few large shoals. The first of these is at the community of High Falls immediately south of the GA 186 bridge. The community gets its name from a series of cascades that includes one sliding drop of over 20 feet. Access to various entry points along this rapid is on river left. This is private property; contact the landowner on site and ask permission before putting in.

This entire rapid should be carefully scouted. Many accidents, some fatal, have occurred here. At certain higher water levels a dangerous hydraulic reversal develops at the base of the falls. Avoid it. These rapids may reach Class IV difficulty in high water.

There are two other significant rapids on the lower section beyond the occasional riffle or easy ledge. The first is at the old Price Mill Shoals Bridge where the river drops 10 feet over a series of ledges. Scout this drop from the left bank. South of US 441, an old railroad bridge marks the start of the second, more dramatic rapid. Stretching for over 200 yards, Pot Leaf Shoals starts out as fairly straightforward Class II ledges and ends as a solid Class III drop through a series of channels created by large and occasionally undercut boulders. High water may push this portion of the drop to Class IV; it should be scouted. Trails along both sides provide good vantage points. The take-out for this section is just below these shoals, offering an opportunity to take a look before starting the run. Off-road vehicle traffic appears to be heavy in this area, suggesting that this might not be the best place to leave a car overnight.

Though the river may look enticing beyond the Old Madison Highway take-out (E), beware. Below this point creeks leave instead of enter the main stream as the river divides into progressively smaller channels. Eventually, these channels become too shallow to float, requiring paddlers to pole, prod, and drag their boats through the resulting swamp in a race to reach downstream access before nightfall.

SHUTTLE: From Watkinsville, take US 441 south. After passing the Oconee Heritage Park, watch for the unpaved Tappan Spur Road on the left as US 441 makes a gradual westward turn. Take Tappan Spur Road 1.3 miles to an intersection with an unmarked gravel road; oncoming traffic has a stop sign. This is Old Madison Highway; turn right here and follow the main road to the river. To return to the put-in, take US 441 north to GA 186. Turn left on

GA 186 and follow to the river. Access is on river left, down the private dirt road close to the bridge. Ask permission before using the land as this is private property.

GAUGE: See the preceding section. The minimum recommended level for the shoals is 350 cfs.

LITTLE RIVER OF PUTNAM COUNTY

A wild stream northeast of Macon, the Little River is pristine and secluded almost all the way to Lake Sinclair, with the entire canoeable section either in or on the boundary of the Oconee National Forest. The river originates in southern Morgan County and runs southeast over a rock and clay bed between thickly wooded banks of 3–6 feet, with an average slope of 40–65 degrees. A major tributary of the Oconee, the river drains portions of Morgan, Putnam, and Jasper Counties.

MAPS: Eatonton, Lake Sinclair West (USGS); Putnam (County); Oconee National Forest (USFS)

GLADES ROAD TO LAKE SINCLAIR

class	I–II
length	16.9 mi
time	Up to 2 days
gauge	Web
level	250 cfs
gradient	4.9 fpm
scenery	B

DESCRIPTION: Runnable downstream of Glades Road northwest of Eatonton in periods of wet weather, the Little sports intermittent Class II rapids and shoals almost all the way to the GA 44 bridge (D). Averaging 30 to 50 feet in width, the river is winding and convoluted throughout its length. The surrounding terrain consists mainly of low, forested hills conducive to camping. Public lands border both sides of the stream for the first 4 miles and continue another 3 miles past this point on the right side of the river.

The 3.4-mile segment of river below Martins Mill Road (B) down to the GA 16 bridge (C) contains most of the river's whitewater rapids, interspersed with long pools. Unfortunately, the Little is high in transported sediment, thus making "whitewater" somewhat a misnomer since the actual color of the water at runnable periods is mustard brown. The most ornery rapid in this section consists of an extended jumble of blasted rock lacking an established channel at lower flows.

Downstream of GA 16 is a dam that must be portaged, followed by the last significant section of shoals. The last take-out on the river is at GA 44, but the trip can be extended another 6.6 miles to the boat ramp off of Twin Bridges Road at Lake Sinclair.

Little River of Putnam County

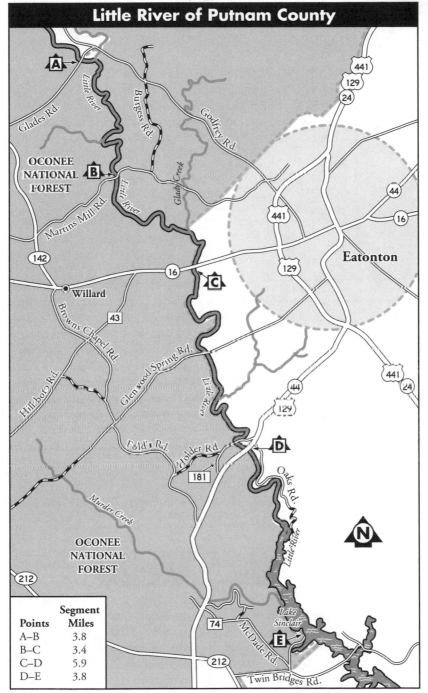

Points	Segment Miles
A–B	3.8
B–C	3.4
C–D	5.9
D–E	3.8

SHUTTLE: From Milledgeville to the take-out, use GA 212 north to reach Twin Bridges Road. Turn right; after 1 mile, turn left and follow signs for the Twin Bridges camping area at the lake. To reach the highest put-in, return to GA 212 and continue north to US 129. Turn right and stay on US 129 as it skirts Eatonton to the west. Turn left onto Godfrey Road, then left at Glades Road. The bridge and highest access point is ahead. Midway access points are found on Martins Mill Road (reached from Godfrey), GA 16 (off of US 129), and US 129 itself.

GAUGE: Online data is available for the Little River near Eatonton on the USGS Web site. The minimum recommended level is 250 cfs; the river is more enjoyable with at least 350 cfs. Maximum is up to flood stage.

ALCOVY RIVER

An easily accessible Piedmont stream rich in beauty and diverse in flora and wildlife, the Alcovy is born in Gwinnett County near Lawrenceville and flows south to drain Walton and Newton Counties before spilling into Lake Jackson where it meets the Yellow and South Rivers to form the Ocmulgee. The river's course offers a little of something for everyone. The upper section near the headwaters is a short, difficult, steep creek run. Farther downstream, the river becomes a full-fledged swamp in the middle section. For most of the lower section, the river's character is mild, with only one shoal mid-run—but it ends with a bang at a long series of rapids that build in intensity to a Class III (IV) finish. This last rapid, or the mostly flatwater section proceeding it, is easily omitted by using the access points above the bridge near the top of the drop.

MAPS: Lawrencville, Covington, Stewart (USGS); Gwinnett, Newton (County)

US 29 TO ALCOVY ROAD

class	III (IV)
length	2.5 mi
time	2 hr
gauge	Web
level	200 cfs
gradient	45 fpm (100+)
scenery	B-

DESCRIPTION: Beautiful at times, especially for its location, the Upper Alcovy is a very narrow and creek-like run just outside Atlanta. The run is Class III difficulty with one Class IV drop; two-thirds of the upper section is whitewater and the remainder flat. Keep an eye out for strainers throughout the run as it is easy for trees to bridge the narrow stream.

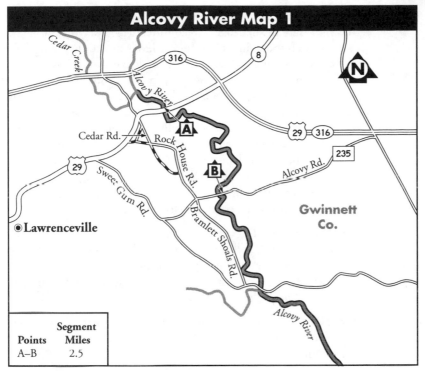

Alcovy River Map 1

Points	Segment Miles
A–B	2.5

At the put-in on US 29, the easiest access is available on river right, upstream of the bridge. The small stacked stone dam located immediately below the bridge is runnable at lower water levels, but with a little more effort, it is possible to put-in immediately below this structure.

There is a larger dam near the take-out for this section that is portaged on the left. Minimize the time spent on this portage and get back into the river near the base of the dam to avoid calling attention to yourself.

The gradient between the two dams is a little over 100 feet per mile, but it does not seem like it when you are on the run. There is one Class IV rapid about one-third of the way into the run that contains a good-sized undercut rock that collects debris. The river's flow leading up to this rapid is continuous with no eddies; get out a good ways upstream to scout it. In this rapid, a midstream boulder splits the current just below the main drop, with half of the resulting current heading to the left into the undercut rocks. The stream twists to the left as it crosses the ledge, then

straightens out after hitting the undercut rocks. A big boof off the right side of the ledge is recommended to stay to the right. This move is more difficult at higher levels due to the strength of the current heading to the left over the ledge; at lower water levels it is hard to get enough momentum for a good boof.

The Upper Alcovy takes a good amount of water to run and is feasible only in the winter most of the time. River levels need to be on the rise to make a run possible, but with the high volume of runoff that the river receives upstream of this section be aware that conditions can change rapidly. If the visual scouting reveals the creek running at medium to high levels during a downpour, it is close to the flashing point and the flow volume can rise exponentially. This is not a condition for boating.

SHUTTLE: From Lawrenceville, take US 29 east and turn right onto Cedar Road, following it to a lefthand turn onto Alcovy Road. The bridge and take-out is ahead. To get to the put-in, return to US 29 and turn right; proceed to the put-in on the southwest side of the bridge.

GAUGE: The USGS Web site provides data for the Alcovy near Grayson. A good minimum for this run is 200 cfs and rising; maximum is 1,000 cfs.

US 278/GA12 TO CR 213

class	I
length	6.1 mi
time	4.5 hr
gauge	None
level	N/A
gradient	7 fpm
scenery	B-

DESCRIPTION: The Alcovy is generally runnable downstream of the US 278 bridge east of Covington from November to early July in years of average rainfall. Unusual for its location in the Piedmont, in this section the river meanders through a wooded lowland swamp terrain complete with bypass islands and oxbow lakes supporting large stands of tupelo gum. Hazards in this section are limited primarily to deadfalls, which hinder forward progress. Fishing is reported to be good in this little-traveled and isolated section of river.

SHUTTLE: From Covington, take GA 36 south turning left at CR 213. Proceed 0.5 miles to the bridge and take-out. For put-in, return to Covington via GA 36 north. Turn right onto Floyd Street at the square; follow Floyd to US 278/GA 12. Turn right onto US 278/GA 12; the river is 1.6 miles ahead. The best access is on the river's left, downstream side.

GAUGE: There is no gauge for this section of river.

CR 213 TO FACTORY SHOALS RECREATION AREA

class	I–II (IV)
length	8.3 mi
time	5 hr
gauge	Visual, phone
level	1.0 ft
gradient	10 fpm (55)
scenery	B-

DESCRIPTION: Passing under the Central Georgia railroad bridge above CR 213, the river emerges from the watery lowlands and continues in a well-defined channel with red clay banks up to 6 feet high that slope at an angle of 45 to 90 degrees. At the start of this section, the river's width varies between 25 and 40 feet, then widens to between 45 and 65 feet for most of its runnable length. The current on the Alcovy is generally moderate and the water color is usually a murky brown, indicative of the high concentration of dissolved clays.

The surrounding terrain remains wooded but is drier than it was upstream. Common tree varieties in the floodplain forests include sweet gum, swamp chestnut, oak, red ash, red maple, dogwood, possum haw, willow oak, and overcup oak. Along the banks, river birch, sugarberry, sycamore, and green ash predominate.

Downstream from the bridge at Henderson Mill Road (E) the Alcovy begins to drop at a greater rate. One short series of ledges punctuates the run a mile below the mouth of Long Branch Creek. Afterwards, the Alcovy remains calm until just upstream of the bridge at Newton Factory Road. It is possible to take-out at the bridge above the bulk of the shoals, or even farther upstream at the campsites within the northern branch of the Factory Shoals Recreation Area.

Here the Alcovy's width expands to 280 feet in spots as it crashes the 55 vertical feet down White and Factory Shoals. This 0.8-mile series of rapids builds to Class III (IV) intensity as the river passes below the bridge and into an extensive rock garden that culminates with a 6-foot plunge into the pool of Lake Jackson. Difficulty and intensity vary according to water level, and it should be scouted. The last rapid of the series can be run to the right or left. The Factory Shoals Recreation Area offers a take-out point below the shoals and scouting trails on river right. Though not included in the mileage for this section, the trip can be extended another 4 miles south into Lake Jackson.

SHUTTLE: From Covington, take GA 36 south approximately 10 miles. Turn left onto Newton Factory Bridge Road and continue 1 mile ahead to the river or Factory Shoals Recreation Area (entrance on the right). To get to the put-in, return to GA 36 and turn right. Continue to a right-hand turn onto CR 213. The bridge is up ahead.

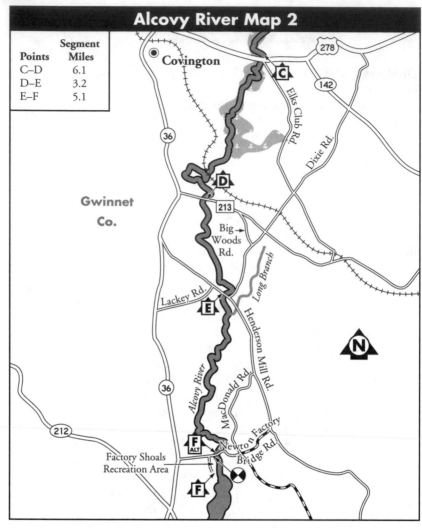

GAUGE: There is a visual gauge at Newton Factory Bridge Road on the river-right, downstream side. If running Factory Shoals, 1.0 is the minimum; the water gets pushy above 2.0. Levels can be provided with some lead time by calling the Factory Shoals Park ranger at (770) 787-6670. The lower section upstream of Factory Shoals can be run at levels below 1.0.

YELLOW RIVER

An intimate river with a consistently Piedmont flavor, the Yellow River stretches from suburban Gwinnett County outside of Atlanta to the south, draining portions of DeKalb, Rockdale, and Newton Counties before entering the backwaters of Lake Jackson. True to its name, the Yellow runs high in sediment, resulting in a water color from light to greenish brown. The upper section has more gradient and contains a sprinkling of significant ledges. The gradient in the lower section is much less, with most of the fall occurring at two lengthy and impressive shoals, each one topped with an equally impressive dam. Higher, and consequently dirtier flows are needed to make running the Yellow's rapids feasible.

MAPS: Snellville, Conyers, Milstead, Porterdale, Stewart, Worthville (USGS); Gwinnett, DeKalb, Rockdale, Newton (County)

US 78 TO YELLOW RIVER MOUNTAIN BIKE PARK

class	II–III (IV)
length	4.2 mi
time	2.5 hr
gauge	Web
level	250 cfs
gradient	15 fpm
scenery	B-

DESCRIPTION: This upper section of the Yellow River begins downriver from a sewage treatment plant stationed north of US 78 and as such has the accompanying water quality problems. On the plus side, it is conveniently located in Gwinnett County near Stone Mountain for whitewater paddlers who can overlook this. Once the water level is high enough to enjoy this section, it also moves quickly, and boaters should be competent in their Class III moves before attempting a run.

The first 3 miles hold a few drops of Class II–III difficulty interspersed with flat water. At high water levels, three keeper hydraulics are formed. The first is preceded by a stretch of fast-moving water that forms potential surfing waves. At the main drop, the riverbed creates a virtual low-head dam that spawns a dangerous pour-over hole. Avoid this by running the ledge on the very far right side, following the river as it cuts into the bank farther than it appears it will. A short distance downstream, an island splits the river into two channels, the right channel giving the better ride as you accelerate through it to the left. There have been confrontations with private landowners in this area; when scouting, keep a low profile and move along quickly.

At Annistown Bridge Road (B), there are two interesting drops: one above the bridge and another immediately below. These can be scouted from the roadway before putting in. Both are considered Class III difficulty at lower water levels, but at

higher flows become far more dangerous given the proximity of the bridge pilings and the size of the hydraulics that form, particularly at the downstream ledge. The route through the groove of the upper ledge is less rocky than appears; this drop can also be run by boofing off the flat rock to the right of the groove. The downstream ledge forms a fun play spot at lower water levels, but above 8 feet it becomes a retentive keeper hydraulic that should be avoided. Regardless of whether you pass to the right or the left of the bridge pilings, the best route is to the right of the hole, even if it means getting up-ended by the large pour-over boulder waiting for you there. Access at Annistown Bridge Road makes this a possible park-and-play spot.

Below this drop, the river moves quickly through the remaining mile to the Yellow River Mountain Bike Park (C), the best take-out for this section.

SHUTTLE: From the highest put-in on Stone Mountain Freeway (US 78), turn right onto Ross Road, east of the river. Turn right at Annistown Bridge Road; after crossing the river, take the first left onto Juhan Road. The park is ahead on the left.

GAUGE: Levels for the gauge located at GA 124 near Lithonia are available on the USGS Web site. A minimum of 250 cfs is needed to run this section, but levels of 1,000 cfs (5.25 feet) create better play spots. Above 2,500 cfs (8 feet), eddies become scarce as the river starts running into the trees; the keepers above the island and below the Annistown Bridge should be avoided.

YELLOW RIVER MOUNTAIN BIKE PARK TO GA 36

class	I–II (III)
length	43.3 mi
time	Up to 2.5 days
gauge	Web
level	175 cfs
gradient	4 fpm (42)
scenery	B- to C

DESCRIPTION: In this section the Yellow River offers nearly 44 miles of mostly placid floating interrupted by two long and dramatic shoals. The river maintains a moderate current as it widens to an average of 45 to 70 feet, running between well-defined red-clay banks. Signs of habitation are common since the Yellow flows along or through several large settlements. Outside of these, the Piedmont wilderness atmosphere remains largely intact. Wildlife is common and the flora is luxurious and diverse.

Other than a stretch of Class II water located downstream of GA 124 (D), the first significant departure from the relaxing repartee is located 0.2 miles below the GA 20 bridge at Milstead (G). A sizeable dam stalls the river's flow, and must be portaged on the left. Below the dam is a series of Class II, borderline Class III rapids—the most accessible stretch of significant whitewater in the lower section. The footpath reached via the gravel

Yellow River Map 1

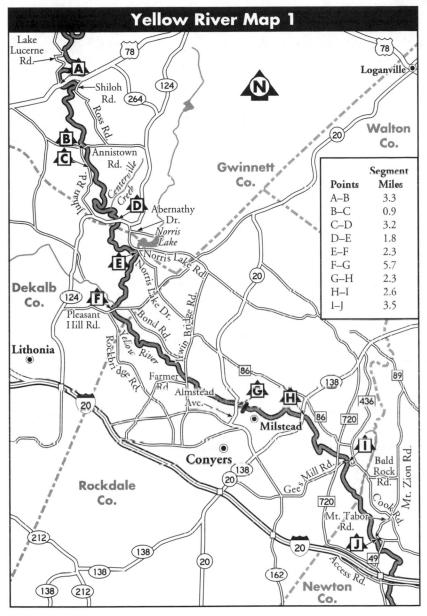

Lake Lucerne Rd.

78

A

Shiloh Rd.

124

264

Ross Rd.

Loganville

N

20

Walton Co.

B

C

Annistown Rd.

Juhan Rd.

Centerville Creek

D

Abernathy Dr.

Norris Lake

Gwinnett Co.

Norris Lake Rd.

E

Norris Lake Dr.

20

Dekalb Co.

124 **F**

Pleasant Hill Rd.

Bond Rd.

Irwin Bridge Rd.

Yellow River

Rockbridge Rd.

Lithonia

Farmer Rd.

Almstead Ave.

86

G

H

138

89

436

20

Milstead

86

720

I

Bald Rock Rd.

Mt. Zion Rd.

Conyers

138

20

Gee's Mill Rd.

Cook Rd.

Rockdale Co.

720

Mt. Tabor Rd.

212

138

20

J

49

138

20

162

Access Rd.

138

212

Newton Co.

Points	Segment Miles
A–B	3.3
B–C	0.9
C–D	3.2
D–E	1.8
E–F	2.3
F–G	5.7
G–H	2.3
H–I	2.6
I–J	3.5

Yarbrough Road allows for many possible put-ins and easy scouting from the granite outcropping on river left. Abundant broken glass and other trash in the area indicate that this might not be the best place to leave a car. An alternate access point for the shoals (and dam) is at the river-left, downstream side of the GA 20 bridge.

These shoals start out wide, with a shallow island dividing the flow as the river passes over numerous small ledges. A Class III move is required to ferry from river left to river right downstream of the dam's boil line if you choose to run to the channel to the right of the island. Below the island, the channels converge into a narrow cinch that creates a powerful mid-river hydraulic; at 1,000 cfs, this keeper hole is nearly river-wide. A large eddy below the hole makes for an easy stopping point for the short carry back up to the top. The gradient continues to drop downstream as the river is once again divided, this time by a larger island. Be prepared to avoid the right bank in the right channel as a considerable amount of the current bounces off the wall.

Continuing downstream below these shoals, the Yellow resumes its tranquil demeanor, and only occasional deadfalls pose a hazard to navigation. Two miles below I-20 and above the Brown bridge west of Covington (L), a pipeline crosses the river. This spot is dangerous at most water levels and should be portaged.

The second significant stretch of rapids on this section, Cedar Shoals, starts beneath the dam located immediately below the GA 81 bridge in the town of Porterdale (M). It is easy to take-out above the bridge on river left, but portaging to continue your trip downstream is problematic. An old factory building on river left blocks passage on that side; some of the river's flow is still diverted into the basement of this building, exiting downstream of the dam. Portaging is physically possible on the right, but the property is private and posted. The rapids below the dam are considered to be Class II–IV depending on the water level; the channel to the right of the island is preferable. For boaters interesting in paddling a portion of these extensive shoals, there is another access point on river left before the end of the rapids at River Front Road. A sewage treatment plant blocks access farther downstream at the end of this road; the next feasible access point is 11 miles downstream at GA 212.

From the end of Cedar Shoals to Lake Jackson, the river runs flat with a few intermittent Class I riffles and very small shoals. The river corridor remains wooded and serene in spite of frequent signs of habitation. Once again deadfalls constitute the major hazard to navigation.

Yellow River Map 2

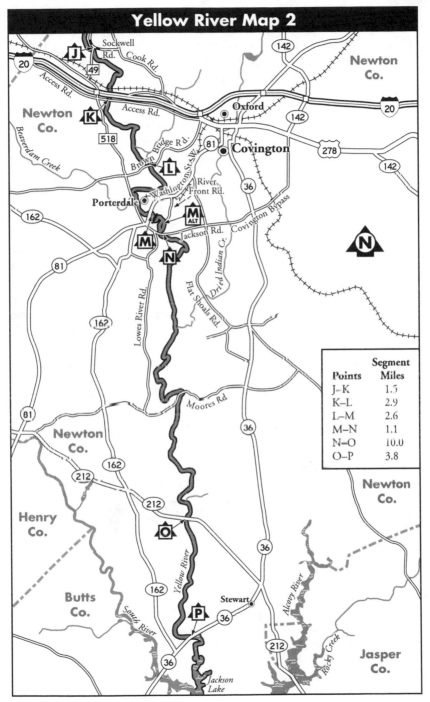

Points	Segment Miles
J–K	1.5
K–L	2.9
L–M	2.6
M–N	1.1
N–O	10.0
O–P	3.8

SHUTTLE: The final take-out (P) is located on GA 36, south of Covington. Without a four-wheel-drive vehicle, the carry down the dirt road on the northwest side of the GA 36 bridge is long. Most of the lower access points can be reached from GA 162. See the map for the locations of the higher access points.

GAUGE: The USGS Web site posts data for gauges located at Pleasant Hill Road and farther downstream at Gees Mill Road. Using Gees Mill Road gauge, the minimum level for the rapids at Milstead is 800 cfs. A minimum of 175 cfs suffices as a starting point for floating the flat sections.

SOUTH RIVER

The saga of the South River, Atlanta's "other" river, is full of twists and turns. Born in the city streets near the state capitol and Zoo Atlanta, many of the river's sources literally crawl underground through a combined sewage/stormwater system before the river emerges to flow southeast through DeKalb, Rockdale, and Newton Counties on its way into Lake Jackson. Despite its urban roots, the river's shores are at times thickly wooded, even in its upper reaches. Plans are in place for improving the water quality by separating Atlanta's sewage from run-off, at the same time that forested land adjoining the river is being acquired for preservation as public green space. Though far cleaner than it was in the early 1990s, the river is best enjoyed in the cooler months and not after heavy rains.

MAPS: Redan, Conyers, Kellytown, Ola, Worthville (USGS); DeKalb, Rockdale, Henry, Newton (County)

SNAPFINGER ROAD TO LAKE JACKSON

class	I–II (III)
length	40.7 mi
time	Up to 4 days
gauge	Web, visual
level	400 cfs
gradient	4
scenery	B- to C

DESCRIPTION: Tree-lined and intimate, the northernmost stretches of the South River run through a narrow wooded valley, skirt some exposed bluffs, and wind along the base of several tall, gumdrop-shaped granite outcroppings that include Panola and Arabia Mountains. Evidence of habitation and development are common along the South River but somewhat surprisingly do not occur in sufficient concentration to spoil the wilderness beauty of the stream. The Arabia Mountain Heritage Area encompasses 2,000 acres of land at the top of this run, with plans to purchase additional acres to further preserve the river corridor.

The river starts this section by cascading over Panola Shoals, an impressive granite rock-outcropping slide topped by the GA 155 bridge. If you choose to run the slide on the left, first scout from the left bank to spot the unfortunately placed rebar near the end of the chute. Quickly settling down, the river stumbles playfully over sandbars and intermittent Class I+ shoals all the way to the Klondike Road bridge (B). Midway in this section is a low-water bridge that can be dangerous at certain water levels. This first segment can be plagued by deadfall which must be portaged around or dodged.

One-half mile below Klondike Road the river doubles in width as it spills over Albert Shoals, a series of ledges requiring a Class III move that starts on the right and runs left to avoid the pour-over extending from the right side. Moderate flows are needed in order to cleanly run the jumble of rocks in the channel on the left. Albert Shoals is close enough to the bridge to allow park and play access.

Smaller rapids and short shoals, not exceeding Class II in difficulty, occur intermittently up to the vicinity of the GA 138 bridge (C). The river calms down after passing GA 138 as it weaves through a broadened valley lined with typical Piedmont bottomland forests. The 10 miles of river from GA 138 to GA 20 remains convoluted and serpentine, and is frequently obstructed by deadfalls. Below the GA 20 bridge are the Class II Peach Stone Shoals; farther downstream the river passes through some marshy spots before reaching GA 81. The best access here is on river left below the bridge.

Immediately below GA 81 (F) is Snapping Shoals Dam, a low head dam that should be portaged on the right. At moderate flows, Snapping Shoals provides several hundred yards of continuous Class I–II entertainment; the shoal's difficulty increases at higher flows. Half a mile below GA 81 is an access point on river left where GA 212 nears the river. After this point, the current slows to a moderate to slow pace and becomes generally incapable of more than a good ripple. As the river approaches the lake, the floodplain becomes increasingly wet and swampy.

SHUTTLE: The Lake Jackson take-out is located on GA 36, north of the town of Jackson. All other access points intersect with GA 212, which is reached by continuing north on GA 36, turning left onto GA 162, and then left again onto GA 212.

GAUGE: The USGS Web site provides levels for the South River at Klondike Road. The minimum runnable level is 400 cfs; maximum is up to flood stage. A gauge is also located in the river at Butler Bridge Road.

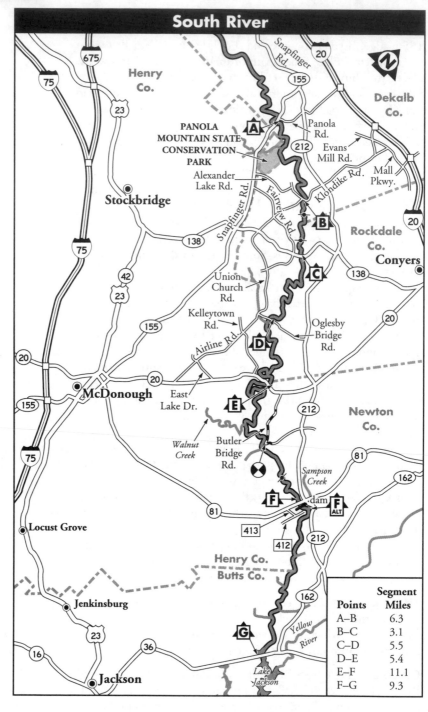

South River

Points	Segment Miles
A–B	6.3
B–C	3.1
C–D	5.5
D–E	5.4
E–F	11.1
F–G	9.3

OCMULGEE RIVER

The Ocmulgee is born at the confluence of the Alcovy and South Rivers in the backwaters of Jackson Lake in Butts and Jasper Counties. Flowing southeast below Lloyd Shoals Dam through the Piedmont, the Ocmulgee winds through steep-to-rolling hills and narrow valleys flanked by a lush, wooded corridor of pine, sweet gum, hickory, willow, red maple, white oak, black oak, and beech. Rock outcroppings occasionally grace the riverside as the stream runs within well-defined red clay banks 6–14 feet high, sharply inclined between 60 and 90 degrees. Scrub vegetation is thick with diverse flora, including ferns, vines, and shrubs. The Ocmulgee carries a high concentration of sediment and therefore appears muddy most of the year.

MAPS: Lloyd Shoals Dam, Berner, East Juliette, Macon East, Warner Robbins Northeast, Warner Robbins Southeast, Haynesville, Westlake, Klondike, Hawkinsville, Finleyson East, West of Eastman, Abbeville North, Abbeville South, Rhine, Queensland, China Hill, Jacksonville, Snipesville, Roper, Lumber City, Hazlehurst North (USGS); Jasper, Butts, Monroe, Jones, Bibb, Twiggs, Houston, Bleckly, Pulaski, Dodge, Wilcox, Telfair, Ben Hill, Coffee, Jeff Davis, Wheeler, Montgomery (County); Georgia Department of Natural Resources; Oconee National Forest (USFS).

LLOYD SHOALS DAM TO MACON

class	I–II (III)
length	45.5 mi
time	Up to 4.5 days
gauge	Web
level	400 cfs
gradient	4 fpm
scenery	A–C

DESCRIPTION: The initial section of the Ocmulgee below Lake Jackson runs through the historic Seven Islands area. Two of the oldest known roads in North America, the Seven Islands Stagecoach Route and the Seven Islands Indian Trail converge in Jasper County and cross the river at Smith Mill Road. Evolving out of a major trading hub for the Native American Creek Tribe, several large mills operated in this stretch during the nineteenth century. After being demolished by one of Sherman's armies in November 1864, some were rebuilt and operated until the cotton collapse of the 1920s and '30s.

Forest has since reclaimed the land and left little obvious evidence of past human activity. One fascinating exception is the ruined Lamar's Mill on the Butts County (river-right) side of Forty Acre Island. Exactly at this point the river spills across its largest rapid, a long, tight series of ledges rated Class III. Most of the current flows left of an island and the gradient is more

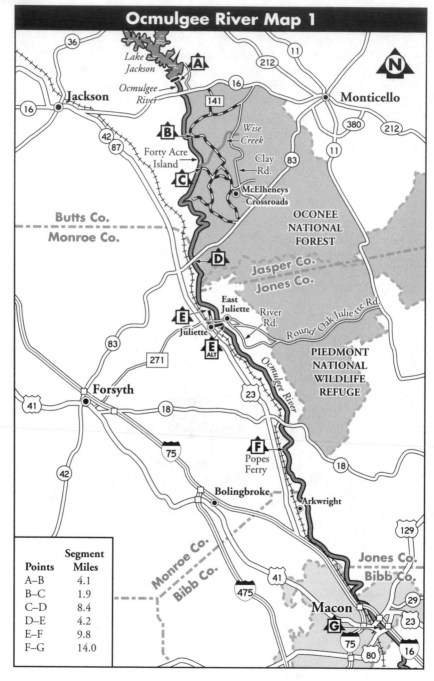

Ocmulgee River Map 1

36

11

212

Lake Jackson

A

N

Jackson

16

Ocmulgee River

16

141

Monticello

380

212

42

87

B

Wise Creek

11

Forty Acre Island

C

Clay Rd.

83

McElheneys Crossroads

OCONEE NATIONAL FOREST

Butts Co.
Monroe Co.

D

Jasper Co.
Jones Co.

East Juliette

River Rd.

Round Oak Juliette Rd.

E

Juliette

83

271

E ALT

PIEDMONT NATIONAL WILDLIFE REFUGE

Forsyth

41

18

Ocmulgee River

23

75

F

42

Popes Ferry

18

Bolingbroke

Arkwright

129

Monroe Co.
Bibb Co.

Jones Co.
Bibb Co.

41

475

29

Macon

G

75

23

80

16

Points	Segment Miles
A–B	4.1
B–C	1.9
C–D	8.4
D–E	4.2
E–F	9.8
F–G	14.0

photo © Tom Welander

Sneak Rapid on the Ocmulgee

gradual the farther left you go. A more abrupt channel right of the island abuses boats; few would consider it worthwhile. Less advanced boaters and those more keen on experiencing history than bruising limbs and busting boats can portage the entire rapid through the mill site on the right shore.

Flows above 2,000 cfs enable you to float down the left side of Forty Acre Island. This mile-long channel is very secluded and pretty, with one significant ledge portaged on the left bank. Two other shoals of moderate difficulty are difficult to portage and pose potentially bad consequences for less-experienced boaters. This secret stream is not hospitable to less than apt paddlers.

Long stretches of smooth water deter most whitewater boaters from the Seven Islands section; the difficulty of the infrequent rapids wards off most others. The few who embrace this quintessential Piedmont conundrum find themselves joyfully isolated. There is no modern development on the upper reaches of the river. A patchwork of private and public lands, the latter acquisitions of the Oconee National Forest, borders the river on the left from GA 16 to below GA 83. Numerous islands present good camping options.

Below Wise Creek (C), the Ocmulgee deepens. The corridor remains pristine as the river's course tends towards broad gentle curves and moderate to long straightaways followed occasionally by a sharp bend. The current continues down to the backwaters of John Birch Dam in the vicinity of GA 83 (D). At Juliette, you

must make a quarter-mile portage on the left around the Birch Dam. Shoals resume at half-mile intervals below the dam, seldom exceeding easy Class II, and continue all the way to Arkwright. The large Arkwright Power Plant signals the end of the Ocmulgee's whitewater and the departure of the river from the Piedmont. The Ocmulgee rejoins civilization below Arkwright as it flows through Macon's industrial suburbs and downtown. On the east side of Macon, the valley broadens and confining hills taper and level off, marking the Ocmulgee's descent into the Coastal Plain.

The river's width in the Piedmont varies from 90 to 120 feet in the upper stretches to 260 feet at some shoals and pools above the shoals. Flows are determined by frequent but irregular releases from Lloyd Shoals Dam. Unfortunately, Georgia Power does not announce its release schedule in advance.

SHUTTLE: To the Wise Creek take-out, head east on GA 16 from Jackson. After crossing the river (the put-in at the Georgia Power boat ramp is located up the paved road on the left), turn right onto Clay Road, then right at the paved Freedonia Church Road/McElheney Crossroads. At the end of the road, turn right and then take the next left, proceeding straight ahead at the next stop sign to reach the take-out at Wise Creek. Other access points include boat ramps at GA 83, Pope's Ferry (downstream of GA 18), and in Macon at Spring Street (G).

GAUGE: The river is generally runnable from Lake Jackson to Macon all year, subject to regular but capricious releases at Lloyd Shoals Dam. Flow volume is reported on the USGS Web site for the river at Jackson. The minimum is 400 cfs; 800 cfs is more enjoyable. The maximum is flood stage. Water released from the dam is cold, increasing the risk of hypothermia in cooler weather.

MACON TO ALTAMAHA RIVER

class	I
length	198.8 mi
time	Up to 4 weeks
gauge	Web
level	N/A
gradient	<2 fpm
scenery	B

DESCRIPTION: As the Ocmulgee slips out of Macon, away from the Piedmont and into the Coastal Plain, it assumes the characteristics of most alluvial Coastal Plain streams. Its course becomes convoluted and serpentine, with horseshoe bends, islands, and some oxbow lakes. To either side of the river, bottomland forests envelope the Ocmulgee in a pristine wilderness

Ocmulgee River Map 2

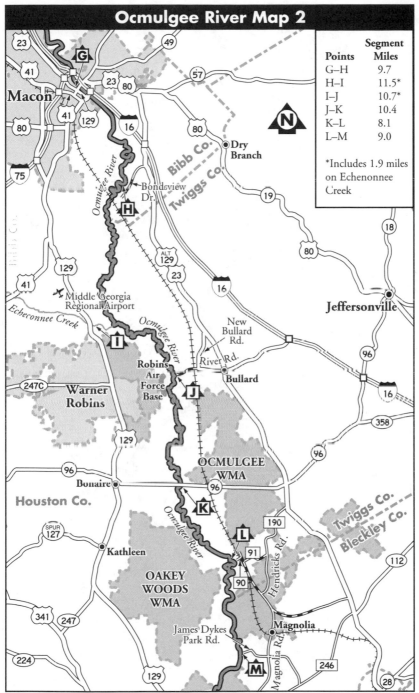

Points	Segment Miles
G–H	9.7
H–I	11.5*
I–J	10.7*
J–K	10.4
K–L	8.1
L–M	9.0

*Includes 1.9 miles on Echenonnee Creek

N

Macon

Dry Branch

Bibb Co.
Twiggs Co.

Bondsview Dr.

H

ALT 129

Middle Georgia Regional Airport

Echeconnee Creek

Ocmulgee River

I

Jeffersonville

New Bullard Rd.

River Rd.

Robins Air Force Base

J

Bullard

Warner Robins

Houston Co.

Bonaire

OCMULGEE WMA

K

Kathleen

L

Hendricks Rd.

Twiggs Co.
Bleckley Co.

OAKEY WOODS WMA

James Dykes Park Rd.

Magnolia

Magnolia Rd.

M

Ocmulgee River Map 3

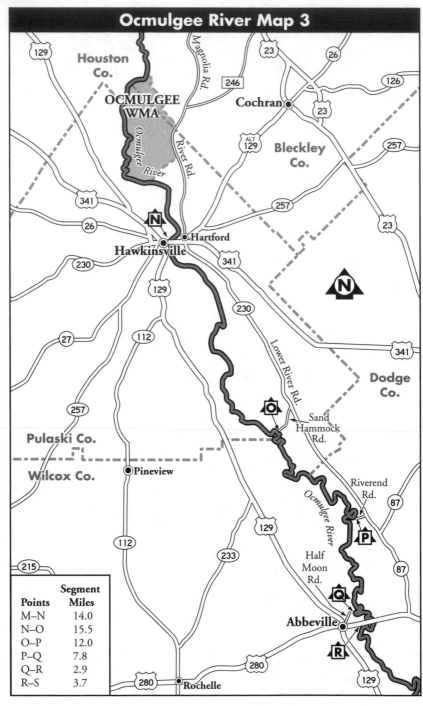

Points	Segment Miles
M–N	14.0
N–O	15.5
O–P	12.0
P–Q	7.8
Q–R	2.9
R–S	3.7

corridor sometimes 4 miles across. Populated by water oak, over-cup oak, cypress, sweet gum, red maple, tupelo gum, and swamp black gum, the bottomland forests are inundated with water much of the year. The river banks, composed of sandy clay and 3–6 feet in height, form a natural levee on which cypress and gum trees grow along with birch, willow, and a variety of under-growth. The current is moderate and the setting is generally wild and remote.

Moving south through Houston and Twiggs Counties, the Ocmulgee flows by Warner Robbins Air Force Base and then past the Ocmulgee Wildlife Management Area on the east (and again farther downstream) and along the western boundary of the Oaky Woods Wildlife Management Area. In Pulaski County near Hawkinsville, a belt of fertile farmland reclaimed from the swamp replaces the wilderness corridor with immense cultivated fields. In Wilcox and Dodge Counties, swamp forest again pre-vails, and beige sandbars on the inside of turns and the down-stream side of islands become common as the Ocmulgee meanders south toward Abbeville. From Abbeville to the mouth of the Ocmulgee at its confluence with the Oconee, the riverside setting remains that of a wooded wilderness, though occasional cabins, boat landings, and powerboat traffic indicate frequent visitation by local outdoorsmen, fishers, and hunters. If you are continuing onto the Altamaha River, be prepared for turbulence at the Ocmulgee's confluence with the Oconee, even if the water appears calm on the surface. The collision of these two Altamaha tributaries has been known to flip unwary paddlers. The Ocmul-gee normally contains the higher flow volume.

River width in the Ocmulgee varies from 140 feet below Macon to about 350 feet as it approaches the mouth at the Altamaha. The level of difficulty is Class I throughout the section below Macon, with powerboat traffic being the primary hazard to navigation. The Ocmulgee is runnable below Macon all year and access is adequate. Wildlife is diverse and plentiful.

SHUTTLE: The first take-out after passing the confluence with the Oconee is the GA 135 Landing located on US 221/GA 135 northeast of Hazlehurst. Upriver access points are numerous and well-developed. See map for locations.

GAUGE: The river is generally runnable all year. The maximum is flood stage. The DNR Fisheries Office at (912) 845-4180 can provide more information, including a map of the most fre-quently used boat ramps.

Ocmulgee River Map 4

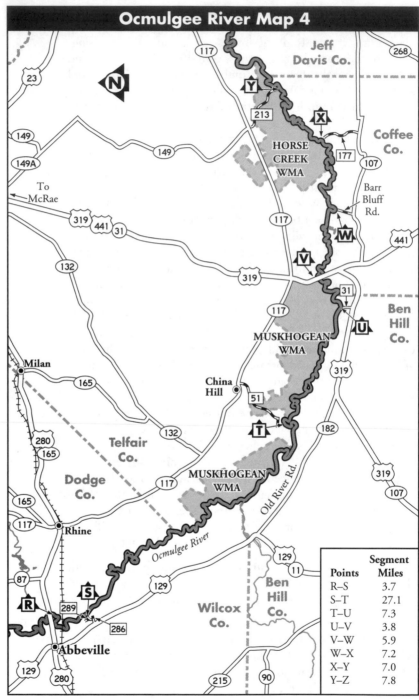

Points	Segment Miles
R–S	3.7
S–T	27.1
T–U	7.3
U–V	3.8
V–W	5.9
W–X	7.2
X–Y	7.0
Y–Z	7.8

Ocmulgee River Map 5

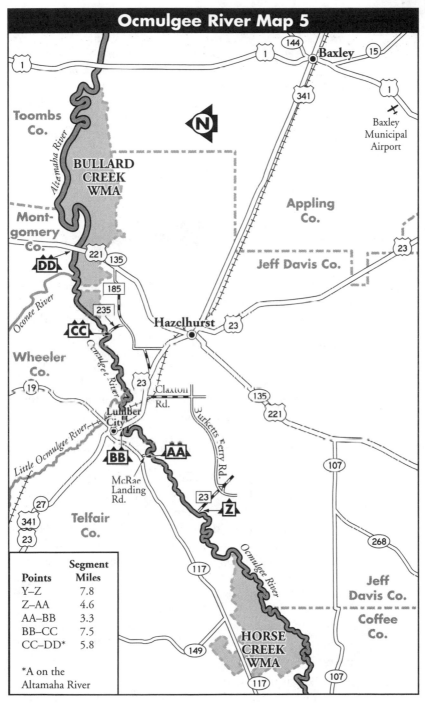

Points	Segment Miles
Y–Z	7.8
Z–AA	4.6
AA–BB	3.3
BB–CC	7.5
CC–DD*	5.8

*A on the Altamaha River

TOWALIGA RIVER

Runnable below the spectacular High Falls in Monroe County from late November to May, the Towaliga is a pleasantly scenic stream with good access. The river begins in the central Piedmont, flowing south out of Henry County before emptying shortly thereafter into the Ocmulgee above Juliette. Along the way it snakes a winding path through an intimate forested valley. If you're looking for excitement, a few tributaries in the area also contain significant drops, including Rocky Creek and the Little Towaliga River.

MAPS: High Falls, Indian Springs, Forsyth, Berner, East Juliette (USGS); Monroe (County)

High Falls State Park to GA 42

class	I–II (III)
length	8.9 mi
time	5–6 hr
gauge	None
level	N/A
gradient	8 fpm
scenery	B

DESCRIPTION: The upper section kicks off with a bang: the spectacular High Falls. The main drop of the falls is below the bridge and off-limits to paddlers. However, a trail along the left bank provides a number of possible put-ins immediately below the falls, depending on which of the subsequent rapids you are willing to tackle. The river here broadens to 300 feet, with large ledges and boulder rapids continuing for several hundred feet. These rapids are technical in low water, but due to the width of the stream, they create numerous sneak routes at higher levels. In any event they would not exceed Class III in difficulty. Easy access is available on river right for those who want to put-in below the rapids.

For the first 5 miles, hills rise sharply from the streamside as the Towaliga runs through 4- to 6-foot reddish clay banks. The river narrows first to 80 feet and then shortly thereafter to its average width of 45 to 60 feet. From here to the Mayfield Road bridge (B) the river is at its best with delightful, bouncy rapids and ledges interspersed with long pools overhung by white oak, sweet gum, red maple, hickory, sycamore, and beech. The occasional rapids approach low Class II in difficulty and get easier as you proceed downstream. The current is moderate to swift, and usually runs brown with a high concentration of sediment. Dangers in this section, other than the rapids mentioned, are limited to deadfalls.

SHUTTLE: To the take-out, take Exit 193 off of I-75. Turn east off of the exit onto Johnstonville Road and continue to GA 42 north. Turn left at GA 42; the access point (C) is at the bridge

Towaliga River

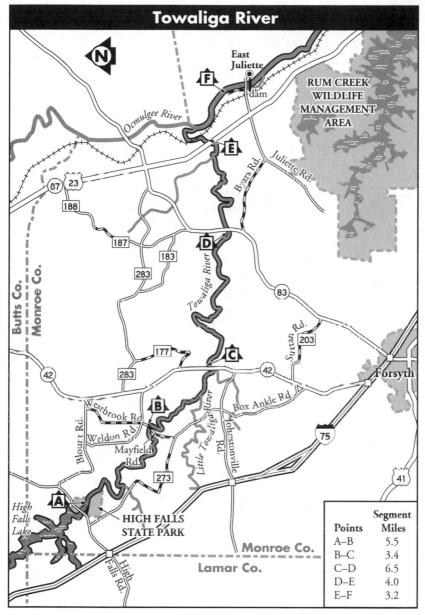

East
Juliette

F

dam

RUM CREEK
WILDLIFE
MANAGEMENT
AREA

Ocmulgee River

E

Brats Rd.

Juliette Rd.

87   23

188

187

183

283

D

Towaliga River

83

177

Surtan Rd.

203

42

283

C

42

Forsyth

Westbrook Rd.

B

Box Ankle Rd.

Blount Rd.

Weldon Rd.

Little Towaliga River

Johnstonville Rd.

75

Mayfield
Rd.

273

41

A

High
Falls
Lake

HIGH FALLS
STATE PARK

Monroe Co.

High
Falls Rd.

Lamar Co.

Butts Co.

Monroe Co.

Points	Segment Miles
A–B	5.5
B–C	3.4
C–D	6.5
D–E	4.0
E–F	3.2

0.8 miles ahead. To return to the put-in, take GA 42 back to Johnstonville Road and turn right. Continue 1.3 miles to a right turn on Boxankle Road; take Boxankle to High Falls Park Road. Turn right and proceed to High Falls State Park. A mid-run access point is at Mayfield Road, 2.7 miles north of the intersection of Boxankle and Johnstonville roads.

GAUGE: None. At a minimum, there should be a couple of inches of water spilling over the dam at High Falls before attempting a run.

GA 42 TO JULIETTE ON THE OCMULGEE RIVER

class	I
length	13.7 mi
time	8 hr
gauge	None
level	N/A
gradient	2 fpm
scenery	B

DESCRIPTION: The hills recede gradually as a corridor of cultivated land encroaches on the river just upstream of the GA 42 bridge. For the next 10 miles, the river runs with only an occasional riffle as the gradient flattens to 2 feet per mile. The greatest obstacle of this section is attributable to the forest, which at times appears to be falling into the streambed, and is also the source of beauty along this section. Portaging around trees slows forward progress, as does the sandy river bottom that keeps you guessing where the deepest channel lies.

Below US 23 (E), the gradient increases to 15 feet per mile for the last short stretch before the river merges into the Ocmulgee, upstream of Juliette. On the banks, catalpa, ash, and birch become more common, and the river continues to be well shaded. The take-out is on river right, 0.5 miles upstream of the dam.

SHUTTLE: The take-out is north of Juliette on the Ocmulgee River. From the intersection with US 23/GA 87, proceed east on Juliette Road. River access is available down the dirt road on the left, immediately after the railroad tracks on the far side of Juliette. To return to the put-in, take Juliette Road west to a right-hand turn onto Byars Road. Continue to GA 83; turn left on GA 83 and continue 3.2 miles to a right turn onto Sutton Road. Follow Sutton to GA 42. Turn right on GA 42 and follow to the junction with the river.

GAUGE: There is no gauge. At a minimum, there should be a couple of inches of water spilling over the dam at High Falls before attempting a run. More water would increase the comfort factor on the lower section, but this section should be avoided in high water situations.

The wide Ocmulgee River below its confluence with the Towaliga

photo © Tom Welander

LITTLE OCMULGEE RIVER

The Little Ocmulgee, overshadowed by its heavyweight neighbors, sneaks through the coastal plain terrain southeast of McRae to meet up with the main Ocmulgee just before its confluence with the Oconee, forming the mighty Altamaha. A small, blackwater stream, white-sand banks of moderate height frame the stream's burgundy-red water.

MAPS: Scotland, Jordan, Lumber City (USGS); Wheeler, Telfair (County)

TOWNS TO LUMBER CITY

class	I
length	10.1 mi
time	7 hr
gauge	None
level	N/A
gradient	<2 fpm
scenery	B–C

DESCRIPTION: Runnable below the community of Towns from December through mid-June in most years, the Little Ocmulgee is pleasant, although frequent signs of habitation, including several small towns and a shadowing railroad, essentially rob it of its wilderness atmosphere. Cypress and sweet gum dominate the banks, along with some black gum, willow, and ash. With a moderate current, the level of difficulty is Class I all the way to its mouth at the Ocmulgee below Lumber City. Hazards to navigation are limited to deadfalls. Camping is available at Little Ocmulgee State Park, about 7 miles upstream of this section.

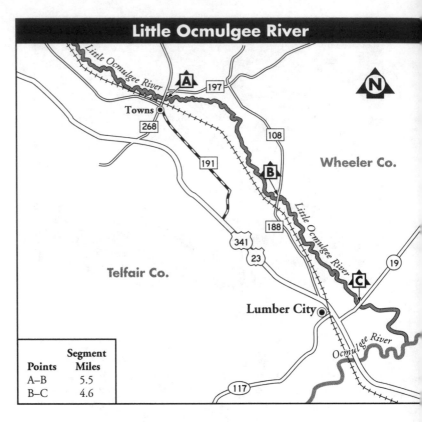

Little Ocmulgee River

Points	Segment Miles
A–B	5.5
B–C	4.6

SHUTTLE: From Lumber City, take GA 19 east to the river for the lowest take-out at access point C. For the highest put-in, return to Lumber City and take US 23 north, turning right onto CR 268 toward Towns. Intermediate access is possible on CR 108 (B), on the east side of the river.

GAUGE: None. Runnable up to flood stage.

ALTAMAHA RIVER

The turbulent confluence of the Ocmulgee and Oconee Rivers near Hazelhurst marks the beginning of the Altamaha River. Occasional bluffs along its southern shores corral the river eastward to the Atlantic Ocean. No dams interrupt the river's massive flow, resulting in a richly diverse habitat for native plants and animals, including fish species unique to this watershed. Though the river is large, bottomland swamps, creek tributaries, and islands offer opportunities for more intimate exploration, particularly as the bluffs recede and the river drifts through the lower Coastal Plain to its mouth at the Atlantic Ocean near St. Simons Island.

MAPS: Hazlehurst North, Grays Landing, Baxley Northeast, Altamaha, Tison, Altamaha Southeast, Glennville Southwest, Jesup Northwest, Doctortown, Jesup East, Ludowici, Everett City, Darien, Altamaha Sound (USGS); Wheeler, Montgomery, Jeff Davis, Toombs, Appling, Tattnall, Long, Wayne, McIntosh, Glynn (County); GADNR Canoe Trail

US 221 TO ALTAMAHA SOUND (DARIEN)

class	I
length	124.1 mi
time	Up to 2 weeks
gauge	Web, phone
level	N/A
gradient	<1 fpm
scenery	B-

DESCRIPTION: The Altamaha is the culmination of one of the largest river basins of the Atlantic Seaboard, with a watershed of 14,400 square miles covering one-quarter of the land mass in Georgia. Its waters maintain a cloudy gray-green hue even in high water due to dams upstream on the Oconee and Ocmulgee Rivers that filter out the muddier sediment of the Piedmont. The river gets a violent start due to the angle, volume, and velocity with which its two massive tributaries meet. There is no rapid here, but paddlers should be wary of boiling currents that may be barely perceptible from the surface.

For its first 68 miles before crossing US 301 (S), the river's course is more winding than it is farther downstream. Tan-colored sandbars and expansive natural beaches abound at lower flow levels and can be found on the inside of most turns and the downstream side of many islands. These provide excellent sites for camping, picnicking, or merely sunning. Sandy bluffs shaded by beautiful stands of live oak and mockernut hickory occasionally buttress the river's southern shore, and offer good camping sites during high-flow periods when the sandbars are submerged. They are also home to unusual stands of vestigial white pine trees, left

behind when their brethren followed the climate change north. The surrounding bottomland swamp forest is composed of over-cup oak, water oak, cypress, sweet gum, water hickory, elm, ash, and red maple. Vegetation on the riverbank also includes silver maple and willow, among others.

With a width of 300–350 feet at its inception, commercial navigation is possible along the entire length of the Altamaha—though most modern-day traffic comes from recreational powerboats that tend to concentrate around public boat ramps. Bullard Creek Wildlife Management Area sits on river right for the first 17 miles from the confluence almost all of the way to Deen's Landing. One of the most jarring intrusions upon the natural beauty of the Altamaha lies at US 1 (G), where a nuclear power plant is prominently visible from the river. The plant and smatterings of fishing shacks are the most notable distractions from the native forests, swamps, and wildlife.

Downstream of US 1 at Morris Landing (I), the river passes the 3,500-acre Moody Forest Natural Area on river right. A joint project of the Nature Conservancy and the Georgia Department of Natural Resources, this parcel protects one of the last known stands of old-growth longleaf pine and black-jack oak. The sloughs bordering the river here are home to tupelo cypress trees over 600 years old, a reminder of what the forests looked like prior to the wholesale lumber harvest that occurred in the early twentieth century.

The entrance of the Ohoopee River marks the approximate beginning of Big Hammock WMA on river left. Below the GA 121 bridge, islands are more numerous and dozens of feeder streams and sloughs, especially in Long and Wayne Counties, tempt off-river exploration into the adjoining swamps. On these side trips the abundant wildlife of the Altamaha is more easily spied. The river's wide floodplain forms a protective habi-tat for a distinctive ecological community that includes alliga-tors, deer, and endangered species such as the gopher turtle, and eastern indigo snake. Among the ducks, egrets, and ibis that frequent the wetlands, the rich tapestry of birds that nest here includes rare bald eagles, osprey, swallowtail kites, and red-cockaded woodpeckers. Wildlife below the surface of the water is similarly lush; mussels and freshwater fish mingle with salt-water species that use the river as a spawning ground in the spring. William Bartram's path crossed this landscape multiple times, his appreciative eye lingering to document the wide vari-ety of life forms he encountered. One plant species that man-aged to elude his scientific survey is the herbaceous Dicerandra radfordiana, a light-purplish flowered mint that is unique to

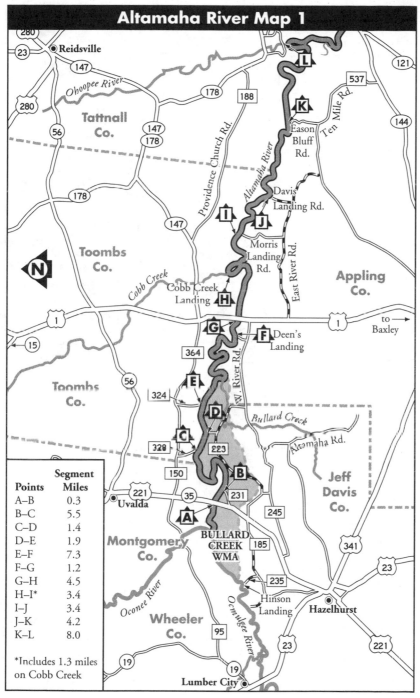

Altamaha River Map 1

Reidsville

Ohoopee River

Tattnall Co.

Altamaha River

Providence Church Rd.

Eason Bluff Rd.

Ten Mile Rd.

Davis Landing Rd.

Morris Landing Rd.

Toombs Co.

Cobb Creek

Cobb Creek Landing

East River Rd.

Appling Co.

to Baxley

Deen's Landing

W. River Rd.

Toombs Co.

Bullard Creek

Altamaha Rd.

Jeff Davis Co.

Uvalda

Montgomery Co.

Oconee River

BULLARD CREEK WMA

Ocmulgee River

Hinson Landing

Hazelhurst

Wheeler Co.

Lumber City

Points	Segment Miles
A–B	0.3
B–C	5.5
C–D	1.4
D–E	1.9
E–F	7.3
F–G	1.2
G–H	4.5
H–I*	3.4
I–J	3.4
J–K	4.2
K–L	8.0

*Includes 1.3 miles on Cobb Creek

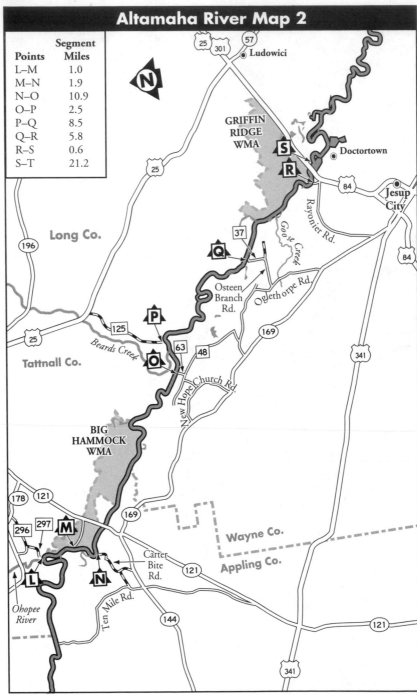

Altamaha River Map 2

Points	Segment Miles
L–M	1.0
M–N	1.9
N–O	10.9
O–P	2.5
P–Q	8.5
Q–R	5.8
R–S	0.6
S–T	21.2

Ludowici

GRIFFIN RIDGE WMA

Doctortown

Jesup City

Long Co.

Rayonier Rd.

Goose Creek

Osteen Branch Rd.

Oglethorpe Rd.

Tattnall Co.

Beards Creek

New Hope Church Rd.

BIG HAMMOCK WMA

Wayne Co.

Appling Co.

Carter Bite Rd.

Ten Mile Rd.

Ohopee River

Altamaha River Map 3

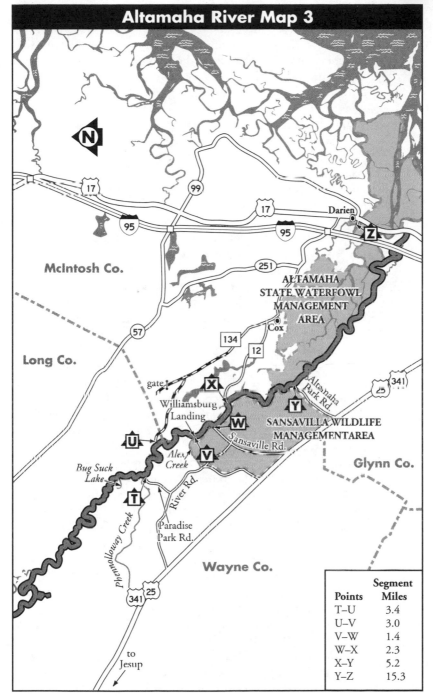

McIntosh Co.

Darien

Z

ALTAMAHA
STATE WATERFOWL
MANAGEMENT
AREA

Cox

Long Co.

gate

X

Williamsburg
Landing

U

Bug Suck
Lake

T

Alex
Creek

V

W

Sansaville Rd.

Altamaha
Park Rd.

Y

SANSAVILLA WILDLIFE
MANAGEMENT AREA

Glynn Co.

River Rd.

Paradise
Park Rd.

Phennollowoy Creek

341 25

Wayne Co.

to
Jesup

	Segment
Points	**Miles**
T–U	3.4
U–V	3.0
V–W	1.4
W–X	2.3
X–Y	5.2
Y–Z	15.3

the Altamaha's banks—it grows in only two locations world-wide, both along the Altamaha.

Back in the main channel, the sandy ridges increase in size, reaching up to 100 feet above the river before they culminate at Doctortown. This is the only sizeable town on the shores of the Altamaha and is home to a pulp mill that monopolizes river views at the crossing of US 301. The industrial plant and other signs of development (including a pre–Civil War railroad bridge above a partially submerged paddle wheel) quickly recede as paddlers enter the lower river. The river's 51-mile course from here to the ocean is protected by a 300-foot scenic-river corridor that buffers the river from development. Commercial pine forests, common in the area, are not visible from the river.

For the remainder of its journey through the Coastal Plain, the river loops in great horseshoe arcs. Banks on this lower section of the Altamaha are generally low, averaging 3–5 feet with an incline varying between 30 and 70 degrees. The cypress trees are larger than those upstream, and sweet gum, tupelo gum, and swamp black gum trees are plentiful. Shrub growth includes black willow, water elm, silky dogwood, alder, swamp privet, and swamp palm.

As the Altamaha moves south through McIntosh and Glynn Counties, the streamside and swamp flora changes somewhat, reflecting the tidal influence. In normal rainfall years, the ocean stills the river's current by the time you reach Altamaha Park. As the river nears the Atlantic Ocean a series of large islands splits the channel. These comprise several wildlife management areas that offer good options for camping, including Lewis Island, which hosts the state's oldest and largest known grove of bald cypress trees. The surrounding terrain shifts from swamp forest to marshland; vast virgin gum and cypress swamps were destroyed in the early 1800s to convert the floodplain to rice plantations. Particularly in the refuges, many of the old rice dikes are maintained to provide winter protection for migrating waterfowl. Cypress and gum trees grow in small, isolated stands in the marsh, surrounded by a watery carpet of tall grasses. Throughout the marsh, small creeks, rivers, and sloughs cut labyrinthine paths to connect larger water courses, offering fascinating paddle trips abounding in wildlife.

On the Class 1 Altamaha, the primary dangers are powerboat traffic and getting lost in off-river explorations. The river's width varies from 350 feet at the confluence of the Ocmulgee and Oconee Rivers to 500–550 feet in Long and Wayne Coun-

ties to 660–700 feet before splitting around the islands in lower McIntosh County. The current is moderate to slow. Access is good; bordering counties the Georgia DNR are promoting and developing the Altamaha Canoe Trail, which links access sites, local facilities, and waypoints of cultural interest. In the delta area, intricate and confusing networks of waterways combine with access points located off the main river channel to demand well-practiced map and compass skills. Good planning is essential for any trip into the delta and should take into account the ebb and flow of the tide.

SHUTTLE: To reach the final take-out at Darien, take Exit 49 from I-95, turning to the east on GA 251. Where the road ends at US 17, turn right and proceed into town. Turn right onto the last road before crossing the bridge; the boat ramp is on the left. Upper access points are shown on the maps. Some access points are located on sloughs and are not visible from the river. Take bridge crossings into consideration when selecting access points for your trip so as to minimize shuttle driving distances; only four bridges cross the river. Local outfitters provide shuttle service, which can be helpful in locating the best access points and negotiating dirt roads that become challenging when wet.

GAUGE: The river is floatable year-round even in periods of drought. USGS gauges provide levels at Baxley and farther downstream at Doctortown. Sand bars, good for camping sites, disappear at levels above 6 feet. High water opens up the opportunity for paddling within the adjoining swamp forests, but danger increases when swift current passes through trees and bushes; skill in maneuvering your craft under these circumstances is required. Call the Waycross Fisheries Office at (912) 285-6094 for more information.

A Brief History of the Altamaha Region
— by Charlie Ford

There was a time when no one walked these lands or drank from these streams.

Humans first arrived in Georgia's the coastal plain in 9500 BC. Descendants of those early inhabitants formed tribes that grew into the civilizations the Spanish met here in the 1400s.

The powers of Europe began establishing settlements in the "new-world" between 1350 and 1540, but explorers passed this particular section of coast several times before landing. They stopped in the Carolinas and what is now Florida, but didn't see much use in dropping anchor amongst Georgia's swamps and barrier islands.

Hernando de Soto was the first European to travel through the state on his ultimately fruitless rampage from Florida, up to the Carolinas, and back southward to Alabama. He never found the gold he sought, but in his wake he left European diseases, which virtually decimated the native tribes. Many natives survived battles with DeSoto's army only to perish of imported diseases.

The Spanish returned in the early 1500's with the more peaceful intention to convert native tribes to Christianity. Spaniard Pedro Menendez is credited with eventually befriending the indigenous tribes and building forts, or "presidios," in south Georgia.

The land between the Oconee and Ocmulgee Rivers, sometimes called "Tama," is reported to have once been home to a Spanish mission between 1610 and 1640, and became a colonial-era trading post in the 1700s. The mission, Santa Isabel de Utinahica, was probably built of pine poles with a roof of palmetto.

As English settlements encroached southward, the Spanish were driven from the area little by little. Many of the missions were burned to the ground in the early 1700s. The royal colonists established an arms-length relationship with indigenous tribes.

The owner of the Tama trading post, Mary Musgrove, was the first interpreter between the Creek tribe and British Governor James Oglethorpe. Although she was very instrumental in Georgia's founding, Musgrove was also an antagonist of sorts. She led a native uprising against the English that quickly came to a peaceful end. The Tama granted to her and her third husband at the start of the Altamaha River was given to appease her.

In the late 1700s and early 1800s, pioneers used the Altamaha to explore and settle middle Georgia. There the settlers built farms and raised families. The fertile soil of this new land provided settlers the opportunity to grow rice, cotton, and indigo, which was shipped downriver and on to England. At one time barges were a regular site along the Ocmulgee, Oconee, and Altamaha.

Agriculture and trade survived the Revolutionary War, but the region's slavery-dependent economy collapsed in the wake of the Civil War. By the early 1900s there were few commodities on earth more valuable than yellow-pine timber from the heart of Georgia. Huge rafts were assembled from cut logs and guided by locals along the Altamaha to Jesup, and eventually on to Darien. Those rafts ferried away the last of the region's indigenous virgin timber, improving the economy but significantly altering the environment. Today, slash pines in neatly planted rows have replaced many wild pine forests.

The Altamaha River looked much different in its natural state, with no dams, bridges, or industry. But there remain stretches that appear as they must have centuries ago.

Successive civilizations have harnessed the river's power and admired its beauty. The area's earliest inhabitants relied on the river for transportation and food, for colonists and Antebellum Southerners it was a vital trade link, and today recreational boats ply its waters— among them canoes not unlike those paddled by Native Americans centuries before.

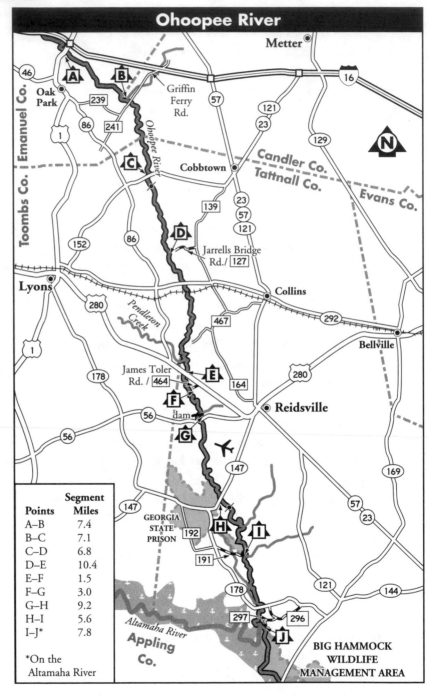

Ohoopee River

Points	Segment Miles
A–B	7.4
B–C	7.1
C–D	6.8
D–E	10.4
E–F	1.5
F–G	3.0
G–H	9.2
H–I	5.6
I–J*	7.8

*On the Altamaha River

OHOOPEE RIVER

Burgundy-red waters run clear and sparkling over the contrasting bottom and banks of sun-drenched white sand on the Ohoopee. A tributary of the Altamaha River, it is the western and northernmost river sporting this Coastal Plain combination. A shading canopy of moss-draped cypress and hardwoods combines with the Ohoopee's natural tranquility and remote, pristine setting to set it apart as a showplace of nature and one of the most exotic and beautiful streams in southern Georgia.

MAPS: Cobbtown, Ohoopee, Reidsville West, Altamaha, Tison, Altamaha Southeast (USGS), Candler, Emanuel, Tatnall, Toombs (County)

GRIFFIN FERRY ROAD TO ALTAMAHA RIVER

class	I
length	58.8 mi
time	Up to 6 days
gauge	Web
level	190 cfs
gradient	<2 fpm
scenery	A

DESCRIPTION: Wildlife is varied and plentiful throughout the wide bottomland swamp corridor that cradles the Ohoopee along its serpentine course. Small islands, meandering by-passes, and oxbows are not uncommon, particularly in the reaches below Pendelton Creek. The current is moderate throughout, and the level of difficulty is Class I, with sharp bends and trees growing in the stream keeping it interesting.

Runnable except during dry periods downstream of the US 1 bridge in Emanuel County, the stream's width ranges from 30 to 45 feet, widens to between 50 and 65 feet at GA 292 west of Collins, and culminates at 80 feet as it approaches the Altamaha. Hazards consist primarily of occasional deadfalls and a dam that must be portaged above the GA 56 bridge outside Reidsville (G).

Numerous white sandbars and beaches lend themselves to swimming, picnicking, and canoe-camping. The banks, also of white sand, are 2–4 feet high and slope at approximately 30–45 degrees. The surrounding terrain is mixed lowland swamp forests of bald cypress, willow, pond cypress, swamp black gum, Ogeechee lime, ash, red maple, water oak, and sweet bay, rising gradually to a low upland plateau.

SHUTTLE: If paddling past the confluence with the Altamaha, the first take-out reached is Tattnall County Landing on river left. To get there from Reidsville, take GA 147 south and turn left on GA 178. After crossing the Ohoopee, turn right on CR 296 and follow

it to the boat ramp. Upper access points are reached from GA 86, US 280, GA 56 and GA 147 out of Reidsville.

GAUGE: Using USGS Web site data for the gauge at Reidsville, the minimum is 190 cfs, and the maximum up to high flood stage. The Metter Game and Fish office, at (912) 685-2145, can provide more information.

OGEECHEE RIVER

The Ogeechee is Georgia's only major riverway that stretches from the Atlantic to the Piedmont unimpeded by dams, forming a rare native environment for indigenous wildlife and a spawning grounds for sturgeon and mullet. After a brief, rarely runnable Class II section formed as the river falls off the Piedmont, the Ogeechee runs wild through broad expanses of lowland swamp and past occasional bluffs carved out of the clay banks before reaching the alluvium marshes of the Atlantic Ocean. Its remote nature holds development at bay—a trip on the Ogeechee opens up a private wonderland virtually inaccessible except by boat.

MAPS: Louisville South, Old Town, Colemans Lake, Midville, Birdsville, Millen, Four Points, Rocky Ford, Hopeulikit, Dover, Rocky Ford 15', Oliver 15', Brooklet 15', Egypt 15', Eden, Meldrim Southwest, Meldrim Southeast, Richmond Hill, Burroughs, Isle of Hope, Raccoon Key (USGS); Jefferson, Burke, Emanuel, Jenkins, Screven, Bulloch, Effingham, Bryan, Chatham (County); Georgia Department of Natural Resources

LOUISVILLE TO MILLEN

class	I
length	52.6 mi
time	Up to 1.5 weeks
gauge	Web, phone
level	Unknown
gradient	<2 fpm
scenery	B

DESCRIPTION: Intimate, serene, and beautiful, in good years the Ogeechee becomes runnable below the impassable Chaulker Swamp at the US 1 bridge crossing south of Louisville. Here the river is from 35 to 50 feet in width and almost completely shaded by sycamore, willow, sweet gum, and cypress laden with moss. The current is slow, in keeping with the tranquil, lazy atmosphere.

For the most part, the Ogeechee runs in the center of a heavily forested lowland swamp as it moves southeastward through Jefferson, Burke, and Emanuel Counties. The course of the river is meandering and convoluted, with numerous horseshoe bends, oxbow lakes, and small meandering islands. Beyond the lowland swamp the terrain rises gradually to a plateau about 20 feet above

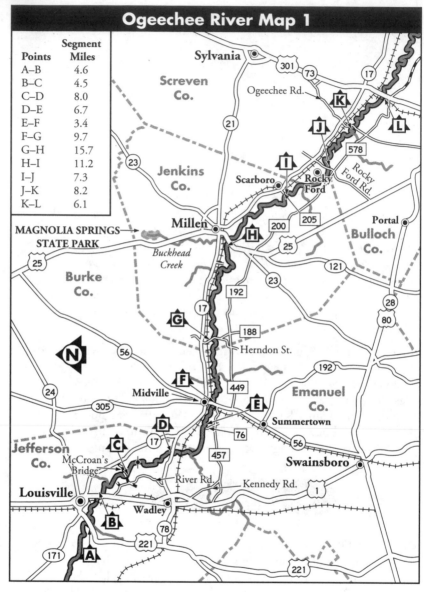

Ogeechee River Map 1

Points	Segment Miles
A–B	4.6
B–C	4.5
C–D	8.0
D–E	6.7
E–F	3.4
F–G	9.7
G–H	15.7
H–I	11.2
I–J	7.3
J–K	8.2
K–L	6.1

the swamp floor. When not marred by logging activity, the setting is primitive in the extreme, with a swamp or woodland corridor ranging for a mile or more to either side of the river.

The same factors that make this section of the Ogeechee enticing constitute the major impediment to paddling it. In high-water years like 2003, trees and accompanying vegetation are dislodged and washed into the stream, clogging the narrow streambed with prolific deadfalls that force frequent hurdling, portaging, and at a minimum, intricate maneuvering. Passage more reliably clear of obstruction begins at in the next section.

SHUTTLE: The lowest take-out for this section is immediately south of Millen on US 25 (H); access is at the northwest corner of the bridge. Upper access points are close to GA 17.

GAUGE: Data for the gauge located at Midville is available on the USGS Web site. The minimum level for using this gauge is unknown; maximum is flood stage. Local outfitters can provide assessments over the phone.

MILLEN TO GA 24

class	I
length	49.5 mi
time	Up to 6 days
gauge	Web, phone
level	3.0 ft
gradient	<2 fpm
scenery	B+

DESCRIPTION: The river's channel below Millen (H) becomes wider and relatively free of the deadfall that can plague the upper sections, although complete stream-wide blockages are still possible. The current moderates from sluggish to surprisingly swift as the river meanders around frequent bends. This, and the trees growing in the stream, keep the paddling lively and sharpen your navigational skills. Scenery is excellent, flora and fauna are abundantly varied, and except following heavy rains, the tannin-stained water is bright and clear.

The surrounding swamp expands and contracts as the Ogeechee flows past tall (65 feet) sand-and-clay bluffs that give the stream a special identity. These bluffs, and many others more modest in size, approach and recede from the river intermittently, leaving vast primeval gardens of backwater sloughs and thickly forested watery lowland in their wake. Continuing almost all the way to the tidewater section below the railroad crossing west of Meldrim (in the lowest section), the bluffs offer the best canoe camping sites on the Ogeechee.

When the cycles of rain and deadfall align to create favorable conditions (more rain, less deadfall), approaches to the river can be made via the Buckhead Creek's crossing of GA 17, west of

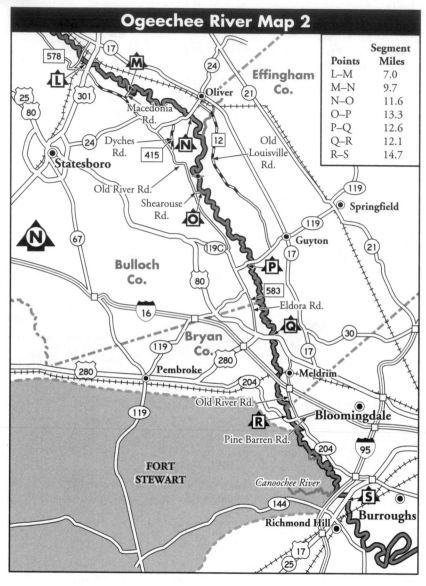

Ogeechee River Map 2

Points	Segment Miles
L–M	7.0
M–N	9.7
N–O	11.6
O–P	13.3
P–Q	12.6
Q–R	12.1
R–S	14.7

Millen. The creek is largely fed by Magnolia Springs which surfaces at Magnolia Springs State Park north of Millen.

SHUTTLE: The lowest take-out on this section is located east of Statesboro on GA 24 (N). Higher access points are easily reached from GA 17, north of the river.

GAUGE: Levels at Rocky Ford are provided on the USGS Web site and over the phone by calling local outfitters. A good level is around 3–3.5 feet; the maximum is flood stage. The Waycross DNR Fisheries Office at (912) 285-6094 can provide more information, including a map of commonly used public access points.

GA 24 TO US 17

class	I
length	64.3 mi
time	Up to 1 week
gauge	Web, phone
level	N/A
gradient	<1 fpm
scenery	B

DESCRIPTION: In this section the river widens to 110 feet and the channel becomes more well-defined. Moving into Bryan and southern Effingham Counties, small islands suitable for canoe-camping become more prevalent. Just downstream from GA 204 (R), the Ogeechee separates into multiple channels 40 to 55 feet in width, which are all runnable. These rejoin and split a second time before coming together to stay.

As the Ogeechee approaches and runs along the eastern boundary of Fort Stewart in Bryan County, the woodland swamp corridor widens to several miles and presents countless opportunities for side explorations into the adjacent sloughs and swamps, especially at high water. Paddlers anticipating off-river explorations should carry a compass and topographical maps and know how to use them to avoid getting lost.

Just upstream of the Ogeechee's main tributary, the Canoochee River, the Ogeechee enters the tidewater zone. From this area downstream the banks and confining low-ridge plateaus bordering the swamp corridor begin to recede and flatten into a vast grassy marsh resembling a giant rice paddy. This topography persists below the last access point all the way to Ossabaw Sound, where the Ogeechee joins the Little Ogeechee and the Vernon River at the edge of the Atlantic Ocean. Powerboat traffic is not uncommon below the mouth of the Canoochee as the river's width averages 190 to 230 feet.

While the tidal marsh is unique in its flora, its diverse fish and bird fauna, and in its labyrinthine creeks that carve graceful swaths through the marsh grasses, the marsh is extremely inaccessible. Paddle trips must begin upriver, proceed down into the marshes, and then return to the point of embarkation or to an

access point up one of the other streams emptying into the sound. Careful attention must be given to the tides when planning such trips, and paddlers should be completely self-sufficient in their equipment and preparations, since dry land is often nonexistent.

SHUTTLE: The final take-out is reached from I-95 south of Savannah. Take Exit 90 and go east on GA 144. Turn left onto US 17, which takes you to the boat ramp at access point S. GA 119, US 80, and GA 204 provide access to upper debarkation points of this section.

GAUGE: See preceding section. Levels near Eden are also provided online, and local outfitters can provide river information. The Richmond Hill DNR Fisheries office at (912) 727-2112 can supply a map of the commonly used access points and annual forecasts of fish harvests by species.

CANOOCHEE RIVER

Pristine, secluded, and rich in wildlife and vegetation, the Canoochee River is a delightful smooth-water stream. Its long stretches of undeveloped land and frequent white-sand beaches make it ideally suited to camping trips. Originating in Emanuel County northwest of Savannah, the river winds its way to the Atlantic, merging with the Ogeechee near I-95.

MAPS: Daisy, Glissons Mill Pond, Willie, Letford, Trinity, Limerick Northwest, Richmond Hill (USGS); Bryan, Liberty (County)

US 280 TO US 17

class	S
length	57.1 mi
time	Up to 6.5 days
gauge	Web
level	2.5 ft
gradient	<2 fpm
scenery	B+

DESCRIPTION: Characterized by its sparkling burgundy-colored water and white banks and sandbars, the Canoochee runs nearly year-round above US 280 (A), though it is not as remote as the section described below. There is good access to this upper section via a state-run boat ramp at GA 169.

Downstream of the US 280 bridge, the riverbanks are 3 to 7 feet in height, average 45 degrees in slope, and are lined with black gum, sweet gum, swamp palm, cypress, willow, and swamp white oak. Adjacent floodplains range from unusually wide to virtually nonexistent when pine forests penetrate almost to the river's edge. Stream width varies from 40 to 60 feet in the upper

Canoochee River

Points	Segment Miles
A–B	14.6
B–C	9.0
C–D	5.7
D–E	11.0
E–F	16.8

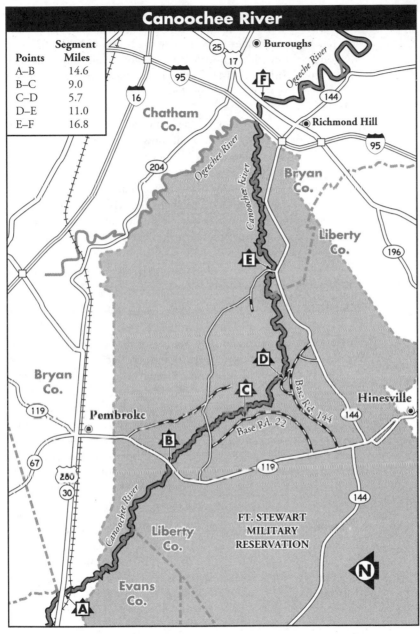

reaches (US 280 to GA 119) where the Canoochee is well shaded, to an alternating pattern of broad and narrow sections for most of the remainder of its length. Below GA 119 (B), the Canoochee constricts to 50 feet or less for several hundred feet and then broadens to 140 feet or more. Near its mouth at the Ogeechee, the Canoochee reaches a width approaching 185 to 210 feet.

The moderate current of the upper and middle Canoochee becomes modified by the ebb and flow of the tide near its confluence with the Ogeechee. The level of difficulty is Class I throughout, with deadfalls in the upper section and powerboat traffic in the lower section being the primary hazards to navigation. Sandbars and well-defined banks provide suitable sites for canoe camping. A pass, available for a nominal fee, is required to camp within the Fort Stewart army base; call the Permits and Passes office at (912) 767-5032 to secure one prior to departure. The military can restrict access to roads within the base, so call first to confirm accessibility.

SHUTTLE: From Exit 90 off of I-95 south of Savannah, take GA 144 east to a left-hand turn onto US 17. Continue on US 17 to its intersection with the Ogeechee River; the boat ramp (F) is on the far side of the bridge. To reach the upper access points, return to GA 144 and head west toward Hinesville. Two access points will be passed along the way: one at GA 144 (E) and another reachable via roads inside the base (D). For higher access, at Hinesville turn right onto GA 119 toward Pembroke. Two more access points are available via this stretch of road: one at another base road to the east of GA 119 (C), and the other where GA 119 crosses the river. For the highest access points, at Pembroke turn left onto US 280/GA 30 and proceed to the bridge at the river.

GAUGE: The USGS Web site provides river levels for the Canoochee near Claxton, Georgia. Over 6 feet is in the trees and should be avoided. The minimum recommended level is 2.5 feet. An ideal level is 4.5 feet, leaving sand banks exposed for camping.

SATILLA RIVER

The Satilla River has the distinction of being the largest blackwater river situated entirely within Georgia. With a dignified and tranquil pace, it oozes along beneath a wooded canopy, bypassing Waycross and the Okefenokee Swamp before looping south to meet the Atlantic at St. Andrew Sound. Undergrowth is thick and luxurious, with swamp cyrilla and azalea setting the reflective river aflame with color in the early spring. Glistening white sandbars occupy the insides of turns and provide resting spots for the traveler, while birds, reptiles, and other animals hurry about their business in the swamp. Although many adjacent acres have been reclaimed for commercial pine planting, the river, cradled neatly by a wet bottomland forest corridor, remains pristine in appearance if not in fact. Since the area is favored by sportsmen, boat ramps are common and fishing camps are frequently encountered along the Satilla's course.

MAPS: Douglas South, Pearson, Axson, Talmo, Dixie Union, Blackshear West, Waycross East, Hoboken West, Blackshear East, Patterson Southeast, Hortense, Nahunta, Boulogne, Woodbine (USGS); Coffee, Atkinson, Ware (County); Georgia Department of Natural Resources.

US 441 TO US 84/GA 38

class	S
length	55.6 mi
time	Up to 1.5 weeks
gauge	Web
level	5.0 ft
gradient	<2 fpm
scenery	A-

DESCRIPTION: The Satilla is runnable below US 441 during the winter and spring. In Atkinson County where this section begins, the Satilla flows in a straighter course than in Ware County and below where the characteristic white sandbars begin to materialize. An umbrella of pine, swamp black gum, water oak, laurel oak, sweet bay, and majestic cypress shade the stream as it winds past white sand banks up to 8 feet high, sandy bluffs, and commercial pine forest plateaus that tower over the stream from time to time. A rather barren strip of cultivated table land parallels the Satilla for about a mile below the GA 158 bridge in Ware County (G), before the stream again slips back into the wooded corridor.

Deadfall blockages above Waycross pose the primary hazards to navigation in this section, impeding downstream progress and acting as a barrier for larger boats. A canoe is the ideal watercraft to portage around any obstructions. Though water levels fluctuate somewhat unpredictably, especially above Waycross, flash flooding is not considered a problem. Campsites, however, should be chosen on bluffs rather than sandbars in the winter and spring.

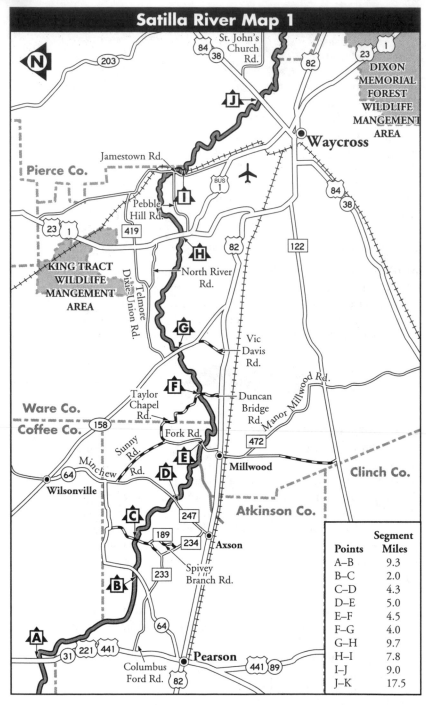

Satilla River Map 1

N

203

84
38

St. John's
Church
Rd.

82

23   1

DIXON
MEMORIAL
FOREST
WILDLIFE
MANGEMENT
AREA

J

Waycross

Jamestown Rd.

Pierce Co.

BUS
1

84
38

I

Pebble
Hill Rd.

23   1   419

82

122

KING TRACT
WILDLIFE
MANGEMENT
AREA

Telmore
Dixie-Union Rd.

H

North River
Rd.

G

Vic
Davis
Rd.

Manor Millwood Rd.

F

Ware Co.

158

Taylor
Chapel
Rd.

Duncan
Bridge
Rd.

Coffee Co.

Fork Rd.

472

Sunny
Rd.

E

Millwood

Clinch Co.

Minchew
Rd.

64

D

Wilsonville

Atkinson Co.

C

247

189   234   Axson

233   Spivey
Branch Rd.

B

64

A

31   221   441

Pearson

441   89

Columbus
Ford Rd.   82

Points	Segment Miles
A–B	9.3
B–C	2.0
C–D	4.3
D–E	5.0
E–F	4.5
F–G	4.0
G–H	9.7
H–I	7.8
I–J	9.0
J–K	17.5

photo © Tom Welancer

A slough on the Satilla

SHUTTLE: To reach the lowest take-out for this section (J), take US 1/23 to the bridge over the river. Access is on the southwest corner of the bridge over the main channel. Most of the upper access points are most easily reached from US 82 south of the river.

GAUGE: Data for the gauge located near Waycross is available on the USGS Web site. Less than 5 feet can make progress difficult. Sandbars are covered above 8 feet, and above 9–10 feet, the current becomes swift. The maximum is up to high flood stage. Call the Waycross Fisheries Office at (912) 285-6094 for more information.

US 84/GA 38 TO GA 252

DESCRIPTION: The Satilla is runnable below Waycross most of the year, although it is still possible to encounter downed trees that completely block the stream as low as the US 301 bridge (N). The river starts this section by broadening to between 55 and 80 feet as it wriggles out from under its tree canopy to some extent. Throughout the circumambient terrain of Waycross, open farm fields intrude on the privacy of the river, and assert themselves once again along the Pierce–Brantley county line below the GA 121 bridge (K), where the white sandbars become rare until the confluence with the Little Satilla 37 miles downstream.

class	S
length	101.8 mi
time	Up to 2 weeks
gauge	Web, phone
level	5.0 ft
gradient	<1 fpm
scenery	A-

Below the mouth of the Little Satilla, sandbars once again become prevalent, as do horseshoe loops, bypass islands, and oxbow lakes, particularly where the river flows near Nahunta. The Satilla continues to broaden, reaching a width of 110–130 feet before passing into Camden County. Flowing along the Charlton-Camden county line, the wilderness hides any sign of civilization as immense woodland swamps settle in and the river widens further to 180–210 feet. Tall sandy bluffs offer high-ground camping above the GA 252 bridge (R), and the ruins of Burnt Fort, a pre-Revolutionary era bastion, make an interesting side-trip.

The next verified public access below US 82 is 29 miles downstream, eliminating everything but the possibility for multiple-day canoe-camping trips.

SHUTTLE: The last take-out for this section is northeast of Folkston on GA 252. See the map for the location of up-river access points.

GAUGE: See upper section.

GA 252 TO WOODBINE

class	T
length	25.5 mi
time	Up to 3 days
gauge	Web, phone
level	N/A
gradient	<1 fpm
scenery	A-

DESCRIPTION: Depending on the water level coming downstream, tidal effects begin to influence the river as high as the 3-R Fish Camp (Q), 10 miles above the GA 252 bridge. Grassy marsh prairies alternate with bottom forest along the river channel, particularly below the mouth of Armstrong Creek. Below the US 17 bridge at Woodbine (S) to the St. Andrew Sound, access is almost nonexistent and tidal currents are tricky. Some sandy bluffs persist in this area, but wet marshes, intricate networks of tidal creeks, and saltwater estuaries are the order of the day. The tidal currents near St. Andrew Sound, along with some powerboat traffic in the lower reaches, pose the primary hazards to navigation in this section.

SHUTTLE: The lowest take-out in this section is at the boat ramp on the southeast corner of the US 17 bridge in Woodbine. See the map for the location of up-river access points.

GAUGE: The gauge at Atkinson as reported on the USGS Web site is more appropriate to this section, though levels will be heavily influenced by the tides. Be familiar with tidal patterns and how to manage them, particularly near the end of this section.

Satilla River Map 2

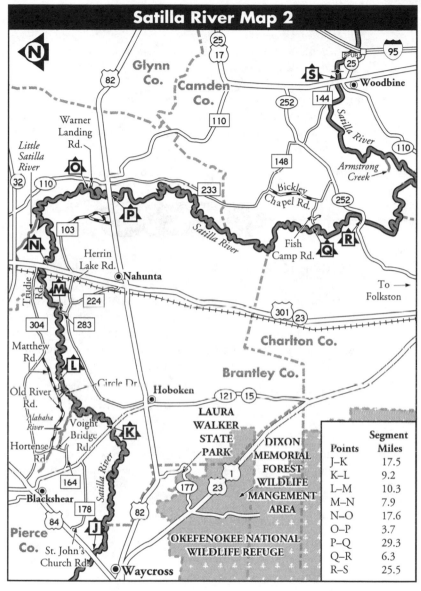

Points	Segment Miles
J–K	17.5
K–L	9.2
L–M	10.3
M–N	7.9
N–O	17.6
O–P	3.7
P–Q	29.3
Q–R	6.3
R–S	25.5

ALABAHA RIVER

Black water reflects a mesmerizing mirror of the gum cypress–dominated floodplain of the Alabaha. Flowing with a slow to moderate current, this diminutive stream passes through a wooded swamp corridor draped with Spanish moss and bordered by palmetto stands occasionally penetrated by pine forests and agricultural development. Banks of 2–8 feet in height hold the river underneath a thick canopy of trees as it sidles through Bacon and Pierce Counties before emptying into the Satilla River east of Waycross.

MAPS: Blackshear East (USGS); Pierce (County)

GA 15 TO THE SATILLA RIVER

class	S
length	16.1 mi
time	1–2 days
gauge	None
level	N/A
gradient	<2 fpm
scenery	B+

DESCRIPTION: Runnable below the GA 15 bridge except in the late summer and fall, the Alabaha is similar to the Satilla in flora, wildlife, and topography but is far smaller and less convoluted in its course. Its small size lends an air of privacy and increases the probability of deadfall encounters, the only hazard to navigation. Access is good, and extended trips onto the Satilla are possible after reaching the mouth of the Alabaha.

SHUTTLE: The last take-out for the Alabaha is located downstream of the confluence on the Satilla. To get there from Blackshear, go east on US 84/GA 38. Take the first right immediately after crossing the Alabaha; follow this road to Old River Road and turn right. Continue straight onto the dirt road when the pavement takes a 90-degree turn to the right (turning into

Voight Bridge Road). Continue straight for 5.2 miles until reaching Circle Drive on the right. Follow Circle Drive to Turkey Ridge Road (CR 312) and the Future Farmers of America (FFA) boat ramp. Intermediate access is available at Voight Bridge Road (C), the boat ramp just downstream (D), at US 84 (southeast corner of the bridge), and at the southeast corner of the GA 15 bridge.

GAUGE: There is none. Call the Waycross Fisheries Office at (912) 285-6094 for more information.

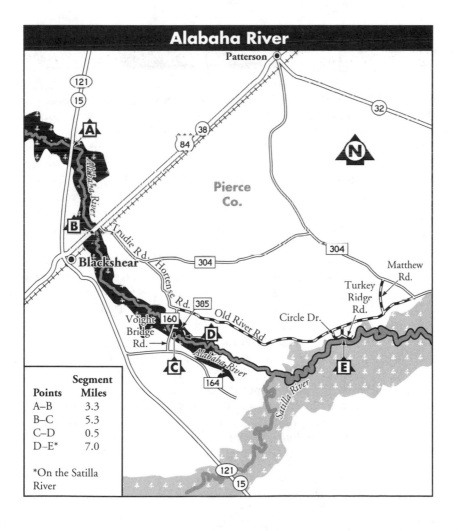

Alabaha River

Points	Segment Miles
A–B	3.3
B–C	5.3
C–D	0.5
D–E*	7.0

*On the Satilla River

LITTLE SATILLA RIVER

Thick, luxurious swamp forest of swamp black gum, sweet bay, pine, and cypress confine this brownish-red stream as it winds an intricate southeastwardly path to the main Satilla. Unlike its larger namesake, which displays massive white-sand bars at low water, the Little Satilla charms by displaying the same scenery on a more intimate scale—making it ideal for paddle craft and little else. Over 10 miles of the river pass through state-owned lands, resulting in an isolated wilderness paddling experience. Small bluffs grace the streamside from time to time and provide good high-water camping areas. Unlike the main Satilla, sandbars are comparatively rare.

MAPS: Screven, Patterson Southeast (USGS); Pierce, Appling, Wayne, Brantley (County)

GA 38/US 84 TO US 301

class	S
length	37.0 mi
time	3 days
gauge	None
level	N/A
gradient	<1 fpm
scenery	B+

DESCRIPTION: Runnable downstream from the US 84 bridge, except in the typically dry season from later summer into fall, the Little Satilla averages 45 to 75 feet in width with a slow to moderate current. Its banks are 2–7 feet high and are composed of an off-white sandy clay. Throughout its runnable length the stream is shaded and the banks buffered with a thick undergrowth. Wildlife, especially birds, abounds and is easily observed by the quiet paddler. Generally remote and pristine, the river corridor is nevertheless occasionally penetrated by agricultural development.

There are no rapids on the Little Satilla, with occasional deadfalls being the only hazard to navigation. Areas of special interest include the Little Satilla Wildlife Management Area, which spans both sides of 10.3 miles of the stream between the US 84 (A) and GA 32 (F) bridge crossings. Check hunting season schedules online at **www.gadnr.org** if you plan on camping here; an off-season float will afford more peace, privacy, and safety.

Access is good, and trips on the Little Satilla can be extended beyond its mouth onto the Satilla River. Just plan on making that a multiple-day camping trip since the next closest public access after passing US 301 on the Little Satilla requires 15.6 miles of paddling (7.3 to the Satilla, and another 8.3 miles to the Warner Landing boat ramp).

SHUTTLE: From Nahunta, take US 301 north to the river for the last take-out on the Little Satilla (E). To reach the next

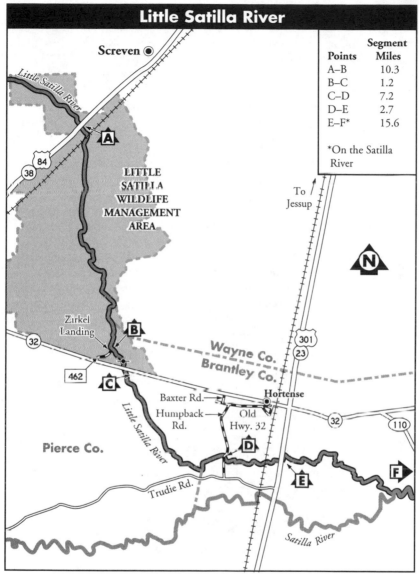

Little Satilla River

Screven ●

Little Satilla River

84
38

A

LITTLE
SATILLA
WILDLIFE
MANAGEMENT
AREA

Points	Segment Miles
A–B	10.3
B–C	1.2
C–D	7.2
D–E	2.7
E–F*	15.6

*On the Satilla
River

To
Jessup

N

Zirkel
Landing

B

32

Wayne Co.

Brantley Co.

301
23

462

C

Little Satilla River

Baxter Rd.

Humpback
Rd.

Old
Hwy. 32

Hortense

32

110

Pierce Co.

D

E

F

Trudie Rd.

Satilla River

upstream access point at Humpback Road (D), use Trudie Road south of the river. The next two highest access points are reached by taking US 301 north to GA 32 west; there is access as the highway crosses the river (southeast corner), and a DNR boat ramp upstream of GA 32 is reached by turning right onto Zirkle Road after crossing the river. The highest access is on US 84/GA 38, which is most easily reached by continuing west on GA 32 into Patterson and turning right. Access is on the right side of the road after crossing the river.

GAUGE: There is no gauge. For additional info, call the Waycross Fisheries Office at (912) 285-6094.

ST. MARYS RIVER

The semi-tropical St. Marys River defines the distinctive tab of land at the southeastern corner of Georgia. Beginning in the bogs of the Okefenokee Swamp that spawn the North Prong of the river, the St. Marys River meanders south through lowland swamp and forests that shelter diverse and abundant wildlife. The river officially begins at its southernmost point, due east of Jacksonville, Florida, with the entry of its other swamp-born tributary, the Middle Prong. White-sand beaches litter the river's progress as it carves an ever-deeper channel, eventually creating low sandy bluffs before the effects of the tidal marshes and the sea wear them down. The St. Marys is a wild black-water stream of beauty and distinction.

MAPS: Moniac, Maclenny Northwest, Maclenny West, Maclenny East, Maclenny Northeast, St. George, Toledo, Folkston, Boulogne, Kings Ferry, Kingsland, Gross, St. Marys (USGS); Charlton, Camden, Baker FL, Nassau FL (County)

MONIAC TO FOLKSTON

class	S
length	78.7 mi
time	Up to 2 weeks
gauge	Web, phone, visual
level	2.0
gradient	<2 fpm
scenery	A

DESCRIPTION: The St. Marys can be run as high as the GA 94 bridge crossing of the North Prong. The river emerges from the Okefenokee Swamp under a dense gum-cypress canopy, but trees in the channel become less prevalent by the time the river reaches this point. Averaging 40 to 55 feet, the North Prong gradually settles into a well-defined channel and becomes more exposed as it nears its confluence with the Middle Prong (flowing out of

St. Marys River

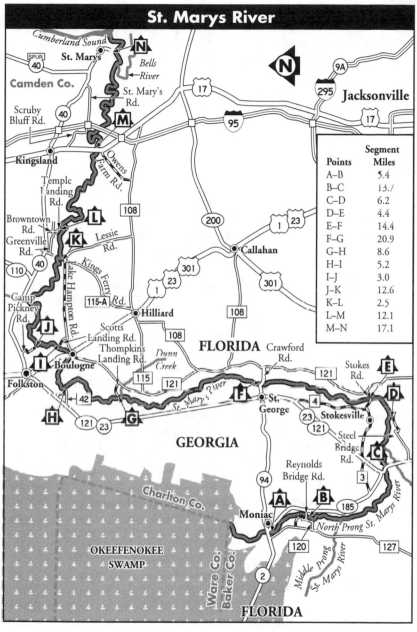

Points	Segment Miles
A–B	5.4
B–C	13.7
C–D	6.2
D–E	4.4
E–F	14.4
F–G	20.9
G–H	8.6
H–I	5.2
I–J	3.0
J–K	12.6
K–L	2.5
L–M	12.1
M–N	17.1

Pinhook Swamp in Florida). Watery wooded swampland extends from both sides of the stream, and swamp cyrilla and palmetto vegetate the banks. Its diminutive size makes this portion of the stream susceptible to deadfall blockages that should be avoided, particularly at high water.

When the Middle Prong joins the North Prong the river doubles in width and its winding habit intensifies. Surrounding lowlands seem, on the average, a little drier, and pine bluffs begin to intermittently extend to the river's edge. White sandbars begin to grace the insides of turns and provide sparkling contrast to the dark, burgundy-red water. The waters are stained from tannins released from decaying organic matter and tree roots; the dark water mirrors a perfect reflection of the above-ground scenery.

Below the GA 121 bridge (C) at the bottom of Charlton County, the South Prong of the St. Marys enters the stream. This prong, rising completely out of Florida and flowing north, is much smaller than the Middle and North Prongs. In the vicinity of the mouth of the South Prong, several small settlements appear along the St. Marys River, and intrude temporarily on its remote wilderness setting.

Swinging north, the St. Marys River remains mostly unspoiled. It widens slightly and entrenches itself in increasingly steeper banks. Bluffs and pine forests intermix with swamp flora, and provide good high-water camp sites. Between St. George and Folkston its banks rise to more than 7 feet, and are often backed by sandy bluffs standing 20 feet or more above the river, forested with a mixture of pine and tropical flora. The channel here is deep and well defined, and powerboat traffic becomes common in the vicinity of Folkston.

SHUTTLE: US 1/23 south from Folkston will bring you to I, the lowest take-out for this section. Turn left onto Lake Hampton Road, then left onto Scotts Landing Road. Up-river access points are easily reached from GA 121/23 south out of Folkston.

GAUGE: The USGS provides data for the telemetry gauge located near Macclenney, Florida. The minimum level is 2 feet, maximum level is high flood stage. Using the visual gauge at Moniac, the minimum level is 5.5 feet. Local outfitters and the Waycross Fisheries Office (at (912) 285-6094) can also provide information.

FOLKSTON TO ST. MARYS

class	T
length	47.0 mi
time	5.5 days
gauge	Web, phone, visual
level	2.0 ft
gradient	<1 fpm
scenery	A-

DESCRIPTION: The river's width below Folkston averages between 90 and 120 feet, but sometimes contracts as intervening bluffs create narrows. All along the St. Marys River, sloughs and feeder creeks provide opportunities for side-trips into the surrounding swamp corridor or between the approaching bluffs. This becomes more pronounced as the stream moves into Camden County, where marsh prairies indicate your entrance into the tidal zone. Amazingly, the St. Marys' high banks persist and, if anything, become more steeply inclined.

Above the US 17 bridge (M), grassy marsh becomes prevalent on one side of the stream while gum and cypress remain dominant on the other. Below I-95, vast lime-colored grassy marshes combine with a complex network of tidal creeks and rivers and an occasional cypress hammock to turn the St. Marys into a tidewater garden. Banks decrease slightly in steepness but continue to form a natural levee between the stream and the surrounding marsh. Opportunities for side explorations remain excellent. Powerboat traffic and tricky tidal currents become more pronounced as the last access point before reaching Cumberland Sound and the Atlantic Ocean are reached at the city boat ramp at the town of St. Marys (N). Hazards include powerboat traffic and tidal effects in Camden County.

SHUTTLE: The lowest take-out for this section is at the end of GA 40 where it meets the river in the town of St. Marys. Taking GA 40 west will lead you to higher access points on the northern side of the river; use FL 115 to access the river from the south.

GAUGE: See the first section.

OKEFENOKEE SWAMP

If Georgia consisted only of the Chattooga River and the Okefenokee Swamp it would still be a water wonderland, beautiful and exciting beyond all expectation. As it is, of course, Georgia is rich in watercourses from top to bottom, and offers paddlers an almost inexhaustible opportunity for exploration. Even so, the Chattooga and the Okefenokee occupy positions of exalted prominence not only in Georgia, but among the natural treasures of the entire United States. The Okefenokee is particularly special. It is unique: a self-contained microcosm of ongoing evolution, an incredible miniature ecosystem in which the drama of the survival of the fittest is performed countless times each day. But more than an ordeal in survival, the Okefenokee is a joyous celebration of everything right and beautiful in nature, and a living testimony to the ability of the citizenry to preserve rather than destroy nature when stirred out of their complacency.

MAPS: Waycross Southeast, Dinner Pond, Fort Mudge, Double Lakes, Chase Prairie, Chesser Island, Moniac, Eddy, Sargent, Strange Island, Blackjack Island, The Pocket, Billys Island, Cravens Island (USGS); Ware, Charlton, Clinch (County)

ALL OKEFENOKEE TRAILS

class	S
length	Varied trails
time	2–6 days, permits required for overnight
gauge	None
level	N/A
gradient	N/A
scenery	A+

DESCRIPTION: Dark and mysterious, bright and colorful, quiet and expectant, shrill and cacophonous, the Okefenokee is a study in contrasts. It epitomizes the swamps of Hollywood and your imagination, while revealing environments and wonders that transcend all expectations. The Okefenokee, says nature writer Franklin Russell, "is a fascinating realm that both confirms and contradicts popular notions of a swamp. Along with stately cypresses, peat quagmires, and dim waterways, the Okefenokee has sandy pine islands, sunlit prairies, and clear lakes."

The swamp is situated in southeastern Georgia, near the Florida border. It extends about 38 miles from north to south, and approximately 25 miles from east to west at its widest part. Covering some 430,000 acres, the Okefenokee is one of the largest, oldest, and most primitive swamps in America. Most of the Okefenokee is under the protection of the Okefenokee National Wildlife Refuge, established in 1937, which occupies 90 percent of the swamp's area. Actually a vast peat bog, the Okefenokee was formed more than 250,000 years ago when the Atlantic Ocean covered an area 75 miles inland from its present coastline. The pounding surf and continuous currents created an elongated sandbar with a large lagoon on its landward side.

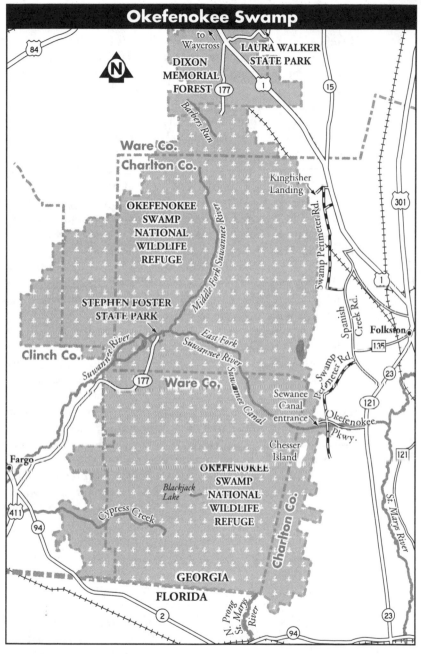

Okefenokee Swamp

84

to Waycross

LAURA WALKER STATE PARK

DIXON MEMORIAL FOREST

177 1 15

Barbers Run

Ware Co.

Charlton Co.

Kingfisher Landing

OKEFENOKEE SWAMP NATIONAL WILDLIFE REFUGE

Middle Fork Suwannee River

Swamp Perimeter Rd.

301

1

Folkston

135

Spanish Creek Rd.

STEPHEN FOSTER STATE PARK

Suwannee River

East Fork Suwannee River

Clinch Co.

177 **Ware Co.**

Suwannee Canal

Perimeter Rd.

Sewanee Canal entrance

Okefenokee Pkwy.

23

121

121

Fargo

411

94

Cypress Creek

Chesser Island

Blackjack Lake

OKEFENOKEE SWAMP NATIONAL WILDLIFE REFUGE

Charlton Co.

St. Marys River

GEORGIA

FLORIDA

2

N. Prong St. Marys River

94 23

When the ocean receded, the sandbar became a ridge. The lagoon drained, leaving a sandy basin that became the bed of the Okefenokee, which is now more than 100 feet above sea level. Today, the entire swamp, except for the islands, is covered with a bed of peat underlain by a huge, saucer-shaped, sand-floored depression. The peat bed exceeds 20 feet in depth in some places and is a mere 6 inches deep in others.

Being higher than much of the surrounding area, the Okefenokee depends on local rainfall to maintain its water level. Draining away from a series of ridges in the center of the swamp, the waters of the Okefenokee are in constant circulation. Moving slowly through the prairies and around the hammocks and islands, the waters of the swamp are colored a burgundy red by tannic acid released into the water as swamp vegetation decomposes. Both the fabled Suwannee and the beautiful but less celebrated St. Marys Rivers originate in the Okefenokee.

Much of the swamp consists of "prairies," expansive shallow lakes clogged with aquatic plant life. Open water in the Okefenokee is surprisingly scarce. All of the lakes (about 60), gator holes, and waterways combined cover less than 1,000 acres.

Known throughout the world for its unusual and diverse wildlife, the swamp is home to 225 species of birds, 43 species of mammals, 58 species of reptiles, 32 species of amphibians, and 34 species of fish. The shrill cries of wood ducks and the hoarse squawks of egrets and herons can be heard resounding everywhere. Turkey vultures ride the hot air currents high overhead, while flocks of white ibis glide along just above the treetops. Old bull alligators bellow their challenges, undisturbed by the beat of woodpeckers hammering on dead trees, while choruses of frogs turn the night into a guttural symphony. In the tangled jungle, raccoon, otter, bobcat, opossum, and whitetailed deer hold court among the pond cypress, bay, black gum, and swamp cyrilla.

The Okefenokee defies summary; no description can do justice to what even unbelieving eyes can scarcely comprehend. Says Russell:

> It is possible to describe the Okefenokee as a peat-filled bog . . . but this reduces the swamp to an unpleasant image of immense dreariness. It is possible to count the islands, about 70, and say that they cover 25,000 acres, but this says nothing of their having been the sites of bitter battles between bears and cougars, of their having sprouted crops of corn and vegetables and great whispering plantations of slash pines surrounded by the stark grandeur of water loving cypresses.
>
> It is possible to talk about 60,000 acres of prairies, the flooded open areas choked with water lilies and neverwets,

photo © Linsay Meeks

Paddling the Suwannee Canal in the Okefenokee Swamp

pipeworts, and ferns, with maiden canes and sedges and moss, but this is only one facet of the great swamp. This is to say nothing of the wildlife, the reptiles, the waterfowl, or even the hammocks, those dense labyrinths of twisted growth, odd collections of hardwoods, water oaks, live oaks, and magnolias clustered together.

In the late 1990s, Trail Ridge, on the eastern edge of the swamp, was the proposed site of a DuPont titanium mine. This was met with significant public and government objection. Fears included that the swamp might be drained or flooded due the proximity of the mine to the swamp. Following extensive negotiations, DuPont retired their mineral rights and donated the 16,000 acres on Trail Ridge to the Conservation Fund, which will disburse the land in consultation with the state and local community. Already 5,000 acres have been earmarked for donation to the National Wildlife Refuge.

SHUTTLE: To reach Stephen Foster State Park, take GA 177 north from Fargo. The Suwannee Canal trails are reached by taking GA 121/23 south from Folkston, turning right onto the Okefenokee Parkway. The Kingfisher access point is reached via US 1 south of Waycross.

GAUGE: There is no gauge in the swamp and is virtually always floatable. The only exception is after multiple-year droughts. Call Stephen Foster State Park at (912) 637-5274 for more information.

Paddling in the Okefenokee

Though the natural panorama of the Okefenokee defies verbal description, first-hand physical exploration of the swamp can be undertaken with a modicum of preparation. The Okefenokee National Wildlife Refuge wilderness offers designated trails that provide the opportunity to spend from 2 to 6 days in the swamp. The trails are well marked. Guides are neither required nor needed, but a permit must be obtained well in advance for the use of these trails. For paddlers interested in a 1-day (or shorter) outing, circuit trips are available in specified areas that depart from and return to the same access point. Permits are not required for 1-day outings.

Partially covered overnight camping shelters are provided at Maul Hammock, Big Water, Bluff Lake, Canal Run, and Round Top. These consist of 20-by-28-foot platforms built above the water. While the maximum allowable group size is 20, this would require sleeping shoulder to shoulder and is not recommended. A group of 10 or fewer is much more realistic. Because these shelters are only partially covered and wind often accompanies any rain, free-standing tents are recommended. They also serve as insect protection. Other campsites are located on dry islands within the swamp at Floyd's Island and Craven's Hammock.

Because of sanitation problems, each group is required to carry a portable toilet with disposable plastic bags. Human waste must be carried out of the swamp and disposed of at the end of the trip. This regulation essentially applies to waste generated en route, since porta-potties are available at each overnight stop. Portable toilets and associated gear are the responsibility of the paddler and are not provided by the refuge management.

Portions of all the canoe trails are open to the general public (paddlers on 1-day trips, tour boats, etc.), and trippers staying longer can expect to encounter other

refuge visitors on these sections of the trails. On those parts of the trails requiring a permit, however, only other paddle groups in transit will normally be encountered. The existing system of scheduling allows only one group at each campsite on any given night.

Fluctuating water levels affect the difficulty of the paddling. Some trails may be closed or difficult to travel during certain times of the year because of low water. These difficulties, according to the refuge management, should be viewed "as an integral part of the wilderness experience." Paddlers should read all regulations carefully and not be reluctant to ask questions before departing. This simple precaution may eliminate considerable discomfort and unnecessary problems.

The spring months (March through early May) with their mild temperatures, high water levels, and profusion of wildflowers, are the most popular period for canoeing in the Okefenokee. In fact, March and April trips are limited to two-night stays.

Reservations can be made only within two months to the day before your trip begins. To make a reservation, call (912) 496-3331 between 7 a.m. and 10 a.m., Monday through Friday (excluding federal holidays). On receipt of an inquiry or permit application, the refuge management will forward a packet containing information on the history, geology, wildlife, and management of the refuge, as well as paddling trip regulations and suggestions for a more pleasant and successful outing. Refuge management advises that first-time visitors carefully digest this information before making their reservations.

All paddlers should remember that temperatures and biting insects can be vary harsh in the Okefenokee, particularly during the summer months. Temperatures can fall into the teens during January and February. Most of the swamp is bathed in direct sunlight and shade is often at a premium. In stormy weather, this

same lack of cover creates uncomfortable moments when heavy rain, high wind, and lightning may assault you. The bottom line is that the Okefenokee offers a true wilderness experience. Careful planning and preparation are key elements of a successful trip.

DESIGNATED CANOE TRAILS

There are a dozen designated canoe trails that can be used, each leaving from one of three access points: Kingfisher Landing, Suwannee Canal, and Stephen Foster State Park. The trips range from overnight to a five-night excursion. All follow the color-coded trails listed below, with descriptions from the Okefenokee National Wildlife Refuge. Contact the Refuge for the latest trip options.

Orange Trail: Follows the historic Suwannee Canal, which was dug in the late 1800s in an attempt to drain the swamp. Canal Run Shelter is 10 straight miles from the east entrance, on the berm of the canal. Past Canal Run Shelter are 5 miles of narrow, winding trail that lead to Billy's Island. Follow Billy's Lake 2 miles to Stephen Foster State Park. Low water levels between Canal Run and Billy's Island often mean navigating stumps, peat blow-ups, and encroaching side vegetation.

Red Trail: Kingfisher Landing to Maul Hammock is a long day of paddling, 12 miles through scrub-shrub, prairie, and small lakes. The 11 miles between Maul Hammock and Big Water go through prairie, narrowly closed channels, and into a wider river channel surrounded by cypress. Both days are long and difficult. The Big Water Shelter is at the north end of Floyd's Prairie. The last 9 miles go through prairie, cypress forest, and Billy's Lake.

Green Trail: Kingfisher Landing to Bluff Lake is 8 miles along a channel originally cut for peat mining and across open prairies full of pitcher plants. The next 9 miles to Floyd's Island take you from Durdin Prairie to Territory and Chase Prairies. Between are narrow closed-sided

channels that may be difficult to paddle during low water levels. The overnight shelter on Floyd's Island is a hunting cabin built in the 1920s for the Hebard family, which at the time owned most of the swamp. There is a short portage across the island. Floyd's Island to Stephen Foster State Park is 8 miles of prairies and cypress forests, ending in Billy's Lake.

Brown Trail: To reach Cravens Hammock, you paddle 5 miles through the Narrows to the Suwannee River Sill. Follow the trail through 5 more miles of cypress, bay, and gum swamp to an oak-covered hammock. The trail condition varies with water levels—there can be a strong current through The Narrows, which may make the return trip difficult.

Purple Trail: The Purple Trail winds through Chase Prairie leading to Round Top Shelter, which boasts a 360-degree view of the prairie. Windy days can make paddling unpleasant, but the shelter is worth the trip, especially when the moon is full.

Blue Trail: The Blue Trail connects the Orange Trail with the Green Trail and skirts the edge of Chase Prairie through deeper holes, which are good fishing areas. It is used mainly as a route from the Orange Trail to Floyds Island.

Note: A short portage across Floyds Island is required on all trips crossing this island. The state charges a camping fee at Stephen Foster State Park.

PADDLING TRIP INFORMATION

Permits: Canoe trips into the Okefenokee wilderness may be arranged in advance or on a first-come, first-served basis. For current reservation procedures and policies, see the Okefenokee National Wildlife Refuge at **http://okefenokee.fws.gov** or call (912) 496-7836.

Physical Conditions: The swamp terrain is flat; there is no fast water and very little dry land. Your paddle will be

used every inch of the way as you wind through cypress forests or across open "prairies" exposed to the sun and wind. You may have to get out of your canoe and push across peat blowups or shallow water. Water levels in the Okefenokee Swamp sometimes become too low to permit use of certain trails; when this occurs, parties holding reservations in these areas will be notified.

Weather: Daytime temperatures are mostly mild. However, during June, July, August, and September, the swamp can be hot and humid, with temperatures ranging above 90 °F. Winter days range from below 40 °F to 80 °F, but much of the time temperatures are in the 50s and 60s. Summer nights are warm, and winter nighttime temperatures can be near or below freezing. Record lows have dipped to 18 °F. The rainy season is normally from June through September. Many summer afternoons are drenched with localized thundershowers. Lightning is probably the most dangerous feature of an Okefenokee experience.

Safety: Each traveler is required by law to have a Coast Guard–approved life preserver in his or her possession. Each canoe must contain a compass and a flashlight. Each paddler must register when entering and leaving the swamp. Due to danger from alligators, pets may not be taken into the swamp. For the same reason, swimming is not permitted. The minimum party size, for safety, is two persons. Parties will not be permitted to launch later than 10 a.m. to ensure that their overnight stop is reached before dark.

Camping: Overnight camping is permitted only at a designated overnight stop. You must register at each stop. No nails should be used and no trees or limbs should be cut. Open fires are not permitted except at specified areas, so gasoline, bottled gas, or similar types of stoves will be required if you plan to cook meals. You must remain at the designated overnight area between sunset and sunrise.

You may camp only 1 night per rest stop. Portable toilets with disposable bags are required, even though overnight camp sites are outfitted with chemical toilets.

Quality Control: Each canoe trail will be limited to one party daily, and each party will be limited to a maximum of 10 canoes or 20 people. Canoeists are responsible for keeping trails free from litter. Pack it in, and pack it out. Motors are not permitted on canoe trips.

Wildlife: Wildlife abounds in the Okefenokee every month of the year. Sandhill cranes, ducks, and other migratory birds are most numerous from November through March. Otter are commonly seen during cold weather when alligators are relatively inactive. Alligators are active in the summer and can be observed sunning on the banks, mostly during spring and fall.

In general, mosquitoes are no problem except after dark from April through October. They are rarely encountered during the daytime. Deerflies, although a biting menace at times during the summer, are not as bad deep in the swamp. There is no need to fear snakes or alligators as long as normal precautions are taken and animals or nests are not molested.

Fishing: Sport fishing is permitted during posted hours in accordance with Georgia state law and Refuge regulations. Live minnows are not permitted as bait in Okefenokee waters. Bass fishing is best in early spring and late fall, but a lot depends on water levels, moon phase, weather, and the skill of the angler.

Suggested Supplies: In addition to regular camping gear, bring along: (1) Rope for pulling your canoe. (2) Drinking water. (3) Insect repellent. (4) Mosquito netting. (5) Rain gear. (6) First aid kit. (7) Snake bite kit. (8) Extra batteries. (9) Litter bags. (10) Free-standing tent with line to tie down to shelters, or jungle hammock and sleeping bag.

SUWANNEE RIVER

Thanks to Stephen Foster, there are few streams in American folklore and culture better known than the Suwannee. The mere mention of its name stirs fanciful visions of stately moss-draped cypress and sultry Southern days. No more beautiful than several dozen other southern Georgia rivers, the Suwannee is nevertheless a living legend in the most literal sense, and therefore something special. The river originates deep in the bowels of the Okefenokee Swamp and winds its way southeast, escaping into Florida and its terminus at the Gulf of Mexico.

MAPS: Billys Island, The Pocket, Strange Island, Fargo, Needmore, Fargo Southwest (USGS); Charlton, Ware, Clinch, Echols (County)

OKEFENOKEE SWAMP TO CR 6

class	S
length	45.5 mi
time	5 days
gauge	Web, phone
level	Unknown
gradient	<1 fpm
scenery	A

DESCRIPTION: Only a small portion of the Suwannee flows within the state of its birth, a fact made much of by Florida tourism promoters. This section, however, is unique among all stretches of the river by virtue of the almost mystical aura conferred by the Okefenokee Swamp.

Deep in the middle of the swamp the Suwannee is born at the confluence of the East and Middle Forks of the Suwannee at the northern end of Billys Lake. Access is available at the nearby Stephen Foster (who else?) State Park. You will quickly find, however, that paddling within Okefenokee is heavily regulated (see the section on the Okefenokee Swamp). If you proceed downstream and out of the swamp, you will have to cross the sill, a man-made levee constructed to stabilize the depth of water in the swamp. The portage is short and easy, but alas, a permit is required. If this sounds like the heavy hand of bureaucracy, remember that this regulation and several dozen more like it (like carrying all human waste out of the swamp), have preserved the pristine integrity of one of America's irreplaceable natural wonders.

Once across the sill, the Suwannee settles into shallow, white, sandy clay banks and flows southward through a watery floodplain forested with pond cypress, swamp black gum, sweet bay, swamp cyrilla, slash pine, magnolia, and palmetto. Since animals and birds do not need permits to cross the sill, the incredibly diverse fauna found in the Okefenokee can also be found along the upper Suwannee.

The water color is dark red, stained by tannic acid from decaying vegetation, and the current is slow. Below the sill to the GA 94 bridge crossing at Fargo, the river flows through several

large midstream stands of cypress and gum, which at higher
water require some heads-up navigation, and present a nice
opportunity to get lost in the surrounding inundated lowlands.
While the flow of the main current is usually easy to follow, there
are times when map, compass, and a little swamp luck are helpful. Access between the state park and Fargo is almost nonexistent, except at a private campground off of GA 177 where
camping and launching are available for a small fee. The state has
purchased 350 acres of land on the river at Fargo; in the future
there may be more access available.

Below Fargo the Suwannee remains isolated in pristine, exotic
wilderness, and flows languidly along a shady, twisting course of

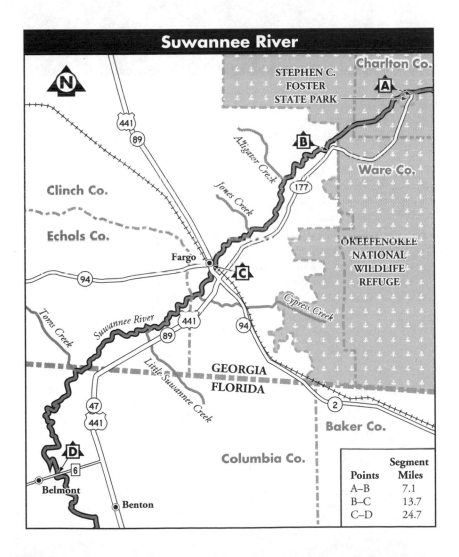

Points	Segment Miles
A–B	7.1
B–C	13.7
C–D	24.7

photo © Tres Hombres del Rio

A Spanish-moss-draped cypress along the Suwannee River

moss-draped cypress. The first access point below Fargo is CR 6, just over the state line. If you continue, you will notice that the banks are higher and more well-defined, and that numerous feeder streams enter the Suwannee. Farther downstream, Florida's largest rapid, Big Shoals, and the Stephen Foster (who else?) Memorial await you. Additional information concerning the Florida sections of the Suwannee can be obtained by writing: Florida Department of Natural Resources, Crown Building, Tallahassee, FL 32304.

The Suwannee's current is slow to moderate. Dangers to navigation are confined to the standard deadfalls in the stream's adolescent reaches, and locals drinking at the GA 94 bridge. Since campsites are rare below access point B, paddlers should launch with sufficient daylight remaining to make Fargo before dark.

SHUTTLE: Out of Fargo, take US 441 south into Florida. Turn right onto CR 6 and follow it to the river. Return to US 441 north for put-in access at its crossing in Fargo, or continue north on GA 177 to the fish camp at access point B (camping and launching are available for a fee) or to the highest access point deep in the swamp at Stephen Foster State Park.

GAUGE: Levels for gauges at and above Fargo are available on the USGS Web site. Runnability levels are unknown. More information can be provided by calling the local outfitters, or by calling the Waycross Fisheries Office at (912) 285-6094.

ALAPAHA RIVER

Jungle-like in its remoteness and luxurious with exotic vegetation, the dark reddish-brown waters of the Alapaha wind through a swampy wonderland teeming with wildlife. Signs of habitation are rare along the river's course; only a few isolated cabins intrude on the remote tranquility. An underlying strata of limestone creates small shoals that approach Class II in intensity, enlivening the paddling. This is, however, mostly a smooth-water run, complete with trees that grow profusely in the river channel, often blurring the dividing line between river and swamp.

MAPS: Alapaha, Tenmile Bay, Willacoochee, Hastings Fish Pond, Lakeland, Naylor, Howell, Statenville, Jennings (USGS); Berrien, Atkinson, Lanier, Lowndes, Echols (County)

GA 135 TO FL 150

class	I (II)
length	85.3 mi
time	Up to 1.5 weeks
gauge	Web, phone
level	2.8 ft
gradient	<2 fpm
scenery	A+

DESCRIPTION: Following a course of extreme and seemingly endless loops and tight turns, it is possible to run the Alapaha as far north as the US 82 bridge, although trees, primarily sweet gum, cypress, and Australian pine, have taken up residence midstream. After a period of high water, dislodged debris collects on these trees, making downstream progress in this upper section technically challenging at best, a dangerous struggle at worst.

When the Alapaha's largest tributary, the Willacoochee River, enters the stream west of the town of the same name, paddling becomes a more relaxing experience. There are still trees found in the stream from the access at GA 135 (A) to the town of Lakeland (C) downstream, but the additional flow increases the stream's width to 45–60 feet. The river's low, sandy banks are relatively newly formed, and trees (pine, water oak, laurel oak, sweet bay, birch, and an occasional live oak) growing on the banks are in a perpetual slow-motion migration into the riverbed, creating a lush canopy that shades the dark-brown waters from the sun.

As it progresses into Lanier County, the Alapaha's course is slightly less curving as it flows in the center of a broad, forested, swamp corridor. Between Lakeland and Statenville, the current gets faster as the river straightens further. White sandbars on the insides of bends continue to provide excellent swimming or camping spots, and persist until crossing beneath the Southern Railroad bridge at access point F. From time to time sand bluffs up to 10 feet high and populated with pine encroach on the

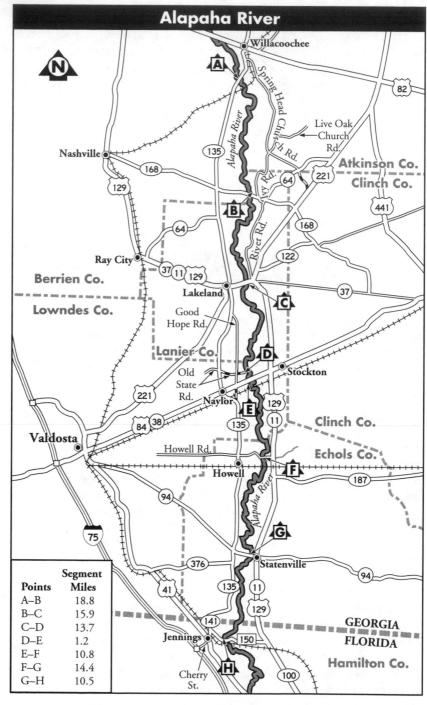

Alapaha River

Points	Segment Miles
A–B	18.8
B–C	15.9
C–D	13.7
D–E	1.2
E–F	10.8
F–G	14.4
G–H	10.5

bottom land, making for good camp sites in absence of sand bars or during periods of higher water. A good camping spot that was formerly a designated stop along the Alapaha Canoe Trail sits a little over two hours below access point F on the river-right bluff.

The current is moderate on the Alapaha, but the river comes up quickly after a good rainfall to create a fast current at high water. With the density of trees crowding the banks, high water can create dangerous conditions for novices or anyone caught outside of a boat. Flat-water paddling prevails throughout the river, except at infrequent shoals. A ledge that approaches Class II difficulty, complete with a surfing wave, is located between US 84 (E) and Howell Road. Avoid sharp limestone rocks at the shoals and where they are exposed at the banks. In low-water periods, the river disappears into the ground-water table downstream of CR 6 before reaching the Suwannee.

SHUTTLE: From Valdosta, take US 41 south into Florida to reach the lowest take-out for this section, east of Jennings. All upper access points are easily reached via GA 135.

GAUGE: The USGS Web site provides data for the Alapaha at the town of Alapaha (upstream of Willacoochee) and at Statenville. Using the Statenville data, 2.8 is a good minimum, with a maximum above 8–10 feet. Additionally, the Echols County Sheriff's Department at (229) 559-5603 can provide runnability assessments, as can the local outfitters. The river is generally runnable from late November through August.

WITHLACOOCHEE RIVER

A list of Georgia's truly beautiful scenic rivers includes the Withla-coochee. Originating in Tift and Berrien Counties, its dark waters flow south along the Cook County line into Lowndes County, where it is joined by its largest tributary, (ironically) the Little River. Intimate, shaded in its northern reaches, mysterious in its beauty—the Withlacoochee is one of the few Coastal Plain streams in which limestone ledges form small shoals. A second distinctive feature of the river is the occasional white sandbar on the insides of bends, which are perfect for swimming or camping.

MAPS: New Lois, Hahira East, Valdosta, Lousley, Nankin, Clyattville (USGS); Berrien, Lowndes, Brooks (County)

GA 37 TO GA 31

class	I (I+)
length	68.8 mi
time	Up to 1 week
gauge	Web, phone
level	Unknown
gradient	<2 fpm
scenery	B+ to C

DESCRIPTION: Runnable from GA 37 to the confluence with the Little River during the winter and spring, and below the confluence of the Little from late November to early August, the Withlacoochee winds a convoluted course through a thickly wooded swamp corridor bordered by cultivated table land and commercial pine forests. The water is a clear, burgundy-red color, which contrasts strikingly with the white sand banks and often appears glossy black where the channel is deep. Formation of bypass islands and oxbow lakes is common.

Both the Withlacoochee and the Little jump their low, sandy, clay banks to inundate their narrow floodplains for long periods of time, giving rise to bottom forests of swamp black gum and cypress. Cypress and gum grow in the stream as well as on the banks, where they are joined by Ogeechee lime, water elm, water oak, laurel oak, and sweet bay. Scrub vegetation is thick with palmetto, swamp cyrilla, and possum haw, among other varieties. Birds, reptiles, and other animals flourish along the Withlacoochee, and are readily observable in all their diversity by the silent paddler.

At the GA 37 crossing (A), the river averages a slim 30 feet in width; it expands to 40 feet as it dips into Lowndes County and broadens to 55 to 70 feet below the mouth of the Little (near G), where the river's course straightens. Shoals occur primarily in Lowndes and Brooks Counties, rarely surpassing Class I+ in difficulty. One small rapid, complete with surfing wave, is found

Withlacoochee River

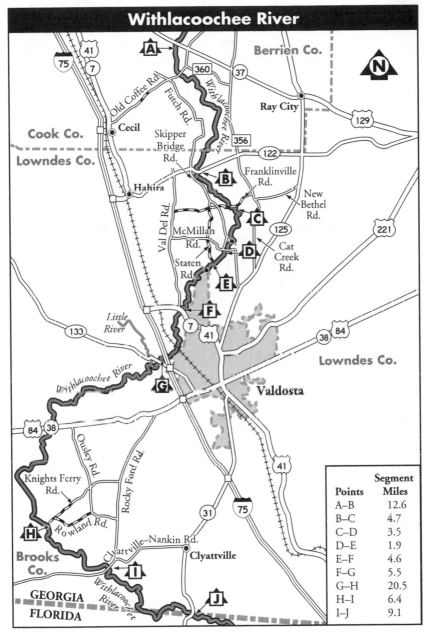

	Segment
Points	**Miles**
A–B	12.6
B–C	4.7
C–D	3.5
D–E	1.9
E–F	4.6
F–G	5.5
G–H	20.5
H–I	6.4
I–J	9.1

upstream of the Clyattsville–Nankin Road bridge (I). Another awaits where the river first crosses the border into Florida. The limestone shoal that forms the foundation of this rapid is jagged; avoid contact with it by running this on the left. Signs of habitation are sparse, although swimmers are frequently encountered at bridge crossings and anglers are likely to turn up anywhere. The current is moderate, and other than the small shoals mentioned, deadfalls create the only hazard to navigation.

Continuing south in a broad loop, the Withlacoochee passes quietly into Florida where it empties into the Suwannee. Although only the Georgia portion of the Withlacoochee is described, the Florida section is equally beautiful and fully worthy of exploration.

SHUTTLE: From I-75, take Exit 11 south of Valdosta. Turn south on GA 31 and continue to the river at the Florida border. Turn right onto the dirt road before the bridge to reach the boat ramp. Access points above Valdosta are easily reached via GA 125 north. Below Valdosta, see the map for the best routes.

GAUGE: The USGS Web site lists data for the telemetry gauge at Quitman and farther upstream at Bemiss. Minimum levels using this gauge are unknown. Maximum is flood stage. Local outfitters can provide assessments of runnability over the phone.

LITTLE RIVER OF SOUTHERN GEORGIA

The Little's tannic acid-stained water bubbles playfully over small limestone ledges and between brilliantly contrasting white sandbars along the way to its juncture with the Withlacoochee River southwest of Valdosta. Remote and enticing, the Little is canopied with Ogeechee lime, water elm, and scattered cypress. The river's course is substantially less convoluted than that of similar blackwater streams in the Coastal Plains.

MAPS: Omega, Ellenton, Berlin East, Cecil, Hahira West, Hahira East, Valdosta (USGS); Colquitt, Cook, Brooks, Lowndes (County)

WEST OF LENOX TO WITHLACOOCHEE RIVER

class	I
length	57.5 mi
time	6 days
gauge	Web, visual
level	Unknown
gradient	<2 fpm
scenery	B+

DESCRIPTION: Runnable below the Cool Springs Bridge (A) west of Lenox in Cook County in winter and spring, the Little is 25 to 30 feet in width and is frequently obstructed by deadfalls. Below the Rountree Bridge west of Sparks (B), the Little enters the backwaters of a beautiful swamp lake at Reed Bingham State Park. A sort of Okefenokee in miniature with a variety of watery flora, this small lake is definitely worthy of exploration.

Downstream of the dam at the lake's southern end, the Little continues in uninterrupted tranquility except for a short section below the GA 122 bridge (G) where a number of small cabins line the stream. For the remainder of its journey to the Withlacoochee, the Little never exceeds 50 feet wide as it hides bashfully beneath the exotic canopy of the surrounding woodland swamp.

The Little River's level of difficulty is Class I throughout. Numerous deadfalls are a primary hazard to navigation, along with the portage required at the dam at the state park. The current is moderate to slow, access is good, and the river is suitable for camping. Trips on the Little can easily be combined with floats on the Withlacoochee.

SHUTTLE: From Valdosta, take GA 133 west of I-75 to its crossing with the Little River; turn left into the Department of Natural Resources Troupville Boat Ramp across the road from the prison. See the map for the locations of upper access points.

GAUGE: The USGS's Web site lists data for the river at Adel. The minimum level is unknown. In order to stay out of the trees, stay off the river during high flood stage in the winter. A visual gauge is painted on the bridge at Morven Road (H), though guidelines using this gauge are unknown.

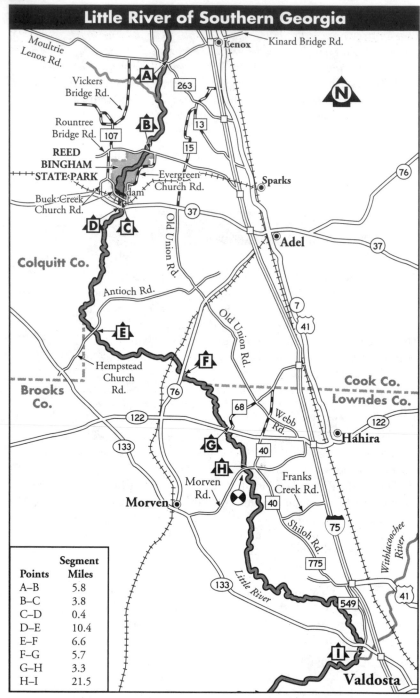

Little River of Southern Georgia

Moultrie Lenox Rd.

Lenox

Kinard Bridge Rd.

A

Vickers Bridge Rd.

263

B

13

Rountree Bridge Rd.

107

15

REED BINGHAM STATE PARK

Evergreen Church Rd.

Sparks

76

Buck Creek Church Rd.

dam

37

D   **C**

Adel

37

Colquitt Co.

Old Union Rd.

Antioch Rd.

7

41

E

Old Union Rd.

Hempstead Church Rd.

F

Cook Co.

Brooks Co.

76

68

Webb Rd.

Lowndes Co.

122

122

133

G

40

Hahira

H

Morven Rd.

Franks Creek Rd.

40

Morven

Shiloh Rd.

75

775

Little River

133

Withlacoochee River

549

41

I

Valdosta

N

Points	Segment Miles
A–B	5.8
B–C	3.8
C–D	0.4
D–E	10.4
E–F	6.6
F–G	5.7
G–H	3.3
H–I	21.5

OCHLOCKONEE RIVER

White sand beaches, dense vegetation, and wildlife conspire to create an exceptionally pretty stream, the Ochlocknee River. Rising in Worth County south of Albany, the Ochlocknee runs southwest before slipping over the state line into Florida on its way to the Gulf of Mexico. Its chocolate-brown waters follow a generally winding and serpentine course through an oak- and gum-dominated bottom land forest corridor; oxbow lakes are not uncommon.

MAPS: Moultrie, Coolidge, Chastain, Merrillville, Ochlockonee, Pine Park, Cairo South, Berachton, Calvary (USGS); Colquitt, Thomas, Grady, Gadsden FL (County)

GA 188 TO FLORIDA BORDER

class	I
length	53.7 mi
time	Up to 1.5 weeks
gauge	Web, phone
level	Unknown
gradient	<2 fpm
scenery	B+

DESCRIPTION: Intimate, pristine, and exotically canopied with cypress, black gum, birch, and willow, the Ochlockonee flows with a moderate to sluggish current between sandy clay banks of 2 to 5 feet. White sandbars and beaches grace the insides of many bends and provide excellent sites for camping or swimming. Otherwise, the banks are dense and luxurious with vegetation including swamp palm, cyrilla, and Sebastian bush. From time to time tall pines line the streamside, as do sweet bay and water oak. Wildlife, particularly birds, make their presence known through continuous activity.

Downstream of GA 188 (A), the stream can be run most of the year and is substantially less plagued by the maze of deadfalls found upstream. The river's channel is deep, providing excellent opportunities for fishing. Passing below the US 19 bridge (C), the watercourse briefly expands into an extensive swamp for about 0.7 miles. Shortly, after passing below GA 3, the Ochlockonee emerges abruptly from the jungle into terrain that has been completely cleared for a powerline crossing, bringing home the stark reality of human intervention on otherwise pristine surroundings with great visual impact.

Continuing downstream and crossing into Florida, the river widens to approximately 60 to 75 feet, but otherwise remains essentially unchanged, except that it picks up a little sediment as it passes through the Tallahassee hills in southern Grady County. The level of difficulty is Class I throughout; dangers to navigation consist primarily of deadfalls that completely block the

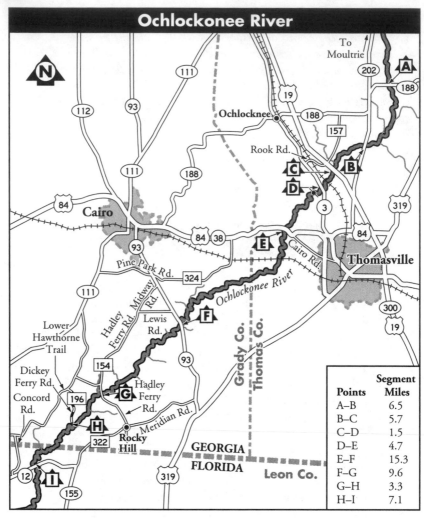

Ochlockonee River

To Moultrie

Ochlocknee

Rook Rd.

Cairo

Thomasville

Ochlockonee River

Cairo Rd.

Pine Park Rd.

Lower Hawthorne Trail

Hadley Ferry Rd. Midway Rd.

Lewis Rd.

Dickey Ferry Rd.

Concord Rd.

Hadley Ferry Rd.

Meridian Rd.

Rocky Hill

Grady Co.

Thomas Co.

GEORGIA
FLORIDA   Leon Co.

Points	Segment Miles
A–B	6.5
B–C	5.7
C–D	1.5
D–E	4.7
E–F	15.3
F–G	9.6
G–H	3.3
H–I	7.1

stream periodically in all Georgia sections and brush strainers that form in the channel along the side of small islands.

SHUTTLE: To the final take-out from Cairo, take GA 111 south to the town of Darsey, located on the state line with Florida. Turn left here onto FL 157, and follow it to another left onto FL 12. Follow FL 12 to the river. See the map for the locations of upper access points.

GAUGE: The USGS Web site provides data for the gauge located at Thomasville. Runnability levels using this gauge are unknown; maximum is flood stage. Local outfitters and the Albany Game and Fish Office (phone (229) 430-4256) can provide more information.

part**Seven**

The Georgia Coast

No paddling guide for Georgia would be complete without mention of the Atlantic coastal waters. Ranging from the mouth of the Savannah River at the South Carolina border south to the mouth of the St. Marys River at the Florida state line, the Georgia coast remains one of the largest undeveloped wilderness areas east of the Mississippi River.

A chain of 13 barrier islands anchors the outer edge of the coastal region, shielding the expansive marshes, smaller islands, and hammocks that stretch from the interior sides of the barrier islands to the mainland. Within this marshy coastal zone, thousands of miles of potential paddling trips wind through a labyrinth of rivers, sounds, and convoluted tidal creeks. Though access points are somewhat sparse, the number and type of trips available are limited only by the paddler's imagination—one access point can be the debarkation point for many different routes. Trip styles range from the serene exploration of smaller sloughs and creeks to a wild ride in the surf. Wide expanses of undeveloped terrain make for excellent camping trips.

Wildlife abounds in the coastal ecosystem. Acres and acres of lime-green grasses form on the lowest lying land, providing habitat for raccoons, mink, and rice rats. Birds, including the willet, great blue heron, and snowy egret, feed in the marshes. Shrubs and trees grow on the higher

land of the islands and hammocks. Here, laurel oak, red-bay, and sprawling live oak trees draped with Spanish moss canopy an understory of palmettos. Larger islands are home to feral pigs, deer, and wild horses in addition to the more recent imports of armadillos.

Marine life is diverse and abundant. Tidal creeks and sloughs provide sheltered nurseries for young fish, shrimp, and crabs. Oyster beds cluster in the muddy zone between the high and low tide. Gregarious dolphins swim beside paddlers, announcing their arrival with a blast of air. Surfacing sea turtles, river otters, and jumping fish all make appearances above the plane of the water, seemingly with little regard for the paddler who has ventured onto the topside of their turf.

While much of the terrain is wilderness, many of the waterways are not. Powerboats and sailboats are common, but typically avoid the smaller sloughs and creeks. Large intracoastal barges can be encountered in the InterCoastal Waterway, which winds through the coastal region.

Compared with traditional river trips, paddling among the tidal islands and marshes demands comprehensive planning and research—do your homework before heading out. Tidal currents, feasible routes, high land access points, and the available freshwater options all require consideration in trip planning. Coastal outfitters and experienced paddlers will happily provide you with advice on all of these counts.

Gathering local knowledge of tides and suggested routes is a highly recommended starting point. The timing and strength of tides vary by area; working with the local tidal pattern can make the difference between a pleasant trip paddling with the flow or an arduous slog with potentially dangerous consequences when working against it. As such, tidal patterns dictate the

best launch and return times. Local information can also help you avoid getting stranded in the tide-dependent channels that are transformed at low tide into impassable muddy channels laced with oyster beds full of sharp cutting shells.

NOAA charts and USGS quadrangle maps are useful in planning a trip. NOAA chart numbers 11,506 through 11,512 encompass the Georgia coast, and a free online index is available to help determine which charts you'll need to order. These charts are also available in marine stores. USGS maps can be found at some outfitters, most surveying supply stores, and also online. Again, use the index map to locate the quadrangle(s) needed for your trip.

Trace your route on paper before getting on the water. Navigation while paddling the Georgia coast is sometimes complicated by the lack of differentiating vertical landmarks. You may be looking for the entrance to a creek a half mile away and all you can see is a solid-green line of marsh. Having important bearings, distances, and landmarks noted in advance on your chart will expedite your trip.

High land access points are limited—again, local knowledge is invaluable in planning where to land and where to camp. Island access (for camping or day visits) is actively controlled by a variety of different jurisdictions; some islands are restricted wildlife preserves, some are private. Camping, where available, is excellent, but requires that you plan in advance and secure the required permissions before leaving. Simply showing up can jeopardize future access for all paddlers. Four of the thirteen barrier islands (Tybee, Sea Island, St. Simons, and Jekyll) are accessible by car and highly developed. Of these, Jekyll and St. Simons Islands offer traditional hotel lodging; Jekyll also hosts a campground. The

family who owns Little St. Simons Island operates an upscale lodge there.

COASTAL CAMPING OPTIONS

Little Tybee is one of the least disturbed of the barrier islands and home to rare and endangered migrating birds. The island is owned by the state and managed by the Department of Natural Resources. Permits are not required for camping, but make sure you obey the rules established to regulate and minimize human impact on the island. For more information, call the DNR at (912) 264-7218.

Ossabaw is the third largest barrier island and home to rare and biologically diverse native plant and animal communities. The island was acquired by the State of Georgia under very specific guidelines. Designated a Georgia Heritage Preserve, the island has been set aside for scientific and cultural study; trips to the island should meet this criteria—that is, have specific research or educational goals related to the unique natural history of the island. Camping permits, visits, and tours are provided; groups should contain at least six people. For more information and applications for day-use and camping permits, contact the Ossabaw Island Foundation at (912) 233-5104.

The State of Georgia also owns Sapelo Island, the fourth largest of Georgia's barrier islands. Pioneer camping for groups of 15–25 people (for a minimum of two nights) is available at the Cabretta Beach facility. Reservations and more information are available by calling (912) 485-2299. Hog Hammock, a small community located on the south side of the island, is home to

African Americans who have maintained the customs and Gullah language of their African ancestors, who worked the plantations formerly located on the island. Bed-and-breakfast-type lodging is available from Lula (912) 485-2270 and the Wallow (912) 485-2206. Primitive camping with a view of the marsh is available in Hog Hammock at Sapelo Sanctuary at (912) 485-2273, or the Weekender at (912) 485-2277.

At 17.5 miles in length, Cumberland is the largest barrier island. The island features maritime forests, dune fields, marshes, mud flats, and tidal creeks in addition to past and present human developments. The National Park Service administers access to the patchwork of public lands spread throughout the island. Camping options include developed campgrounds and remote backcountry sites in the wilderness areas. Competition for permits is fierce; call up to six months in advance. Contact the Cumberland Island National Seashore at (888) 817-3421 or (912) 882-4335.

To say that the maritime forests and marshes of the Georgia coast are merely special would be misleading. They are in fact a magical, fragile ecosystem that shields the inner coast from the brutal vagaries of the sea. Deference to the natural environment and the regulations that preserve it is not just recommended but necessary to ensure the continued health of this unique environment. That so much of this region remains undeveloped is truly remarkable—no other eastern state can boast a similar expanse of wild coastal lands.

CROOKED RIVER

For paddlers voyaging to Cumberland Island National Seashore, Crooked River provides the shortest and most enjoyable route starting from a public boat ramp on the mainland. Even if the destination is the chief attraction, journey by paddle enhances the overall Cumberland experience. The river is a typical coastal estuary, the safe passage of which requires deference to tides and wind.

MAPS: National Park Service; Harrietts Bluff, Cumberland Island South, Cumberland Island North (USGS); Camden (County)

CROOKED RIVER STATE PARK TO BRICKHILL BLUFF

class	T
Length	13.1 mi
time	4 hr (ideal conditions)
Gauge	Web
Level	Tidal
scenery	B-

DESCRIPTION: Paddling trips to Cumberland Island may take the form of a day trip or an overnight stay. The 13-mile round-trip to Plum Orchard (B) packs plenty into a single day. Campers either continue up Brickhill River to camp at Brickhill Bluff (C) or take out at Plum Orchard and backpack into Cumberland's interior. Your choice of backcountry campsites must be arranged in advance with the Park Service. Permits are issued at the Cumberland Island Ferry Landing Visitor Center in St. Marys. Obtaining a permit requires a reservation or luck; there is a strict cap on the number of campers allowed on the island and reservations are often exhausted months in advance. In the absence of a reservation, all is not lost; no-shows sometimes free up permits for walk-ons. Phone (888) 817-3421 or (912) 882-4335 for reservatoins. Additionally, there is a $2 per day parking fee at the Crooked River State Park boat ramp.

The trip can be a leisurely jaunt or an odyssey, depending on conditions. With the wind and tide going your way, the 6-mile trip to Plum Orchard takes a couple hours. Going against a stiff wind can exhaust the entire 6-hour tide window, particularly for open canoes. Along the way, the surrounding terrain of coastal-marsh mud flats is covered with grass slightly higher than a paddler's eyes. The width and openness of the scene, combined with the absence of stopping points along the way, can make inland paddlers feel vulnerable. Above the grass, forests are visible in the distance. Boat traffic consists of pleasure craft: anglers fishing from motorboats and the occasional sailboat. You may encounter commercial traffic where Crooked

Crooked River

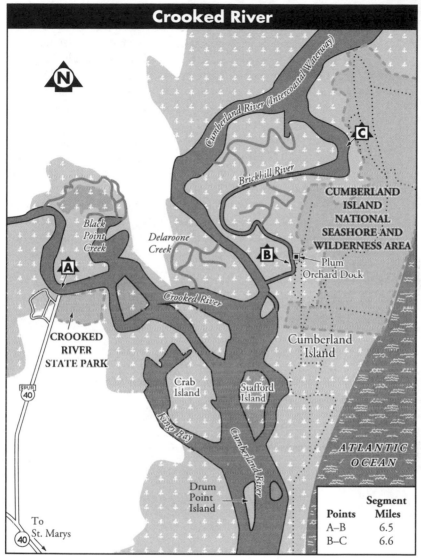

N

Cumberland River (Intercoastal Waterway)

C

Brickhill River

Black
Point
Creek

Delaroone
Creek

CUMBERLAND
ISLAND
NATIONAL
SEASHORE AND
WILDERNESS AREA

A

B

Plum
Orchard Dock

Crooked River

CROOKED
RIVER
STATE PARK

Cumberland
Island

SPUR
40

Crab
Island

Stafford
Island

Kings Bay

Cumberland River

ATLANTIC
OCEAN

Drum
Point
Island

To
St. Marys

40

Points	Segment Miles
A–B	6.5
B–C	6.6

River crosses the Intercoastal Waterway. Needless to say, stay out of the way and make your crossing snappy.

Regardless of the weather, bring apparel or insect repellent that protects exposed flesh, not least of all your hands, from biting insects. The bug nuisance peaks at the boat ramps. The bites continue to torment long after your paddle strokes outdistance the swarms, so cover yourself preemptively before you start packing your boat for launch.

Time your launch carefully with all of the following phenomena in mind: sunrise and sunset; high and low tides; the lag between tide reversal and when the current gets moving in the desired direction; wind direction and strength; the time of day at which you can pick up your permit; and the time required to drive from St. Marys to Crooked River boat ramp. Given that some of these variables are not known in advance, arrive knowing the next feasible launch time in case conditions don't allow you to launch when you want to.

SHUTTLE: Crooked River State Park is located at the end of GA Spur 40. Take I-95 to Exit 3 for GA 40 East. Turn left at GA Spur 40 and proceed to the boat ramp.

GAUGE: For tidal flows on Crooked River, use the National Weather Service's Web site for Jacksonville tides at **www.srh. noaa.gov/jax/tides.shtml.**

CATHEAD CREEK

Cathead Creek is a tributary of the Altamaha River above Darien. It drains part of Buffalo Swamp, a rare tidal forest containing bald cypress, sweet blackgum, and water tupelo. Cathead Creek flows for 8 miles through an undeveloped section of McIntosh County that was once cultivated with rice for over a hundred years. Today paddlers can explore the irrigation canals of the abandoned rice fields, which are overgrown with freshwater vegetation and abundant with wildlife. The fields and swamps are inundated twice a day by the tides, which average about 7 feet.

MAPS: Ridgeville (USGS); McIntosh (County)

COX STREET TO DARIEN

class	T
length	8.9 mi
time	3–4 hr
gauge	Web, phone
level	Tidal
gradient	N/A
scenery	B+

DESCRIPTION: The upper reaches of this tidal creek can be accessed from a culvert landing on Cox Road north of Darien, just past the GA 251 junction. Although it appears to be a freshwater stream, the creek's flow changes with the ingress and departure of the tide. The easiest trip involves putting in at high tide and paddling downstream to the boat ramp in Darien.

The creek starts out narrow and intimate as it passes beneath overhanging trees. The only departure from the solitude is the anachronistic crossing of I-95 encountered two hours into the trip. In the lower sections, the creek becomes very broad with vast salt marshes and exposed sandbars at low tide. One notable surviving feature of the area's history is the grid of canals that formed the borders of rice paddies, a reminder of the rice plantations built by enslaved labor. Today, these irrigation canals and impoundments provide sanctuary for migrating birds and waterfowl.

Just before Cathead Creek empties into the Altamaha River, it runs along the high banks of Darien's west side bordered with private homes and docks. The take-out is at the boat ramp in Darien at the foot of Scriven Street. There is limited access and very few places to get out along the banks of the creek before reaching the private docks near Darien. Runnable year-round, the only hazards are deadfall, tricky tides, and getting lost in the swamps or irrigation canals.

SHUTTLE: The take-out is at the boat ramp in Darien. From there to the put-in, take US 17 north, turn left onto GA 251, and continue straight onto Cox Street when GA 251 turns to the

north. The put-in is ahead on the right where the road crosses the culvert. Shuttle service is available from the local outfitter.

GAUGE: Get information on tidal flows before leaving via phone from local outfitters, or through the National Weather Service's Web site. Moving with the tide makes the trip easy; against it can be arduous.

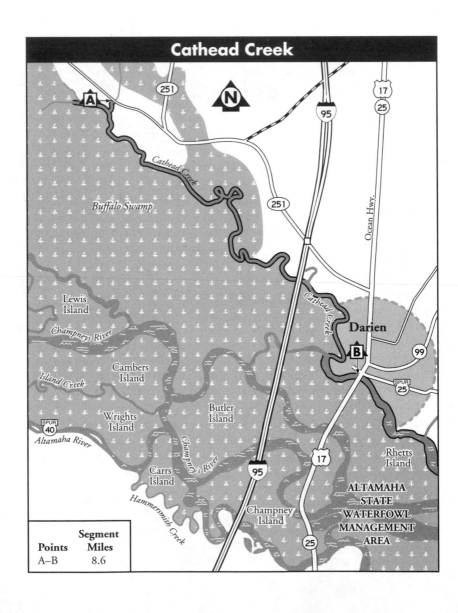

Canoeing the Coast? Try Kayaking
— by Steve Cramer

A canoe may not be the perfect vehicle for sightseeing along Georgia's diverse and scenic coast. Rather, a touring kayak is the preferred craft for coastal exploration, as it is both highly efficient and highly seaworthy, allowing the paddler to confidently traverse salt marsh creeks, large rivers, and even open ocean. Increasingly, paddlers and outfitters are turning to these long kayaks as the best way to explore estuaries and inlets along the coast. The terms "touring kayak" and a "sea kayak" are used interchangeably, though the former term is more comprehensive, since it makes it clear that you don't have to go out to sea to enjoy the ride.

So what is a touring kayak? Generally, it's a decked boat 14–18 feet long and quite narrow at 20–25 inches wide. But isn't that narrow beam tippy? Well, yes, compared to most tripping canoes. A canoeist accustomed to standing up to scout the route will have to give that up in a touring kayak. On the other hand, the touring kayak is a direct descendant of the Inuit *qajaq*, literally the "hunter's boat," which has been used for centuries to hunt seals in the open ocean. Although a bit tender initially, most touring kayaks have good secondary stability to cope with the bumpy water of the open sea—or even coastal rivers on a windy day. And if you do manage to flip, the Eskimo roll remains an option.

So, do you need to be able to roll before kayaking the coast? Not unless you plan to venture out into the surf zone or for long stints off shore. Most touring kayakers can't roll, but safety-minded ones practice techniques for re-entering the boat in deep water in case of an unplanned exit. (Remember, in the marsh there may be no solid land for miles.) Usually you'll have a paddling companion to help, but even if you get

isolated there are reasonably easy re-entry techniques that can be done solo.

Although it seems like a narrow kayak shouldn't haul much gear—and in fact they don't rival canoes of similar length—a 17-foot touring kayak can easily hold gear and provisions for a week or more, especially if two or more paddlers share tent, stove, and other equipment. For example, the Dagger Cortez, at 17.5 feet long and 20.5 inches wide, has hatch volumes of 5,200 cubic inches forward and 9,150 cubic inches aft, the equivalent of three large backpacks. A touring kayaker should pack lots of long, narrow bags, because gear has to be stowed through hatches typically no more than 18 inches wide. Packing a kayak is a three-dimensional jigsaw puzzle, but one that gets easier each time you do it—and as the days pass and food stores dwindle. Kayak manufacturers claim that hatches are dry, but very few are totally waterproof. Invest in some good nylon drybags for items that must stay dry like sleeping bags, clothes, and rice.

Besides the basic gear, kayakers on the coast should consider bringing a few extras for security: signaling equipment such as flares, a signal mirror, a fog horn or loud whistle; a small VHF marine radio to talk to other vessels in the area, get weather reports, and, if necessary, summon the Coast Guard for assistance; cellular phones, which work well near towns in this flat landscape but aren't always reliable; and a Global Positioning System (GPS) receiver, especially one with mapping capabilities—one stand of spartina grass looks a lot like another.

Planning is important because it's easy to traverse wide swaths of Georgia's coastal marsh in a touring

kayak. Paddlers accustomed to canoes will be pleasantly amazed at the effortless glide of a touring kayak. Most can cruise at 3–4 knots without undue strain. Of course, that straight ahead ease comes at a price. Touring boats are notoriously difficult to turn, especially compared to whitewater boats or flat-bottomed canoes. You've got a long waterline, so if you try to turn the boat flat you're pushing a lot of water at the bow and stern. The solution is to put the boat up on its edge to shorten the waterline. Beginners may be nervous about edging, but your boat is probably more stable than you think.

Regardless of your skill level, practice launching and beaching at a beach before attempting even short trips. In all cases, travel in groups of no fewer than three craft. Weather conditions should be carefully evaluated before paddling off shore in the Atlantic. Calm seas and slack to moderate winds are essential for all but the most skilled kayakers. On extended trips, monitor weather forecasts on a marine VHF radio. Also consider tidal conditions, particularly when entering or crossing a sound. If you're paddling 4 knots into a 3-knot tide current (not unusual in the cuts between islands), you'll be going about 1 knot. That's an hour paddling to go a mile. Conversely, put the tide behind you and you can almost double your speed.

There are so many different ecosystems along the coast: open ocean, beachfront, tidal rivers, marsh creeks, and even blackwater swamps a bit inland. With a little practice and planning, a touring kayak provides an efficient vehicle to get you there, allowing you to see more of Georgia's coastal beauty up close.

part**Eight**

NOTEWORTHY RIVERS IN NEIGHBORING STATES

OCOEE RIVER, TENNESSEE

The Ocoee is arguably the most popular whitewater run in the Southeast. Its rollicking style and nonstop action have proven to be irresistible—when it's running, some boaters simply lose the will to go anywhere else. The river is divided into three sections by dams controlled by the Tennessee Valley Authority, who tightly control water releases in the interest of reserving flow for power generation. When the water is flowing, both upper sections of the Ocoee described here are solid Class III and IV difficulty; with flow rates of 1,200+ cfs, the river should not be taken lightly. Do not attempt this river in craft not specifically designed for whitewater, or without Class III technical skills—you will need both. Many of the rapids are closely spaced, and some are long and continuous, with rescue being difficult. Swims can be long and unpleasant. On the other hand, US 64 is right next to the river, making it somewhat easier to get off the river if you find yourself in trouble.

MAPS: Ducktown, Caney Creek (USGS); Polk TN (County)

OCOEE NO. 3 DAM TO OCOEE NO. 2 DAM (UPPER OCOEE OR OLYMPIC SECTION)

class	III–IV
length	5.0 mi
time	2–3 hr
gauge	Web, phone
level	1,400+ cfs
gradient	50 fpm
scenery	B+

DESCRIPTION: This section begins just below Ocoee Number 3 dam (A) with a couple of miles of playful Class II rapids on which to warm up and get ready for the bigger stuff to follow. The first major rapid, the Gauntlet or Mikey's Ledge, is marked by the main flow starting to move to river right just above a large rock ledge outcropping right of center. This is a pretty solid Class III+ run. Scouting can be done from the rock ledge, or by pulling out on river right above the approach and walking down the old road bed. If you get out on river right to scout, you may want to continue on down the roadbed to scout the next drop as well. Like most rapids on the Ocoee, the Gauntlet has more than one line. On the right side of the outcropping, there is a chute on river right close to the bank. There is also a "jump" off the nose

of the main ledge over the hole in the center of the run. And there is a line over a 4-foot drop on the left side of the outcropping. The water is fast and pretty technical below the first drop.

Not far below, you'll see the first signs of the Olympic course and the Whitewater Center. Just above the Olympic course is a river-wide broken ledge with several chutes leading into a series of serious holes and strong crosscurrents. This rapid is called either Blue Hole or Box Car. It can be very wet in an open canoe. Several of the chutes are runnable, with the better run being on the far right.

The Olympic course is a fast, constricted section of water with several drops, lots of eddies, and water that is pushier than it looks. You can take-out on either side at the top and walk the entire run on either side or both sides to scout it. Virtually every drop here has been named. In order, they are: Best Ledge, Smiley Face, Slam Dunk, a wave train called Conveyor Belt, Callihan Ledge, and last, but certainly not least, is Humongous. This area is a great park-and-play section, with several good surfing holes and the ability to take-out at the bottom and carry back up and

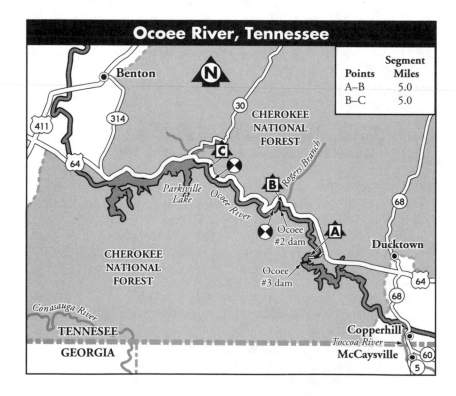

run again as many times as you want, using the deluxe, paved foot trails along the course.

Near the end of the course, there is a large man-made rock out-cropping in the middle with a lot of water going to either side. This is Humongous, an aptly named Class IV rapid that is partic-ularly unpleasant to swim, and can result in a swim of more than a quarter mile if you aren't a very aggressive swimmer. The right side of Humongous features a nearly channel-wide retentive hole that can routinely flip large commercial rafts and recirculate boats and boaters. If you run that side, skirt the hole on the far right. The left side features a series of very large wave-holes that will fill up an open canoe in a heartbeat. Eddy-hop far left to skirt the holes. The last eddy on the left (under the footbridge) is the take-out to carry back up and do it again. All these eddies have very strong eddy lines that require a good punch to get across.

A few hundred yards below the Olympic course is a rapid whose common name isn't printable, but also goes by Trash Can and Roach Motel. The main flow moves toward river left, and the river narrows dramatically and goes through three very large holes, each one bigger than the one before. Again, a very wet run for an open canoe. Skirt the holes down the far right, dodging the rocks and smaller holes. Alternatively, skirt the first two holes on the right and do a quick ferry across to the left to skirt the last hole on the left. There is an easy run-out at the bottom with a good recovery area if you swim or swamp out. This is the biggest water on the entire section, possibly the entire river.

Next, there is a section of easy Class II water until you get to the bridge going to Power House Number 3. The channel then splits, and if you follow the main current to the left, you'll quickly reach a man-made drop sometimes called Edge of the World, where the river channel drops into a canal carrying the outflow of Power House Number 3. If there is water coming down the canal from the powerhouse, this can be a very tricky 3–4-foot drop into a strong crosscurrent, which forms a danger-ous hydraulic. There are also serious pinning spots in the drop if you are not on the right line. You can avoid this drop by staying to the right where the current splits and picking your way down a rocky channel to the right of an island until you rejoin the main flow coming out of the canal. The river becomes flat at this point, and runs into the pond above Ocoee Number 2 Dam (B), which feeds the flume to Power House Number 2. Take-out on river right just above the dam.

SHUTTLE: The take-out for the Upper Ocoee run is Rogers Branch Access Area on US 64, about a mile west of the Ocoee

Whitewater Center, which is west of Ducktown, Tennessee. There is a large parking area, a staging area for the commercial outfitters, and a boat loading/unloading area. Tennessee Parks and Recreation assesses a fee for parking at this access point. To get to the put-in, go east on US 64, past the Whitewater Center about a half mile, to a paved, gated road to the right that goes to Ocoee Number 3 Dam. Follow the road to the put-in area, which is well marked by signs. The gate to the road is closed and locked unless there is an official recreational release from Ocoee Number 3 Dam.

GAUGE: The TVA Web site at www.tva.gov has information on recreational and event releases. Typical release flows are in the 1,400–2,500 cfs range. River characteristics do not change a lot within this flow range, but the rapids become much more pushy, and the moves are more difficult to make at the higher end of the flow range.

OCOEE NUMBER 2 DAM TO PARKSVILLE LAKE (MIDDLE OCOEE)

class	III–IV
length	5.0 mi
time	2–3 hr
gauge	Web, phone, visual
level	4.5 ft or 1,250 cfs
gradient	57 fpm
scenery	B

DESCRIPTION: The powers-that-be strongly prefer that boaters use the facilities provided by those agencies for put-ins and take-outs on this section of the river. Use the boat loading/unloading area at Rogers Branch (B) only for its intended purpose, and park in the designated parking area. There is a large concrete ramp leading from the unloading area to the put-in. If you want to put-in below the first rapid (a common desire for first-timers), a footpath has been constructed from the unloading area to the alternate put-in (called the Old Raft Put-in), just below Grumpy's Ledge. The path has traffic barriers separating pedestrians from the heavy motor traffic on US 64, a much safer alternative than trying to unload on the roadside with vehicles zooming by and the exhaust fumes choking your lungs.

Once in the water, you will find the Ocoee to be synonymous with continuous action. The pace is intense and the eddies are not always where you would like them to be. Below the put-in, Class II and III rapids follow one after the other, and consist primarily of big waves and some respectable holes. These rapids are agreeably straightforward for the most part and have recognizable routes.

The first rapid, Bulldozer, begins right at the put-in—there's absolutely no warm-up. You come out of the eddy at the bottom of the ramp and you're in the middle of it. Bulldozer is punctu-

ated in the middle by a nearly river-wide ledge hole called Grumpy's Ledge, that has frequently been known to retain both boats and paddlers. Consequently, most boaters prefer a far-left line, eddy-hopping down past the hole, or a far-right "sneak" that has some respectable holes and some pinning spots of its own. There is a bit of a tongue through Grumpy just left of center, but the drop is pretty blind from above, and if you're off-line, you can get munched badly. Scout carefully or follow someone who knows the lines well.

Following Bulldozer is a really nice play wave above Staging Eddy, a drop feeding into a large eddy on river right where people regroup and warm up for the rest of the run, taking advantage of some nice surf spots without unpleasant consequences. After this stretch of warm-up rapids, the river broadens and runs over a long series of wide, shallow ledges known as Gonzo Shoals. Route selection is anything but obvious, and the going, particularly at minimal flow, is extremely technical.

Below the wide, shallow stretch, the river begins to narrow slightly and bend to the right. This is the approach to Broken Nose, a.k.a. Veg-O-Matic, a series of three drops in rapid succession. The drops are near the right bank. Powerful crosscurrents surge between each of the drops, and a keeper hydraulic lurks at the base of the final drop. There is a cheat route to the left for those who prefer not to encounter the main activity in Broken Nose Rapid. It is separated from the main channel by a large rock outcropping and consists of three quick ledge drops as well, but not quite as tricky or potentially retentive as the holes on the right.

Action continues and bears back to the left through a Class II–III series that includes Second Helping, a.k.a. Slice–Dice, and Moon Chute. When the river begins to turn back toward the right, prepare for Double Suck. Double Suck gets its name from two closely spaced souse holes. You will recognize the rapid by the large granite boulders thrusting upwards and blocking the center one-third of the stream. Go just to the right of these boulders and over a 4-foot drop into the first hole. Don't relax after this one, however, because the second hole follows immediately, and it will eat the unwary. Staying to the far left side of the chute, you can skirt these holes, but a little too far left can pin you in a cleft in the rocks that's not particularly dangerous but is hard to get out of. Eddy out behind the large boulders in the center if you need time to recover your composure or bail the water from your boat.

Continuing downstream, the river swings away from paralleling US 64. This is the approach for Double Trouble, a double set

of holes and waves. These can be run down the middle for a big ride, or you can sneak left or right to skirt the holes. Below Double Trouble, a number of smaller rapids, including Flipper, lead into a long pool known as the Doldrums, at the head of which is a good play hole named Hollywood. Hollywood is very forgiving to certain boat designs and very unkind to others. Its characteristics change with the water level.

The Doldrums is the longest pool on the river, and signals the presence of Class IV Table Saw about three-fourths of a mile ahead. At the end of the Doldrums the stream broadens conspicuously and laps playfully over the shallows with little riffles and waves. Protruding from the right bank above Table Saw, a large rock shelf or boulder beach funnels the water to the left. The river narrows and the current deepens and picks up speed as it enters what was once the most formidable rapid on the Ocoee. Table Saw is named for a feature that has disappeared from the river, but the name has remained. A large, sharp rock that was once situated in the middle of the main chute split the current and sent up an impressive rooster tail, giving the appearance of the blade of a table saw when viewed from the shore. Before the rock fell over and ceased to be a problem, it was known to damage or destroy boats that got too close. It could smash in a bow, or split the bottom of a boat very easily, and would have made a nasty pinning rock. Below the old location of the "saw" is a violent diagonal hole that, fortunately, is not a keeper. The current then tends to push toward the right, piling up on a large boulder called Pilgrim Rock. This rock is partially undercut and should be avoided. There are eddies on the left (preferred) and right at the bottom.

Table Saw can be scouted from the boulder beach on the right or from eddies on the left. The best straightforward run is right of center, down a tongue of relatively smooth but fast-moving water, bracing hard as you hit the diagonal hole at the bottom, and going hard left to avoid the large boulder. Rescue can be set on river right just below the hole where there is a nice, if not overly spacious, eddy, or on the rocks on the left at the bottom. Speedy rescue of people and equipment is important here, due to the proximity of Diamond Splitter, just downstream.

Consisting of yet another river-dividing boulder, Diamond Splitter rises ponderously out of the water, presenting a potential for broaching or entrapment. The generally preferred route is to the right of the boulder. The line left of the boulder leads into Witch's Hole, a fairly popular play spot.

From here, Class II and III rapids rampage more or less continuously, with only one significant intervening pool as the Ocoee

approaches the powerhouse. These are all pretty straightforward and many have some decent play spots. Slingshot, also called Accelerator, has some very fast water and some nice standing waves at the bottom. A quarter of a mile upstream of the powerhouse is Torpedo, a.k.a. Cat's Pajamas, a long, confusing, technical rapid with several powerful holes. Frequently omitted in descriptions of the Ocoee, this rapid can be very rough on a boater who chooses the wrong route. Most easily scouted from the road while running the shuttle, Torpedo should be of particular interest to first-timers. The big hole at the bottom can be a keeper.

Torpedo is separated from Hell Hole, an enormous, deep, aerated, river-dominating hole, by a pool just upstream of the powerhouse and bridge. Situated toward the right bank of the river on the upstream side of the new bridge, Hell Hole can be played, surfed, or punched with the happy prospect of being flushed out in case of an upset.

Note: This is a major park-and-play spot on the river, and if there are no rafts coming down the approach, there will be boaters in the hole, whether you can see them or not. (Yes, it's a deep hole!) If you plan to run the middle and punch the hole, it's best to follow a raft trip through or signal your intentions to be sure there are no boats surfing when you hit the hole. A collision here can be a nasty event. While Hell Hole monopolizes the channel, a technical run skirting the hole on the left is possible (and generally advisable).

It is hard to consider Hell Hole, however, without mentioning that it is only the first part of a double rapid with an obstacle course inserted neatly in the middle. Not 20 yards beyond the fearsome hole itself is the drop known as Power House Rapid. Power House consists of a 4-foot vertical ledge and nasty hydraulic spanning the left two-thirds of the stream, with a more manageable tongue spilling down on the right. Arriving safely at the bottom of all this requires making it through or around Hell Hole, fighting the current at the bottom of the hole (which tries to carry you left), and working hard to the right to avoid the ledge and to line up for the tongue through Power House. Have a good roll if you try to play Hell Hole, and anticipate the current kicking you left as you wash out. When the water is high (1,800+ cfs), Hell Hole tends to wash out a little, while the Power House hydraulic becomes worse. Scout this complex stretch either while running the shuttle or from the TVA plant bridge.

If you make it this far, you can drift the next 0.75 mile downstream to the take-out facility constructed for the exclusive use of

the boating public on the right shore of Parksville Lake. Do not use the commercial take-out located just below the powerhouse to load your boat on your vehicle, unless you want a confrontation with the rangers. Even when there is no commercial traffic at the commercial take-out, you are likely to be hassled by the authorities if you try to load your boat there. Possession or consumption of alcoholic beverages or illegal drugs is also prohibited at all access areas, and authorities are always looking for an excuse to check for these prohibited items.

Hazards for this section include hydraulics at Grumpy's Ledge, Broken Nose, Double Suck, and Torpedo; heavy raft traffic; and occasionally obnoxious raft guides.

Note: The Ocoee River is subject to major flooding events, some in recent history exceeding 100,000 cfs. These flows can cause significant changes in the riverbed and the characteristics of the rapids. The descriptions here contain the latest information available at the time of publication, but major changes can and do occur fairly regularly.

SHUTTLE: The take-out is on US 64 west of Cleveland, Tennessee, and east of Ducktown, Tennessee. Parking and boat loading are on the shore of Parksville Lake, about 0.75 miles below Ocoee Power House Number 2. To get to the put-in, go east on US 64 about 5 miles to Ocoee Number 2 Dam, then turn right into Rogers Branch Access Area, just above the dam. Self-service parking fees apply at both locations.

GAUGE: Release schedules are available on the Internet at the TVA Web site (www.tva.org) and are updated annually. Check the schedule before you go! There is a gauge located on river left about 150 yards downstream of the Number 2 Power House. Normal release levels start at 4.5 on the gauge (about 1,250 cfs). Unfortunately, to check this gauge, you will need to be on the river, or have a good set of binoculars. A new gauge has been added in an eddy on river right about 0.25 miles below the put-in. Releases are generally a bit higher if the Upper Ocoee is running. River and rapid characteristics change very little with higher flows, except that everything gets a good bit pushier, and the action happens a bit faster. Above 3,000 cfs (about 5.8 on the gauge), the river does start to change character, with many eddies disappearing, and preferred routes changing. The maximum level is around 4,000 cfs, but some crazies have made runs as high as 12,000 cfs. At flows above 3,500 cfs (about 6.2 on the gauge), the river is a big flush; there are few eddies, and swims will be long, possibly all the way to the lake.

photo © Rob Maxwell

Alien Boof on Tennessee's Ocoee River

The Birth of the Modern Ocoee
— by Allen Hedden with Bob Sehlinger and Don Otey

For years paddlers traveling the Old Copper Road (US 64) in southeastern Polk County, Tennessee, would marvel at the dry, rocky Ocoee riverbed beside the highway. Some couldn't help but conjecture about potential souse holes, rapids, and falls. But high on the mountainside, also beside that stretch of roadway, a leaky, ancient wooden flume carried the river's entire flow to a powerhouse several miles downstream.

One day in 1976, that old wooden boxway could carry the liquid load no more; the water that had generated 17 megawatts of power was transferred back into the riverbed. Paddlers would conjecture no more. Double Trouble, Diamond Splitter, Table Saw, and Hell's Hole were exciting manifestations of the reborn whitewater with a 57-foot-per-mile drop. The Ocoee gained

instant notoriety as river runners tried to learn how various flow levels might affect their crafts on this new whitewater run. Commercial raft outfitters sprang up. National decked-boat championship races followed.

However, the Tennessee Valley Authority, responsible for much of the region's power production, proposed repairing the flume. A long battle ensued between the TVA and the paddlers and commercial outfitters who sought recreational releases after the flume was rebuilt. The result was a Congressional mandate for a recreational release schedule of a minimum of 116 days per year at a minimum flow rate of 1,200 cfs. This arrangement was an economic boon to the historically impoverished area.

For more than a decade, the Upper Ocoee was still, for the most part, a dry riverbed, with an average of one or two weeks per year of "maintenance releases" and occasional heavy rain events offering the only opportunities to paddle. Then in the early 1990s, a proposal was put forward to create a venue for the whitewater slalom event of the 1996 Olympics, held in and around Atlanta. A multi-million dollar Ocoee Whitewater Center was proposed, as well as the constriction of a quarter mile of the riverbed to less than half its original width to create world-class rapids for the slalom event. Some man-made obstacles would add a few more river features, and walkways, footbridges, and temporary grandstand seating would be constructed along the course.

The expensive proposal included the TVA agreeing to continue recreational and event releases for this section of the river for at least five years after the Olympics. The Olympic proposal was approved and accepted, and commercial and public boating of the

river on a regular basis began. At the end of the five-year period, the TVA wanted to return the riverbed to its former dry state, but reluctantly agreed to extend the release agreement. In 2003, a long-term agreement was reached extending the recreational and event releases well into the future, guaranteeing 54 recreational release days per year for 15 years. TVA is compensated for lost generation revenue on both the Middle and Upper Ocoee by fees levied on the commercial outfitters who operate on the river.

The Olympic proposal and subsequent release agreement ensured that paddlers will continue flocking to the Ocoee in the years ahead. However, they will find human impact on the environment that extends well beyond diverting the stream for power production. Sulfuric acid leached from 40 years of mining and smelting in the Copperhill mining basin at the Georgia–Tennessee border has completely sterilized the Ocoee's tributaries. Years of airborne acid also denuded the forested hillsides in the basin. (This little red dot amid the sea of smoky green, along with the Great Wall of China, was once one of the few man-made earth modifications visible to the orbiting astronauts.) The bare hillsides of the basin choke the same dead Ocoee tributaries with fine-grained red silt. By-products from a chemical plant in Copperhill released into the river once compounded the problem. Fortunately, the chemical plant is no longer in operation, much reforestation has occurred throughout the Copper Basin, and the EPA and other organizations continue working to clean up the watershed. Water quality in the Ocoee remains poor, however. If you make the run, keep your mouth closed.

HIWASSEE RIVER, TENNESSEE

Georgia's Hiawassee River leaves the state headed north, cuts across the forested foot of a couple of North Carolina peaks, and plunges into Tennessee via the frigid Appalachian powerhouse releases as the Hiwassee River. After all its mountain meandering, this river still has one ridge left to clear in its surge towards the Tennessee River. It's a fun ride; the Hiwassee is a forgiving stream, but one that accelerates a desire to hone your skills. Swift current and the river's width, between 200 and 400 feet, can make recovery a difficult, chilly experience. In a beautiful, scenic setting, the clear water of the bouncing river makes a dramatic horseshoe bend at the foot of Tennessee's Hood Mountain. It is truly a worthy member of the state's scenic river system.

MAPS: McFarland, Oswald Dome (USGS); Polk TN (County)

POWERHOUSE TO RELIANCE

class	II
Length	5.5 mi
time	3.5
Gauge	Web, phone
Level	1,500 cfs
gradient	15 fpm
scenery	B+

DESCRIPTION: For a non-paddling experience on the Hiwassee, take a look at the interesting and scenic 15-mile section of the river between the dam and the powerhouse. This bed is now mostly dry and only carries water during periods of extremely high natural flow from heavy rainfall. Hiking access is via the railroad tracks (still in regular use) for the entire distance. The scenery is beautiful, with mountains on both sides and unusual rock formations. There are high train trestles crossing over brooks, and at one point the track crosses over itself, which is famous in railroad circles. The railroad makes more than a complete circle, known as the Hiwassee Loop, to gain altitude. Nearer the powerhouse is the abandoned town site of McFarland and the Narrows, where the river is constricted between the tracks and high rocks of unusual formation.

Downstream from the powerhouse where the river is canoeable, the water is cold. Releases come from deep in the impoundment. It is rather unusual to find such cold water in a wide, shallow stream. Trout thrive; dunked canoeists shiver. Anglers and canoeists have almost learned to coexist on this stretch of rockbound water. When there's no dam release, the waders line the rocky outcroppings in the riverbed, hunting the pooled-up fish. When the 1,500-cfs dam release comes along, tubers, rafters, and paddlers of all types come with it, plunging

over those same rock ledges and recovering in those same fished-out pools.

The first 5 miles of the Hiwassee below the powerhouse is Class I and II, with a couple of rapids rating a strong Class II. The put-in is at the powerhouse access ramp, about a quarter mile below the powerhouse. Another 2 miles downstream is the Big Bend parking lot, hidden in the trees at the foot of a series of ledges. If rain, cold, or mishap creates a need to take-out early, you should know how to find that access—there isn't another one until the ramp at Reliance. Between the powerhouse and Reliance, you'll encounter a mixed bag of paddling possibilities: swift current and bouncy waves at Cabin Bend; big, unstable drops at Number 2 Rapids and Oblique Falls; tricky crosscurrents at Bigneys Rock; follow-the-flow, water-reading exercises at the Ledges and the Stairsteps; peel-off and eddy-turn practice at the Needles; and big swamper waves at Devils Shoals.

Below Reliance, the river flattens out as it makes its final run out of the mountains. Downstream another 6 miles on river left is the U.S. Forest Service Quinn Springs Campground, located across Tennessee 30 from the fishing access. The Tennessee State

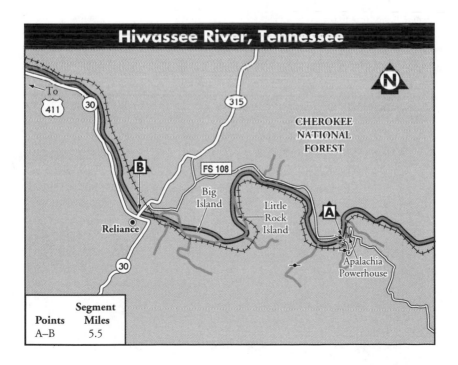

Hiwassee River, Tennessee

Points	Segment Miles
A–B	5.5

Park's Gee Creek campground is on river right, just below. The Gee Creek ramp is up the creek a few yards; the creek's entrance is marked by an old Native American V-shaped fishing weir below the mouth of the creek in the Hiwassee.

SHUTTLE: From Blue Ridge, take GA 5 north through McCaysville and into Tennessee, where it turns into TN 68. Go west on US 64 along the Ocoee, then north on TN 30 to Reliance and the take-out. The take-out can also be reached from the west via TN 30 from US 411. To reach the put-in, take the bridge across the river and take the first right onto FS 108, following it to the put-in at the Apalachia Powerhouse.

GAUGE: The TVA provides flow data on their Internet site or by calling (800) 238-2264 and following prompts for releases at Apalachia Dam. The minimum required flow is 1,500 cfs. The recommended maximum is 5,000 cfs for open boats, 10,000 cfs for decked.

LITTLE RIVER CANYON, ALABAMA

Located approximately 40 miles west of Rome, Georgia, the Little River Canyon is an impressive sandstone-granite gorge through which a sparkling clear stream runs. The Little River has deep mirror-surfaced pools, gentle ripples, and boulder-smashing, highly technical whitewater. The water is usually clear, with deep, shimmering, turquoise pools. Cedars, pines, hardwoods, and, in spring, a profusion of wildflowers adorn the cliffs on either side of the river. Small tributaries plummet to merge with the primary flow, creating many intimate coves with excellent photographic potential. Paddlers shouldn't become too enthralled with the scenic vistas, however, becauser the river demands your full attention at times. Rapids are numerous and good boat control is essential. If dependable eddy turns, ferrying skills, and good judgment are not part of your paddling program, then do not venture here. Boaters should have at least intermediate skills before attempting the easier Chairlift section of.

MAPS: Jamestown, Little River, Fort Payne (USGS); De Kalb AL, Cherokee AL (County)

AL 35 TO UPPER TWO PUT-IN (SUICIDE)

class	IV–V
Length	3.0 mi
time	2–3 hr
Gauge	Web, phone, visual
Level	-3 in
gradient	120, 80, 20 tpm
scenery	A+

DESCRIPTION: The Suicide Section of Little River Canyon is the best-known run in Alabama. It is a measure of the progress whitewater sport has made since the early 1970s that a run once considered death-defying is now made with regularity. But it's a cool name, anyway.

Class III and IV rapids abound, undercut penalties are numerous, and the Class Vs are each distinctive. Put-in above AL 35 and the falls, or down the trail at the first AL 176 pull-off on river right. The double-drop portion of the 33-foot-high falls can be run on river left by the skilled and psyched when the level is above 6 inches.

After a couple squirrely rapids, a river-wide and very easy 8-foot drop can be run almost anywhere. Class IV+ Mammoth Rock rapid is easily recognized by its namesake on river left at the bottom of a boulder garden. It can be run left, or by an easier sneak right. Terminal Eddy is best run out of the back of the eddy on river right. Watch out for the undercut on the left, which can harbor wood. Of course, calling attention to undercuts on Little River Canyon is somewhat redundant, because they are everywhere.

You have now arrived at the big three: Avalanche, Cable, and

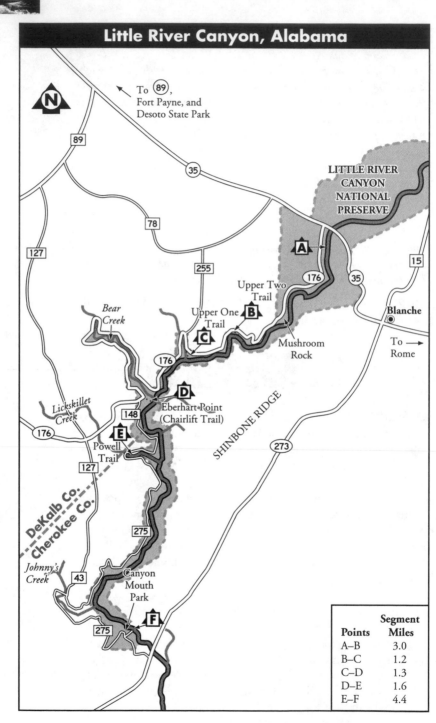

Little River Canyon, Alabama

To 89,
Fort Payne, and
Desoto State Park

N

89

35

LITTLE RIVER
CANYON
NATIONAL
PRESERVE

78

127

255

15

Upper Two
Trail

Bear
Creek

Upper One
Trail   **C**

B

176

35

A

Blanche

To →
Rome

Mushroom
Rock

D

SHINBONE RIDGE

Lickskillet
Creek

148

Eberhart Point
(Chairlift Trail)

176

E

273

Powell
Trail

127

DeKalb Co.
Cherokee Co.

275

Johnny's
Creek

43

Canyon
Mouth
Park

275

F

Points	Segment Miles
A–B	3.0
B–C	1.2
C–D	1.3
D–E	1.6
E–F	4.4

Pinball. Avalanche is quite obstructed, and most paddlers who run it boof into the pin-rich, river-left eddy and then re-enter the main flow. Avalanche gets easier as the water rises; below 3–5 inches it can abuse boat and body, but it goes. Walk or scout the rapid easily on the left. After some fun Class II and III water, look for cables above you to identify Cable Falls, a 12-foot water-fall followed by a boof to the right. This rapid is a straightfor-ward Class V with consequences. The first 10-foot drop is a major pain when the water gets below 2 inches on the AL 35 gauge; alternate lines are required below 0 inches. The second drop is not trivial. Run close (but not too close) to the right edge of the main drop. If you swim left, you may go into an undercut. A short distance downstream is Pinball, a bona-fide Class V—not a place to make mistakes. Above it, go left over a 4-foot drop, then ferry across to the eddy on river right to scout or walk. Scout right if you have not seen Pinball's required moves and large undercuts before. The walk is pretty easy. Again, watch for wood here. Once you get past Pinball, it is surprisingly flat for quite a while until you encounter the beginning of the Upper Two stretch.

Suicide is almost always run in combination with Upper Two. Some paddlers continue through the Chairlift section to the Canyon Mouth. Another take-out option exists at the Powell Trail (E) a short distance below Bottleneck on the Chairlift section.

SHUTTLE: From Atlanta, take I-75 north to Exit 290 for GA 20 west. Follow GA 20 as it threads north through Rome and turns west again. After crossing the border (GA 20 turns into AL 9 here), turn right onto AL 35 and proceed to the Little River Canyon National Preserve. If taking out at the canyon mouth, return on AL 35 to AL 273 south; if using the Chairlift put-in (D) as your take-out, take AL 176 south along the river-right side.

GAUGE: Check levels at the southeast (river-left) corner of the AL 35 bridge. Using USGS Internet levels for Little River Canyon near Blue Pond, levels at the bridge can be estimated with the following formula: inches = (cfs volume-600)/100. However, this method will often underestimate the true level. The streambed at the USGS gauge is sandy, so readings can shift from year to year. Check the American Whitewater Web site for correlation updates. Suidcide can be run as low as -3 inches; 1 inch is better. At about 7 inches it is pushy, and at 12 inches it is very serious. At levels higher than 8–12 inches, paddlers opt for the creeks feeding the canyon. Alabama Power provides level

information at the same location as the USGS gauge, but levels may differ slightly from the more accurate USGS flows. Call (800) 525-3711 and follow the prompts: 6, 2, 2.

UPPER TWO PUT-IN TO EBERHART POINT (UPPER TWO)

class	III–V
length	2.5 mi
time	1.5 hr
gauge	Web, phone, visual
level	-4 in
gradient	80, 100 fpm
scenery	A+

DECRIPTION: This is a really fun part of the canyon. The Upper Two begins below a good surfing wave at the bottom of the Suicide section. After some warm-up, Screaming Right Turn (Class IV) appears immediately followed by Roadblock (Class IV+, maybe V) and Humpty-Dumpty. Roadblock, an 8-foot V-hole drop, is the stickiest and most dangerous spot on any commonly run Alabama whitewater river. One boater has died here, and near-death experiences are not uncommon. Be aware of the line and consequences before you run it. Portage is easy on the left. Humpty-Dumpty is a three-part Class IV+ or V with undercuts that gets harder at each drop. Listen for the sound of toilets as you scout or walk on river right. At lower levels (-2 inches or so), the true ugliness of Humpty-Dumpty can be seen. You will see a vortex flow going under rocks on the right next to the second drop, while the center line becomes too narrow to run on the last drop. Next there is some really good Class IV fun, includ-

photo © Jed Dugger

Cresting a falls in the Little River Canyon, Alabama

ing Mr. Bubbles and the Narrows. Deep Throat forms a spectacular plume at levels around 12 inches. It is run left at the bottom to avoid the pin-friendly throat. Deep Throat signals the end of the Upper Two.

The Upper Two put-in trail (B) is off CR 176, and is amusingly labeled "Lower Two" on a large National Park Service sign. Some people take out at the top of the Chairlift section (D) if they started their day with Suicide, but almost anyone who puts in on the Upper Two goes to Canyon Mouth Park at the bottom of Chairlift. Another take-out option exists at the Powell Trail a short distance below Bottleneck on the Chairlift section. A put-in just below Humpty-Dumpty (Upper One) is also a possible starting point for trips extending onto the Chairlift.

SHUTTLE: The shuttle is not short. The best way is probably up AL 176 to AL 35 east, then down AL 273 to the Canyon Mouth Park.

GAUGE: See first section. Zero inches is a preferred minimum on the AL 35 bridge gauge, but it can be run as low as -4 inches or approximately 225 cfs. The run gets pushy at 10 inches.

EBERHARTS POINT TO AL 273 (CHARLIFT)

class	II–III (IV-)
length	6.0 mi
time	3–4 hr
gauge	Web, phone, visual
level	0 in
gradient	33 (50) fpm
scenery	A+

DESCRIPTION: The put-in for this section is one of the more memorable parts of the trip. It is an arduous carry to the river, but do not succumb to the urge to weep and toss your boat into the abyss. The river is well worth the struggle. Begin near the original site of the old chairlift at Eberharts Point on the Canyon Rim Parkway (AL 275/CR 176) and hike approximately 600 feet from the rim to the canyon floor. The lift itself now sits rusting a few hundred yards from the put-in trail.

Aspiring intermediate paddlers, who will greatly enjoy this run, will find the first 1.5 miles of this section challenging. Circle Back and Eddy Hop are the first two Class IIIs. Be aware that Eddy Hop harbors an undercut. Blue Hole Memorial (Class III+), with another undercut on the left, is the final warm-up for the main course, Bottleneck. Bottleneck is a forgiving but tricky Class IV-. Above the final drop, there is a series of fun drops with big eddies. The key to Bottleneck is arriving at "the highway" on the last drop at the right spot with the proper angle. The final drop will show you if you are on line. Bottleneck will often flip you, but to date it hasn't proven to be a keeper. Run a bit too far left and you are going to flip. Approach at too much of a right

angle, even on the highway, and you stand a good chance of flipping. After Bottleneck, the run is pretty much Class II and II+. However, at high water (over 12 inches) Chairlift is big-time Class III and IV and Bottleneck is meaty. Towards the end it gets pretty flat, especially for paddlers tired by Suicide or Upper Two. The last rapid is at the confluence with Johnnies Creek at mile 5.

Another option for those seeking the easiest possible run is to put in on the Powell Trail below Chairlift. Camping is available in the area at Desoto State Park on AL 89.

SHUTTLE: From the put-in, take AL 176 east (downstream). Turn left onto CR 127, which turns into CR 43. Then take CR 275 into Canyon Mouth Park.

GAUGE: See first section. Zero inches is a preferred minimum on the AL 35 bridge gauge, and 10 inches near the maximum.

appendixes

Appendix A:
Paddling Organizations

REGIONAL

Besides promoting healthy waterways and river access, Georgia's paddling clubs provide services including instruction, scheduled cruises, competitions, social outings, roll practice sessions, and regular meetings. In addition, most clubs regularly publish newsletters. Dues vary between clubs, as do services.

Atlanta Whitewater Club
P.O. Box 11714
Atlanta, GA 30355
(800) 231-6058 ext. 8
www.atlantawhitewater.com

Canoe and Kayak Club of Augusta
2328 Washington Road
Augusta, GA 30904
(706) 738-8500
www.ckca.homestead.com

Georgia Canoeing Association
P.O. Box 7023
Atlanta, GA 30357
(770) 421-9729
www.georgiacanoe.org

Georgia Wilderness Society
1927 Thomas Drive
Macon, GA 31201
www.georgiawildernesssociety.org

Ohoopee Canoe Club
www.ohoopeecanoeclub.com

NATIONAL

Two national organizations are very prominent proponents of safety within the paddling community; both are cited in the Hazards and Safety section (page 10) for their contributions in that arena. American Whitewater is the only national organization dedicated to whitewater paddling; their efforts to conserve and restore whitewater rivers and negotiate boater access are renown. The American Canoe Association represents all paddle sports, and is the leader in creating education programs and certifying instructors. Both organizations work to secure cleaner and safer river experiences, sponsor competitions, and regularly publish magazines for their members.

American Whitewater
1430 Fenwick Lane
Silver Spring, MD 20910
(866) BOAT-4AW
www.americanwhitewater.org

American Canoe Association
7432 Alban Station Blvd. Suite B-232
Springfield, VA 22150-2311
(703) 451-0141
www.aca-paddler.org

Appendix B: River Outfitters

Don't want to bring an extra car along to set shuttle? Need to rent a boat? Following is a list of outfitters in Georgia who supply rental boats, run shuttles, or both.

MOUNTAIN REGION

Appalachian Outfitters
2084 S. Chestatee Hwy 60
Dahlonega, GA 30533
(800) 426-7117, (706) 864-7117
www.canoegeorgia.com; theriverguy@hotmail.com
Shuttles: Etowah and Chestatee

Chattooga Whitewater Outfitters
14239 Long Creek Highway
Long Creek, SC 29658
(864) 647-9083
www.chattoogawhitewatershop.com
Shuttles: Chattooga

Go with the Flow
4 Elizabeth Way
Roswell, GA 30075
(770) 992-3200, (888) 345-FLOW
www.gowiththeflow.com; david@gowiththeflowsports.com

Mountaintown Outdoor Expeditions
122 Adventure Trail
P.O. Box 86
Ellijay, GA 30540
(706) 635 2524 or (706) 635 2726 (evenings)
Shuttles: Cartecay River, Mountaintown Creek

River Right Outfitter Inc.
2218 US Hwy 52 East
Ellijay, GA 30540
(706) 273-7055
www.riverright.com; riverright@ellijay.com
Shuttles: Cartecay River

Toccoa Valley Campground
11481 Aska Road
Blue Ridge, GA 30513
(706) 838-4317
Shuttles: Toccoa River

MOUNTAIN REGION (continued)

Whitewater Learning Center
3437 Rockhaven Circle NE
Atlanta, GA 30324
(404) 231-0042, (800) 294-6548
www.whitewatergeorgia.com

Wildwood Outfitters
7272 S. Main Street
Helen, GA 30545
(706) 878-1700 or (800) 553-2715
www.wildwoodoutfitters.com; info@wildwoodoutfitters.com
Shuttles: Chattahoochee River (upper)

PIEDMONT REGION

Broad River Outpost
7911 Wildcat Bridge Road
Danielsville, GA
Mailing Address: 112 Witcher Rd.
Carlton, GA 30627
(706) 795-3242
www.broadriveroutpost.com; info@broadriveroutpost.com
Shuttles: Broad, Hudson, Middle and North Fork Broad, and
Oconee Rivers

Flint River Outdoor Center
4429 Woodland Road
Thomaston, GA 30286
(706) 647-2633
www.flintriverfun.com
Shuttles: Flint River

COASTAL PLAIN AND GEORGIA COAST

Altamaha Wilderness Outfitters
(aka Altamaha Coastal Tours, Altamaha Outpost)
229 Fort King George Rd.
Darien, GA
Mailing Address 112 Witcher Rd.
Carlton, GA 30627
(912) 437-6010
www.altamaha.com; info@altamaha.com
Shuttles: Altamaha, Ohoopee, Satilla Rivers, GA Coast, Okefenokee Swamp

American Wilderness Outfitters Limited (AWOL)
2328 Washington Road
Augusta, GA 30904
(706) 738-8500
awolmanager@aol.com
Shuttles: Savannah River, Augusta Canal, GA Coast

CanoeCanoe
3008 Hwy 280 East
Lyons, GA 30436
(912) 526-8222
www.canoecanoe.com; cc@canoecanoe.com
Shuttles: Altamaha, Oconee, Ocmulgee, Ohoopee Rivers, Okefenokee Swamp

Canoe Country Outpost
2818 Lake Hampton Road
Hilliard, FL 32046
(904) 845-7224 or (866) 845-4443
www.canoecountryoutpost.com
Shuttles: St. Marys River

Flint River Outpost
11151 GA Highway 3
Albany, GA 31705
(229) 787-3004, (888) 572-6697
www.flintriveroutpost.com
Shuttles: Flint River

High Country Outfitters
3906 B Roswell Road
Atlanta, GA 30342
(404) 814-0999
www.highcountryoutfitters.com

Ogeechee Outpost
182 Rose Drive (Morgan's Bridge)
Ellabelle, GA 31308
(912) 748-6716
www.ogeecheeoutpost.com
Shuttles: Ogeechee River, Ebenezer Creek

Ogeechee Park Rentals
318 Dublin Road
Pooler, GA 31322
(912) 964-0202 or (912) 663-0442
www.ogeecheecanoe.com; ogeecheecanoe@aol.com
Shuttles: Ogeechee River, others

COASTAL PLAIN AND GEORGIA COAST (continued)

Okefenokee Adventures
Rt 2 Box 3325
Folkston, GA 31537
(912) 496-7156 or (866) THE SWAMP
www.okefenokeeadventures.com
info@okefenokeeadventures.com
Shuttles: Suwannee Canal, Okefenokee Swamp

Oke Trailmasters
RR1 Box 123
Fargo, GA 31631
(912) 637-5163
Shuttles: Alapaha, Withlacoochee, Ochlockonee,
Suwannee Rivers, Okefenokee Swamp

Okefenokee Pastimes
RR2 Box 3090
Folkston, GA 31537
(912) 496-4472
www.okefenokee.com
Shuttles: St. Marys, Satilla and Suwannee Rivers, Okefenokee
Swamp

Sea Kayak Georgia
1102 Highway 80
Tybee Island, GA 31328
(912) 786-8732, (888) KAYAK-GA (529-2542)
www.seakayakgeorgia.com; info@seakayakgeorgia.com

South East Adventure Outfitters
313 Mallory Street
St. Simons Island, GA 31522
(912) 638-6732
www.southeastadventure.com; kayak@southeastadventure.com
Shuttles: GA Coast, Altamaha and Satilla Rivers, Okefenokee
Swamp

Suwannee Canoe & Kayak
2105 Westfield Drive
(229) 247-0408
suwannee9@bellsouth.net
Shuttles: Withlacoochee, Little, Suwannee, Alapaha Rivers

Suwannee Outpost
2461 95th Drive
Live Oak, FL 32060
(800) 428-4147
www.canoeoutpost.com
Shuttles: Withlacoochee, Alapaha, Suwannee Rivers

Three Rivers Expeditions
13 Victor Street
Hazelhurst, GA 31539
(912) 379-1371
www.3riverexp.com
Shuttles: Altamaha, Oconee, Ocmulgee, Little Ocmulgee, and
Ohoopee Rivers

Turkey Creek Outfitters
991 Highway 280 West
Cordele, GA 31015
(229) 271-1997
www.turkeycreekoutfitters.com; tcoutfitters@infospree.net
Shuttles: Flint River

Up the Creek
111 Osborne Street
St. Marys, GA 31558
(912) 882-0911 or 887-upthecreek; www.angelfire.com/ga/utcx
utcx@angelfire.com
Shuttles: St. Marys River, Cumberland Island

Appendix C: Safety Code of American Whitewater

Adopted 1959, Revision 1998
Lee Belknap, *Safety Chairman*
Charlie Walbridge, *Safety Vice Chairman*
Mac Thornton, *Legal Advisor*
Rich Bowers, *Executive Director*

This code has been prepared using the best available information and has been reviewed by a broad cross section of whitewater experts. The code, however, is only a collection of guidelines; attempts to minimize risks should be flexible, not constrained by a rigid set of rules. Varying conditions and group goals may combine with unpredictable circumstances to require alternate procedures. This code is not intended to serve as a standard of care for commercial outfitters or guides.

I. PERSONAL PREPAREDNESS AND RESPONSIBILITY

1. Be a competent swimmer, with the ability to handle yourself underwater.

2. Wear a life jacket. A snugly-fitting vest-type life preserver offers back and shoulder protection as well as the flotation needed to swim safely in whitewater.

3. Wear a solid, correctly-fitted helmet when upsets are likely. This is essential in kayaks or covered canoes, and recommended for open canoeists using thigh straps and rafters running steep drops.

4. Do not boat out of control. Your skills should be sufficient to stop or reach shore before reaching danger. Do not enter a rapid unless you are reasonably sure that you can run it safely or swim it without injury.

5. Whitewater rivers contain many hazards which are not always easily recognized. The following are the most frequent killers.

    a. High water. The river's speed and power increase tremendously as the flow increases, raising the difficulty of most rapids. Rescue becomes progressively harder as the water rises, adding to the danger. Floating debris and strainers make even an easy rapid quite hazardous. It is often misleading to judge the river level at the put in, since a small rise in a wide, shallow place will be

multiplied many times where the river narrows. Use reliable gauge information whenever possible, and be aware that sun on snowpack, hard rain, and upstream dam releases may greatly increase the flow.

b. **Cold.** Cold drains your strength and robs you of the ability to make sound decisions on matters affecting your survival. Cold water immersion, because of the initial shock and the rapid heat loss which follows, is especially dangerous. Dress appropriately for bad weather or sudden immersion in the water. When the water temperature is less than 50 degrees F, a wetsuit or drysuit is essential for protection if you swim. Next best is wool or pile clothing under a waterproof shell. In this case, you should also carry waterproof matches and a change of clothing in a waterproof bag. If, after prolonged exposure, a person experiences uncontrollable shaking, loss of coordination, or difficulty speaking, he or she is hypothermic, and needs your assistance.

c. **Strainers.** Brush, fallen trees, bridge pilings, undercut rocks or anything else which allows river current to sweep through can pin boats and boaters against the obstacle. Water pressure on anything trapped this way can be overwhelming. Rescue is often extremely difficult. Pinning may occur in fast current, with little or no whitewater to warn of the danger.

d. **Dams, wiers, ledges, reversals, holes, and hydraulics.** When water drops over a obstacle, it curls back on itself, forming a strong upstream current which may be capable of holding a boat or swimmer. Some holes make for excellent sport. Others are proven killers. Paddlers who cannot recognize the difference should avoid all but the smallest holes. Hydraulics around man-made dams must be treated with utmost respect regardless of their height or the level of the river. Despite their seemingly benign appearance, they can create an almost escape-proof trap. The swimmer's only exit from the "drowning machine" is to dive below the surface when the downstream current is flowing beneath the reversal.

e. **Broaching.** When a boat is pushed sideways against a rock by strong current, it may collapse and wrap. This is especially dangerous to kayak and decked canoe paddlers; these boats will collapse and the combination of indestructible hulls and tight outfitting may create a deadly trap. Even without entrapment, releasing pinned

boats can be extremely time-consuming and dangerous. To avoid pinning, throw your weight downstream towards the rock. This allows the current to slide harmlessly underneath the hull.

6. Boating alone is discouraged. The minimum party is three people or two craft.

7. Have a frank knowledge of your boating ability, and don't attempt rivers or rapids which lie beyond that ability.

   a. Develop the paddling skills and teamwork required to match the river you plan to boat. Most good paddlers develop skills gradually, and attempts to advance too quickly will compromise your safety and enjoyment.

   b. Be in good physical and mental condition, consistent with the difficulties which may be expected. Make adjustments for loss of skills due to age, health, fitness. Any health limitations must be explained to your fellow paddlers prior to starting the trip.

8. Be practiced in self-rescue, including escape from an overturned craft. The eskimo roll is strongly recommended for decked boaters who run rapids Class IV or greater, or who paddle in cold environmental conditions.

9. Be trained in rescue skills, CPR, and first aid with special emphasis on the recognizing and treating hypothermia. It may save your friend's life.

10. Carry equipment needed for unexpected emergencies, including foot wear which will protect your feet when walking out, a throw rope, knife, whistle, and waterproof matches. If you wear eyeglasses, tie them on and carry a spare pair on long trips. Bring cloth repair tape on short runs, and a full repair kit on isolated rivers. Do not wear bulky jackets, ponchos, heavy boots, or anything else which could reduce your ability to survive a swim.

11. Despite the mutually supportive group structure described in this code, individual paddlers are ultimately responsible for their own safety, and must assume sole responsibility for the following decisions:

   a. The decision to participate on any trip. This includes an evaluation of the expected difficulty of the rapids under the conditions existing at the time of the put-in.

   b. The selection of appropriate equipment, including a boat design suited to their skills and the appropriate rescue and survival gear.

c. The decision to scout any rapid, and to run or portage according to their best judgment. Other members of the group may offer advice, but paddlers should resist pressure from anyone to paddle beyond their skills. It is also their responsibility to decide whether to pass up any walk-out or take-out opportunity.

d. All trip participants should consistently evaluate their own and their group's safety, voicing their concerns when appropriate and following what they believe to be the best course of action. Paddlers are encouraged to speak with anyone whose actions on the water are dangerous, whether they are a part of your group or not.

II. BOAT AND EQUIPMENT PREPAREDNESS

1. Test new and different equipment under familiar conditions before relying on it for difficult runs. This is especially true when adopting a new boat design or outfitting system. Low volume craft may present additional hazards to inexperienced or poorly conditioned paddlers.

2. Be sure your boat and gear are in good repair before starting a trip. The more isolated and difficult the run, the more rigorous this inspection should be.

3. Install flotation bags in non-inflatable craft, securely fixed in each end, designed to displace as much water as possible. Inflatable boats should have multiple air chambers and be test inflated before launching.

4. Have strong, properly sized paddles or oars for controlling your craft. Carry sufficient spares for the length and difficulty of the trip.

5. Outfit your boat safely. The ability to exit your boat quickly is an essential component of safety in rapids. It is your responsibility to see that there is absolutely nothing to cause entrapment when coming free of an upset craft. This includes:

a. Spray covers which won't release reliably or which release prematurely.

b. Boat outfitting too tight to allow a fast exit, especially in low volume kayaks or decked canoes. This includes low hung thwarts in canoes lacking adequate clearance for your feet and kayak footbraces which fail or allow your feet to become wedged under them.

c. Inadequately supported decks which collapse on a paddler's legs when a decked boat is pinned by water

pressure. Inadequate clearance with the deck because of your size or build.

d. Loose ropes which cause entanglement. Beware of any length of loose line attached to a whitewater boat. All items must be tied tightly and excess line eliminated; painters, throw lines, and safety rope systems must be completely and effectively stored. Do not knot the end of a rope, as it can get caught in cracks between rocks.

6. Provide ropes which permit you to hold on to your craft so that it may be rescued. The following methods are recommended:

a. Kayaks and covered canoes should have grab loops of ¼" + rope or equivalent webbing sized to admit a normal sized hand. Stern painters are permissible if properly secured.

b. Open canoes should have securely anchored bow and stern painters consisting of 8–10 feet of ¼" + line. These must be secured in such a way that they are readily accessible, but cannot come loose accidentally. Grab loops are acceptable, but are more difficult to reach after an upset.

c. Rafts and dories may have taut perimeter lines threaded through the loops provided. footholds should be designed so that a paddler's feet cannot be forced through them, causing entrapment. Flip lines should be carefully and reliably stowed.

7. Know your craft's carrying capacity, and how added loads affect boat handling in whitewater. Most rafts have a minimum crew size which can be added to on day trips or in easy rapids. Carrying more than two paddlers in an open canoe when running rapids is not recommended.

8. Car top racks must be strong and attach positively to the vehicle. Lash your boat to each crossbar, then tie the ends of the boats directly to the bumpers for added security. This arrangement should survive all but the most violent vehicle accident.

III. GROUP PREPAREDNESS AND RESPONSIBILITY

1. Organization. A river trip should be regarded as a common adventure by all participants, except on instructional or commercially guided trips as defined below. Participants share the responsibility for the conduct of the trip, and each participant is individually responsible for judging his or her own capabilities

and for his or her own safety as the trip progresses. Participants are encouraged (but are not obligated) to offer advice and guidance for the independent consideration and judgment of others.

2. River conditions. The group should have a reasonable knowledge of the difficulty of the run. Participants should evaluate this information and adjust their plans accordingly. If the run is exploratory or no one is familiar with the river, maps and guidebooks, if available, should be examined. The group should secure accurate flow information; the more difficult the run, the more important this will be. Be aware of possible changes in river level and how this will affect the difficulty of the run. If the trip involves tidal stretches, secure appropriate information on tides.

3. Group equipment should be suited to the difficulty of the river. The group should always have a throw line available, and one line per boat is recommended on difficult runs. The list may include: carbiners, prussick loops, first aid kit, flashlight, folding saw, fire starter, guidebooks, maps, food, extra clothing, and any other rescue or survival items suggested by conditions. Each item is not required on every run, and this list is not meant to be a substitute for good judgment.

4. Keep the group compact, but maintain sufficient spacing to avoid collisions. If the group is large, consider dividing into smaller groups or using the "buddy system" as an additional safeguard. Space yourselves closely enough to permit good communication, but not so close as to interfere with one another in rapids.

a. **A point paddler sets the pace.** When in front, do not get in over your head. Never run drops when you cannot see a clear route to the bottom or, for advanced paddlers, a sure route to the next eddy. When in doubt, stop and scout.

b. **Keep track of all group members.** Each boat keeps the one behind it in sight, stopping if necessary. Know how many people are in your group and take head counts regularly. No one should paddle ahead or walk out without first informing the group. Paddlers requiring additional support should stay at the center of a group, and not allow themselves to lag behind in the more difficult rapids. If the group is large and contains a wide range of abilities, a "sweep boat" may be designated to bring up the rear.

c. **Courtesy.** On heavily used rivers, do not cut in front of a boater running a drop. Always look upstream before leaving eddies to run or play. Never enter a crowded

drop or eddy when no room for you exists. Passing other groups in a rapid may be hazardous: it's often safer to wait upstream until the group ahead has passed.

5. Float plan. If the trip is into a wilderness area or for an extended period, plans should be filed with a responsible person who will contact the authorities if you are overdue. It may be wise to establish checkpoints along the way where civilization could be contacted if necessary. Knowing the location of possible help and preplanning escape routes can speed rescue.

6. Drugs. The use of alcohol or mind altering drugs before or during river trips is not recommended. It dulls reflexes, reduces decision making ability, and may interfere with important survival reflexes.

7. Instructional or commercially guided trips. In contrast to the common adventure trip format, in these trip formats, a boating instructor or commercial guide assumes some of the responsibilities normally exercised by the group as a whole, as appropriate under the circumstances. These formats recognize that instructional or commercially guided trips may involve participants who lack significant experience in whitewater. However, as a participant acquires experience in whitewater, he or she takes on increasing responsibility for his or her own safety, in accordance with what he or she knows or should know as a result of that increased experience. Also, as in all trip formats, every participant must realize and assume the risks associated with the serious hazards of whitewater rivers. It is advisable for instructors and commercial guides or their employers to acquire trip or personal liability insurance:

    a. an "instructional trip" is characterized by a clear teacher/pupil relationship, where the primary purpose of the trip is to teach boating skills, and which is conducted for a fee.

    b. a "commercially guided trip" is characterized by a licensed, professional guide conducting trips for a fee.

IV. GUIDELINES FOR RIVER RESCUE

1. Recover from an upset with an eskimo roll whenever possible. Evacuate your boat immediately if there is imminent danger of being trapped against rocks, brush, or any other kind of strainer.

2. If you swim, hold on to your boat. It has much flotation and is easy for rescuers to spot. Get to the upstream end so that you cannot be crushed between a rock and your boat by the force of

the current. Persons with good balance may be able to climb on top of a swamped kayak or flipped raft and paddle to shore.

3. Release your craft if this will improve your chances, especially if the water is cold or dangerous rapids lie ahead. Actively attempt self-rescue whenever possible by swimming for safety. Be prepared to assist others who may come to your aid.

  a. When swimming in shallow or obstructed rapids, lie on your back with feet held high and pointed downstream. Do not attempt to stand in fast moving water; if your foot wedges on the bottom, fast water will push you under and keep you there. Get to slow or very shallow water before attempting to stand or walk. Look ahead! Avoid possible pinning situations including undercut rocks, strainers, downed trees, holes, and other dangers by swimming away from them.

  b. If the rapids are deep and powerful, roll over onto your stomach and swim aggressively for shore. Watch for eddies and slackwater and use them to get out of the current. Strong swimmers can effect a powerful upstream ferry and get to shore fast. If the shores are obstructed with strainers or under cut rocks, however, it is safer to "ride the rapid out" until a safer escape can be found.

4. If others spill and swim, go after the boaters first. Rescue boats and equipment only if this can be done safely. While participants are encouraged (but not obligated) to assist one another to the best of their ability, they should do so only if they can, in their judgment, do so safely. The first duty of a rescuer is not to compound the problem by becoming another victim.

5. The use of rescue lines requires training; uninformed use may cause injury. Never tie yourself into either end of a line without a reliable quick-release system. Have a knife handy to deal with unexpected entanglement. Learn to place set lines effectively, to throw accurately, to belay effectively, and to properly handle a rope thrown to you.

6. When reviving a drowning victim, be aware that cold water may greatly extend survival time underwater. Victims of hypothermia may have depressed vital signs so they look and feel dead. Don't give up; continue CPR for as long as possible without compromising safety.

V. UNIVERSAL RIVER SIGNALS

These signals may be substituted with an alternate set of signals agreed upon by the group.

Stop: Potential hazard ahead. Wait for "all clear" signal before proceeding, or scout ahead. Form a horizontal bar with your outstretched arms. Those seeing the signal should pass it back to others in the party.

Help/emergency: Assist the signaler as quickly as possible. Give three long blasts on a police whistle while waving a paddle, helmet or life vest over your head. If a whistle is not available, use the visual signal alone. A whistle is best carried on a lanyard attached to your life vest.

All clear: Come ahead (in the absence of other directions proceed down the center). Form a vertical bar with your paddle or one arm held high above your head. Paddle blade should be turned flat for maximum visibility. To signal direction or a preferred course through a rapid around obstruction, lower the previously vertical "all clear" by 45 degrees toward the side of the river with the preferred route. Never point toward the obstacle you wish to avoid.

I'm ok: I'm ok and not hurt. while holding the elbow outward toward the side, repeatedly pat the top of your head.

VI. INTERNATIONAL SCALE OF RIVER DIFFICULTY

This is the American version of a rating system used to compare river difficulty throughout the world. This system is not exact; rivers do not always fit easily into one category, and regional or individual interpretations may cause misunderstandings. It is no substitute for a guidebook or accurate first-hand descriptions of a run.

Paddlers attempting difficult runs in an unfamiliar area should act cautiously until they get a feel for the way the scale is interpreted locally. River difficulty may change each year due to fluctuations in water level, downed trees, recent floods, geological disturbances, or bad weather. Stay alert for unexpected problems!

As river difficulty increases, the danger to swimming paddlers becomes more severe. As rapids become longer and more continuous, the challenge increases. There is a difference between running an occasional Class IV rapid and dealing with an entire river of this category. Allow an extra margin of safety between skills and river ratings when the water is cold or if the river itself is remote and inaccessible.

Examples of commonly run rapids that fit each of the classifications are presented in the document "International Scale of River Difficulty—Standard Rated Rapids" (at **www.american whitewater.org/archive/safety/bnchmark.htm**). Rapids of a difficulty similar to a rapids on this list are rated the same. Rivers

are also rated using this scale. A river rating should take into account many factors including the difficulty of individual rapids, remoteness, hazards, etc.

THE SIX DIFFICULTY CLASSES:

Class I: *Easy.* Fast moving water with riffles and small waves. Few obstructions, all obvious and easily missed with little training. Risk to swimmers is slight; self-rescue is easy.

Class II: *Novice.* Straightforward rapids with wide, clear channels which are evident without scouting. Occasional maneuvering may be required, but rocks and medium sized waves are easily missed by trained paddlers. Swimmers are seldom injured and group assistance, while helpful, is seldom needed. Rapids that are at the upper end of this difficulty range are designated "Class II+".

Class III: *Intermediate.* Rapids with moderate, irregular waves which may be difficult to avoid and which can swamp an open canoe. Complex maneuvers in fast current and good boat control in tight passages or around ledges are often required; large waves or strainers may be present but are easily avoided. Strong eddies and powerful current effects can be found, particularly on large-volume rivers. Scouting is advisable for inexperienced parties. Injuries while swimming are rare; self-rescue is usually easy but group assistance may be required to avoid long swims. Rapids that are at the lower or upper end of this difficulty range are designated "Class III-" or "Class III+" respectively.

Class IV: *Advanced.* Intense, powerful but predictable rapids requiring precise boat handling in turbulent water. Depending on the character of the river, it may feature large, unavoidable waves and holes or constricted passages demanding fast maneuvers under pressure. A fast, reliable eddy turn may be needed to initiate maneuvers, scout rapids, or rest. Rapids may require "must" moves above dangerous hazards. Scouting may be necessary the first time down. Risk of injury to swimmers is moderate to high, and water conditions may make self-rescue difficult. Group assistance for rescue is often essential but requires practiced skills. A strong eskimo roll is highly recommended. Rapids that are at the upper end of this difficulty range are designated "Class IV-" or "Class IV+" respectively.

Class V: *Expert.* Extremely long, obstructed, or very violent rapids which expose a paddler to added risk. Drops may contain large, unavoidable waves and holes or steep, congested chutes with complex, demanding routes. Rapids may continue for long

distances between pools, demanding a high level of fitness. What eddies exist may be small, turbulent, or difficult to reach. At the high end of the scale, several of these factors may be combined. Scouting is recommended but may be difficult. Swims are dangerous, and rescue is often difficult even for experts. A very reliable eskimo roll, proper equipment, extensive experience, and practiced rescue skills are essential. Because of the large range of difficulty that exists beyond Class IV, Class 5 is an open ended, multiple level scale designated by 5.0, 5.1, 5.2, etc. Each of these levels is an order of magnitude more difficult than the last. Example: increasing difficulty from Class 5.0 to Class 5.1 is a similar order of magnitude as increasing from Class IV to Class 5.0.

Class VI: *Extreme and exploratory.* These runs have almost never been attempted and often exemplify the extremes of difficulty, unpredictability and danger. The consequences of errors are very severe and rescue may be impossible. For teams of experts only, at favorable water levels, after close personal inspection and taking all precautions. After a Class VI rapids has been run many times, its rating may be changed to an appropriate Class 5.x rating.

© 2003 American Whitewater
1424 Fenwick Lane
Silver Spring, MD 20910
(866) BOAT-4-AW
info@amwhitewater.org

glossary

Boil line Located immediately downstream of a hole, the point (or area) at which current begins passing downstream again instead of rushing upstream into the hole.

Boof To launch over and off of a rock at the top lip of a drop. A successful boof lifts the bow so that the angle of the boat is more shallow than the angle of the water falling off the drop.

Bow The forward end of the boat.

Brace Paddle stroke used to prevent the boat from flipping over.

Breaking wave A wave that intermittently curls back on itself, falling upstream.

By-pass A channel cut across a meander that creates an island or oxbow lake.

Chock-stone A stone that the current flowing over a falls lands onto.

Chute A channel between obstructions that has faster current than the surrounding water.

Curler A wave with a top that is curled over onto the face of the wave.

Deadfall Trees or brush that have fallen into the stream totally or partially obstructing it.

Decked boat A kayak (usually) or canoe that is completely enclosed and fitted with a spray skirt that keeps the hull from filling with water.

Downstream V A river feature often marking the best route through obstacles, with the point of the V facing downstream. Formed by the eddy lines resulting from two obstacles bracketing a faster channel of water, or by turbulent water bracketing a smooth tongue.

Drop-and-pool Term used to describe a river characterized by rapids separated with long, placid stretches. The rapids act as natural dams that still the current preceding the drop.

Eddy The water downstream of an obstruction in the current or below a river bend. The water in the eddy may be relatively calm or boiling, and will flow upstream.

Eddy line The boundary at the edge of an eddy separating two currents of different velocity and direction.

Eddy turn Maneuver used to enter or exit an eddy.

Eddy-out Exit the downstream current into an eddy.

Ferry A maneuver for moving laterally across a stream, executed facing upstream or downstream.

Flood stage The point at which a river is out of its banks. The level associated with flood stage is location-specific and depends on the depth of the river bed, height of the banks, and flow.

Gradient A river's change in altitude over a fixed distance, usually expressed in feet per mile.

Hair Turbulent, foamy whitewater.

Haystack A pyramid-shaped standing wave caused by deceleration of current from underwater resistance, commonly found at the end of a chute where the faster current collides with the slower moving water pooled below the rapid.

Hole A river feature created where water flows over an obstacle with sufficient flow and velocity to create a wave that violently and continuously breaks (recirculates) upstream against its face.

Hydraulic General term for souse holes and holes.

Keeper Any hole that is difficult to exit. Can take the form of a hole whose right and left edges curve upstream and fold back into the hole, or a very large hole whose boil line is found more than a boat-length downstream.

Ledge The exposed edge of a rock stratum that acts as a low, natural dam creating a falls or rapid as current passes over it.

Line A viable route through a rapid.

Low-head dam A usually man-made obstacle that laterally spans a river from the left to the right bank, creating a pool upstream and a keeper hydraulic immediately below. Grimly referred to as the "perfect killing machine" for their lack of exit points once a boater is caught in the hydraulic.

Meander A large loop in a river's path through a wide floodplain.

Ox-bow A U-shaped lake formed when a river's meander is bypassed by the main channel.

Peel-out A maneuver for exiting an eddy and quickly entering the downstream current.

Pencil in When a boat pierces the water below a drop in a vertical position.

PFD Personal flotation device. Better term for "lifejacket." The Coast Guard recognizes five classes of PFDs. The ACA recommends US Coast Guard-approved Class III PFDs.

Pile The frothy whitewater on top of a wave or in a hole.

Pillow Bulge on the surface of the river created by water piling up against an underwater obstruction, usually a rock.

Pinning When an object (usually a boat) is pushed onto an obstacle (usually a rock) and held there forcefully by the pressure of the current.

Pool A section of river where the prevailing current has been stilled, and the water is usually deep and quiet.

Portage To avoid an obstacle, hazard or rapid by exiting the river, carrying boat and gear downstream, and re-entering the river below the obstacle.

Pot-hole Formed by erosion, a depression in the river bed at the base of a steep drop.

Pour-over A sticky hole formed by water flowing over an abrupt drop.

Punch Approaching and passing through a hole aggressively, boat perpendicular to the hole, in order to reach the current moving downstream beyond the boil line.

Rapids Portion of a river where there is appreciable turbulence usually accompanied by obstacles.

Riffles Slight turbulence with or without a few rocks tossed in, usually found where current is swift and very shallow.

River right The right side of the river as determined when facing downstream.

River left The left side of the river as determined when facing downstream.

Rock garden Rapids that have many exposed or partially submerged rocks necessitating intricate and technical maneuvering.

Roll The technique of righting a capsized kayak or canoe with the paddler remaining in the paddling position.

Scout To evaluate a rapid (either from the shore or while your boat is in an eddy) to decide whether or not to run it, or to facilitate selection of a suitable route through it.

Sieve A hazard formed by channels of swift water flowing through menacingly tight spaces between and underneath boulders, usually accompanied by undercuts. Water can flow freely through, but debris and paddlers are easily pinned underwater by the forceful currents.

Shuttle Using vehicles to transport people and boats on land between river access points prior to or after a run.

Slide rapid An elongated ledge that descends or slopes gradually rather than abruptly, usually covered by shallow water.

Sneak An alternative route through a rapid that avoids the main flow. Usually, but not always, an easier route than the main channel.

Souse hole *See* Hole.

Spray skirt A hemmed piece of neoprene or nylon clothing that resembles a short skirt, having an elastic hem fitting around the boater's waist and an elastic hem fitting around the cockpit of a decked boat.

Standing wave A wave that does not move in relation to the riverbed. *See* Haystack.

Stern The rear end of the kayak or canoe.

Strainer Branches, trees or vegetation partially or totally submerged in the river's current. A serious hazards for paddlers, they only allow water to pass through freely. The current will pull anything else down, plastering it into place, similar to the action of a kitchen colander.

Surfing The technique of situating your boat on the upstream face of a wave.

Swamp To fill a canoe or kayak with water.

Tongue *See* Chute.

Undercut rock A hazard in which the river has eroded a boulder below the surface of the water, creating a cavity with potential for entrapment not visible above the surface.

index

Making the World a Better Place to Paddle

The American Canoe Association
Canoeing, Kayaking and Whitewater Rafting

Join Today!